Management Development Strategies for Action

Alan Mumford

Jeff Gold

Alan Mumford is a consultant professor of management development at International Management Centres. He has worked with senior managers and directors in a number of organisations, including Ford of Europe, Unilever and Unison

Jeff Gold is principal lecturer in organisation learning at Leeds Business School. He has published on a variey of topics relating to management, as well as being a textbook author.

The Chartered Institute of Personnel and Development is the leading publisher of books and reports for personnel and training professionals, students, and all those concerned with the effective management and development of people at work. For details of all our titles, please contact the Publishing Department:

tel: 020–8263 3387

fax: 020–8263 3850

e-mail: publish@cipd.co.uk

The catalogue of all CIPD titles can be viewed on the CIPD website:

www.cipd.co.uk/bookstore

Management Development
Strategies for Action

Alan Mumford

Jeff Gold

Chartered Institute of Personnel and Development

Published by the Chartered Institute of Personnel and Development,
CIPD House, Camp Road, London, SW19 4UX

First published 2004

Designed and typeset by Fakenham Photosetting, Fakenham, Norfolk
Printed in Great Britain by The Cromwell Press, Trowbridge, Wiltshire

British Library Cataloguing in Publication Data
A catalogue of this publication is available from the British Library

ISBN 0 85292 984 6

Chartered Institute of Personnel and Development, CIPD House,
Camp Road, London, SW19 4UX
Tel: 020-8971 9000 Fax: 020-8263 3333
E-mail: cipd@cipd.co.uk Website: www.cipd.co.uk
Incorporated by Royal Charter. Registered Charity No. 1079797

Contents

List of Figures and Tables

Preface

Management Development: Strategies for action is a fully revised and updated version of Alan Mumford's well-known book, the first edition of which was published in 1989. In subsequent editions, published in 1993 and 1997, new material was inserted but essentially the original structure and objectives was retained. This continuity was partly a reflection of the popularity of the book but also the viability of the key ideas and approach. Previous editions were primarily aimed at practitioners working in the field of management development, including many managers themselves. As the book title suggested, a key purpose was to prompt action – it was important that practitioners and managers actually worked out what they could do with the material covered. Then, as now, learning is the central issue – and without a strategy for action which is realised *as action*, can any manager claim that learning has occurred?

This edition has been totally rewritten, partly to bring it up to date but also to meet the needs of a wider range of readership. We still provide the guidance for practitioners which gave unique strength to earlier editions. We are aiming in addition to meet the needs of the large number of students who now study management development as subject for either a professional qualification with the Chartered Institute of Personnel and Development or as part of their MBA or other Master's-level qualifications. You will see that each chapter, for example, provides a *Chapter Outline* and the *Learning Outcomes* in terms of what *you should be able to understand, explain, analyse and evaluate.* Students will find that these relate to the CIPD's national Standards for the Management Development subject. Similarly, the 12 chapters cover the main features of most syllabuses for management development for professional and Master's programmes. The schema below shows the logical structure we have used for the coverage of management development.

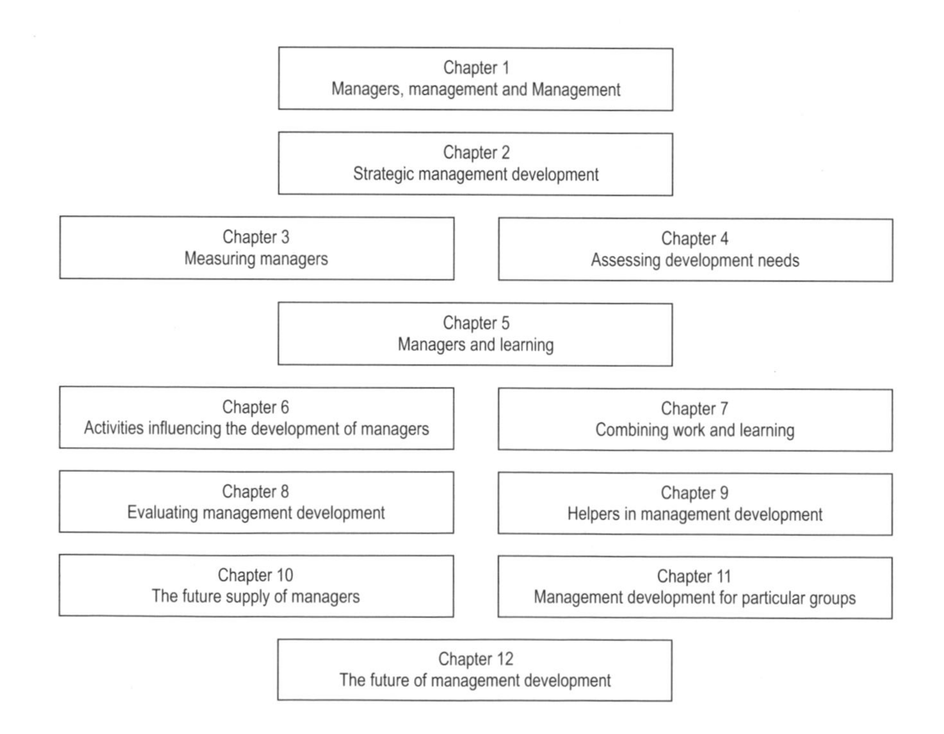

Chapter 1: *Managers, management and management development* seeks to set out the purpose of management development by considering what managers do in various contexts, and how they learn. We will make a clear distinction between what all managers are supposed to do and what they actually do, and note how there are many reasons why implementing management development may be less than effective. We also consider the thorny issue of whether management is different from leadership.

Chapter 2: *Strategic management development* takes a high-level view of the value of management development, seeking a link at national and organisation levels between management development and overall performance. We consider the growing pressure for countries, especially the UK, organisations and managers themselves to take a more strategic view of management development. This sets the scene for two connected chapters, Chapter 3: *Measuring managers* and Chapter 4: *Assessing development needs*, in which we consider the various models for measuring management performance, including management competences which are seen by many organisations as a way of ensuring the strategic link. We also consider the various systems, devices and activities which purport to help managers identify what, how and why they need to develop to improve their performance as managers.

Chapter 5: *Managers and learning* emphasises the centrality of learning in management development. This retains the prominence of the importance of effectiveness in management development and considers the range of theories and ideas that have specifically been applied to learning for managers. Whichever theory is applied, for us the key principles relating to effectiveness must be considered. These inform all the remaining chapters, especially Chapter 6: *Activities influencing the development of managers* and Chapter 7: *Combining work and learning.* In these chapters we seek to explore the many activities that are employed in management development but also the difficulties that occur in making learning relevant to a manager's practice. We give careful attention to some of the barriers that managers face in learning and note the importance of reflection in helping managers overcome some of the difficulties and identify new opportunities for their development.

Chapter 8: *Evaluating management development* continues the theme of helping managers learn by considering the importance of purpose and approach. Management development is, by tradition, poorly evaluated. We attempt to explain why, and consider some alternative approaches. We suggest that an organisation's learning climate has a strong impact on managers, especially if there are sources of help. In Chapter 9: *Helpers in management development* we explore how help might be provided.

Chapter 10: *The future supply of managers* considers further features of the environment for management development, paying particular attention to how managers are selected and supported through their careers, even when managers are increasingly expected to manage their own careers. Chapter 11: *Management development for particular groups* considers the increasingly important issues of diversity management, managing professional staff and the problems of management development in small and medium-sized enterprises (SMEs).

The final chapter, Chapter 12: *The future of management development* takes a view of some of the trends affecting managers and management development and how managers must learn to deal with complexity and unpredictability. We also revisit the link between management development and strategy and extend this link to organisation learning and innovation.

Throughout the book, although we provide extensive coverage of theory and research, we did not want to lose the connection to action and practice. There are therefore a number of features that we believe will appeal to both students and practitioners alike. They include:

- *Reflect – conclude – plan boxes*: these provide questions in the text that will prompt you to think about the material, apply any ideas to your own organisation, and then consider what you might do.
- *Web links*: we recognise that nearly all students now have access to the Internet, so we have provided links throughout the book to some key websites that will enable students to follow up and explore some of the key ideas and examples.
- *Discussion questions*: these appear at the end of each chapter and are designed for class discussion
- *Further reading*: we have drawn upon many sources of information in writing this book, but we also indicate particular sources that enable students to further their understanding and interest.
- *Group activity*: this is designed for groups of three or four students to examine an issue in detail, consider applications to an organisation – their own where possible – discuss conclusions and jointly prepare a presentation.

One of the important enhancements in this edition is the attention paid to many of the ideas from research and practice that have constructed the field of management development. As we suggest in Chapter 1, there are vast numbers of books about what good management is, and what effective managers do, and just as many 'experts' in business schools, consultancies and elsewhere offering advice on how to be a manager. There are many answers to the problems of how to develop managers and how managers learn. As a consequence, there is a burgeoning stock of ideas and an ever-growing list of books, journals, conferences and websites devoted to the subject of management development. One of our key points, which we emphasise in Chapter 1, is that there are no single statements about management which can be applied to all managers in all organisations, and that what managers do and what they have to learn is contingent on the specific demands of a particular environment. We therefore seek to provide in addition a critical view of what is happening, especially where broad generalisations are made about what managers should learn and how they should be developed. We encourage you to take a sceptical view of some of the grandiose claims that characterise management development. Feel free to let us know about your experiences as you do this.

In writing this book we acknowledge the help we have received. Alan Mumford was given his introduction to management development by Don Stradling, who gave him his first opportunities in this field. We thank Vicky Harte at the HRD Unit at Leeds Business School who sought out and printed many papers to bring the book up to date. We would also like to thank Rick Holden, Stuart Watson, John Hamblett and Judith Barras at Leeds Business School, Mike Rix at NTP Meridian, David Firth at Foolweb and Peter Mullinger at Croda Chemicals. Professor Richard Thorpe at Leeds University provided valuable comments on a number of chapters, as did two anonymous reviewers. Many thanks also to Robert Foss and then Ruth Lake at CIPD Publishing for bringing us together and supporting our progress. Last but not least, thanks and much love to our respective wives, Denise Mumford and Susan Gold, who encouraged our efforts to meet the deadlines for this book.

Finally, thanks to you for buying this book. Whether you are a student studying management development as a subject, a practitioner responsible for helping managers develop or a manager seeking ideas for your own learning, we hope that we have stimulated and provoked you to not just think about management development but actually *do* something with those thoughts. We would like to know just what you did.

Alan Mumford

Jeff Gold
j.gold@lmu.ac.uk

Managers, management and Management Development

CHAPTER 1

Chapter outline

Introduction
Management and managers
Managers and professionals
What do organisations do about management development?
Management and learning
What is management development for?
The benefits of management development
Dilemmas about management development
Summary

LEARNING OUTCOMES

After studying this chapter, you should be able to understand, explain, analyse and evaluate:

- **the dangers of generalising about what managers do**
- **the link between professionalism and management**
- **whether managers and leaders are different**
- **the crucial relationship between what managers do and how they learn**
- **alternative purposes and definitions of management development, from which individuals might choose to operate in their own organisations**
- **issues which may cause conflict, uncertainty and ineffectiveness in implementing management development.**

INTRODUCTION

In October 1939 Winston Churchill said, 'I cannot forecast to you the action of Russia. It is a riddle wrapped in a mystery inside an enigma.' The number of books written about what good management is, and what effective managers do, is so large as to make one feel that both these topics are like Churchill's description of Russia. If management and the work of managers were simple, we would not need so many books which attempt to elucidate them, nor would there be so many 'experts' in business schools, consultancies and elsewhere offering advice on how to be a manager. Rather, management is a complex process involving a confusing and sometimes contradictory mix of objective factors about the nature of the work to be done, more subjective factors emerging from the reality of the people involved, the culture of the organisation, and the kind of purposes which that organisation attempts to meet. One of the most valuable results of effective management development (MD[1]) can be to create a recognition that there are no single statements about management which can be applied to all managers in all organisations. What managers do is contingent on the specific demands of a particular environment. Even so, there have been continuing concerns in the UK about the quality of managers and the desire to extend good management practice into areas such as the health services, professional firms, schools and small businesses. Whatever effective management is, we need more of it (CEML, 2002).

MANAGEMENT AND MANAGERS

'Management' can be an expression about a group of people holding the title of management, carrying authority for activities within an organisation. Or 'management' can mean the processes by which those activities are defined, resourced, controlled and evaluated.

For the purpose of this book the 'management' part of MD is taken to mean the description of activities carried out by managers. Management in the sense of a group of individuals holding power and authority is an important but less useful focus. To say that 'management here is too autocratic' or that 'management is insufficiently caring about customer needs' may be a useful precursor to analysis of exactly who has these failings, and therefore what kind of development needs and solutions may emerge. But use of 'management' in the rather pejorative way that people talk about 'they' is less useful. A major reason for this is that management development has consistently overprovided for general statements of need, and generally applicable solutions to those needs.

The greater the degree of generalisation in MD and the lower the attention to the particular needs of individuals in particular situations, the less effective MD will be.

REFLECT – CONCLUDE – PLAN 1[2]

An Oxford University philosophy paper is supposed to have included the following question:

All generalisations are untrue. Discuss.

- What is your reaction to the last generalisation? How applicable is it in your experience of defining management, and of management development?
- What impact could it have on the provision of effective MD?
- What might you do as a result of your argument?

What managers do

Oscar Wilde wrote, 'The truth is never pure and rarely simple.'[3] Just as there are grave dangers in generalising about what 'good management' is, so attempts to provide a simple statement of what 'good managers' do can be misleading. The major issues relevant to effective MD must be identified by looking at some of the more familiar theories.

The American F. W. Taylor sought to define the role of managers and is recognised as the pioneer of scientific management. Through analysis of work tasks, managers could find the 'one best way' to control work and eliminate waste – a process referred to as Taylorism. This search for the 'one best way' model of management has continued ever since. Henri Fayol (1949) identified five basic managerial functions – planning, organising, co-ordinating, commanding and controlling. Early forms of management education in the UK and USA used these categorisations, supplemented by additional aspects such as staffing, directing and budgeting. Extensions to Fayol's view, supplemented by the experience of Alfred P. Sloan's *Forty Years in General Motors* (1945) became in a sense the classic descriptions of managerial work because they were the first serious attempts.

These classic descriptions of managerial work, however, and derivations of them were neither particularly helpful in causing managers better to understand what they needed to do, nor seriously helpful in facilitating the development of managers to meet these requirements. They do not usefully describe in behavioural terms what managers have to be able to do, and therefore what development actions are appropriate. In the 1930s the famous Hawthorne investigations resulted in what became referred to as the Human Relations School, supported by the application of psychology to work issues after the Second World War. This required managers to think about key factors such as the influence of groups, the effect of work conditions and the causes of conflict.

A subsequent line of thought began to focus rather on the characteristics of managers, such as decisiveness, courage and initiative. This idea of what managers needed to be able to display through their work was particularly popular as a result of the Second World War and studies and anecdotes about the kind of leadership (as it was called rather than 'management') displayed during it.

The major change in views about, and actions on, what managers had to be able to do came through the research and books by Rosemary Stewart (1975) in Britain, and Henry Mintzberg (1973) and John Kotter (1982) in the United States. Stewart's work is particularly compelling because her research was conducted with hundreds of managers. The main features of her discoveries were:

- Managers do not work according to the neat, well-organised themes of the classical management schools.
- Their activities are characterised by brevity, variety and fragmentation.
- They spend most of their time interacting with other people rather than thinking well-organised thoughts.
- They work at a brisk and continuing pace, with little free time.
- So far from being subject to extremely generalised comments about 'what all managers do' there is a substantial variety in the objective demands of managerial jobs.
- In addition to objective differences – for example, between a sales manager and a research manager – personal choices are made by managers which affect what they actually do.

These statements now seem obvious, partly because they so clearly are supported by the experience of those of us who have actually worked as managers.

Mintzberg, in a much smaller but interestingly indicative study, found much the same pattern of pace, variety and fragmentation as Stewart. However, he identified some roles which he believed to be common, particularly for the chief executives who were the basis of his studies. Table 1 shows the roles.

Table 1 *Mintzberg's role analysis*

Interpersonal roles	Informational roles	Decisional roles
figurehead leader liaison	monitor disseminator spokesperson	entrepreneur disturbance-handler resource allocator negotiator

Source: adapted from Mintzberg (1973)

Although Mintzberg's analysis has subsequently been criticised, it can usefully be employed in a formal management development context. Managers can benefit from discussing, for example, what proportion of time they spend on any of these roles, and other aspects of the significance of what they are doing.

John Kotter (1982) also looked at a relatively small number of senior executives. Like Mintzberg and Stewart he emphasised the degree to which managers were not strategic, reflective or well organised, but he defined five characteristics of effective behaviour (Kotter, 1982):

- developing an agenda (often different from a formal plan)
- building networks involving other managers, colleagues, direct reports, outsiders
- execution by establishing and working to multiple objectives and maintaining relationships to achieve those objectives, especially by spending time with other people
- working through meetings and dialogues
- spending time with others.

Kotter created a stunningly significant concept – the effectiveness of seemingly inefficient behaviour. The fact that executives rarely plan their days in advance in much detail but rather react to the day's needs through conversations that are short, disjointed and often deal with a variety of issues within the space of a few minutes is seemingly inefficient. These inefficiencies are often the subject of formal management development processes. While not arguing for the wasteful use of time, Kotter observed that apparent waste was not the same as being ineffective. Information and understanding crucial to effectiveness were created often by accidental experiences.

The utility of such accidental opportunities, however, should not dissuade us from attempting to remove the genuine inefficiencies of the ways in which managers use their time – perhaps those useful accidental experiences can be replaced by useful planned experiences, both in general managerial behaviour and in creating more effective learning experiences from managerial behaviour.

Another major researcher and theorist who has affected the basis of our understanding of what managers do has been Richard Boyatzis (1982). His case research with 2,000 managers at different levels and in different kinds of organisations in the United States identified 18 characteristics or skills which he claimed all successful managers have in common. While at first sight his 18 competencies (see Chapter 3) might be seen as a more sophisticated version of generalised statements about what 'all' managers need to be able to do, in fact he qualified this view to the extent of saying that there will necessarily be variations of requirements in different organisations. Boyatzis indeed specifically recommended that organisations should work on their particular understanding of these characteristics in their own organisations, rather than accepting someone else's general view of the applicability.

Boyatzis' ground-breaking study has been followed by a number of sometimes equally detailed research studies showing variations on his competencies. In the UK, the most ambitious attempt was that through the Management Charter Initiative (see Chapter 3).

The significance of what could be called the 'competency movement' is that it has led to a more refined understanding of what managers do, and in at least some cases to an emphasis on organisations producing their own adjusted list more relevant to their particular needs. In Chapter 3 we extend this examination considerably to show its significance in MD. This is an illustration of Wilde's dictum, in that it would be simple for most people to take an existing list and then apply it and assess their development needs against it. The convenience and simplicity of this approach – which requires no additional effort in defining what managers do in your organisation – is likely to be misleading in terms of its effect on developing managers in those competencies which are crucially required in their particular organisation – or at least identifying and working on the most crucial. Managers live in a changing world, in organisations whose objectives can change, whose priorities can shift. The things which managers have to do effectively must be responsive to these changed circumstances. Even organisationally-derived competencies are generalised statements about managerial work in that particular organisation. Both the content of a competence and its level of priority might in fact differ within an organisation according to a specific function or level. It is doubtful that any framework of management can fully account for a process of managing that must remain 'inherently problematic' (Hales, 1993; p.15).

What generalisations are possible? Firstly, we would suggest that most effective MD will derive from the most specific statements of what particular managers need to be able to do well. Further, the more that individual or group development is focused on requirements which in themselves represent a closely-drawn derivation from organisational or unit strategy, the more effective the development will be. There are, however, at least some issues that are likely to be of concern in the job of any manager:

- The manager is an individual with accountabilities and responsibilities (preferably set down in writing).
- The manager is part of a social interaction, working with relatively permanent groups and teams but also occasional relationships – issues of power and influence are always present.
- In managing resources (finance, material, information and people) the manager is a problem-solver and decision-maker.
- Managers have to make decisions about how much they will allow others to do without significant reference to them ('empowerment').
- Direct management of others is accompanied by necessary indirect influence on internal colleagues and the external world: hence the significance of being able to network effectively (and to understand political skills).
- Most managers work in conditions of uncertainty and risk.
- The clear definition of those objectives and priorities which most managers would prefer to work to must be constantly updated.
- The only unchanging thing is that change will be ever-present.

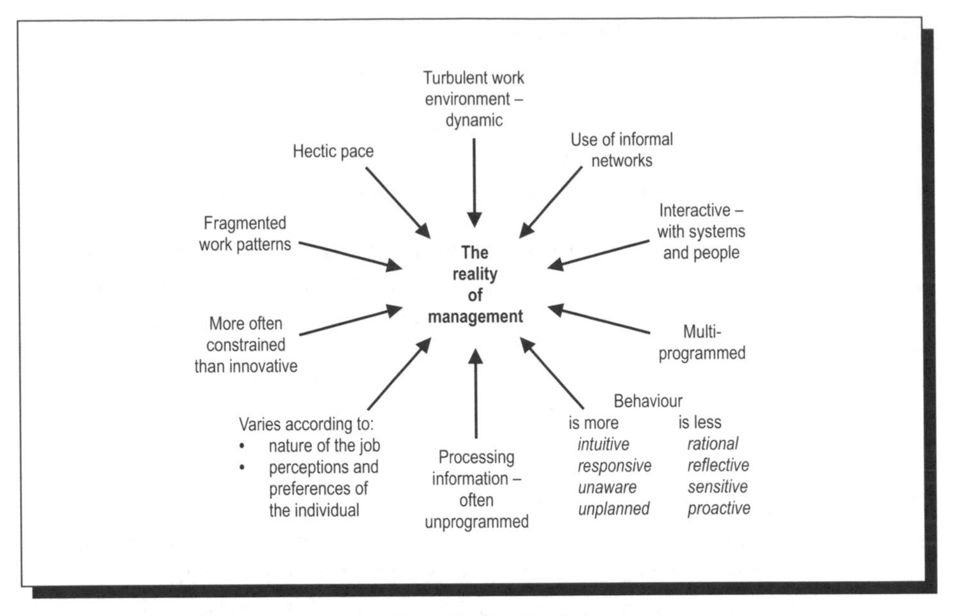

Figure 1 *The reality of management – as experienced by Alan Mumford*

- Change, and accompanying differences in priorities, may be best coped with if there is a specific organisational understanding of mission and values.
- Some organisational cultures encourage particular management styles; however, even within one organisation several different styles may be displayed effectively.
- Peter Drucker told us (1974) that there was a difference between being efficient – doing things right – and being effective – doing the right thing (see also Kotter's behavioural characteristics, earlier).

It should be noted that all these statements, though perhaps helpful in enabling MD advisers to determine their own approach to advising others, apply similarly to the content of the management developer's own job. There are, of course, much more substantial descriptions of managerial skills and the context in which those skills are applied (see Chapter 3). Some MD advisers might want to pursue these issues in greater depth. Figure 1 provides an image of the reality of management, as experienced by Mumford in his role as a manager, researcher and developer. It attempts to avoid both complexity and oversimplification.

Ethical values

A concentration on what managers actually do is crucial. However the 'what' ought to be accompanied by 'why'. This has been the concern of Watson (1994) and others who have been interested in the reality of management as experienced by managers themselves. One of the most important conclusions to emerge was the value-laden and moral positions of those who perform management roles. As Watson suggests (p.223),

> **Management is a essentially and inherently a social and moral activity [in which success is achieved by] building organisational patterns, cultures and understandings based on relationships of mutual trust and shared obligation among people involved with the organisation.**

Another study by Luthans (1988) pointed to the presence of dubious behaviours such as discussing rumours, hearsay and the grapevine; complaining, griping, and putting others down; politicking and gamesmanship. Other behaviours included non-work-related chit-chat and informal joking around.

WEB LINKS

Watson and Luthans were both using an ethnographic approach to research. As Watson explained, he was able to 'get close to managers as individuals' and involve himself 'in their organisation context' (p.6). Find out more about ethnographic research at
http://www.questia.com/Index.jsp?CRID=ethnography&OFFID=se1
and
http://www.sas.upenn.edu/anthro/CPIA/methods.html

These views of management include something rarely addressed specifically in MD – values and ethics of the organisation. It may well be that those in power in an organisation are saying 'These are our values, this is the way in which we want to do things and these are our ethics.' They are rather more likely to imply all of these rather than to state them, and they are certainly less likely to make explicit any statement about ethics. In our view ethics is an understated issue in MD. A first reason for this is that there ought to be concern about the extent to which individuals are required to support and lend themselves to the values and ethics of an organisation, when their personal values and ethics are in conflict. One example is the issue of the form of conduct either encouraged or required by an organisation in terms of how its managers behave in other countries. Behaviour which would not be accepted in this country may be allowed or indeed encouraged in relation to other countries 'whose values are different from ours'. Similarly, there are important implications for managers in valuing difference among staff within organisations, as we will note when we consider the emerging trend towards diversity management in Chapter 11.

A different ethical issue may arise in the course of some of the formal methods adopted for developing managers. When outdoor training reached a peak of popularity, there were issues about the extent to which managers ought to be required to attend a form of training which was physically, mentally and emotionally stretching beyond the bounds of acceptability to some individuals.

Issues about strategy and values occur within an organisational context, and this must also be understood in order to create effective MD. Is the organisation centralised or decentralised? Is it more autocratic or democratic in the way it operates? Of course one of the purposes of MD might be to assist a move from centralised to decentralised operation, or from relatively autocratic to relatively democratic decision-making processes.

MANAGERS AND PROFESSIONALS

One of the changes referred to earlier is that individuals who previously regarded themselves primarily if not solely as 'professionals', rather than as managers, are no longer able to place themselves in discrete categories of that kind. In the UK, the National Health Service senior professionals have been helped to see that they are managers within their professional role, even though they have not made what some would see to be the great shift of moving into a purely managerial role. The same characteristic can be seen, for example, in large legal partnerships and in trade unions. This process is following that of the evolution of management in industrial and commercial organisations, where 'professionals' – for example, in the finance department – start as pure professionals but may finish by becoming the managers of professionals. In the public sector in the UK, there has been a trend towards what is referred to as New Managerialism with an implicit aim of curtailing the power of professionals (Exworthy and Halford, 1999). Within professional organisations such as firms of accountants and lawyers, the trend towards a more managerial approach has seen the emergence of the 'managed professional business' (Cooper *et al*, 1996) with an emphasis on becoming more businesslike in response to changing market demand using the language, techniques and structures of management. However, as argued by Vermak and Weggeman (1999), traditional styles of command and control are a recipe for conflict with professionals, and 'it is easy to get into a vicious circle: the manager tries to control things – the professionals sabotage this' (p.33).

The issue about professionals as managers – as we have discovered for example in projects with lawyers and trade unionists – is whether the people who are actually carrying out managerial functions see themselves as managers. There are specific features about trying to engage in MD for senior professionals. Many of them are discussed by Raelin (1986), who examines the differences of view that may occur in the way professionals see themselves as compared with the way they see people who are more clearly identified as managers. Dawson (1994) also reviews potential clashes in the older professions between what may be seen as professional standards and ways of behaving and managerial requirements. Nevertheless, a recent survey of professional associations by Perren (2001), involving those bodies responsible for setting out a profession's specification for membership, suggested that management and leadership were seen as highly relevant for their members, although few went so far as to specify MD as a requirement. See Chapter 11 for further examination of this.

A further issue relates to whether the practice of management can be regarded as a profession itself. Certainly, in the UK we can point to a number of professional associations that are regarded as 'management professions', such as the Institute of Chartered Accountants in England and Wales, the Chartered Institute of Marketing or the Chartered Institute of Personnel and Development. Such professions do provide a professionalisation route to management with reference to specific domain of knowledge and practice. However, can management more generally be regarded as a profession? According to Freidson (2001) professionalism is composed of five interdependent elements:

- specialised work that is grounded in a body of theoretically-based discretionary knowledge and skill that is given special status
- exclusive jurisdiction created and controlled by occupational negotiation
- a sheltered position with labour markets based on qualifying credentials of the occupation
- a formal training programme to provide qualifying credentials
- an ideology that asserts a commitment to doing good and quality.

We would suggest that in general management does not yet match these elements, although each can be debated. For example, consider the first element relating to knowledge and skill. From what we have said about generalisations in management, it is difficult to point to a unified body of knowledge and a set of standardised skills. Further, managers, while they often act with discretion, are constrained by organisational requirements. What is allowed in one organisation may be disallowed in another.

WEB LINK

In the UK, there have been significant attempts by the Institute of Directors and the Chartered Management Institute to enhance the status of management as a profession: www.managers.org.uk will take you to the Chartered Management Institute in the UK, and
http://www.iod.com/ is the homepage of the Institute of Directors.

REFLECT – CONCLUDE – PLAN 2

1. Review any document you may have setting out the skills/knowledge/competencies required in your own job.
2. Review any document you may have setting out skills, knowledge and competence requirements for managers in your organisation for whom a management development programme or course has been designed.
3. Review any information you may have demonstrating the utility of the documents you may have in response to 1 and 2.
4. In the light of the data you have, and the comments made in this section, what conclusions do you draw?
5. What actions might you take?

Are managers and leaders different?

Reference was made earlier to the impact of the Second World War on ideas about management, drawn from what were seen as effective leadership practices during that War. This concept never entirely lost its popularity, and it has become a much more serious issue in MD over the last 20 years. It primarily revolves around the question of whether managers and leaders are different people, or perhaps whether managers and leaders behave differently and require different skills. These are questions which will be the subject of further discussion later, particularly in Chapter 2.

The concept of leadership as a discrete process is undoubtedly attractive to many people – not least those who might think they have the required characteristics. The word carries with it, often explicitly, concepts such as 'vision', 'charisma', 'transformational leadership'. Authors such as Bennis (1989) and Kotter (1990) encourage the view that leadership is separate and distinct from management, which implies a different level or type of development need. Because of its attractiveness as a proposition it can provide motivation for development which may not otherwise be present in an organisation or in an individual. Certainly the term has often been used as a marketing tool for courses which propose to deal with leadership rather than management and therefore hope to attract some managers because of the title.

The attractiveness of the concept is indeed recognised by the number of books and articles on the subject, which really became a respectable academic issue following the publication of an article by Zaleznik (1977), supported by a book in 1990. There are now a multitude of institutions, programmes and even academic departments devoted to the notion of leadership rather than management. It is noticeable that in education, health, public administration and local government, a number of leadership colleges and programmes have been established, although much of their approach to delivery and content are based on ideas drawn from MD. In the UK, CEML (2002) identified a particular deficit in leadership skills and it is leadership that is highlighted by government reports as the key to making the changes necessary for 'modernisation' and effectiveness in the 21st century (PIU, 2000).

WEB LINKS

Go to http://www.ncsl.org.uk/ for the National College of School Leadership.
For an example of a current leadership programme in the UK public sector, go to http://www.publicserviceleadersscheme.gov.uk/

We feel that there are at least two problems with the submergence of management by leadership. The first is that the list of leadership characteristics or behaviours turns out on examination to be very much the kind of list that would be produced in relation to any effective manager. Leadership characteristics such as being a stimulator of thought and action in others, of being creative and 'getting out of the box' and producing direction-changing processes are surely those we would look for in effective managers.

Secondly, to say that these are the requirements for a leader, whereas a manager need only be concerned with the most routine and basic 'transactions' or the least exciting parts of the direction of a unit or organisation, is demeaning of the managerial context, and of the majority of people who thereby become defined as 'only' managers rather than leaders. Throughout this book, we will therefore take the position that by necessity leadership is a feature of management work, and that those who perform such work – whatever their job title – will act as leaders as well as managers.

WHAT DO ORGANISATIONS DO ABOUT MANAGEMENT DEVELOPMENT?

Some organisations offer absolutely nothing – no individual reviews, no plans for individual development, no annual review of succession, no nominations for courses. Others provide a full range of formal opportunities. Inevitably, a lot are in the middle, providing something but not everything, or providing for lower-level managers but not for the most senior. The phrase 'management development' has probably existed in the UK only since 1951. While some commercial and industrial organisations have been carrying out at least some of the processes identified below for even longer than that, formal MD has been put in place much more recently in most organisations.

Four stages in management development can be seen, in different organisations or in one organisation over time, as shown in Figure 2.[4]

The characteristics of each stage are:

Stage 1 – Unplanned experiential management development

This is an approach to management development based on the assumption that managers emerge from experience. Typical expressions of this are:

- 'Managers are made through doing things, not by going on courses.'
- 'The cream rises to the top.'
- 'I made my way without any help from anyone else.'
- 'I learned the hard way.'

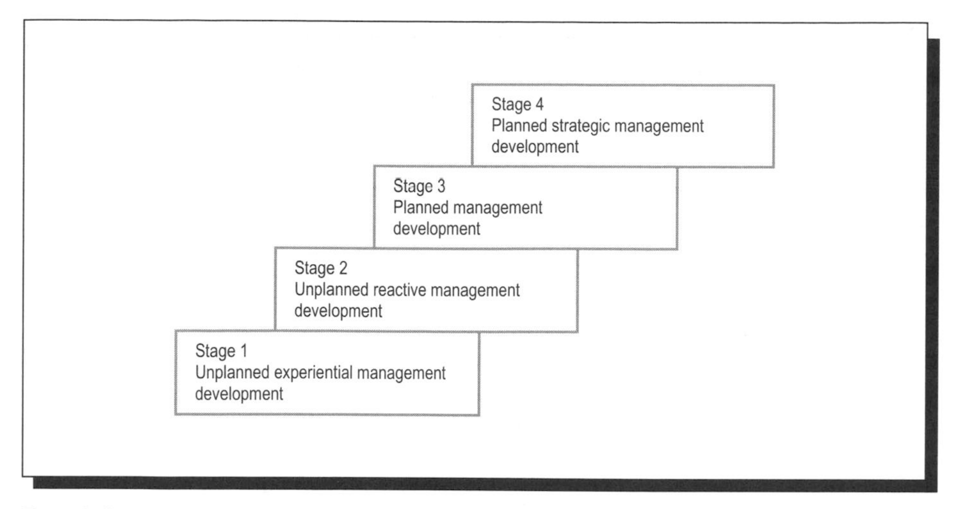

Figure 2 *Stages in management development*

Stage 2 – Unplanned reactive management development

This is a management development approach dominated by immediate pressures.

- 'These customer satisfaction reports are terrible. We must run some courses on customer care.'
- 'None of our people seems to have much knowledge of how our European competitors work. We should send them off on a tour of companies over there.'
- 'What are you doing about improving our effectiveness in handling change?'

Stage 3 – Planned management development

Many organisations now have structures, procedures, forms through which development needs are assessed and provided for. This may be done as part of appraisal or performance reviews, or through a separate development review; needs and solutions may be identified. Personal development plans are produced.

There may also be catalogues of internal courses, the identification of regularly used external centres, the identification of possible job changes or secondments, the provision of formal coaching and mentoring. The more effective use of informal relatively accidental learning opportunities within, for example, projects or from normal management work is encouraged.

Stage 4 – Strategic management development

Some organisations have worked from the development needs of the organisation, identified through, for example, a business plan. Although focused on defined organisational needs, and therefore in some respects looking like the reactive management development mentioned above, it tends to deal in longer-term issues, probably identifying key management capabilities in a competency framework.

- 'How can we develop managers more capable of handling mergers or acquisitions?'
- 'How are we going to develop, over the next three years, managers capable of handling decentralised powers?'

One of the other changes in MD (other than the introduction or recognition of new methods of development) over the last 20 years has been the recognition that MD is most effective when it matches the strategy or mission of an organisation, and indeed is developed and implemented in order to facilitate the implementation and success of that strategy. Although there are now doubts about the effectiveness of some of the more mechanical, strategic and business planning processes favoured from the 1970s through to the mid-1990s, the idea that an organisation ought to establish a clear statement of where it wants to get to and how it needs to get there is still fundamental to good management. How the strategy is defined and implemented is of course a management development issue! (See Chapter 2.)

REVIEW – CONCLUDE – PLAN 3

1. Where is your organisation in terms of the stages described above?

   Stage 1 ☐ Stage 3 ☐ Stage 2 ☐ Stage 4 ☐
2. Review other organisations in which you have worked. At which stage would you assess them to have been?
3. Does your own organisation need to move from one stage to a later stage?
4. What could you do to help secure movement?

One of the authors was asked to carry out a review of the MD policies and processes of a large UK-based company. It had been active in formal MD for 30 years. The documents, plans, processes and brochures available from its files were reviewed. A number of people from personnel departments were interviewed. Finally, the questions were discussed with 20 senior managers and directors (see checklist below). You could ask the same questions about your own organisation. (See our Group Activity at the end of this chapter.)

Checklist of questions about an organisation's management development

- What do you believe to be the purpose of your organisation's management development policies? How effective have they been for yourself and for the managers reporting to you?
- How helpful has the appraisal process been in defining the effectiveness of individual managers and their development needs?
- Do you use other processes for reviewing performance and development?
- Do you believe that the processes for collecting and reviewing individual potential have worked satisfactorily – eg succession planning?
- What contribution has been made by processes such as job rotation, and internal or external courses?
- Can you quote cases of managers who are more effective as a result of these management development processes?

MANAGEMENT AND LEARNING

Some authors (see Chapter 5) differentiate between learning and development, some differentiate between education, training and development. For us, development embraces all activities through which people learn. A great deal of this book emphasises the importance of recognising individual needs and proposed development solutions related not only to needs but to the ways in which individuals prefer to learn. Although the association of these two

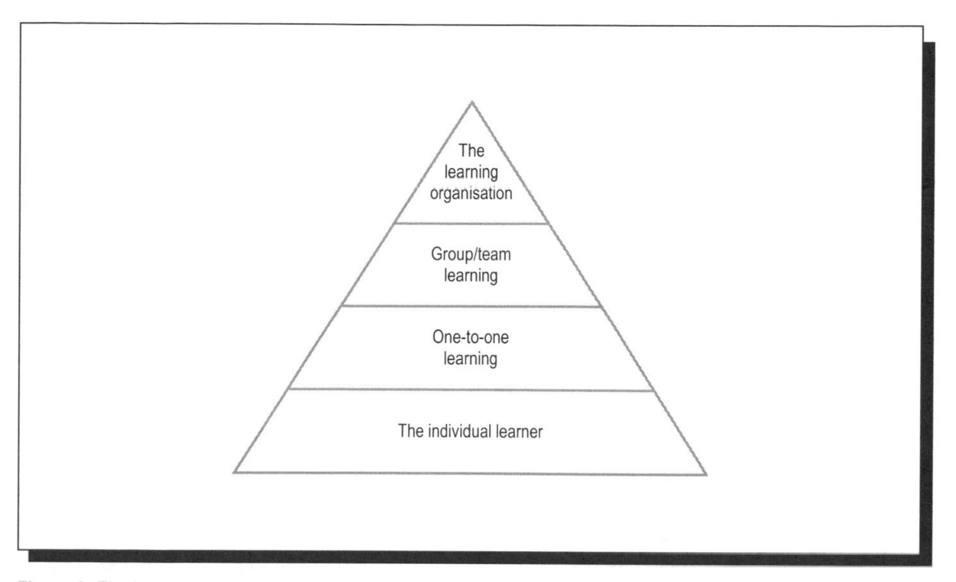

Figure 3 *The learning pyramid*

points is crucial for effective learning, focus on the individual does not mean that we believe individuals exist in a cocoon of self-appraisal and individual action. They work and learn in a context of other people, and opportunities to learn exist and can also be created in that context, which is set out in the learning pyramid shown as Figure 3.

The peak of the pyramid, the learning organisation, represents the highest challenge for learning. We say much more about the learning organisation in Chapter 12. The conceptual point presented through the pyramid is not only that learning exists at four levels but that it needs to progress through the first three levels if the fourth – the learning organisation – is to be reached.

WHAT IS MANAGEMENT DEVELOPMENT FOR?

In 1977, MD was defined by the Training Services Agency as

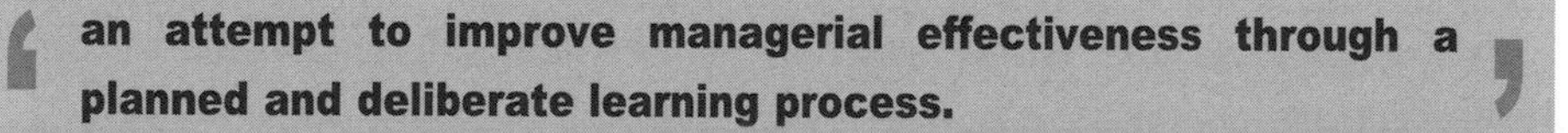

‘an attempt to improve managerial effectiveness through a planned and deliberate learning process.’

In many ways that definition illustrates the issue about whether MD is conceived as embracing both formal and informal processes of development. The definition reflected current beliefs and practices, which emphasised formal, planned and deliberate processes which originate from and are often monitored and controlled by people and forces other than the individual manager involved. It does not include those unplanned, accidental, undeliberate experiences that so many managers record as a significant part of their development.

A great deal of MD is not ‘planned and deliberate’ and even more significantly probably cannot be. Yet the practice of management developers should certainly include attempts to shift at least some experiences from the accidental, informal, undeliberate more towards at least being reviewed and deliberately assessed as learning experiences after the event. Mumford's (1997) revised definition was and remains

> **an attempt to improve managerial effectiveness through a learning process.**

There are alternative definitions, which vary not just according to the literary skills of the definer but on the different understanding of the purposes of MD and the processes involved in it:

> **I define management development as the management of managerial careers in an organisational context.**
>
> **Burgoyne (1998)**

> **At the personal level, (management development) is the process by which you and the others gain the skills and abilities to manage yourself and others.**
>
> **Margerison (1991)**

> **Management development has a deceptively simple sound to it. Clearly it means developing the ability of people to manage in their own organisational environment.**
>
> **Sadler (1998)**

> **That entire system of corporate activities with the espoused goal of improving the managerial stock in the context of organisational and environmental change.**
>
> **Lees (1992)**

A definition helps to establish what management development is about. It also needs to be clearly associated with a definition of purposes. One of the most interesting studies of MD, comparing processes in the UK and Japan by Storey *et al* (1994), suggested a number of objectives for MD:

- as a device to engineer organisational change – in particular culture change
- as a tool in pursuit of quality, cost reduction and profitability
- to structure attitudes
- to contribute to the development of a learning organisation
- to assist with self-development.

Although not explicit in their book, their discussion of these purposes enables us to look at the extent to which they may not be mutually supportive, or indeed might be contradictory of each other. The first four purposes quoted above clearly relate explicitly to organisational needs, whereas the last should contribute to those organisational objectives, but in some respects might not do so. It could be in the interests of individuals even acting within a planned MD system to develop themselves in ways and for needs which are not priorities for the organisation – and indeed might relate to longer-term ambitions outside the organisation. There is scope for confusion here – partly related to definitions of what you mean by self-development, which is discussed further in Chapter 7.

There are other areas in which confusion about purposes – perhaps enhanced by a failure to agree the meaning of particular words – may arise. For example, there may be issues about the extent to which MD policies, systems and actions are designed to create individuals who are wholly in tune with the prevailing beliefs and methods of working in an organisation. Yet at the same time an organisation may claim that it wants to develop managers who are keen on taking initiatives, who will break the mould of current thinking and methods of working, who will introduce styles of behaviour that challenge the existing styles. Such contradictions may appear within MD programmes. For example, Höpfl and Dawes (1995) reported a programme designed to empower middle managers in a water company so that management style could move directing and controlling toward support and trust. However, as soon as the managers started to make suggestions, senior management found themselves under threat – leading to the curtailment of the programme.

Formal and structured processes for development have depended on the creation or use of courses, of detailed planning, of succession, promotion, career moves, the latest schemes for appraisal and assessment of managerial performance. Gradually the MD world has accepted that this is too limited a view of what MD is about (Storey *et al*, 1994; Woodall and Winstanley, 1998). This book certainly takes the view that it is the task of MD to get recognition and increased use of learning opportunities of a much more informal nature, especially those in and around the day-to-day work which managers do.

The benefits of management development

Lees (1992) identified ten very different reasons why organisations support MD, shown listed below. In his view the first four have a functional and performance emphasis; the remainder are 'political, legitimate, symbolic and defensive'.

Lees' ten faces of management development

- functional – performance
- agricultural
- functional – defensive
- socialisation
- political reinforcement
- organisational inheritance
- environmental legitimacy
- compensation
- psychic defence
- ceremonial.

We agree with his view that the first of these is the most frequent as an explicit rationale for undertaking MD. Some of his other 'faces' need further explanation. 'Agricultural' is a way of repeating the view of some organisations that 'we need to grow our own managers'. The metaphor of growing in the sense of enabling people to develop by fertilising and supporting development is both attractive and helpful because it encourages movement away from some of the more mechanistic ideas about management development. His case for the functional – defensive face is that it is a statement about the relatively poor use that some companies make of the formal training that they provide. In this context managers then become cynical about what is being provided for them and why. We have already commented on the socialisation case – that organisations often like to have managers thinking and behaving in a way which they see as coherent but which others might see as requiring people to stick to a standard norm. Political reinforcement engages the idea that management development processes try to make sure that contribution by managers to organisational performance is encouraged and supported through a defined set of characteristics and required behaviours.

Organisational inheritance captures the idea that movement between jobs is set by formal criteria for promotion and movement. Lees commented that these formal statements are often at odds with the actuality of what happens. 'Environmental legitimacy' is the term Lees used to describe a process through which a supposedly professionalised management is supported by a professionalised MD system, and thereby adds to the supposed legitimacy of management generally and within a particular organisation.

'Compensation' is the rather odd term he used to describe the process through which MD activities become in some sense a reward for continued employment. (While this may have been true in perhaps the first 30 years of MD in the UK, it seems unlikely that it is any longer the case that most managers are simply sent on courses because it is their turn or because a month in a relatively pleasant environment is perceived as a sort of holiday.)

For psychic defence, Lees offered a rather subtle explanation which included the smoothing away of some of the worries and anxieties that managers feel about their own promotion – or the promotion of others over them. Finally, 'ceremonial' is a good term for describing MD as including rituals which confirm the passages of managers through the organisation, and which bind the manager further into the organisation by celebrating achievement.

Lees' article is particularly a challenge to MD advisers who can assess to what extent in their view their schemes exhibit or show the ten faces. It also reminds us that MD can serve different purposes and different interests, even in the same organisation. In our view there are three important stakeholders in MD:

- the individual whose development is being encouraged
- the manager of the individual
- the organisational unit to which the individual belongs.

There are different benefits for each stakeholder.

Benefits for the individual include:

- an increased ability to develop improved performance
- a reduction in stress about untackled gaps in personal performance requirements
- an increased chance of holding on to a desired current job
- an increased chance of developing potential for other jobs
- a clearer process for establishing personal aspirations

- a clear process for establishing the commitment of my manager and the organisation to my development.

Benefits for the manager of the individual include:

- a reduction in performance problems
- an increased use of additional opportunities for effective work in the unit
- a reduction in the belief that my manager does not believe in development
- more individuals capable of dealing with new or difficult tasks or complete jobs.

Benefits for the organisational unit include:

- increased ability to meet current and future organisational needs
- increased effectiveness for the unit, via improved performance
- increased likelihood that development for individuals will be more sharply focused on organisational needs
- improved motivation for individuals, leading to greater commitment to the organisation
- increased provision of continuous learning rather than 'one-off' training.

REFLECT – CONCLUDE – PLAN 4

Which of the above stimuli do you believe to be strongest –

- in your own development?
- for your manager?
- in the unit to which you belong?

Dilemmas about management development

Considering the benefits of MD for different stakeholders along with the various purposes outlined by Lees (1992) counters the orthodox belief of unified organisations with a single purpose. As Burgoyne and Jackson (1997) suggest, a more pluralist understanding is required to appreciate political dynamics and the cultural and symbolic context in which MD occurs.

We see the choice between shifting the balance in MD to giving more attention to informal and accidental processes and perhaps less to formal structured MD not as an either/or but as a dilemma that has to be reconciled so that each can support the other. Thus senior managers and HR directors may desire MD programmes, systems and policies to be designed primarily to meet organisational requirements, as compared with meeting individual needs – for example, for easier job mobility. Reconciliation requires differing perspectives to be surfaced and shared so that common ground can be identified.

Another dilemma is the extent to which the MD agenda balances today's needs with tomorrow's. Very often in practice management development seems to be looking back even at yesterday's needs rather than today's. Yet forecasting what will be needed tomorrow, although an engaging pursuit on an away day, is not in reality often an activity which produces very useful results. Somehow a balance has to be struck so that at least for the most relevant people attention is paid not just to what they need immediately but what may be needed in the future. The short-term/long-term dilemma was one identified by Taylor (1994), requiring managers to learn to operate across a range of skills, at the same time.[5]

A final dilemma is drawn from the issue of the requirement often to act for a large number of managers, with whom there is an inevitable justification for producing generally applicable answers. There may be easily identifiable general needs – accompanied by clear solutions, such as 'Put everybody through a management of change programme.' We are all familiar with the economics of size, of dealing with relatively large numbers of people through a standard process rather than reinventing the wheel for small groups, let alone individuals. The dilemma here is in two parts. The first is the extent to which even with the large group there will be significant differences of need – for example, in relation to different functional and job requirements. Do all managers really need to be given an understanding of strategy – a very familiar element in many general management courses? The second part of the dilemma relates to individuals. MD has too often ignored the relevance of difference. The difference occurs observably in relation to culture between, for example, British companies and others overseas – but increasingly it also involves consideration of ethnicity and gender (see Chapter 11). Within these relatively large differences there is a further crucial difference – individuals differ in their own particular needs in relation to their own immediate job and their potential for other jobs; they also differ crucially in the ways in which they prefer to learn. It is not only the 'one size fits all' that is a problem in relation to individuals – it is the one method suits all that makes for difficulties.

SUMMARY

- The emphasis in this chapter is on the contingent nature of management.
- The most effective MD is based on that contingent view – what should managers do in this particular organisation?
- MD has to embrace informal, accidental learning opportunities as well as formally created ones.
- Organisation ethics and values must be addressed in the development of managers.
- There is a growing emphasis on management among professionals and the professionalisation of management.
- We see leadership as a feature of the practice of management, not separate from it.
- There is wide variation in MD activity between organisations.
- MD can serve a variety of purposes and provide benefits for different stakeholders.
- Organisations must balance and reconcile a variety of MD dilemmas.

DISCUSSION QUESTIONS

1. How are definitions of management related to the practice of managers?
2. What is the link between management development and organisational learning/development? How does organisation size affect this link?
3. Can management ever be fully considered a professional occupation?
4. 'Leaders transform, managers transact.' Discuss.
5. Should management development always serve the needs of the organisation?
6. What are the benefits for employees of management development for their manager? What blocks might employees set on their manager's learning?

FURTHER READING

GARAVAN, T. N., BARNICLE, B. and O'SUILLEABHAIN, F. (1999) 'Management development contemporary trends issues and strategies', *Journal of European Industrial Training*, Vol. 23, No. 4; pp.191–207.

LINSTEAD, S., JEFFCUTT, P. and GRAFTON-SMALL, B. (eds) (1996) *Understanding Management*. London, Sage.

PAAUWE, J. and WILLIAMS, R. (2001) 'Management development revisited', *Journal of Management Development*, Vol. 20, No.2; pp.180–191.

TALBOT, C. (1997) 'Paradoxes of management development – trends and tensions', *Career Development International*, Vol. 2, No. 3; pp.119–146.

WATSON, T. J. (2001) 'The emergent manager and processes of management pre-learning', *Management Learning*, Vol. 32, No. 2; pp.221–236.

GROUP ACTIVITY

- Form a group of four, each person from a different organisation.
- Re-examine the *Checklist of questions about an organisation's management development* on page 12 in this chapter.
- Each person should answer the questions with respect to their own organisation and draw conclusions. What actions are necessary to secure improvement?
- Meet to share your findings.
- Prepare a short presentation based on your meeting.

REFERENCES

BENNIS, W. (1989) *On Becoming a Leader*. Reading, MA, Addison Wesley.

BOYATZIS, R. (1982) *The Competent Manager*. New York, Wiley.

BURGOYNE, J. (1988) 'Management development for the individual and organisation', *Personnel Management*, June; pp.40–44.

BURGOYNE, J. and JACKSON, B. (1997) 'Management development as a pluralistic meeting point', in J. Burgoyne and M. Reynolds (eds) *Management Learning*. London, Sage.

COOPER, D., GREENWOOD, R., HININGS, C. R. and BROWN, J. (1996) 'Sedimentation and transformation in organizational change: the case of Canadian law firms', *Organization Studies*, Vol.17, No. 4; pp.623–647.

CEML (2002) *Managers and Leaders: Raising our game*. London, Council for Excellence in Management and Leadership.

DAWSON, S. (1994) 'Changes in the distance in order to reappraise the meaning of management', *Journal of General Management*, Vol. 20, No. 1; pp.1–21.

DRUCKER, P. F. (1974) *Management Tasks, Responsibilities, Practices*. New York, Harper & Row.

EXWORTHY, M. and HALFORD S. (eds) (1999) *Professionals and the New Managerialism in the Public Sector*. Buckingham, Open University Press.

FAYOL, H. (1949) *Administration Industrielle Générale*. English translation. London, Pitman Harper.

FREIDSON, E. (2001) *Professionalism*. Cambridge, Polity Press.

GARAVAN, T. N., BARNICLE, B. and O'SUILLEABHAIN, F. (1999) 'Management development contemporary trends, issues and strategies', *Journal of European Industrial Training*, Vol. 23, No. 4; pp.191–207.

HALES, C. (1993) *Managing Through Organisation*. London, Routledge.

HÖPFL, H. and DAWES, D. (1995) 'A whole can of worms!: the contested frontiers of management development and learning', *Personnel Review*, Vol. 24, No. 6; pp.19–28.

KOTTER, J. P. (1982) *The General Managers*. New York, Free Press.

KOTTER, J. P. (1990) *A Force for Change*. New York, Free Press.

LEES, S. 'Ten faces of management development', *Management Education and Development*, Vol. 23, No. 2; pp.89–105.

LUTHANS, F. (1988) 'Successful *v* effective real managers', *Academy of Management Executive*, Vol. 2, No. 2; pp.127–132.

MARGERISON, C. (1991) *Making Management Development Work*. Maidenhead, McGraw-Hill.

MINTZBERG, H. (1973) *The Nature of Managerial Work*. New York, Harper & Row.

MINTZBERG, H. (1975) 'The manager's job: folklore and fact', *Harvard Business Review*, July/August.

MUMFORD, A. (1988) *Developing Top Managers*. Aldershot, Gower.

MUMFORD, A. (1993) *How Managers Can Develop Managers*. Aldershot, Gower.

MUMFORD, A. (1997) *Management Development: Strategies for action*. London, Chartered Institute of Personnel and Development.

PERREN, L. (2001) *Management and Leadership in the UK Professions*. London, Council for Excellence in Management and Leadership.

RAELIN, J. (1986) *The Clash of Cultures: Managers and professionals*. Boston, MA, Harvard Business School Press.

SADLER, P. (1998) 'Concepts and components of management development', in J. Propokenko (ed.) *Management Development*. Geneva, International Labour Organisation.

SLOANE, A. P. (1945) *My Forty Years with General Motors*. New York, Doubleday.

STEWART, R. (1975) *Contrasts in Management*. Maidenhead, McGraw-Hill.

STOREY, J., EDWARDS, P. and SISSON, K. (1994) *Managers in the Making*. London, Sage.

TAYLOR, F. J. W. (1994) *Management Development to the Millennium*. The Taylor Working Party Report. London, Institute of Management.

VERMAK, H. and WEGGEMAN, M. (1999) 'Conspiring fruitfully with professionals: new management roles for professional organisations', *Management Decision*, Vol. 37, No. 1; pp.29–44.

WATSON, T. J. (1994) *In Search of Management*. London, Routledge.

WOODALL, J. and WINSTANLEY, D. (1998) *Management Development*. Oxford, Blackwell.

ZALEZNIK, A. (1977) 'Managers and leaders: are they different?', *Harvard Business Review*, September/October; pp67–78.

ZALEZNIK, A. (1990) *A Managerial Mystique: Restoring leadership in business*. New York, Harper & Row.

ENDNOTES

1 We use the abbreviation MD to indicate Management Development throughout the book.

2 The questions posed here take readers through three elements of the Learning Cycle, which is described in Chapter 5. 'Reflect' is part of the 'Review' element in the Cycle.

3 The quotation is from Wilde's last play, *The Importance of Being Earnest.*

4 In Chapter 2 an alternative model by Burgoyne is presented.

5 Other dilemmas identified by Taylor (1994) included:

- local/global
- task/process
- internal/external
- individual/team
- action/reflection
- operational/strategic.

Strategic management development

CHAPTER 2

Chapter outline

LEARNING OUTCOMES

After studying this chapter, you should be able to understand, explain, analyse and evaluate:

- **the value of management development to the nation**
- **the link between management development and organisation performance**
- **the link between strategy and management development**
- **how management learning may or may not contribute to strategy**
- **the significance of power in management development.**

INTRODUCTION

There is considerable and ongoing debate about the precise meaning of 'strategy', and we will refer to some of this discussion below. However, for both the nation and organisations, there is a recognised need to do something about the quality of managers so that there is a response to such forces as:

- competitive pressures and globalisation
- the demands of reform and modernisation in the provision of public services
- the requirements for change, including technology and knowledge production.

Reminding ourselves that the word *strategy* has its origins in the Greek term *stratēgos*, meaning a general set of manoeuvres for overcoming an enemy, we can suggest that these forces represent the 'enemy' and that the notion of 'the general set of manoeuvres' is a call to seek ways to integrate the development of managers with organisation goals.

In this chapter, we will be concerned with some of the strategic considerations of MD. First of all we will consider some of the national concerns regarding MD, and we will then relate such concerns to how UK organisations make decisions that provide (or do not provide) for MD activity. A key feature of the discussion will be the extent to which MD is linked to considerations of organisation strategy. We will find that one approach is that MD is valued because it has to be linked and determined by business needs as expressed in its strategic plan. This allows a particular kind of response with a declaration of a policy of how requirements should be met and how the value of any provision should be measured. However, we shall also see that this essentially top-down approach can be contrasted with one that gives emphasis to the way managers learn and develop through the opportunities that occur in the hectic reality of managerial life. This is a more opportunistic and emergent view, and one that could provide a bottom-up link to strategy. It recognises that the value of MD is that it could provide an input to strategic considerations as well as being determined by them. However, we will also suggest that this optimistic view could be made ineffective by particular value/reward systems which strongly influence what managers learn. We will conclude by examining how the values and beliefs that form an organisation's culture have a significant influence on what MD is provided and how managers learn.

THE VALUE OF MANAGEMENT DEVELOPMENT IN THE UK

Questions concerning value usually refer to the worth or the overall usability of something or process. In relation to MD, a key consideration for many organisations and indeed the nation as whole is the extent to which MD, whatever its shape or composition, can be shown to improve the performance of managers leading to success of some kind, however judged, in organisations and then the nation. Underpinning such reasoning is what is often referred to as a 'functional performance rationale' for MD (Garavan *et al*, 1999; p.193), so that there is linear chain of connections between MD and national economic success, shown in Figure 4.

At each point in this chain, worth and usability might be assessed, feeding what Holmes (1995) rather sceptically refers to as 'the formula for success'. Indeed, one of the key purposes of the evaluation of MD is to prove that claims about the success of MD at various stages of the chain can be made.[1]

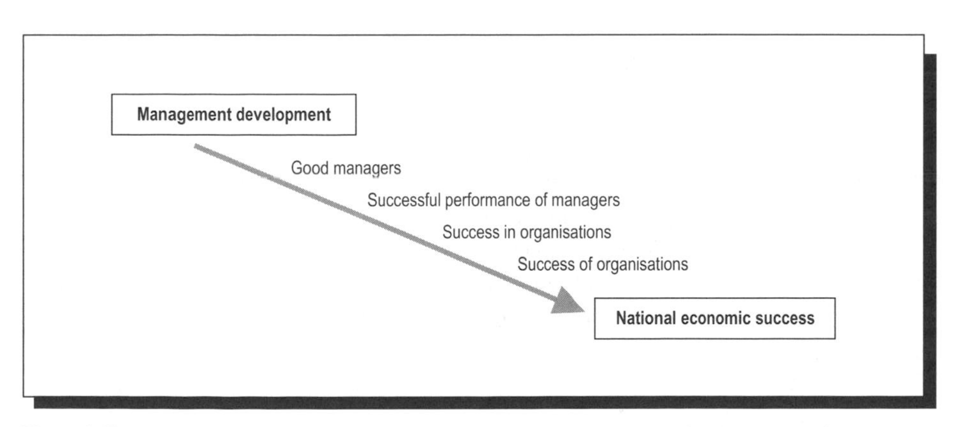

Figure 4 *The connection between management development and organisational and national economic success*

REFLECT – CONCLUDE – PLAN 1

- Do the various claims in the formula for success seem valid to you? Is it possible to show how MD leads to better managers, who in turn improve organisation performance, resulting in national economic success?
- What evidence is there in your own organisation to support the linear chain of connection?
- What could you do to provide better evidence?

In Chapter 8 on *Evaluating management development* we will explore various aspects of this link in more detail. However, for the moment it is enough to say that proving the effectiveness of MD is a difficult process. Very frequently, therefore, more restricted assessments of value are made – for example, the number of people attending a training programme or the overall satisfaction of participants at the end of a programme. Sometimes no formal assessment is made at all so the value of MD is assessed informally or just becomes an act of faith. The link to an organisation's strategy is often therefore thin or nonexistent.

National concerns

Whatever the restrictions on assessing the value, adherence to the links within the formula for success have become a taken-for-granted feature of strategic considerations of management development. Certainly, at national level there have been ongoing concerns about the quantity of managers and MD and the commitment of organisations stretching right up to the present day. During the 1960s there was a general view in the UK that there was not enough training where the lack of skills was leading to low productivity compared to other nations. This resulted in the Industrial Training Act in 1964 and the establishment of Industrial Training Boards. In addition, the publication of the Robbins Report on Higher Education in 1963 identified a lack of management education and recommended the establishment of two postgraduate management schools. Under the guidance of Lord Franks, the two schools were opened in London and Manchester in 1965. In addition, new universities established in the 1960s, such as Lancaster, began to offer management and business qualifications to undergraduates, and this extended to polytechnics as they began to open.

Although the number of people with graduate and postgraduate management qualifications began to rise, this did not alleviate concerns about the vast numbers of managers and employees generally who had no qualifications at all and little opportunity for training and development at work. By the 1980s there was continuing concern over the UK's industrial situation, and an under-investment in human capital – usually referred to as 'Britain's training problem' – was identified as one of the causes, along with a failure to modernise capital equipment, poor development practice, outmoded financial structures, an anti-industrial culture and class system, and poor management of strategic change (Sparrow and Pettigrew, 1987). Intriguingly, one particular feature of the UK situation was that managers, in contrast with those in other countries, did not value training because it was not perceived as strongly linked to profit (Hayes *et al*, 1984). We can see here an important theme – managers who do not see the value of training and development for themselves are unlikely to see the value of training and development for others. Further, failure to make the link between learning and improving skills and performance could become an accepted feature of an organisation's values and beliefs or culture. It also allows others to blame managers for their lack of support for learning.[2]

REFLECT – CONCLUDE – PLAN 2

- Do managers in your organisation provide support for the training and development of staff?
- Do they make a link between training and development and improved performance and the overall success of their area of responsibility?
- What can you do to establish and use the link?

The attention given to the education of managers and their continuing development once they started work was one of the key findings of Charles Handy's report (1987). Whereas Japan, the USA, Germany and France all took the preparation and development of managers 'seriously' (p.2), Britain did not – apart from some particular exceptions in larger organisations. The findings from the Handy Report were supported by those from the Constable/McCormick Report (1987) and others.[3] Underpinning all such research was the key strategic assumption that there is there is value in investing in the development of managers because good management provides the foundation for improvements in productivity in organisations and, hence, overall national economic prosperity. Some of the key features of these reports are listed in the box below.

THE PICTURE IN 1987

- Over half of UK companies made no provision for the training and development of managers (of companies employing more than 1,000 people, one fifth made no provision for the training of their managers).
- Over half of companies in West Germany, the USA and Japan gave their managers more than five days off-the-job training each year. In Britain, managers received an average of just one day, most getting none.
- 90,000 entered management each year – very few had any formal management education or training.
- 24 per cent of UK senior management held degrees – it was close to 85 per cent in the USA and Japan.

– findings from the Handy and Constable/McCormick Reports

In 1987 Handy set out two problems – one for the short term and one for the long term. In the short term there was a need to improve the competence of existing managers. In the long term Britain needed a pattern of formation for managers so that they were fully prepared for their roles. What happened next?

If the results of surveys in the late 1990s are anything to go by, there seems to have been something of a sea-change in the UK. A large survey by Thomson *et al* (1997) of over 900 organisations using questionnaires and interviews found that MD had been given a higher priority compared with 1987. This was evidenced by more organisations providing training, only 4 per cent of large companies and 20 per cent of small companies offering no training. The average number of days of formal training per annum per manager had increased to 5.2 – an apparent five-fold increase since 1987. This particular finding showed little variation according to size of organisation or sector. There was also a claim for more informal development. There had additionally been an increase in the formal qualifications of managers, 77 per cent of junior managers and 44 per cent of senior managers undertaking measures to gain qualifications.

However, there were some words of warning. Various commentators have suggested that the general nature of the results hides important variations. For example, some organisations might report large amounts of training and others might report little or none (Thomson *et al*, 2001) although they had similar patterns for priority, the achievement of objectives and written statements of policy. Storey and Tate (2000), in their contrast with corporate MD in Japanese organisations, refer to the 'fickle' nature of British MD provision where programmes could be cut or changed over time. For example, there could be a tendency to institute new programmes every few years – leading to 'programmitis' (p.211). In addition, there could be swings in the type of provision. For example, one year the emphasis could be on self-development, followed by its de-emphasis in the next. The result might well be confusion and cynicism among managers. So while acknowledging the improvements since 1987, the case for MD was not yet fully proven.

From 1997, with the election of a new UK Government that placed an emphasis on 'Education, education, education' and a commitment to the idea of Lifelong Learning, there have been a number of attempts to set out a strategy for skills development at all levels in the country as whole. Even though there is a lack of specific evidence between training and economic growth (Machin and Vignoles, 2001), the importance of skills was identified as a requirement for national competitiveness and the prevention of social exclusion. A Skills Task Force was set up in 1998 to develop a National Skills Agenda to (NSTF, 1998; p.38):

> **ensure that Britain has the skills needed to sustain high levels of employment, compete in the global marketplace and provide opportunity for all.**

To develop such an agenda, 18 research reports were commissioned and two Employer Skills Surveys (ESS) conducted. Management skills were among the areas covered, the report reinforcing much of the previous research that managers in the UK tended to be under-qualified with low levels of qualifications and an inadequate amount of training (Johnson and Winterton, 1999). One particular highlight of this report was the attention given to MD in small and medium-sized enterprises (SMEs), which employ about one third of all employees in the UK (p.29) and are seen as significant for future growth in the economy. In general, most managers in SMEs do not hold formal management qualifications, nor do they undertake much management training, although they may recognise the value of MD for their business and considerable learning about management occurs informally, by working on business problems (Gibb, 1997). (See also Chapter 10.)

WEB LINK

The work of the Skills Task Force, including access to all reports and research can be found at: www.skillsbase.dfes.gov.uk/reference/reference.asp

After the STF made its final report in 2000, the work was continued by two national bodies. Firstly, the Performance and Innovation Unit of the Cabinet Office examined workforce development, concentrating mainly on lower and intermediate skills. Secondly, management and leaderships skills were explored by the Council for Excellence in Management and Leadership (CEML).

The Council for Excellence in Management and Leadership

CEML was established to 'develop a strategy to ensure that the UK has the managers and leaders of the future to match the best in the world' (CEML, 2002; p.1) because 'good management and leadership is pivotal to investment, productivity, delivery of service and quality of performance' (p.4). Its work was based on a number of working groups and advisory groups. This provided for a very broad scope including SMEs, professional bodies, higher education authorities and other bodies such as government agencies and consultants. More research was commissioned and several reports were produced, providing significant detail and adding to the stock of knowledge provided by previous reports, but also some interesting quandaries about managers and their skills. For example, the report on the management population in the UK (Williams, 2002) found it difficult to identify a reliable measure of the gap in skills at managerial level. Do rising salary levels for managers indicate skills shortages? Possibly, but it could also be the case that managers earn more because they deserve it through adding more value. Further, it would appear that most organisations can fill their managerial posts, although this says little about the quality of those who occupy the posts.

Some of the key findings of the work of CEML were (CEML, 2002):

- There was an increase in the award of management qualifications, but there was continuing dissatisfaction with the level and spread of management skills and especially leadership.
- There was no lack of learning opportunities for managers but there were restrictions on the ability to take up the opportunities.
- There was a need to stimulate demand from all organisations and from individuals, improve supply by paying attention to what the customer wanted, and build links between demand and supply.
- Many organisations were unclear and unfocused about what they needed, which often resulted in dissatisfaction with outcomes.
- Significant amounts of money were being invested in management and leadership development, but there were difficulties in showing a positive return.

WEB LINK

CEML's website contains access to all reports and research and can be found at:
http://www.managementandleadershipcouncil.org/
If you want to examine the latest figures relating to skills, qualifications, Employers Skills Survey results, etc, go to
http://www.skillsbase.dfes.gov.uk/

One result of all the research has been a build-up of a significant amount of knowledge about MD and the extent to which it is valued in organisations. What becomes readily apparent as these various research efforts show is how embedded the notion of the link between MD and economic improvement has become, and how difficult and intractable the problems remain. There clearly have been some improvements since the 1970s as the 1997 survey (Thomson *et al*, 1997) showed, but there remain widespread concerns about the inadequacies and variations. There are examples of good practice and excellence, but in the main there is still not a great deal of evidence that the value of MD is proven. For example, Bosworth *et al* (2002) set out to use the results of the 1999 ESS to show the link between the qualifications and proficiency of managers, the strategies adopted by establishments and their performance. Using descriptive statistics and multivariate analysis, the report highlights some very interesting but paradoxical results. Overall, there seems to be no direct link between management qualifications and performance but evidence for a link between proficiency and performance. The authors suggested that this might be due to the acquisition of their skills through experience. We will explore this particular theme later in the chapter and throughout the book.

STRATEGY AND MANAGEMENT DEVELOPMENT

According to most orthodox views, if MD is to have any purpose in an organisation, it should be linked and driven by organisational strategy. As organisations respond to environmental changes such as globalisation, technological change and customer demands, MD can be seen as a 'strategic tool' to implement the strategy developed and improve business performance. A survey by the Chartered Institute of Personnel and Development (CIPD, 2002) of nearly 1,000 senior managers found that 86 per cent said 'integrating management development with the implementation of organisational goals' was the priority in terms of improving the contribution to organisational performance (p.1). The survey discerned two key purposes of MD:

- Developing managers to sustain the current business model – managers need to have the skills to carry out their roles and new managers need to become productive very quickly. MD provides the means by which an organisation's 'winning proposition' can be sustained.

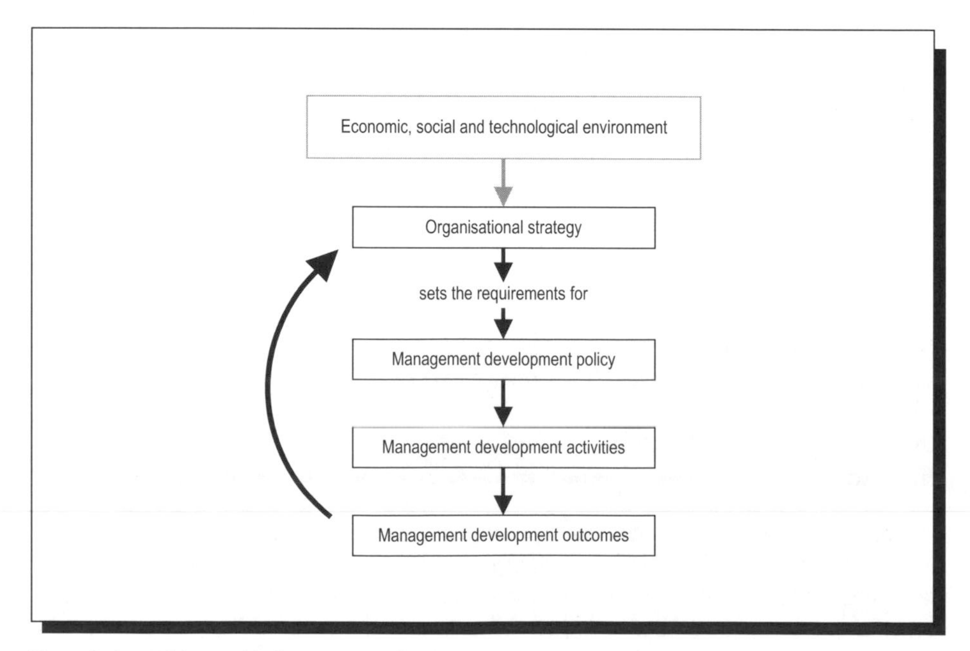

Figure 5 *A sustaining model of management development*

- Developing managers to create future business models – because business models have a limited life and stability is becoming more unusual, managers can learn to develop new models. In fast-moving sectors, such as telecommunications, involvement in change initiatives leads to new understandings and new possibilities.

These purposes provide an interesting and contrasting view of the strategic link. The first is perhaps still dominant, apparently more uncomplicated, and reflects the 'functional performance rationale' referred to above with a causal chain of connection between strategy and performance.

Figure 5 provides a representation of this view of the link.

The obvious points about the model are that:

- Strategy is set in response to an assessment of changes in the environment.
- Strategy provides guidance on the requirements for managers in terms of numbers, skills and performance requirements.
- Management development policy translates the requirements to provide management development activities.
- The outcomes of activities are assessed and valued, providing feedback for organisational strategy.[4]

An example of how a MD strategy is prompted by environmental conditions is the research carried out for the Voluntary Sector National Training Organisation. It suggested that the voluntary sector would face a management skills shortage. Further research was then undertaken to set out the strategy that could then be used for funding proposals. The basic parameters of the strategy were defined as:

- working with funders to persuade them to recognise and reward good management practice in organisations they fund
- liaising with training providers to ensure that the voluntary sector is well served
- working with managers of voluntary organisations to provide them with a range of information and support services
- working with voluntary organisations to promote management development approaches and good practice
- working on standards of competence and qualifications – for example, adapting existing management standards to the needs of the sector and developing new standards and qualifications appropriate for voluntary sector managers.

– Source: http://www.vsnto.org.uk/mandev.htm, accessed 21 May 2003

Other reasons for forming a management development strategy include:

- change of technology, work design, organisation structure
- mergers and acquisitions
- entering new markets and providing new services
- responding to identified weaknesses and poor performance.

WEB LINKS

You can find other examples of management development strategies at:
Sheffield University –
http://www.shef.ac.uk/stdu/policy/mdstrat.html#leaders
Isle of Wight County Council –
http://www.iow.gov.uk/education/learning_centre/Management_Development_Events/
Go to
http://www.bp.com/includes/global/ernst_young.asp?p=/environ_social/employees/global/first.asp to find details of BP's First Level Leaders Programme, which they are rolling out to 12,000 participants. Included are a strategic rationale for the programme and the plan up to 2005.

The second view – developing managers to create future business models – would seem to be more challenging. It provides for the possibility that MD can have a role in making strategy as well as being determined by it. It is a view which may be becoming more evident, especially where organisations face more unstable and capricious environments.

For many organisations however, debates about the strategic purpose of MD are still unlikely, and this may be a reflection of the belief about its value to organisation performance. In the 1980s, Burgoyne (1988) suggested that how an organisation responded to MD was an indication of its maturity. Table 2 shows Burgoyne's 'ladder' of organisation maturity in terms of MD.

The first point to note is that Burgoyne defined MD as 'the management of managerial careers in an organisational context', and managerial careers as 'the biography of a person's managerial worklife'. He said that processes of 'natural' MD happen – they are not deliberately planned or contrived for MD. They are inevitable, usually good, and destined always to be the major provider of MD. However, in most situations they are not enough. In particular he saw these processes as essentially effective in new entrepreneurial firms, usually small in size. Because such organisations need to cope with increasing scale and complexity, natural career structuring and learning alone are not sufficient, so the journey to what he called 'organisational management development maturity' begins.

Beyond Levels 1 and 2, a visible policy for MD provides a form and shape for activities, exemplified by structural and developmental activities. Structural activities include succession planning, assessment centres and various methods and techniques to allocate managers to specific roles. Developmental activities are those which help a manager learn and develop, such as courses, mentoring, coaching, etc. At Level 4 and beyond, these activities and the policy that provides their integration and co-ordination are strongly connected to corporate policy. In 1988, according to Burgoyne, possibly the majority of organisations were at Levels 1 and 2, and Levels 3 and 4 described the limits of current best practice achieved. Levels 5 and 6 apparently existed as 'occasional achievements often precariously achieved and lost, and often only occurring in some relatively autonomous part of large organisations'.

Table 2 *Levels of maturity of organisational management development*

Level 6 Strategic development of the management of corporate policy	MD processes enhance the nature and quality of corporate policy-forming processes, which they also inform and help implement.
Level 5 Management development strategy input to corporate policy formation	MD processes feed information into corporate policy decision-making processes on the organisation's managerial assets, strengths, weaknesses and potential, and contribute to the forecasting and analysis of the manageability of proposed projects, ventures, changes.
Level 4 A management development strategy to implement corporate policy	A management development strategy plays its part in implementing corporate policies through managerial human resource planning, and providing a strategic framework and direction for the tactics of career structure management and of learning, education and training.
Level 3 Integrated and co-ordinated structural and development tactics	The specific MD tactics that impinge directly on the individual manager, of career structure management, of assisting learning, are integrated and co-ordinated.
Level 2 Isolated tactical management development	There are isolated and *ad hoc* tactical MD activities, of either structural or developmental kinds, or both, in response to local problems, crises, or sporadically identified general problems.
Level 1 No systematic management development	No systematic or deliberate MD in structural or developmental sense: total reliance on natural, *laissez-faire*, uncontrived processes of MD.

Source: Burgoyne (1988; p.41)

REFLECT – CONCLUDE – PLAN 3

- Are you able to use Burgoyne's ladder to plot your own organisation's level of maturity?
- If you are at Level 4 or below, what steps would be needed to move you up the ladder?
- What action can you take to facilitate this?

Levels 5 and 6 imply that MD can have a reciprocal link to strategy by which manager learning is both driven by strategy but also provides an input into strategy-making. It also proposes a link between MD and such ideas as the learning organisation (Burgoyne and Reynolds, 1997) and Burgoyne had a significant involvement with the latter.[5]

The strategic management of management development

During the early 1990s, the move to Levels 5 and 6 seemed to be put on hold; many organisations were 'downsizing' and 'delayering', processes which put the job security of many managers at risk. At the same time, there were significant changes in many organisations and managers were often required to take the lead. For example, the implementation of business process re-engineering (BPR) was based on the view of a radical change of business processes by applying information technology to integrate tasks to produce an output of value to the customer. It was often accompanied by removal of unnecessary processes and layers of bureaucracy so that staff became more empowered to deliver high-quality service and products. Managers were very much involved in identifying the processes but might also suffer the consequences where this resulted in the loss of particular roles and disruptions to planned career paths (see Chapter 10).

In the public sector, there has been a significant shift towards 'managerialist' language and techniques as part of a response to deregulations and competition. This trend has been referred to as New Managerialism or New Public Management (Pollitt, 2000). Although this has certainly resulted in a renewed interest in MD in the public sector, with the establishment of new institutions such as the National College for School Leadership, in general there has been considerable resentment towards managerial processes (Exworthy and Halford, 1999).

WEB LINKS

The ESRC-funded Business Processes Resource Centre can be found at http://bprc.warwick.ac.uk/index.html
– what resources are available for MD on this site?
The National College for School Leadership can be found at http://www.ncsl.org.uk/
– examine the emerging requirements for head teachers and managers in schools.

In the 2000s there is renewed interest in the reciprocal connection between MD and organisational strategy to enhance a company's sustainability, profitability and competitive advantage as suggested by the 'Developing managers to create future business models' purpose identified by the CIPD (2002) survey above. There are indeed examples of how some organisations are seeking or hoping to achieve this. For example, Shell have systematic and integrated processes which focus on business results (p.22). They have:

- a 'talent review' process – to identify future requirements and assess talent availability by examining the ratio of candidates for every senior level position
- 'strategy development' – an annual process which includes HR considerations and relating business improvement to the 'capabilities required of our managers'. The process allows 'challenging dialogue about leadership and management capability'
- 'potential assessment' – each person is assessed in terms of the job level they could ultimately achieve in Shell.

For Holbeche (1999), the vital requisite for success is alignment of organisational strategy and employee performance at every level. In this process, there has to be a way of measuring and appraising performance and, as is evident from the example of Shell, allowing strategic changes to be expressed in terms of capabilities required from managers. In many organisations, competency frameworks have been developed to facilitate alignment. As we will explore in Chapter 3, competences express the behaviour needed by managers to allow organisational strategy to be achieved. Competences also allow key HR activities such as reward, selection and the identification of MD needs to be integrated around strategy.

There is, however, little evidence that MD is connected to strategy in the UK. Part of the reason is related to the low attention generally given to strategic management in the UK, especially to considerations for the medium to long term. Even in organisations where strategic management is seriously considered, often the focus is on profit maximisation and cost minimisation (Coleman and Keep, 2001). Skills and HRD are generally a fourth-order consideration, seldom regarded either as an input to strategy or a direct outcome. An exception to this is what is referred to as the resource-based view of the firm. Successful performance is a function of a firm's core competences which can include skills of the workforce or of part of the workforce (Prahalad and Hamal, 1990). Organisational performance can therefore be improved and strategic objectives achieved by focusing development on key groups such as managers.

The importance of the HR context

In addition to interest in core competences, throughout the 1990s there have been attempts to show the link between HRM practices and the bottom line involving studies that show the benefits of what is referred to as a 'high-road' HRM strategy of high training, high involvement, high rewards and quality commitment (Cooke, 2000; p.2). Further, it is suggested that key HR practices must be introduced and implemented in a 'bundle' (p.5) so that they enhance and support each other, contributing to a positive HR context.

The importance of a positive HR context was highlighted as the most influential determinant of MD processes in a model presented by Mabey (2002). Drawing further on data from the 1997 survey (Thomson *et al*, 1997), Mabey developed the model composed of the following elements:

- structural context – including size, centralisation, growth and HRM context
- MD processes – including policy, diagnosis and review, organisational responsibility, the priority given to MD
- volume and type of MD – including the amount, formality/informality, external
- MD outcomes – meeting the objectives of programmes, the impact on the organisation.

Figure 6 shows the relationship between the elements: bold lines indicate statistically significant paths at $p<0.01$ and dotted lines inidcate paths at $p<0.05$.

As mentioned above, Mabey found that HR context – composed of the use of planned career structures, succession planning and fast-tracking – was linked to all the process measures. It suggested that taking a long-term view about managers is more likely to result in attention to their development over time and viewing their contribution as strategic. Another key finding from the model, and clearly related to the idea of a positive context, was the importance given to informal learning and development. This finding highlights again an important feature of our own position on successful MD which we will explore below. These findings will give much support to adopting HR practices and giving priority to people (including managers) in strategic considerations. However, as Guest (2000) reported from a survey of over 1,000

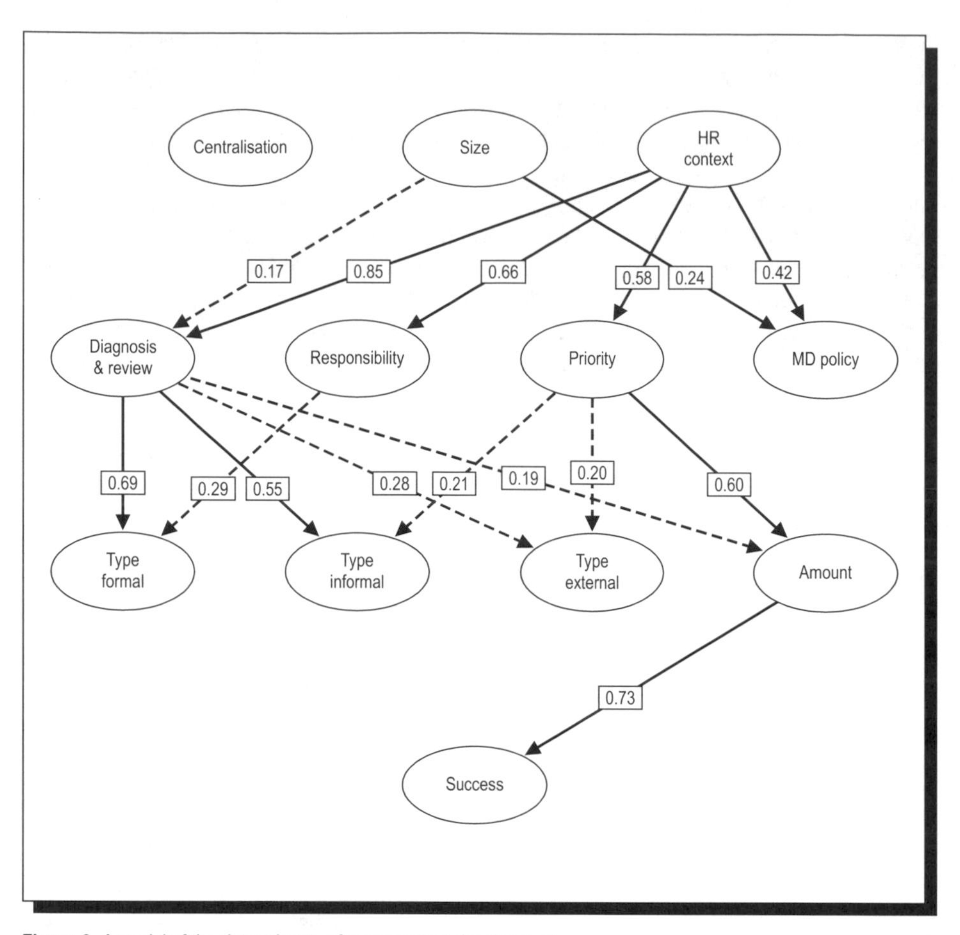

Figure 6 *A model of the determinants of management development*
Source: Mabey (2002, p.1153)

managers and chief executives, most respondents (90 per cent) did not put people issues as a top priority even though those that adopted 'high-commitment' HRM practices showed a good link to business performance.

What is interesting here is that there seems to be a difference between the rhetoric of a strategic approach to MD and the reality. For example, MD specialists may be keen to point out how they always consider business strategy in whatever they provide, but this may often have the effect of having to cut back when required by business circumstances (Storey and Tate, 2000). Further, Mabey and Thomson (2000), in comparing the views of HRD managers and MBA managers found a strong difference of views on whether MD linked to business strategy. A majority of MBA managers saw little link, probably because they had a more precise view of what is meant by strategy. What seems to be evident is that in many cases, even where there is a high priority given to MD, there is still an adherence to a top-down view of how the connection between strategy and MD should work. What is missing is an appreciation of the everyday dynamics, difficulties and uncertainties that managers learn to cope with and how this can easily diverge from the requirements of expressed strategy. MD systems can easily become sealed off from the realities that managers face too (Doyle, 1995). However, there are other ways the connection can be considered, and what is important is that organisations do have a choice, irrespective of their size, structure and sector. As argued by Mabey and Thomson (2000; p.12):

> **enhancing the outcomes of management development is ... within the hands of the organisations themselves and the way they organise and prioritise their management development processes and systems.**

REFLECT – CONCLUDE – PLAN 4

- Other than a top-down view, what other ways can you see of linking strategy to MD?
- Is there too strong a conflict with everyday pressures and practice of managers?
- What could you do to enhance the link?

LEARNING AND STRATEGY

Mintzberg provided the following example of how learning from work can become strategic (Mintzberg, 1987; p.68):

> **A salesman visits a customer. The product isn't quite right, and together they work out some modifications. The salesman returns to the company and puts the changes through; after two or three more rounds, they finally get it right. A new product emerges, which eventually opens up a new market. The company has changed strategic course.**

We might add that if the salesman's manager was performing effectively, the manager would be playing a vital role in this process, learning quite naturally through the work with the salesman and the customer with the result that has a strategic effect. This example highlights for us the importance of natural and informal learning for managers and how this could work as contrast to the top-down, formal views of strategy and MD.

If you refer back to Burgoyne's (1988) model in Table 2, the feature of what he described as 'natural' MD processes and as 'usually good and destined always to be the major provider of MD' seemed to disappear from his model after Level 1. It may be that he meant to imply that such natural processes continued at all levels, but in fact no further attention was paid to them. However, as we have suggested above, natural or informal MD activities would seem to have a vital role to play in organisations. Indeed, we could argue, along with others (Burgoyne and Hodgson, 1983; Stuart, 1984) that managers cannot help but learn informally and naturally by working on the problems and solutions in a particular work context. While much of this learning will occur in an unplanned manner and often without clear intention, we argue that it also has a potential to become more deliberate and feed into an organisation's strategy. We believe that it is important to include both informal and formal learning experiences to capture the totality of MD in an organisation, and in Chapter 6 we will provide such a model. However, it should not be too difficult to work out that managers have many opportunities in the performance of their work which may in turn result in new organisation strategies.

REFLECT – CONCLUDE – PLAN 5

- Can you think of any examples of where ideas for new products or services emerged from unplanned activities in your organisation?
- How could your organisation support this process?

We argue that organisations can make a stronger link between the learning of managers and their strategy. To do this, we draw on the work of Henry Mintzberg and his colleagues (1998) who, in an intriguingly entitled book called *Strategy Safari*, set out to take us on 'A guided tour through the wilds of strategic management'. At the start of the tour, the authors outline what for many organisations is the orthodox version of strategy as a deliberate and purposeful process passing through distinct phases of formulation, implementation and control. Mintzberg *et al* (1998) suggest that this orthodoxy is represented by a range of techniques and prescriptions developed within three schools of strategic management: the Design School, the Planning School and the Positioning School.[6] We do not intend to provide further details of these schools except to say that each contributes to a prescription of how strategies should be made and carried out, and this could include guidance for the nature and type of MD provision. However, a key purpose of the book is to contrast prescriptive schools with other approaches which are less prescriptive and pay more attention to processes that make strategy (or not). In particular, we will draw on two of these schools: the Learning School and the Power School.

The Learning School works on the difficulties of prescriptive approaches and the frequent failure of strategic plans. A crucial feature is attention to the way strategy is formed through ongoing actions and decisions from a variety of sources which lead to small changes at work but eventually a change in direction. In this way, strategy is said to emerge, sometimes accidentally and unplanned, through the learning of people in organisations and the work that they do. Much of Mintzberg's work has been concerned with emergent strategy (see Mintzberg and Waters, 1985). One particularly striking image, which highlights how strategy can emerge often unconsciously without clear direction, is the idea that strategies are like 'weeds in a garden' which take 'root in all kinds of strange places' (Mintzberg *et al*, 1998; p.195). If we apply this to MD, we can see that managers can learn in any context, probably unintentionally or by accident. Such learning cannot be planned or pre-determined; indeed, its overall shape and direction may take the organisation away from any attempts to formally specify what managers should learn. Thus a MD strategy that provides formal activities which are meant to provide managers with an indication of organisation preferences on how they should perform, can easily become distorted or countered by the emergent processes that occur in everyday activity.

Of course, there is no guarantee that the emergent learning (the weeds) will be fully recognised and translated into strategies from which the organisation may benefit. As Mintzberg *et al* (1998; p.195) suggest, 'Real learning takes place at the interface of thought and action, as actors reflect on what they have done.' This is the prompt for management learning where the integration of management work and attention to learning from that work not only creates the potential for both a critique of existing ideas and actions but the development of new ones. An important part this is the opportunity to reflect on work completed, and this provides the space for understanding what has happened and for identifying how improvements can be made. Such improvements can relate both to the manager's performance and the work carried out. Through successive activity, and reflection, both aspects can work as a 'bottom-up' process to change organisational strategy.

WEB LINK

In recent years, the idea of emergent strategy has been developed to incorporate ideas on chaos and complexity. You can find out more about these developments at
http://www.santafeassociates.com/
and
http://is.lse.ac.uk/complexity/default.htm

Mintzberg *et al*'s (1998) presentation of the Power School is an important reminder that power and politics frequently influence what strategies are formed and, we would suggest, have an important impact on MD. The process by which new ideas emerge from management learning seldom take a smooth path. Such ideas require friends and allies but there may also be contests over resources and the approval of key stakeholders in making ideas work or move on. Increasingly it is being recognised that talk and the use of language in negotiating and persuading others are vital management skills (Holman and Thorpe, 2002). Even in the context of formal strategy-making activities there are always likely to be certain voices that are more privileged and dominate others (Gold *et al*, 2001).

We suggested that the Learning School offered the potential of allowing emergent learning from management activities to feed into organisational strategy. However, there is also the possibility that this might be prevented by the working of power and influence in organisations. There is also the possilility that managers learn not to learn or resist learning. How can MD be cast as antithesis of learning? Salaman and Butler (1990) suggested that hierarchic structures and the cultures where managers are located had an effect on managers and learning through particular value/reward systems. For example, they identified the way power is excerised as a source of what managers must learn and which behaviours are rewarded or penalised. This structures much of the everyday experience of managers, causing them to resist change or new forms of behaviour advocated in training courses. Indeed, the gap between new ideas and allowed behaviour can easily breed cynicism about courses (p.187) and, we would argue, any approach to learning which deviates from what is valued. Managers thus learn what they are supposed to learn and what is in their interests to learn to survive on an everyday basis.

This consideration of the Power School of strategy also prompts awareness that managers always learn and develop in a specific context comprising specific tasks and activities using tangible resources but also composed of values, beliefs, symbols, stories, myths and legends. The latter are usually referred to as the organisational culture, an issue which has received considerable attention for the last 25 years and which undoubtedly has played a key role in influencing the nature, style and effectiveness of MD activity. Indeed, the desire to create strong cultures or simply change culture to bring about more positive attitudes is often an underpinning feature of many MD programmes.

SUMMARY

- It is a frequent assumption that there is a linear connection between MD, good managers and the successful performance of managers, success in organisations and national economic success.
- In the 2000s, a Council for Excellence in Management and Leadership found continuing problems with respect to the ability to undertake learning opportunities, the amount of MD in small and medium-sized organisations, and the professions.
- MD can be seen a 'strategic tool' to implement organisational strategy development and improve business performance.
- The HRM context has been found to be a key factor in leading to more MD in an organisation.
- A learning approach to making strategy highlights how ongoing actions and decisions by managers at work can lead to small changes at work but eventually a change in direction.
- Power and influence from different sources through particular value/reward systems may affect the potential of managers to learn.

DISCUSSION QUESTIONS

1. 'Management development should be aligned to corporate strategy.' Discuss.
2. Research has suggested that 45 per cent of organisations give a high priority to management development in the UK. Why do you think there has been an increase in the priority given to management development, and does this reduce or remove concerns about the quality and quantity of managers in organisations?
3. Does management development become more important as an organisation matures?
4. Is there a difference between our beliefs about management development and what we actually do and achieve?
5. Is there a link between management development and the nation's productivity performance?
6. Could the link between strategy and MD be improved in your organisation?
7. How can management learning from everyday activities become strategic?

FURTHER READING

CIPD (2002) *Developing Managers for Business Performance*. London, Chartered Institute of Personnel and Development.

CLARKE, M. (1999) 'Management development as a game of meaningless outcomes', *Human Resource Management Journal*, Vol. 9, No. 2; pp.38–49.

HIRSH, W. and CARTER, A. (2002) *New Directions in Management Development*, Report 387. Brighton, Institute of Employment Studies.

SYRETT, M. and LAMMIMAN, J. (1999) *Management Development: Making the investment count*. London, Economist Books.

WINTERTON, J. and WINTERTON, R. (1997) 'Does management development matter?', *British Journal of Management*, Vol. 8, June; pp.65–76.

GROUP ACTIVITY

- Form a group of four, each person should be familiar with one organisation.
- Focusing on his or her organisation, each person should consider some of the key stakeholders in relation to management development in that organisation. For example, the chief executive, managing rirector or equivalent, the head of finance, the HR manager, trainers, senior managers, junior managers, staff, etc. Try to identify at least six stakeholders per organisation.
- Now complete the following:
  - Considering each stakeholder identified in turn, try to identify their expectations and goals for management development and how they far they value management development. You may be able to assess these from past meetings, documents or actions. You may have to ask them, if possible.
  - Map your findings on a large sheet of paper. Consider how far the stakeholders' interests in management development complement each other and how far they differ.
  - What implications do the findings have for the management development strategy in the organisation?
- Meet with the other members of your group to share your findings.
- Prepare a combined presentation on the importance of stakeholder views for management development strategy and implementation.

REFERENCES

BOSTWORTH, D., DAVIES, R. and WILSON, R. (2002) *Managerial Qualifications and Organisational Performance: An analysis of ESS 1999*. Warwick Institute for Employment Research, Warwick University.

BURGOYNE, J. (1988) 'Management development for the individual and the organisation', *Personnel Management*, June; pp.40–44.

BURGOYNE, J. and HODGSON, V. (1983) 'Natural learning and managerial action: a phenomenological study in the field setting', *Journal of Management Studies*, Vol. 20, No. 3; pp.387–399.

BURGOYNE, J. and REYNOLDS, M. (1997) 'Introduction', in J. Burgoyne and M. Reynolds (eds) *Management Learning*. London, Sage.

CEML (2002) *Managers and Leaders: Raising our game*. London, Council for Excellence in Management and Leadership.

CIPD (2002) *Developing Managers for Business Performance*. London, Chartered Institute of Personnel and Development.

COLEMAN, S. and KEEP, E. (2001) Background literature review for PIU project on workforce development. London, Cabinet Office Performance and Innovation Unit.

COOKE, F. L. (2000) *Human Resource Strategy to Improve Organisational Performance: A route for British firms?* Working Paper 9, ESRC Future of Work Programme. Swindon, ESRC.

CONSTABLE, J. and McCORMICK, R. (1987) *The Making of British Managers*. London, BIM/CBI.

DOYLE, M. (1995) 'Organisation transformation and renewal', *Personnel Review*, Vol. 24, No. 6; pp.6–18.

EXWORTHY, M. and HALFORD, S. (eds) (1999) *Professionals and the New Managerialism in the Public Sector*. Buckingham, Open University Press.

GARAVAN, T., BARNICLE, B. and O'SUILLEABHAIN, F. (1999) 'Management development: contemporary trends, issues and strategies', *Journal of European Industrial Training*, Vol. 23, No. 4/5; pp.191–207.

GIBB, A. (1997) 'Small firms training and competitiveness: building upon the small business as a learning organisation', *International Small Business Journal*, Vol. 15, No. 3; pp.13–29.

GOLD, J., SMITH, V. and RODGERS, H. (2001) 'Strategy and struggle: exploring strategic learning with participatory action research'. Paper presented to 2nd Researching Work and Learning Conference, Calgary, July.

GUEST, D. (2000) 'Piece by piece', *People Management*, Vol. 6, No. 15; pp.26–30.

HANDY, C. (1987) *The Making of Managers*. London, NEDO.

HAYES, C., ANDERSON, A. and FONDA, N. (1984) *Competence and Competition: Training and education in the Federal Republic of Germany, USA and Japan*. London, NEDO.

HOLBECHE, L. (1999) *Aligning Human Resources and Business Strategy*. London, Butterworth-Heinemann.

HOLMAN, D. and THORPE, R. (2002). *Management and Language*. London, Sage.

HOLMES, L. (1995) 'The making of real managers: ideology, identity and management development'. Available at http://www.re-skill.org.uk/relskill/realmgr.htm

JOHNSON, S. and WINTERTON, J. (1999) *Management Skills*. Research Paper 3. London, Skills Task Force.

MABEY, C. (2002) 'Mapping management development practice', *Journal of Management Studies*, Vol. 39, No. 8; pp.1139–1160.

MABEY, C. and THOMSON, A. (2000) 'The determinants of management development', *British Journal of Management*, Vol. 11, Special Issue; pp.3–16.

MABEY, C. and THOMSON, A. (2000a) 'Management development in the UK: a provider and participant perspective', *International Journal of Training and Development*, Vol. 4, No. 4; pp.272–286.

MACHIN, S. and VIGNOLES, A. (2001) *The Economic Benefits of Training to the Individual, the Firm and the Economy: The key issues*. London, Centre for the Economics of Education.

MINTZBERG, H. (1987) 'Crafting strategy', *Harvard Business Review*, July/August; pp.66–75.

MINTZBERG, H. and WATERS, J. A. (1985) 'Of strategies, deliberate and emergent', *Strategic Management Journal*, Vol. 6; pp.257–372.

MINTZBERG, H., AHLSTRAND, B. and LAMPEL, J. (1998) *Strategy Safari*. London, Prentice-Hall.

NSTF (1998) *Towards a National Skills Agenda*. London, Department for Education and Employment.

POLLITT, C. (2000) 'Is the emperor in his new underwear: an analysis of the impacts of public management reform', *Public Management*, Vol. 2, No. 2; pp.181–199.

PRAHALAD, C. K. and HAMEL, G. (1990) 'The core competence of the corporation', *Harvard Business Review*, May/June; pp.79–91.

SALAMAN, G. and BUTLER, J. (1990) 'Why managers won't learn', *Management Education and Development*, Vol. 21, Part 3; pp.183–191.

SPARROW, P. and PETTIGREW, A. (1987) 'Britain's training problem: the search for a strategic human resources management approach', *Human Resource Management*, Vol. 26, No. 1; pp.109–127.

STOREY, J. and TATE, W. (2000) 'Management development', in S. Bach and K. Sisson (eds) *Personnel Management*. Oxford, Blackwell.

STUART, R. (1984) 'Towards re-establishing naturalism in management training and development', *Industrial and Commercial Training*, July/August; pp.19–21.

TUC (2002) *The Low Road*. TUC Employment Research. Available from http://www.tuc.org.uk/em_research/tuc-5459-f0.cfm

THOMSON, A., STOREY, J., MABEY, C., GRAY, C., FARMER, E. and THOMSON, R. A (1997) *A Portrait of Management Development*. London, Institute of Management.

THOMSON, A., MABEY, C., STOREY, J., GRAY, C. and ILES, P. (2001) *Changing Patterns of Management Development*. Oxford, Blackwell.

WILLIAMS, S. (2002) *Characteristics of the Management Population in the UK: Overview Report*. London, Council for Excellence in Management and Leadership.

ENDNOTES

1. In Chapter 8, we will examine other purposes of evaluation in MD.
2. A pamphlet published by the TUC (2002) specifically identified the attitudes of managers as responsible for a failure to adopt a 'high road' approach to competitive success based on high value-added product strategies, high levels of training and investment, high productivity and high wages and good terms and conditions. Managers might prefer to adopt a 'low road' approach based on control, lack of respect for staff and a belief that their staff cannot cope with greater consultation and participation in decision-making.
3. The Constable/McCormick Report (1987) was the result of four working parties: the Thomson Working Party – Perspectives on Management Training and Education: the Results of a Survey of Employers; the Stoddart Working Party – Demand as Perceived by Those who have Passed through a Course of Management Education either Undergraduate or Postgraduate Level; the Mangham Working Party – A Review of Management Education – A Survey of the In-House Activities of Ten Major Companies; and the Osbaldston Working Party – The Supply of Management Education

4 The processes of policy formation and auditing management development might be included in this model. We will consider these processes in more detail in Chapters 6 and 3 respectively.

5 The 'learning company' idea was promoted by, among others, the publication of Pedler, M., Burgoyne, J. and Boydell, T. (1991) *The Learning Company: A strategy for sustainable development*, Maidenhead: McGraw-Hill. We will consider the learning company/organisation in more detail in Chapter 12.

6 Minzberg *et al* (1998) refer to ten schools of strategic management, organised into three categories:

Prescriptive	**Process**	**Fit**
Design	Entrepreneurial	Configuration
Planning	Cognitive	
Positioning	Learning	
	Power	
	Cultural	
	Environmental	

Measuring managers

CHAPTER 3

Chapter outline

LEARNING OUTCOMES

After studying this chapter, you should be able to understand, explain, analyse and evaluate:

- **the difficulties of measuring management performance**
- **the value of a management development audit**
- **varying approaches to the meaning, development and use of management competences in organisations**
- **the use of competences for measuring management performance.**

INTRODUCTION

This chapter is concerned with processes and activities that enable an organisation to develop the means to measure management performance as a precursor to MD. A manager's job should be linked to the direction of the organisation and development based on a clear, formal view of the content of the job. At an individual level this means that there ought to be a job description and some statement of priorities and objectives, preferably drawn up on a three- to twelve-month cycle. To attempt to develop managers for jobs of which the purpose and nature are unclear, where the constraints and opportunities are unspecified, and where the boundaries are undefined, is to risk losing both sharpness and commitment to any subsequent development process. However, as we have seen in previous chapters, the link between a manager's job in terms of how it is performed and the requirements of strategy have not been well made in many organisations.

MODELS AND MEASURES

One of the difficulties relates to competing versions of what managers actually do in their work – the hub of management performance. While not all models are explicitly expressed, a model of management performance requirements provides a kind of organisation template to measure managers. The extent to which a manager meets the specification for performance can then be accurately assessed. Any deficiency reveals a need for improvement and at least some of these needs can be met by a development process. It is best if such models are explicitly stated since models of management and measurement which are implicitly held and used on an everyday basis, without being written down, are not helpful for focused development.

The search for a model

As we mentioned in Chapter 1, throughout the last century there has been a search for a 'true' model of management performance in terms of the knowledge, skills, abilities, attitudes, behaviours and results – a search which continues into the 2000s. Further, at particular moments the search is flavoured by such terms as 'excellence', 'effective', competent', 'high-performing', and more recently 'transformational'.[1] Of course, we can point to the methods of F. W. Taylor and those that followed him, who attempted to provide a scientific explanation for human performance at work. However, there have always been many disputes relating to the extent to which such methods can be regarded as scientific even though the influence remains strong. There has been a growing interest in industrial or organisational psychology as part of an ongoing attraction for scientific explanations of human performance at work, especially the performance of managers.

WEB LINK

http://www.psychnet-uk.com/industrial_psychology/management_personnel_training.htm provides links to many resources relating to organisational and industrial psychology, including various measurement devices that claim scientific status.

Models of management performance that make a claim for scientific status will usually provide evidence, through various measurement devices, by reference to the concepts of reliability and validity. What model of management performance is present in such devices, and how can you decide which is appropriate? Firstly, it would seem important to make a distinction between models which seem to apply to all managers in all contexts (or specified subcontexts such as professional organisations) and those which apply only to managers in particular situations. The first are referred to as generic models and the second as organisation-specific models. For example, there have been various attempts to provide competency models of performance that could be used for all managers, such as the Management Standards in the UK (see below). We might also include as generic all the efforts to provide integrated models of management abilities based on texts and research on management. For example, Perren and Burgoyne (2002) sought to set out a framework of management and leadership abilities from 'well-known' texts and frameworks as well as primary data. The result was a framework of 83 management and leadership abilities shown as Figure 7.

Organisation-specific approaches recognise the importance of context, particularly how the expression of abilities or competences must reflect the meanings of an individual organisation. Many organisations prefer to develop their own models of management performance the specificity of which can help to provide more effective MD.

A second issue to consider is what is meant by performance in management. One way of thinking about performance is as a relationship between means and ends. A manager thus starts off with a set of abilities consisting of skills, knowledge and attitudes which are applied to work. Through such application, particular results or outputs are achieved. Between means and ends lies the process of managing. Figure 8 represents such a view.

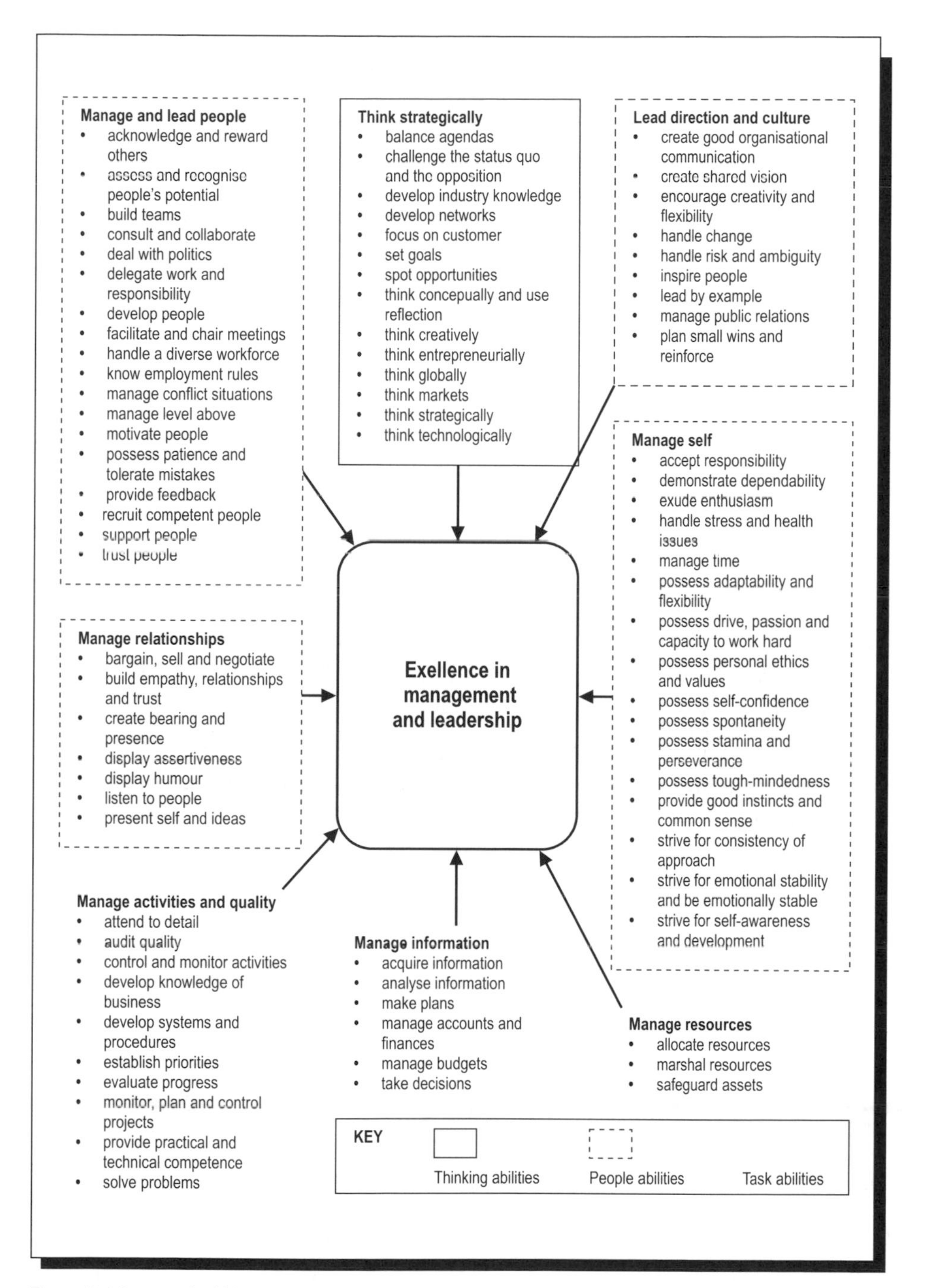

Figure 7 *A framework of 83 management and leadership abilities*

Source: Perren and Burgoyne (2002)

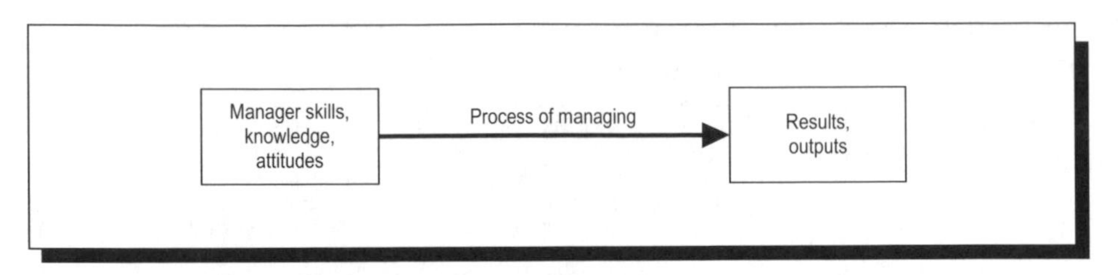

Figure 8 *Performance as a relationship between means and ends*

One obvious result of this view is that it is easier to focus on either the means or the ends (or both) in considering how managers could be assessed and development needs determined. A means focus might therefore be concerned with producing a typology of desired skills, knowledge and attitudes which could be measured. An ends focus would consider either quantitative or qualitative results achieved and whether these met particular criteria or standards. As a consequence, many models of management performance tend to favour either a means approach to measurement – for example, inventories of skills and attitudes – or an ends approach – for example, the achievement of objectives and targets, proof against standards.

REFLECT – CONCLUDE – PLAN 1

- Which view does your organisation favour?
- What limitations are there with the approach used?
- What could you do about any limitations?

The large number of possible management abilities and the very many measurement devices for both means and ends does raise considerable doubts about our knowledge and understanding of management performance. Perhaps the growing number of measurement devices on offer is proof that we are getting closer to the truth and that by combining various measurements a fairly accurate picture (valid and reliable) of a manager can be obtained. However, a critic might believe that such measurements do not provide the full reality but play a vital role in constructing it (Astley, 1985). For example, a manager might be assessed as being in need of planning skills or as representing a Myers-Briggs type of ISTJ.[2] Problems arise in the interpretation of such descriptions and in the credibility of measurement devices in the eyes of managers. Potentially, this gives tremendous power to those who have knowledge and expertise relating to the descriptions in measuring and assessing managers – as we will see below when we examine competency frameworks. It may also lead to responses by managers that the assessments do not relate to their own experiences or feelings.

One of the reasons for the difficulty in measuring performance is that how a manager performs may not always be visible or accessible to those seeking to measure performance. Process always occurs in a time and place, usually with other people, and such contextual factors can have a significant bearing on what actually happens – but it also complicates the picture of management performance. Further, process is concerned with dynamic activity and movement involving more than one person. It could therefore become very difficult to isolate the part played by a manager in such a process. However, access to process will disclose how managers have applied their abilities in particular situations and how work is carried out. Attention to process will provide key information about a manager and the needs for

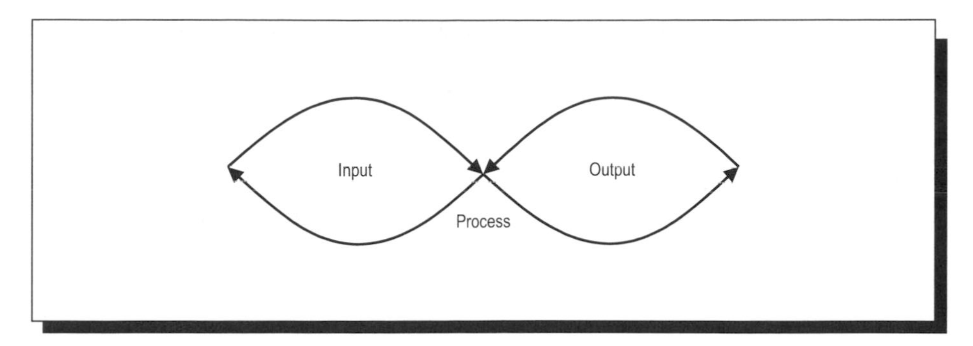

Figure 9 *An integrated view of management performance*
Source: Leary et al (1986)

development. One view of management performance that included attention to process was provided by Leary *et al* (1986). It was argued that effectiveness in management required a consideration of inputs, outputs and processes, and that bringing these dimensions together integrates management performance and has a 'holistic quality' (p.6). Attention to process will allow an assessment of the 'quality of the connection' between means and ends. Figure 9 shows a representation of this integrated view.

Giving more prominence to process is more likely to accord with a manager's experience of work as a dynamic and living activity. Recently, Watson (2001) has spoken of the idea of the 'emergent manager', which highlights management as an ongoing process of interaction. To think about management – better stated as managing – in this way requires a shift in perspective from a view of the world as entities, things and individual managers whose needs can be objectively assessed towards a view of the world as movement, processes and relations between managers and others. Measuring and assessing managers requires consideration of the various processes of interaction with others, and this is one of the reasons for the growing interest in multi-source feedback and self-assessment, which we will consider in Chapter 4. It also highlights assessing MD needs as an ongoing process of interaction with those involved, not asking them to act as distant and objective observers.

THE MANAGEMENT DEVELOPMENT AUDIT

The various tensions that may surface in the assessment of MD needs might be accommodated by a management development audit (MDA). Auditing, of course, is a term borrowed from the field of accountancy and carries with it an image of independence and professional standards. Indeed, according to Easterby-Smith *et al* (1980), an MDA is 'designed to establish a clear picture of management development within an organisation' (p.12) by the use of an unbiased process which does not advocate a particular point of view or solution. Notwithstanding our previous comments relating to the difficulty of adopting an objective stance, an MDA provides an opportunity for an organisation to find out what managers want, how they feel about what they are getting, and whether management development is effective, adding value and in line with organisation requirements. You can see that an MDA, concerned as it is with effectiveness and adding value, has a clear connection to evaluation. Indeed, it is probably best to see MDA as a continuous activity of gaining a broad view of MD needs and assessing its value.

In the UK, as part of its endeavours to give more prominence to management and leadership capability, the Council for Excellence in Management and Leadership (CEML) has sought to develop a national scheme of indicators relating to development and utilisation of management and leadership capability. The result was a framework to show the chain of impact from management capability to business performance and outcome measures (Tamkin *et al*, 2002). Figure 10 shows the framework.

The framework in use could highlight a number of deficiencies in management capability and gaps in information, and therefore could be a part of an MDA. A key factor in organisations is how such information is managed and used in decisions about MD.

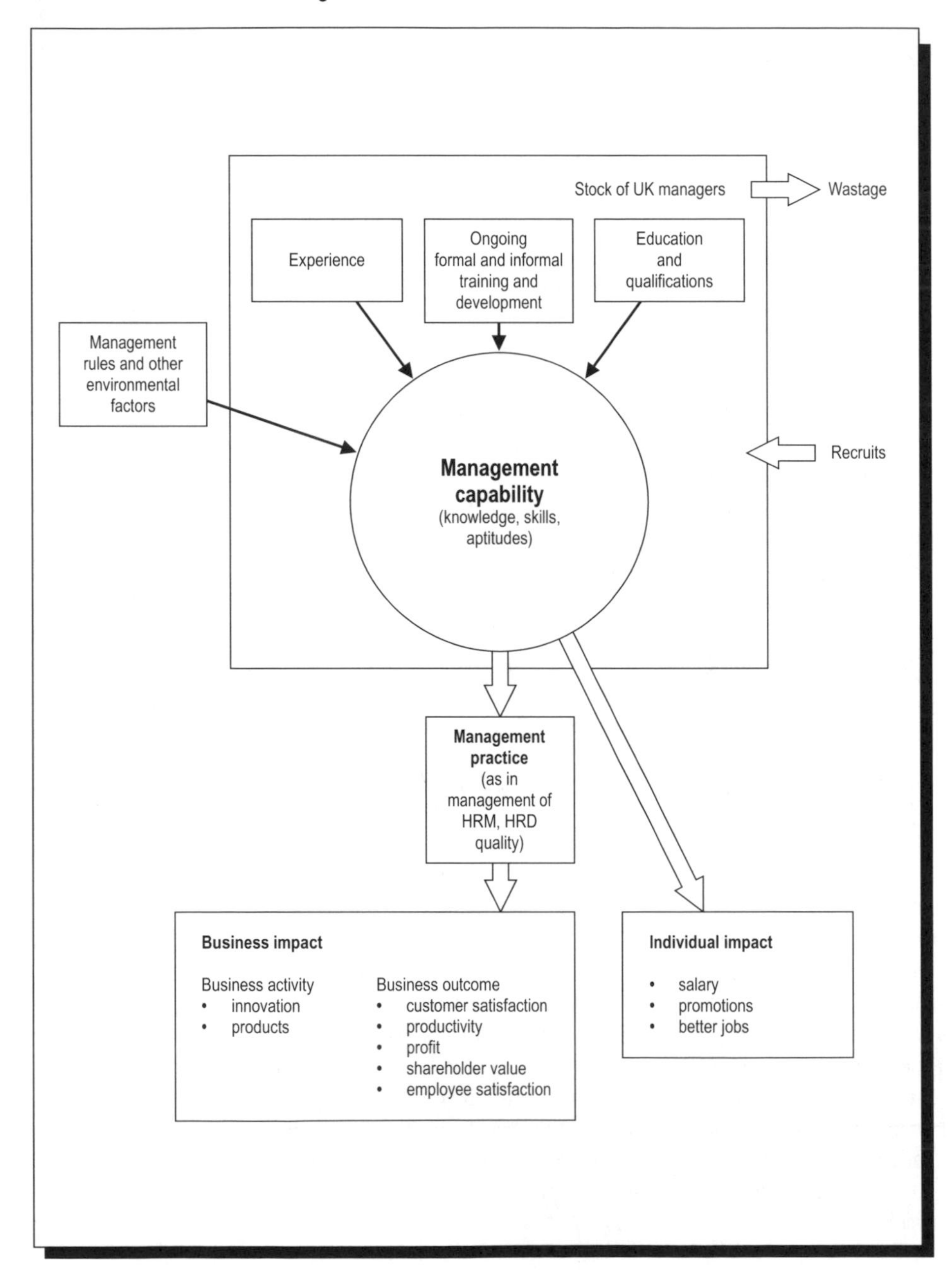

Figure 10 *A framework for the measurement of management capability*
Source: Tamkin et al (2002)

Organisation-level MDA

At a basic level, an MDA is a data-gathering exercise concerning the whole MD framework within an organisation and the operation of the key activities. Because MDAs can be rather intensive activities, and might involve considerable expense and time as well as the generation of large amounts of data, it is important to establish the main purpose and whose expectations must be considered. An MDA can serve a variety of purposes, such as assessing needs for MD, proving added value and/or controlling cost. It might also lead to the improvement of MD activities as a whole. In addition, MDAs could have a role in initiating activities and interventions (Easterby-Smith *et al*, 1980) such as an organisational change programme.

In Chapter 2, we presented a sustaining model of management development (Figure 5) within which MD policy responded to organisation strategy, and in turn MD activities responded to policy, outcomes occurring as a consequence. An MDA will be concerned with all these aspects, but particular attention will be paid to MD activities.

Table 3 suggests what might be considered within an MDA.

Of course there will be links between each of these activities, and the activities themselves can be thought of as sub-systems within a whole. For the activity of appraisal, there will thus be:

- inputs for the activity such as documents, briefing sheets, appraisal skills of the interviewer and interviewee
- the process of the activity such as the interview itself, documents and resources used
- outcomes of the activity such as documents with MD needs identified, feelings about the process.

If an MDA is concerned with the gathering and then the analysis of data, it should be possible to identify data sources for each activity and a variety of techniques such as:

- interviews
- surveys
- observations
- documents.

In the light of our previous consideration of multiple interests in MD, it is evident that an MDA can also become rather a political process, different interests vying for influence on the

Table 3 *Management development activities for audit*

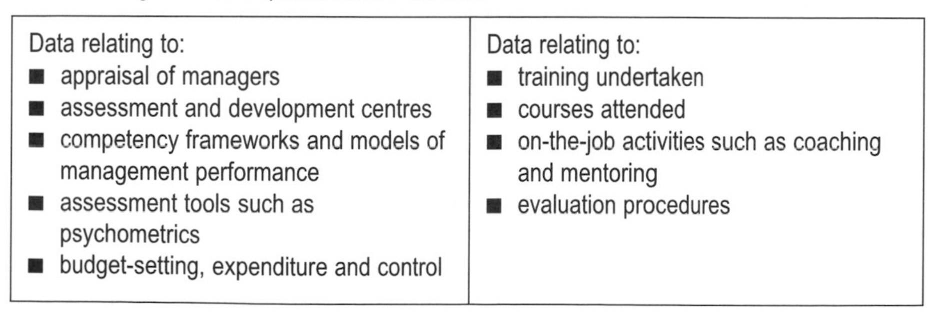

Data relating to:	Data relating to:
■ appraisal of managers ■ assessment and development centres ■ competency frameworks and models of management performance ■ assessment tools such as psychometrics ■ budget-setting, expenditure and control	■ training undertaken ■ courses attended ■ on-the-job activities such as coaching and mentoring ■ evaluation procedures

results. For example, if one consequence of MDA is an organisational MD initiative, the shape of the initiative and its overall aims and objectives will be the concern of different interests affected.

It has become important for MD to show its connection to organisational strategy, and an MDA is likely to provide a means to achieve this. It can serve to prevent MD activities from becoming isolated from organisational objectives and help those involved in MD specify clearly how provision contributes. The CIPD (2002) found that the link between business plans and MD was seldom made, mainly due to the quality of strategic management processes which depended on good-quality information, broad stakeholder involvement, rigorous analysis and debate and clear success criteria. It is suggested that senior managers need to develop their understanding of organisation and management preconditions for business success so that they gain sufficient insight to initiate change or other developments in the organisation. An MDA can thus become part of a business, organisation and management review (BOMR) process to provide 'a clear view of the contribution expected from managers to today's and tomorrow's business models and a business-centred brief for managers and developers to work from' (p.19).

WEB LINK

Another approach is to try CEML's online Best Practice Guide for Leadership Development at
http://www.managementandleadershipcouncil.org/GPG/launch.asp
It is designed to help organisations review their leadership development strategies where leadership development activity is aligned with the values and visions of the organisation.

There are other approaches which provide senior managers with a diagnosis of the whole organisation and which can reveal MD needs. The value of such approaches is that they provide key information which can be used in forming a strategy while at the same time they reveal possible areas for MD and more generally HRD for the whole organisation. For example, the Total Quality Management (TQM) movement which emerged in the 1980s can be seen as set of tools or an attempt to bring about lasting change and a culture of continuous improvements. To promote the latter, the European Foundation for Quality Management (EFQM) has developed a model which can be used to assess an organisation against nine criteria of excellence. In the UK, the model is referred to as the Business Excellence Model (BEM). The crucial feature of the model is that by understanding how the whole organisation works, managers can identify ways to make improvements sometimes by assessing and responding to development needs. An alternative approach is to use Investors in People (IiP). Since 1991, IiP has provided criteria or a set of 'national' standards which focus more specifically on training and development. Crucially, the standards require the development of a business plan which includes plans to develop all employees and the evaluation of the results. Like EFQM, the main benefits from IiP are seen to come when it is used to assess performance requirements and continuous improvement (Alberga *et al*, 1997). Recent developments of IiP include a module focused on management and leadership development.

In the public sector, a Best Value framework was introduced in 1997 to encourage a reorientation of service delivery towards citizens and customers and produce a quality-driven organisation (Sheffield and Coleshill, 2001). Best Value forms part of a statutory framework for performance management in local government, and initial evidence suggests that Best

Value can be used flexibly, highlighting strategic priorities and requirements for continuous improvement including MD (Martin and Hartley, 2000).

WEB LINKS

Further information about EFQM can be found at http://www.efqm.org/welcome.htm and details about its UK application, the Business Excellence Model can be found at http://www.businessexcellence.co.uk/business-excellence-model.htm
The Investors in People website at http://www.iipuk.co.uk/ provides access to copies of the national standard and the latest research on the future of IiP.
There is a government site on Best Value at
http://www.local-regions.odpm.gov.uk/bestvalue/bvindex.htm
and more information at
http://www.bvpps.audit-commission.gov.uk/
You might also visit http://balancedscorecard.com/index.htm. This is a site that shows how an organisation's strategy can be translated into key performance measures and requirements for learning and development.

These various approaches and tools all provide a means by which senior managers can take a whole-organisation approach to assessing MD needs, and simultaneously form a link with organisation objectives. To cement the link in place, so that needs assessed at organisational level become needs for managers, a means of translation is required – and in many organisations this has been provided by a management competency framework.

MANAGEMENT COMPETENCES[3]

Management competences (MC) are descriptions of behaviours, attributes, skills needed to perform management work effectively and/or the outputs to be achieved from such work which can be assessed against performance criteria. It is possible to use such descriptions as a central link in the determination of HR activities for managers (and others). Further, the link with strategy can be explicitly made – the descriptions used in MC frameworks are directly connected to organisational objectives and, in theory at least, provide the means by which those objectives can be achieved or the outputs which prove that the objectives have been met. The key point here is that organisational objectives and the various HR activities such as selection, appraisal, training and development and reward can be aligned (Holbeche 1999). Whiddett and Hollyforde (1999) suggest that there are two important benefits for HRM:

- Competences provide a language for describing effectiveness in an organisation. Throughout an organisation, a common understanding could thus be gained of such attributes as good leadership or planning.
- Competences allow a more consistent way to assess people because all assessors have the same understanding of what is to be assessed.

REFLECT – CONCLUDE – PLAN 2

- What is your view of the use of competences in MD?
- How are competences used to align HR activities in your organisation?
- What action can be taken to improve alignment?

The meaning of management competences

MC can be considered in different ways. For example, competency could be concerned with a manager's behaviour, the skills or attributes the manager has, or the outputs of management work and the standard achieved. These differences reflect various interests and debates that have occurred over the last 25 years relating to people's abilities and performance at work – debates between for example psychologists, educationists, policy-makers, HR and management specialists. However, the outcome of the debates is two approaches to MC:

- the behaviour approach
- the standards approach.

The behaviour approach principally stems from the work of Boyatzis (1982) in the USA, referred to in Chapter 1. He was mainly concerned with the characteristics of effective performance in management work, defined as the results achieved through specific actions by a manager's taking account of the particular policies, procedures and conditions of an organisation. Focusing on the specific action which leads to results, attention turned to identifying the characteristics or abilities of the person that enabled a person to demonstrate the appropriate actions. Management competences are therefore underlying characteristics or abilities[4] a manager brings to a situation which allows him or her to achieve results that are effective. However, because underlying characteristics and abilities are difficult to assess directly, most definitions of MC concentrate on the behaviours of managers for effective performance. For example, Woodruffe's (1992; p.17) definition is

> **'the set of behaviour patterns that the incumbent needs to bring to a position in order to perform its tasks and functions with competence.'**

One limitation of such a definition is the tendency to focus on individualising management performance, but it is worth stating that Boyatzis was always careful to specify that effective job performance was also affected by the environment in which the performance occurs and the requirements of the job. The MC identified by Boyatzis are shown in Table 4.

WEB LINK

You can read an interview with Richard Boyatzis at http://www.trainingjournal.co.uk/articles/boyatzis.htm

The work of Boyatzis and others who followed him led to a growing interest in MC that could be applied in any context – ie that were generic to all organisations. However, there has been an ongoing debate about whether this is possible, especially given the growing diversity of managers (Miller *at al*, 2001). Tovey (1993) argued that generic approaches did not take account of specific business needs and critical success factors with the result that incomplete pictures of management performance are formed which miss vital information on values, climate and culture. Further, there are likely to be different clusters of MC both within organisations and between organisations. Also, there may be very common terms that are used to describe managers' tasks – eg decision-making, planning – but these terms

Table 4 *Boyatzis' competency clusters*

Goal and action cluster	Leadership cluster	Human resource cluster	Directing subordinates cluster	Focus on others cluster
■ efficiency orientation ■ proactivity ■ diagnostic use of concepts	■ self-confidence ■ use of oral presentations ■ logical thought ■ concep-tualisation	■ use of socialised power ■ positive regard ■ managing group process ■ accurate self-assessment	■ developing others ■ use of unilat-eral power ■ spontaneity	■ self-control ■ perceptual objectivity ■ stamina and responsibility ■ concern with close relationships

Source: Boyatzis (1982)

often mean different things in different organisations. So from the mid-1980s onwards many organisations sought to develop MC frameworks that reflected the particular characteristics of their organisations as expressed in the language that was used to describe a good manager. Such frameworks are constructed by a research process that could include the following:

- interviews with senior managers to obtain views on current and future issues facing the organisation
- observation of managers and self-reports by managers (diaries)
- interviews with managers to identify characteristics of high performance and underperformance – use of critical incident technique, repertory grid and/or behavioural event interview
- focus groups to identify key competences
- benchmarking against other MC frameworks.

The result of the process is a framework of MC. Table 5 provides an example, which was developed for a financial services organisation in the UK. Note how the competences are grouped in five clusters.

Table 5 *A management competences framework for a UK financial services organisation*

Personal focus	Customer focus	Future focus	Business focus	People focus
■ self-control ■ self-development ■ personal organisation ■ positive approach	■ creating customer service ■ delivering customer service ■ continuous improvement	■ delivering the vision ■ change and creativity	■ delivering results ■ providing solutions ■ systemic thinking ■ attention to detail	■ developing people ■ working with others ■ influencing ■ leadership

Each competence is specified further by a *description* and *dimensions of behaviour*. For example, for the competence 'delivering results', the description is:

> **Sets clear, realistic but challenging objectives for self and others. Creates effective plans for self and/or others to contribute towards the achievement of business results. Regularly monitors and reviews progress and results.**

The dimensions of this competence are:

> **Dimension 1: Ensures strategy is converted into operational objectives and ensures delivery of plan.**
> **Dimension 2: Manages the achievement of operational plans.**
> **Dimension 3: Achieves results through peers within own team.**

Managers can then be assessed against the dimensions by identifiers of performance ranging from 'less than effective' to 'fully effective' to 'outstanding'. For example, 'outstanding performance' is identified as

> **Having an excellent track record of delivering to time, matching resource requirement to task needs.**

For this organisation, there are thus clear requirements for management performance which are aligned with business requirements in language that is meaningful to managers in the business. Notice how the focus is on behaviours although this still leads to the identification of outputs at different levels of effectiveness. This links the behaviour approach to MC to the standards approach.

The standards approach

The standards approach to MC was the outcome of two streams of activity that were occurring in the UK during the 1980s. Firstly, Government policy from 1981 was directed towards the development of standards of competence for different occupational areas which would lead to qualifications – later to be called National Vocational Qualifications or NVQs (SVQs in Scotland). Secondly, following the Handy/Constable Reports in 1987, a commitment to build long-term improvements in the way British managers were developed resulted in the establishment of a Management Charter Initiative (MCI). The MCI sought to achieve two major objectives:

- the development of a widely acceptable inventory of the main competences required by a manager
- the designation of 'chartered manager' as a professional qualification for those who successfully acquired and demonstrated such competences.

The idea of a chartered manager at that time proved rather contentious, but there was agreement on the need for a policy-making, standard-setting and accrediting body for national management qualifications in the context of the NVQ framework based on competences that were concerned with abilities to perform within an occupational area to standards required in employment. The crucial feature of this approach is that a manager is said to have achieved competence in an aspect of work if the output of his or her performance meets written standards and performance criteria and required evidence. Note also that there was an intention to develop an 'inventory' that was 'widely acceptable'. In other words, the standards approach for managers has been concerned with a generic model of MC.

The standards were developed through the use of Functional Analysis, a process which begins by clarifying the 'key purpose' of management and exploring the 'key roles' that managers have to perform. Each role is then broken down into units and elements with competence statements expressed as outcomes including performance criteria, allowing judgement of a manager's ability to carry out a particular element. The result was a generic model of management, first published in 1991, which was claimed to reflect best practice in management.

The model was revised in 1997, allowing for more choice, but the broad structure remained in line with the NVQ framework in England and Wales and the SVQ framework in Scotland.

Figure 11 shows the key purpose and key roles.

Each key role is further broken into:

- units of competence
- elements of competence for each unit
- performance criteria for each element.

In addition, there are 'knowledge requirements', 'evidence requirements' and 'examples of evidence' for each element. Management qualifications at different levels of the NVQ framework are formed from the various key roles and units and grouping them together, some units defined as compulsory and some as optional.

In 2000 responsibility for the management standards in the UK was passed from the MCI to the Management Standards Centre, an independent unit of the Chartered Management Institute.

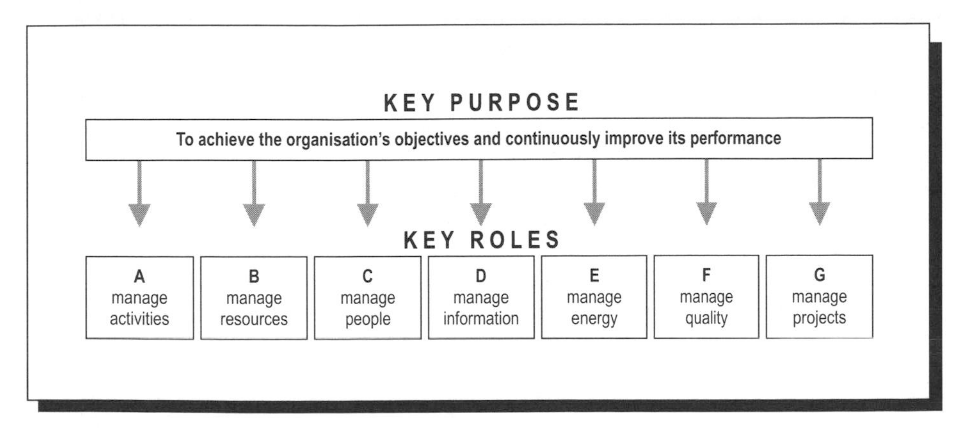

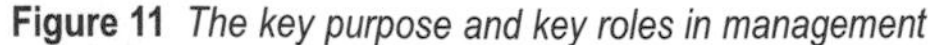
Figure 11 *The key purpose and key roles in management*

WEB LINKS

Details on the NVQ framework can be obtained from
http://www.dfes.gov.uk/nvq/
and http://www.sqa.org.uk/sqa/ in Scotland.
Go to http://www.management-standards.org/, the home page of the Management Standards Centre which is now the Standards Setting Body for the National Occupational Standards for Management.

There have undoubtedly been some benefits identified from the introduction of MC. For example, Strebler and Bevan (1996) found that MC were of assistance in the identification of training needs and the design of training programmes. This made the training more relevant and allowed the development of modules of training. Strebler *et al* (1997) found that multi-sourced feedback was facilitated and added value in assessment. Winterton and Winterton (1997) found that MC led to more coherence in the training structure, allowing for gaps to be more easily identified in training and a more precise specification of training needs. MC can also lead to managers taking more responsibility for the development of others where this is specified as part of the MC framework (Miller *et al*, 2001). In recent years, the behaviour approach has been augmented by interest in the idea of emotional intelligence (EI) (Goleman, 1998). EI is concerned with the ability of a person to understand his or her emotions and the emotions of others, and to manage these appropriately. Drawing on data from an annual benchmarking survey, research suggested that over one-third of employers, mostly in the private sector, had included EI in their competency frameworks (Miller *et al*, 2001).

Despite the benefits, there are also some recognised difficulties with MC. Since the first appearance of MC in the 1980s, there has been an ongoing debate on whether either the behaviour or the standards approach can succeed in providing accurate (valid and reliable) models of the work of managers, and whether MC are acceptable to managers in the assessment of needs for MD.

Technical difficulties

Organisations claim to introduce MC and competency frameworks more generally for a variety of reasons, such as to make the link between organisational objectives and individual objectives clearer and to facilitate organisational change. However, the introduction can be subject to a variety of responses, depending on the history of initiatives within the organisation. Strebler *et al* (1997) found that suspicions may be raised about the real purpose of competences, especially if there is a link to pay. There is also a problem related to the language used and the use of jargon. For example, Rankin (2001) suggested that inappropriate language hampers communication and understanding, and that organisations may need to spend considerable time training and explaining the use of competency frameworks in order to ensure commitment to use them.

MC frameworks may suffer from vague terms and attributes which are difficult to assess. This partly relates to continuing lack of clarity over the meaning of competence as either an aspect of personality such as a trait, characteristic, skill, etc, or an aspect of behaviour or an output to be achieved against a standard. The result may be difficulties concerning the use of MC as measurement in assessment. For example, the following description is taken from an organisation's MC framework:

> **Acts professionally, keeping personal feelings to one side.**

It might be argued that this includes terms that are difficult to explain and even more difficult to observe and measure. For example, what does it mean to act 'professionally'? How would you know it if you saw it? How do we know a manager is able to keep 'personal feelings to one side', and is this something that a manager can learn? The difficulty here is that MC do seek to clarify and specify management work, providing the means to measure management performance and set objectives for performance improvement and MD activities. However, such clarification is not without difficulties because management work is seldom clear-cut and is often carried out under conditions which cannot be controlled. Seeking to provide descriptions that clarify may also lead to a simplification of the complex and ambiguous realities that managers have to face. This seems particularly the case with MC that are concerned with interpersonal performance and that are difficult to observe and measure directly.

A further difficulty emerges from the proliferation of terms and documents which MC generate. Indeed, MC frameworks often produce significant amounts of paper and, even though much of this can now be stored electronically, the result is a bewildering and complex array of material which managers and others need to understand. This is partly due to the means that are used to produce MC, by which management performance is broken down into parts that are said to make a whole. The process of 'atomisation' leads to the expression of MC as many parts. This has been a particular issue with the standards approach in the UK, where there have been ongoing concerns relating to the levels of bureaucracy and paper-chasing to complete management NVQs and a variety of assessment practices (Swailes and Brown, 1999). Research by Holman and Hall (1996) into the use of management standards found that assessment had produced a 'tick-box approach' (p.199) and that achievement of standards against performance criteria became an end in itself rather than a means to challenge or change management practice. There is also a problem with the behaviour approach where the specification of categories of behaviour can result in a growing number of complex measures that become very difficult to manage and use in assessment – eg as part of a performance management system (Strebler *et al,* 1997).

The behaviour approach ought to have one benefit over the standards approach in the way that MC reflect business needs and have a future orientation. The standards approach by definition is concerned with managers' meeting performance criteria which allow assessment of performance as competent. This difference was recognised in some of the early commentaries on MC in the 1980s (Jacobs, 1989). However, this may create tension between the use of MC to improve current performance or as requirements for managers in the future. Strebler *et al* (1997) suggest that MC with future orientation can lead to raised career expectations which the organisation may not be able to match.

Paradoxically, the behaviour approach, which may attempt to consider the language and values of an organisation, may also suffer from being seen as lacking a technical or professional component for many managers. A good number of managers do not see themselves as general managers but as managers within a technical or professional context. Such managers are likely to see their work and their development as requiring attention to both management and technical and professional capabilities.

The behaviour approach may also serve to reinforce existing notions of effective management, and this may affect equal opportunities within an organisation. For example, the language to explain success in management and leadership may reflect particular gender stereotypes. Adams (1996) suggests that there are differences in how men and women may understand successful management styles, and in how behaviour by male managers may be interpreted and categorised differently compared to female managers' behaviour.

REFLECT – CONCLUDE – PLAN 3

- Do you use MC in your organisation? Are these behaviour- or standards-based?
- What is your view on their effectiveness?
- What improvements could you make?
- How would you carry out such improvements?

Theoretical critique

Since the early 1980s there has been a theoretical critique which seeks to problematise the whole notion of MC, questioning their development and underpinning rationale and highlighting the deleterious effects. Although there are a variety of strands to the critique, at the heart of the argument is the view that MC represent another 'one best way' attempt to describe what managers must be and/or do to be competent, effective, excellent, superior, etc. Furthermore, MC adopt a technical orientation which attempt to describe human actions in functional terms (Garavan and McGuire, 2001). By adopting a stance that particular skills, characteristics, behaviours and outputs can be tied to the purpose of achieving organisational objectives, claims can be made for the neutrality, objectivity and even scientific basis of the process of developing MC and the result. MC can therefore easily become a prescription for management performance which can be utilised to define the requirements of a whole range of HR practices relating to managers. As one senior manager jokingly responded to the MC developed by Watson (1994; p.222):

> **This should come in useful when I have to decide which of my first line I am going to sack.**

Both the behaviour and standard approaches to MC are prone to reduce management performance into a set of parts – ie skills, knowledge, characteristics, behaviours, outputs – which are said to make a whole if combined together, as if they were a set of building bricks. In this sense MC are atomistic in the way they break up management performance into fragments. In addition, MC have an individualistic bias which focuses attention and development on individual managers, to the neglect of their participation in teams and their relationship with others in a particular context. This occurs despite warnings by Boyatzis (1982) and others that such a simple view could not be adopted. Further, since MC define management performance, all MD needs stem from them and there can be no other reasons for MD other than those specified by the MC framework. The standards approach in particular has been criticised for its emphasis on outputs and assessment against standards which lead to training and development underpinned by behavioural psychology (Marshall, 1991) where the desired effect of learning is the achievement of the standard, caused by behavioural adjustments. Managers and others learn in far more complex ways, however (see Chapter 5).

Much of the theoretical critique is concerned with the way MC give power to those who seek to control management performance. Holmes (1995), for example, explains how the expression of competences through discourse and language serves not just to describe and identify them but to play a key role in constructing them. That is, if MC describe an attribute for management performance as 'Setting clear objectives for self and others', this may make a great deal of sense to those making an MC framework, but the very act of making sense produces the knowledge as a requirement for management performance and provides power to those who make judgements about performance. Once accepted – and MC are usually subject to a degree of discussion and argument before acceptance – they become 'taken as a rational and legitimate way of talking about' (Holmes 1995; p.36) management performance and participating in the various activities in which they are utilised.

MC as discourse also provides a source for critique by those who take a stance based on the work of the French philosopher Michel Foucault. The particular interest here is how MC act as a form of distant governance on managers who respond by self-regulating their activities according to the values and norms set by the MC. Once again attention is focused on the power of MC to make something known – ie the requirements for competent management performance – which makes it potentially governable and subject to a 'system of domination' (Townley 1993; p.225). The more managers become involved in the use of MC, the greater the possibility they will accept them as the truth about their own performance as managers, although a Foucault analysis points to the historically contingent and unfixed nature of any claims about truth in human existence. Managers may thus fail to recognise themselves within MC frameworks, but such might be the power of the system of domination that this might be considered a failure to recognise the truth about themselves. Managers must therefore define their weaknesses in terms specified by the MC. In this way, MC produce the self-knowledge required for managers to make improvements (Brewis, 1996).

WEB LINKS

The work of Michel Foucault has been a very important source of writing for those who wish to take a critical stance towards management learning and development. If you wish to find out more about Foucault, try
http://www.theory.org.uk/foucault/
or
http://www.thefoucauldian.co.uk/

That MC seem to be used by many organisations to define or 'redefine' management performance was one of the findings by Salaman and Taylor (2002). They found that organisations were able to use MC to state the qualities needed for change, such as customer focus, commercial awareness and market sensitivity in a variety of contexts. Indeed, MC were seen as a key method to communicate new requirements to managers and this often involved alignment with organisational goals and an intensification of effort to achieve them. Managers were thus required to take on new responsibilities previously performed by others such as HR. The findings support other critiques that MC in defining the qualities required of managers, simultaneously provide a means to control them and reinforce the view of organisations as 'rational, machine-like and consensual structures' (p.21).

At first glance, MC would appear to provide the solution to many organisational concerns about management performance and improvement through the specification of either behaviours or standards for managers. In addition, such specification can be aligned with the overall function of management and/or organisational strategy and objectives. In times of change, and as a means to bring that change about, MC provide a common language to define the qualities needed and/or the outcomes to be achieved. Where managers do not meet the requirements specified, this can lead to the identification of needs for MD. However, we have also seen that MC as a movement have been subject to an ongoing technical and theoretical critique. One particular point must shine through – management performance is a complex and multi-faceted phenomenon frequently characterised by flux, movement, ambiguity and uncertainty which cannot be reduced to or explained by a fragmented typology as represented by MC. Burgoyne (1989; p.60) questioned how MC could account for the 'holistic nature of management', and this question has not been and perhaps cannot be answered. We have seen the power effects of the specification of MC but we might also consider what such specification leaves out or cannot include. For example, spontaneity, creativity, and telling stories or good jokes might be considered important management activities, but it would be difficult to measure the skills needed, the knowledge required or the standard to be reached. There are also ethical and moral concerns to consider. As we noted earlier, management performance considered as a process occurs in a time and place as a dynamic activity involving more than one person. As well as creating difficulties for measuring the part played by a manager in such a milieu, the language of measurement may simply not be adequate to represent the movement that occurs and out of which needs for MD emerge.

REFLECT – CONCLUDE – PLAN 4

- Do you or your organisation ever refer to the development of managers as a building process? Do you refer to foundation skills or blocks, for example?
- Is MD limited by MC in your organisation?

SUMMARY

- Management work should be determined by organisational strategy, but it is not always possible to clarify the link between a manager's job in terms of how it is performed and strategy requirements.
- Models of management performance can be explicitly stated or implicitly held.
- Management performance may be considered a relationship between means – skills, knowledge, attitudes – and ends – results and outputs.
- Management development audits (MDAs) are used to find out the state of affairs with reference to management development in an organisation and to assess the effectiveness of activities.
- Management competences seek to link organisational strategy and the performance of managers. Competences provide a language for describing performance and a consistent means to assess managers.
- There are both technical and theoretical criticisms of management competences as a 'one best way' attempt to describe management performance.

DISCUSSION QUESTIONS

1. 'If it can't be measured, it can't be managed.' Discuss, with reference to the performance of managers.
2. Can the performance of managers be measured scientifically?
3. What is the benefit of Investors in People or the Business Excellence Model or Best Value in providing an indication of the requirements for management development in an organisation?
4. Can management competences provide an indication of best practice in management performance?
5. 'Competence is the embodiment of a technically-oriented way of thinking.' Discuss, with reference to management competences.
6. Are management competences a means of controlling management performance?

FURTHER READING

ANTONACOPOULOU, E. and FITZGERALD, L. (1996) 'Reframing competency in management development', *Human Resource Management Journal*, Vol. 6, No. 1; pp.27–48.

DREJER, A. (2002) *Strategic Management and Core Competencies: Theory and application*. Westport, CT, Quorum Books.

GRUGULIS, I. (1998) '"Real" managers don't need NVQs: a review of the new management "standards"', *Employee Relations*, Vol. 20, No. 4; pp.383–403.

HOFFMAN, T. (1999) 'The meanings of competency', *Journal of European Industrial Training*, Vol. 23, No. 6; pp.275–285.

JAMES, K. and BURGOYNE, J. (2001) *Leadership Development: Best practice guide for organisations*. London, Council for Excellence in Management and Leadership.

GROUP ACTIVITY

Emotional Intelligence (EI) has become a more recent addition to many management competence frameworks.

- Form a group of four.
- One person of each four should go to one of the following Internet sites:
  - Find out the meaning of EI at http://www.bbc.co.uk/science/hottopics/intelligence/emotional.shtml
  - Find out about EI Quotients at http://quiz.ivillage.co.uk/uk_work/tests/eqtest.htm
  - Consider how awareness of EI can be used by managers at http://www.expressitpeople.com/20020318/management1.shtml
  - Offer a more critical and balanced interpretation at http://trochim.human.cornell.edu/gallery/young/emotion.htm
- Meet to consider your findings.
- Prepare a presentation on EI for managers.

REFERENCES

ADAMS, K. (1996) 'Competency: discrimination by the back door?', *Competency and Emotional Intelligence Quarterly*, Vol. 3, No. 4; pp.34–39.

ALBERGA, T., TYSON, S. and PARSONS, D. (1997) 'An evaluation of the Investors in People standard', *Human Resource Management Journal*, Vol. 7, No. 2; pp.47–60.

ASTLEY, W. (1985) 'Administrative science as socially constructed truth', *Administrative Science Quarterly*, Vol. 30; pp.497–513.

BOYATZIS, R. (1982) *The Competent Manager: A model for effective performance*. New York, John Wiley & Sons.

BREWIS, J. (1996) 'The "making" of the "competent" manager', *Management Learning*, Vol. 27, No. 1; pp.65–86.

BURGOYNE, J. (1989) 'Creating the managerial portfolio: building on competency approaches to management development', *Management Education and Development*, Vol. 20; pp.56–61.

BURGOYNE, J. and JACKSON, B. (1997) 'Management development as a pluralistic meeting point', in J. Burgoyne and M. Reynolds (eds) *Management Learning*. London, Sage.

CEML (2002) *Managers and Leaders: Raising our game*. London, Council for Excellence in Management and Leadership.

CIPD (2002) *Developing Managers for Business Performance*. London, Chartered Institute of Personnel and Development.

EASTERBY-SMITH, M., BRAIDEN, E. and ASHTON, D. (1980) *Auditing Management Development*. Farnborough, Gower Press.

GARAVAN, T. N. and McGUIRE, D. (2001) 'Competencies and workplace learning: some reflections on the rhetoric and the reality', *Journal of Workplace Learning*, Vol. 14, No. 4; pp.144–163.

GARAVAN, T. N., MORLEY, M., GUNNIGLE, P. and COLLINS, E. (2001) 'Human capital accumulation: the role of human resource development', *Journal of European Industrial Training*, Vol. 25, Nos. 2/3/4; pp.48–68.

GOLEMAN, D. (1998) *Working With Emotional Intelligence*. London, Bloomsbury.

HOLBECHE, L. (1999) *Aligning Human Resources and Business Strategy*. Oxford, Butterworth-Heinemann

HOLMAN, D. and HALL, L. (1996) 'Competence in management development: rites and wrongs', *British Journal of Management*, Vol. 7, No. 2; pp.191–202.

HOLMES, L. (1995) 'HRM and the irresistible rise of the discourse of competence', *Personnel Review*, Vol. 24, No. 4, pp.34–49.

JACOBS, R. (1989), 'Getting the measure of management competence', *Personnel Management*, June.

LEARY, M., BOYDELL, T., VAN BOESCHOTEN, M. and CARLISLE, J. (1986) *The Qualities of Managing*. Sheffield, Manpower Services Commission.

LEES, S. (1992) 'Ten faces of management development', *Journal of Management Development*, Vol. 23, No. 2; pp.89–105.

MARSHALL, K. (1991) 'NVQs: an assessment of the outcomes approach to education and training', *Journal of Further and Higher Education*, Vol. 15, No. 3.

MARTIN, S. and HARTLEY, J. (2000) 'Best value for all?', *Public Management*, Vol. 2, No. 1; pp.43–56.

MAYO, A. (2002) 'A thorough evaluation', *People Management*, Vol. 8, No. 7; pp.36–39.

MILLER, L., RANKIN, N. and NEATHEY, F. (2001) *Competency Frameworks in UK Organisations*. London, Chartered Institute of Personnel and Development.

PERREN, L. and BURGOYNE, J. (2002) *Management and Leadership Abilities: An analysis of texts, testimony and practice*. London, Council for Excellence in Management and Leadership.

RANKIN, N. (2001) 'Raising performance through people: the eighth competency survey', *Competency and Emotional Intelligence Annual Benchmarking Survey 2000/01*, pp.2–21.

SALAMAN, G. and TAYLOR, S. (2002) 'Competency's consequences: changing the character of managerial work'. Paper presented at ESRC Workshop on Managerial Work, Critical Management Studies Seminar. Cambridge, June.

SCHRODER, H. (1989) *Managerial Competence: The key to excellence*. Dubuque, IA, Kendall and Hunt.

SHEFFIELD, J. and COLESHILL, P. (2001) 'Developing best value in a Scottish local authority', *Measuring Business Excellence*, Vol. 5, No. 2; pp.31–38.

STREBLER, M. and BEVAN, S. (1996) *Competence-Based Management Training*. Report 302. Brighton, Institute of Manpower Studies.

STREBLER, M., ROBINSON, D. and HERON, P. (1997) *Getting the Best Out of Your Competences*. Report 334. Brighton, Institute of Manpower Studies.

SWAILES, S. and BROWN, P. (1999) 'NVQs in management', *Journal of Management Development*, Vol. 18, No. 9; pp.794–804.

TAMKIN, P., HILLAGE, J. and WILLISON, R. (2002) *Indicators of Management Capability: Developing a framework*. London, Council for Excellence in Management and Leadership.

TOVEY, L. (1993) 'Competency assessment: a strategic approach – Part 1', *Executive Development*, Vol. 6, No. 5.

TOWNLEY, B. (1993) 'Performance appraisal and the emergence of management', *Journal of Management Studies*, Vol. 30, No. 2; pp.221–238.

WATSON, T. J. (2001) 'The emergent manager and processes of management pre-learning', *Management Learning*, Vol. 33, No. 2; pp.221–235.

WHIDDETT, S. and HOLLYFORDE, S. (1999) *The Competencies Handbook*. London, Chartered Institute of Personnel and Development.

WINTERTON, J. and WINTERTON, R. (1997) 'Does management development add value?', *British Journal of Management*, Vol. 8, Special Issue; pp.65–76.

WOODRUFFE, C. (1992) 'What is meant by a competency?', in R. Boam and P. Sparrow (eds) *Designing and Achieving Competency*. Maidenhead, McGraw-Hill.

ENDNOTES

1 The term 'transformational' is usually used to distinguish between leadership and management.

2 ISTJ means Introverted Sensing with auxiliary extraverted Thinking, one of 16 Myers-Briggs types – see http://www.mtr-i.com/ad.html

3 In common with others we will use the term 'competences' to refer all approaches to providing descriptions relating to management performance.

4 The terms 'characteristics' and 'abilities' include skills, knowledge, understanding, traits, motives, self-image and social role.

Assessing development needs

CHAPTER 4

Chapter outline
Introduction
Performance management systems
Feedback
Development centres
Appraisal
Multi-source feedback
Summary

LEARNING OUTCOMES

After studying this chapter, you should be able to understand, explain, analyse and evaluate:

- **approaches to managing management performance at work through performance management systems**
- **the importance and value of giving and receiving feedback in assessing needs**
- **the difference between assessment and development centres**
- **various approaches to the appraisal of managers**
- **the incorporation of management development needs into personal development plans**

INTRODUCTION

The assessment of development needs for managers frequently requires a reconciliation of competing and potentially contested tensions. There are tensions between who assesses needs and how, and those whose needs are assessed, as well as tensions caused by the language used in the expression of needs identified. As we saw in Chapter 3, *Measuring managers*, the description of management performance can also become a means of controlling performance and defining managers' identities in a prescriptive fashion. There are other tensions. Assessment is inevitably a judgemental process concerning a manager's performance and, given the variety of purposes or rationales for MD, there are bound to be competing responses to judgements made. One obvious stress point concerns the degree to which judgements about managers' performance are deemed to be valid by the managers themselves or whether such feedback provokes a defensive response which may also impact on performance. Assessing needs in MD is a prime candidate for Burgoyne and Jackson's (1997) Arena Thesis by which MD becomes an arena for different purposes, different values to be discussed, perhaps contested and possibly reconciled.

PERFORMANCE MANAGEMENT SYSTEMS

For the HR profession, 'performance management' has over the last decade become something of a panacea as a means of establishing its credibility as a business-oriented equal in the formation and implementation of organisation strategy (Strebler and Bevan, 2001). If strategy and business plans concern an organisation's response to key changes in the environment and progress into the future, these need to be cascaded throughout the organisation so that every section, department and unit is able to set priorities and targets for delivery. At each stage, managers are able to determine with others performance requirements and, where appropriate, how these will be measured. In addition, such is the speed of global and technical change, goals and targets must be reviewed and reset throughout the year. Performance management can be said to play a vital role in ensuring that organisational objectives are communicated and met, and that each person's needs are aligned with organisational requirements. For example, when the mobile communications company O_2 prepared for its launch in 2002, all senior managers were assessed against a competence framework using structured interviews, data from performance reports and 360-degree feedback using web-based surveys. Each manager was then provided with a personal report including detailed feedback. Where skills gaps were identified, coaching sessions were provided.

According to Holbeche (1999), the key elements of performance management are:

- common understanding of the organisation's goals
- shared expectations of how individuals can contribute
- employees with the skill and ability to meet expectations
- individuals who are fully committed to the aims of the organisation.

REFLECT – CONCLUDE – PLAN 1

- On the basis of these key elements, how viable is performance management in your organisation?
- What can you do to improve viability?

Integrating HRM activities

One important aspect of performance management is the opportunity to show integration of HRM activities and how such activities can be linked to organisation goals. Armstrong and Baron (1998) in a survey of over 500 personnel practitioners in the UK found that the term included a broad variety of activities, as shown in Table 6.

Table 6 *The features of performance management*

Feature	Percentage
Objective-setting and review	85
Annual appraisal	83
Personal development plans	68
Self-appraisal	45
Performance-related pay	43
Coaching/mentoring	39
Career management	32
Competence assessment	31
Twice-yearly appraisal	24
Subordinate (180-degree) appraisal	20
Continuous assessment	17
Rolling appraisal	12
360-degree appraisal	11
Peer appraisal	9
Balanced scorecard	5

Source: Armstrong and Baron (1998)

A key task therefore is to show how such activities can be linked together to form a performance management system (PMS) by which information from one activity can feed into another. Figure 12 shows a possible performance management cycle.

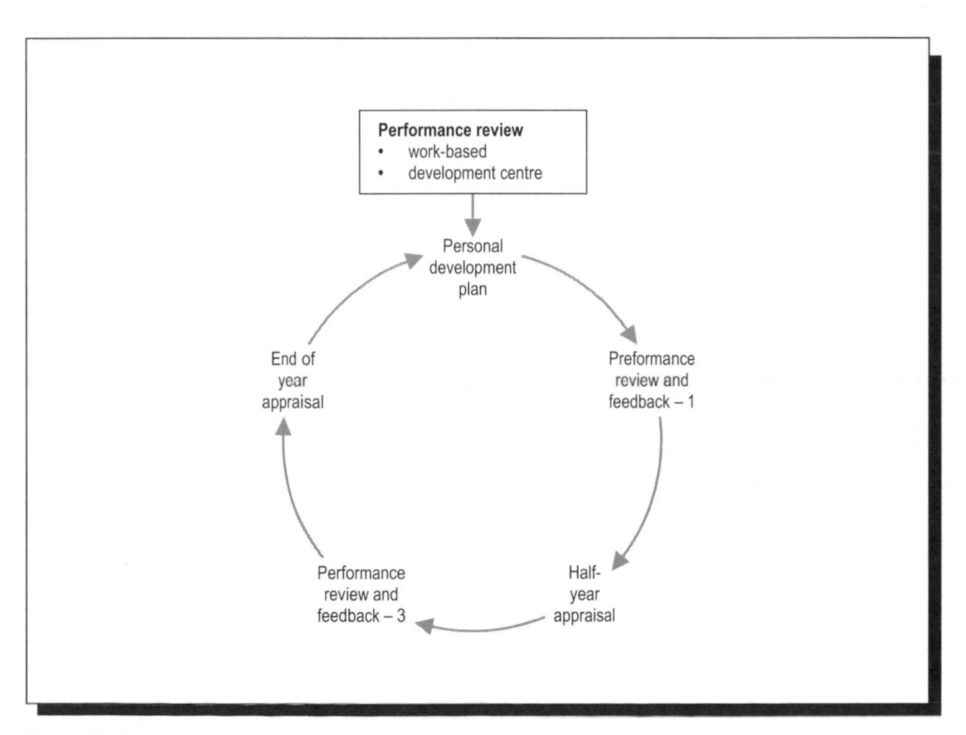

Figure 12 *An integrated performance management cycle*

The operation of a PMS relies heavily on the flow of information between the various activities of:

- a work-based review
- development centre attendance
- personal development plans
- performance reviews and feedback
- appraisal.

Managers require information from such processes to identify how performance might be improved and to assess whether the objectives of plans are being met. Each PMS therefore requires a measurement process or metrics to allow decisions to be made, and it is here that the various approaches to measuring managers – especially competences – come to the fore. In Chapter 3, competences were shown to provide a language for describing performance and a consistent means to assess managers. However, there remains the key question of the overall purpose of a PMS and how information relating to performance will be used. These questions are underpinned by an ongoing tension within any PMS between the need to monitor and control management performance and the need to identify MD requirements. One particular manifestation of this tension occurs where reward and remuneration are tied to performance. There is a long history of difficulties in relating the performance of managers to judgements about pay and other reward outcomes such as promotion. For example, during the 1960s there were various schemes for Management by Objectives (MBO) which were designed to control management performance and stimulate development. However, research soon revealed that such schemes were self-defeating because they were based on a 'reward-punishment psychology' which pressurised managers who had little choice on the objectives to be achieved (Levinson, 1970). More recently, Fletcher and Williams (1996) suggested that the equation of performance management with goals or performance-related pay was likely to reduce the effectiveness of performance management and that job satisfaction and commitment could be enhanced by an approach which combined a number of activities. This is a finding confirmed by recent work attempting to explain how the link between HRM and performance occurs (Guest *et al*, 2000).

WEB LINK

Go to
http://www.leeds.ac.uk/esrcfutureofwork/projects/project_outlines/workplace_reorganisation.html
– this is the site of a research project that is examining the relationship between HRM systems and corporate performance.

One area in which the tension between control and development in a PMS has become evident is Government attempts to modernise the provision of public services through Best Value, which became operative from April 2000. The Best Value framework requires performance review over a five-year period and reports within a national framework of performance measures and standards. The framework is underpinned by a regime of audit and inspection with powers of intervention where 'performance failure' is evident. One consequence is that performance measurement has become the dominant feature of Best Value in order to meet targets rather than as a source for learning and change (Sanderson, 2001).

FEEDBACK

A key feature of any system to assess the development needs of managers is how managers will respond to feedback. Research suggests that this a very sensitive issue. For example, one of the key findings from a classic piece of research carried out in the 1960s into the impact of feedback on managers during performance appraisal (Meyer *et al*, 1965) was that, on average, there were 13 criticisms during an appraisal interview. This often resulted in defensive behaviour on the part of the managers being appraised, such that the more criticism a manager received, the more he or she would react defensively by denying shortcomings and blaming others. One reason for such behaviour was the difference between a person's rating of performance and the degree to which it was confirmed or not by the appraiser. The research showed that most managers rated themselves as above-average before appraisal, and most found the assessment by the appraiser to be less favourable than their own. It was further found that criticism continued to negatively affect performance after the interview.[1]

Self-awareness

One of the main aims of feedback to managers is to increase the level of self-awareness of their strengths and weaknesses as managers so that areas for performance improvement may be recognised and needs for MD identified. All managers will hold views about how they perform their work – ie self-assessment – but this may not be the view held by others, and the aim of feedback is to foster comparison between such views so that greater understanding can be gained (London and Smither, 1995). In recent years, managers have been increasingly subjected to feedback from a variety of sources. Here, we should make a distinction between feedback that occurs naturally during the course of everyday working and feedback provided more formally. Managers will get the former from interactions with others and from results achieved in their work. Managers can also provide feedback for themselves by reviewing and reflecting on their activities as managers. In addition, there are more formal occasions for the provision of feedback including:

- performance reviews and appraisals with managers
- 180-degree or 360-degree feedback from staff, peers, managers, customers and others
- feedback from assessment or development centres.

On such occasions, feedback may be used to identify areas for performance improvement and MD needs by raising self-awareness, but, as we have noted, there might also be decisions on remuneration and career progression. In all cases it is difficult to escape the judgemental features of feedback which may militate against the prospects of managers' really accepting that they have a development need.

WEB LINK

There are many ways to help managers understand the need to increase self-awareness. One of the most popular is the 'Johari window' which explores how feedback and disclosure can help managers (and others). You can find out more about the Johari window at
http://sol.brunel.ac.uk/~jarvis/bola/communications/johari.html

Response to feedback

The response of managers to feedback partly depends on how they think about themselves and their abilities. This is referred to as self-concept and is related to other ideas about self such as self-esteem.[2] All managers, to a greater or less degree, value who they are, what they can do and what they have achieved. This sense of value is usually built up through life experience and provides an important input into how managers negotiate and establish their role and identity as a manager with others (Holman *et al*, 2002). It is not surprising therefore that feedback which provides significant challenge to self-esteem might be resisted or ignored – hence the need to help managers increase their self-awareness.

REFLECT – CONCLUDE – PLAN 2

Look back on an occasion when you received feedback on your performance at work.

- In what respects was it helpful or unhelpful? Why?
- What could you do to improve the feedback you give to others and the feedback others offer you?

WEB LINKS

If you would like some basic advice on giving feedback, try
http://www.mapnp.org/library/commskls/feedback/basc_gde.htm
and the following provides a link to a page which provides good advice on listening skills,
http://www.casaa-resources.net/resources/sourcebook/acquiring-leadership-skills/listening-skills.html

Of course, not all feedback is negative, and many managers recognise the value of getting feedback and take a proactive stance towards it. Such managers can be referred to as 'feedback-seekers' and research by VandeWalle and Cummings (1997) suggests that such behaviour can lead to improved performance. It is argued that a key contributor to feedback-seeking is goal orientation with a distinction between:

- learning-goal orientation – the willingness to develop new skills and mastering new situations

and

- performance-goal orientation – seeking to show and prove that competences are adequate by avoiding negative judgements in favour of positive ones.

Longitudinal research suggested that learning-goal orientation was positively related to feedback-seeking and that performance-goal orientation had a negative relation. It also suggested that a preoccupation with proving the adequacy of competences tended to drive out learning and feedback-seeking. Further testing of this idea showed that contextual factors such as leadership could influence goal orientation and therefore feedback-seeking (VandeWalle *et al*, 2000).

DEVELOPMENT CENTRES

Development centres (DCs) can play a significant role in helping managers assess MD needs although their similarity to assessment centres (ACs) can cause a continuation of the tension between assessment for judgement purposes and assessment for development. This may lead some managers to believe that DCs are ACs in disguise. Both ACs and DCs draw their strength and popularity from a belief in the power of the measurement of management performance by trained observers backed up by psychometrics to provide valid and reliable information about managers (and others). In addition, where ACs and DCs are combined with competence frameworks and other models which set out the requirements for management performance, they become a linking mechanism to support an organisation's strategic approach to HRM and change (Iles, 1992). Indeed, as we noted in Chapter 3, management competences can be seen as a method of communication to managers regarding their alignment to organisational goals and the qualities required of managers.

Woodruffe (2000) suggests that ACs and DCs have the defining and common characteristics of:

- their objective to obtain an indication of people's current or potential competence to perform a job
- the achievement of the objective through assessment techniques such as exercises and work simulations to capture people's behaviour.

Woodruffe (2000) goes on to outline four generalisations about typical centres. These are:

- Participants are observed by assessors – assessors are trained in the use of measurement dimensions such as competences and the skills of rating.
- Assessment is by a combination of methods and includes simulations of the key elements of the work.
- Information is brought together from all the techniques – usually under competences headings.
- Several participants are assessed at the same time – six is very usual to make group exercises feasible.

Methods and purpose

Typically, both ACs and DCs use similar methods which yield information about participants. Research by Jackson and Yeates (1993) on DCs in particular found a mix of the following activities:

- ability tests – especially in centres for selection and promotion: ability tests are considered to be better predictors of future performance
- personality questionnaires, including the Occupational Personality Questionnaire and Cattell's 16 PF
- group discussions, involving problem-solving discussions and negotiations
- presentations, based on preparation before the centre
- in-tray exercises, to simulate management work
- role plays – less common but usually requiring the assessor or someone else to adopt a difficult role

- other group exercises, including outdoor activities
- individual interviews – mainly to provide feedback and assist in identifying development needs which could lead to the formation of a personal development plan.

WEB LINK

The UK's biggest provider of some of the methods for DCs is Saville & Holdsworth. Check their website at
http://www.shlgroup.com/uk/#
You can read various case studies concerning development at
http://www.shlgroup.com/uk/cases/default.htm

DCs ought to serve different purposes from ACs although in practice some organisations combine purposes and this can cause confusion among those who participate (Bolton and Gold, 1994). Jackson and Yeates (1993) found a variety of terms used such as 'development programme', 'career evaluation programme', 'development workshop' as well as 'AC' or 'DC' which reflected the emphasis of a centre. The research found that organisations were using centres for recruitment, for fast-track promotion, for assessing high potential as well as for identifying needs.[3] The crucial questions are whether participants are fully aware of the purpose and whether the stated purpose matches the process enacted. As Woodruffe (2000; p.32) argues,

> **Assessment centres masquerading as development centres are wolves in sheep's clothing.**

He points out that emphasising the purpose of development requires that information generated should be used for development and not to make decisions about a person's potential or future. Individuals who may be prepared to participate honestly in a centre whose objective is their personal development may be less prepared to do so when they think that the results of their performance may provide material for judgements against them later.

The crucial signifier of the intentions of a DC concern the ownership and use of the information generated. Is the information owned by the assessors on behalf of the organisation to make decisions about participants? Or does the information belong primarily to the participant to be used to identify needs? In most organisations, the answers to these questions probably lie somewhere in between pure AC and pure DC, although this may lead to a blurring of the boundary between assessment and development purposes and uncertainty among managers. Figure 13 shows Woodruffe's (2000) presentation of the differences between centres for development and centres to make decisions about selection.

REFLECT – CONCLUDE – PLAN 3

- Do you have any experience as a participant and/or designer of assessment or development centres?
- How far does your experience confirm or conflict with the points about confusion in objectives?
- What could you do to reduce any conflict?

Purpose	development/career-planning	promotion/development	selection
Label	**development centre**		**selection centre**
Philosophy	done by the participant	done with the participant	done to the candidate
Method	self-assessment/peer assessment plus observer's view	assessment with feedback	testing/no feedback
Assessor's role	witness		judge
Includes	self-insight matererials		cognitive test
Output	personal development plan	report	selection decision
Information on exercises	open		secret
Feedback given	after each exercise	after centre	not given
Owner of information	participant	participant and organisation	organisation
Duration	two–three days	one–two days	one day

Figure 13 *A continuum from development centres to selection centres*
Source: Woodruffe (2000; p.36)

During the 1990s many organisations moved toward a developmental emphasis in centres so that MD needs could be identified. Woodruffe (2000) suggests this was partly a reaction to the judgemental and demotivating features of ACs but also partly a reaction to the fast-moving environment which requires constant revisions to roles and the need for managers (and others) to engage in continuous learning. DCs can also be a means to retain staff when promotion opportunities in lean organisations become more limited (Holbeche, 1998). The key issues still remain:

- Do DCs lead to an awareness of what managers must learn to improve their performance?
- Does awareness and learning improve performance?
- Does learning and learning-to-learn form a feature of the DC process?

In general, there has been very little research on the value of DCs. One study by Halman and Fletcher (2000) of 111 customer service staff, however, found that attendance at a DC was associated with adjustments in self-assessment in line with the ratings of assessors, especially where participants underrated their performance before the DC. Over-raters on the other hand made less adjustment, possibly due to a view that there was less need to improve performance and, therefore, attend to the feedback provided at a DC. An interesting result was obtained from participants who rated their performance accurately – ie whose self-assessment matched the ratings of assessors: after the DC their self-assessment rating increased! The findings suggest the need to identify over-, under- and accurate self-raters so that feedback could be adjusted accordingly.

It would seem that there remains the continuing difficulty of separating assessment and development. The credibility of DCs rests in part on the accepted standing of AC methods with respect to reliability and validity. However, Carrick and Williams (1999) argue that there are doubts about validity and there is a problem for some participants of attendance leading to demotivation through the diagnosis of many development needs. Further, the expected outcome for some managers may be negative, and this will affect their willingness to participate and their performance if they do.

APPRAISAL

In many ways appraisal is the Holy Grail of MD, and in principle it deals with one of the major issues about improving management performance – yet the practice is often profoundly unsatisfactory. However, regardless of the record of appraisal, it remains a significant symbol of an organisation's attempt to measure, monitor and control the activity of managers. Further, without appraisal, an organisation may be considered to be acting irrationally and ineffectively (Barlow, 1989).

Purpose

The purpose of control in appraisal may be significant but usually remains in the background. In many organisations, however, appraisal schemes are designed to achieve a number of objectives – explicit or not. Possible objectives for an appraisal scheme include:

- providing information for succession and resource planning
- providing a basis for improved communication between boss and subordinate
- providing clarity of roles and purpose
- identifying and recording performance weaknesses
- providing a basis for analysis of performance and identification of required standards and improvements
- identifying potential
- providing mutual feedback between boss and subordinate
- providing a basis for training and career counselling
- providing a basis for salary decision-making.

This list of objectives would suggest that appraisal represents something of a 'panacea' (Taylor, 1998; p.185) for organisations. No single appraisal scheme or single appraisal interview will meet all of these diverse objectives. In addition, some of the objectives actually conflict with each other. The most familiar instance is that appraisal related to salary decisions is generally found to be ineffective at providing realistic performance-improvement discussion or improved feedback between managers and their bosses.

Conflicts in purpose, particularly where a boss is required to make judgements about managers, lie at the heart of difficulties with appraisal. In the 1950s, for example, the classic study by McGregor (1957) found that managers disliked 'playing God' (p.89) when they were required to make judgements about the worth of their employees. This finding was repeated in the study by Maier (1985), who found that managers were being asked to adopt inconsistent roles in the appraisal interview – that of judge and helper. There is also, of course, the study by Meyer *et al* (1965), which we referred to above, that suggested that feedback, especially critical feedback, had a tendency to result in defensive behaviour by managers, reduced motivation and no change in performance.

REFLECT – CONCLUDE – PLAN 4

- What are the objectives for appraisal in your organisation? Is there any evidence that the objectives are met?
- What is your experience about the effectiveness of appraisal interviews personally and through others in your organisation?
- What could you do to improve appraisal by yourself and with others?

Appraisal and MD needs

Organisations can make a choice to orientate appraisal towards development, but research suggests that in many organisations there is a gap between the desire for a developmental orientation and the achievement of it. For example, a study of appraisal in the NHS certainly found a policy of development and rhetoric to support it, but managers generally used it to exert authority (Redman *et al*, 2000). Training and development always took second place to work objectives and sometimes did not take place at all. Even where development was discussed, the discussion often occurred in a mechanical and tick-box fashion, although there were also some benefits including setting objectives, personal development plans and mini-reviews of progress towards goals.

At the very least there should be separate discussions about performance with the objective to identify MD needs from those that focus on pay, other aspects of reward and promotion. In addition, based on lessons learned from the problems of Management by Objectives, there is the need to attend to the process used to setting plans and the criteria used to make judgements about performance. For example, research by Pettijohn *et al* (2001) found that morale and performance is affected if managers do not feel they can control the factors that affect the criteria by which their performance is judged.

A traditional approach to appraising management performance includes a listing of traits or personality attributes. For example, a manager might be assessed on his or her ability to show loyalty, or passion, or determination, etc. Some appraisal schemes might still include such terms, but attractive as such ideas might be, there is inevitably a difficulty in defining these concepts (one person's loyalty might be another's betrayal), and this has the knock-on effect of making it difficult for appraisers to agree about how to rate managers – ie there may be a low level of inter-rater reliability. A second problem concerns the value in identifying MD needs – it might be argued that even if it could be recognised that a manager was lacking particular traits, it might not be feasible to create a development solution for all of them.

WEB LINK

Traits remain a popular way of thinking and talking about managers especially as leaders. Go to http://www.mapnp.org/library/ldrship/traits.htm
– which is a free library of management resources. This particular link is a page devoted to Suggested Traits and Characteristics of Highly Effective Leaders, and contains many further links to articles and resources.

In addition to traits and personality, appraisal discussions could centre on specific types of management skills – eg planning, time management, building teams, and so on. These do have the value of directly relating to MD activities and processes.

In Chapter 3, we saw that the behaviour approach to management competences (MC) was concerned with behaviour patterns which stem from characteristics and abilities that lead to effective performance. There is also the claim that such competences provide an integrating link between PMS and organisation strategy, although there is evidence too that the competencies identified are not always included in the appraisal process (Abraham *et al*, 2001; p.850). A value of MC is that they can be used to develop ratings scales to be used in appraisal discussions. Two forms of ratings scales can be developed:

- behaviour-anchored ratings scales (BARS) – descriptions of effective and ineffective performance
- behavioural observation scales (BOS) – observable job-related behaviours which raters can assess for frequency.

As well as such ratings concerned with management performance, there has also been some interest in contextual performance which is non-job-specific. It includes such features as co-operation and enthusiasm which contrubute to an enhancement of organisational climate. According to Conway (1999), contextual performance is concerned with personality and motivation, although how such performance is demonstrated will require assessment from those others who interact with managers. This opens the door to a growing interest in multi-source feedback (MSF).

MULTI-SOURCE FEEDBACK

According to Kettley (1997), multi-source feedback (MSF) has become increasingly popular because:

- it empowers employees and promotes teamwork by allowing them to appraise their managers
- it increases the reliability of appraisal feedback and gives more balance to feedback in the context of flatter organisations
- it reinforces good management behaviour by allowing managers to see themselves as others see them.

MSF incorporates six types of appraisal of managers:

- appraisal of managers by staff – upward appraisal
- appraisal by fellow managers – peer appraisal
- appraisal by the boss – top-down appraisal
- appraisal by boss and staff/or peers – 180-degree appraisal
- appraisal by boss, staff and peers – 360-degree appraisal
- appraisal by boss, staff, peers, customers, suppliers and others who are in an interdependent relationship with a manager – 540-degree appraisal.

Figure 14 shows how MSF can cover all the angles of management performance.

There is an undoubted potential for so many types of feedback to help managers increase their self-awareness and identify areas for development, but it can also be a very demanding process. As Handy *et al* (1996) found, feedback from people who can observe what a

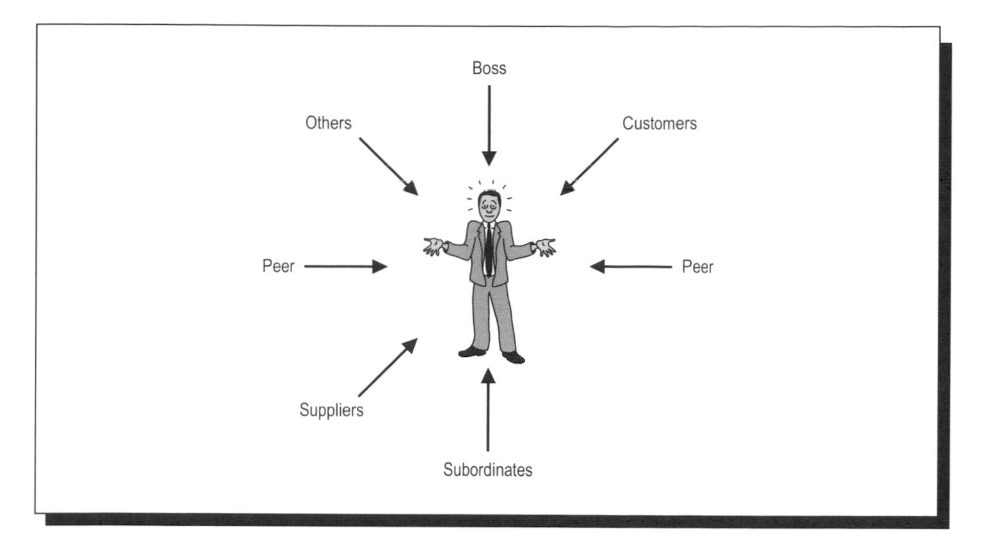

Figure 14 *Covering the angles of management performance*

manager does is difficult to deny. Here's what one manager felt about 360-degree feedback (Handy *et al*, 1996; p.23):

> **360-degree feedback is scary . . . It asks questions I would have preferred not to have answered. But what is so powerful is that I can no longer pretend that I don't know what is being said about me.**

Before we examine these varieties of MSF further, it is important to remember that the process of feedback can provoke a variety of responses from managers. As we suggested above, all managers value who they are, what they can do and what they have achieved. This would suggest that MSF must include another angle of appraisal – self-appraisal.

Self-appraisal

Self-appraisal is based on the simple notion that the best person to make an assessment and judgement about a manager's performance and to determine needs for learning and development is the manager himself or herself. Following Campbell and Lee (1988), it can be suggested that self-appraisal is a four-step process:

1. The manager has beliefs and ideas about what the work requires and what needs to be done to meet goals.
2. The manager attempts to meet work requirements and goals informed by beliefs and ideas.
3. The manager judges whether behaviour achieves the desired results.
4. The manager uses judgements to reinforce or change beliefs and ideas about work requirements and what needs to be done.

It might also be suggested that others such as boss, staff, etc, also move through the same steps to make their judgements about the performance of a manager – albeit from different angles. One of the crucial factors in the success of self-appraisal concerns whether the orientation is towards evaluation for performance control or development. Where the emphasis is on the former, and especially where self-appraisal judgements about performance are contrasted with the ratings of others, there are likely to be discrepancies. Campbell and Lee identified three types of discrepancy:

- *informational* – disagreements about work to be done, how it is done, and the standards to be used in judging results
- *cognitive* – the simplification of complex behaviour and performance, resulting in differing perceptions about what happened
- *affective* – the triggering of defence mechanisms due to the evaluative nature of appraisal, resulting in bias and distortions in interpreting appraisal data.

None of this is surprising, especially if we remember some of the earlier research findings on appraisal in which most people tend to overrate their performance and inflate their self-appraisal (Meyer, 1980).

The distortions identified and others are likely to be present in all forms of MSF, especially where evaluation for performance control is the main purpose. However, where development is favoured, self-appraisal may be more effective. Managers may, for example, be modest about their ratings and more critical if the purpose is development. Further, with the use of management competences, self-appraisal can focus on specific behaviours in particular contexts rather than on general impressions. For instance, the following self-appraisal items are taken from the management competency framework of a software company in the UK relating to 'Educating, Training and Developing Staff',[4] in which managers rated themselves on a scale of 1 to 5.

a) I take responsibility for the effective induction of new staff.
b) I am able to identify the training needs of new staff and agree a training plan.
c) I understand how to evaluate the effectiveness of training.

Upward appraisal

Of course, managers may wish to include the views of others as part of an MSF process. If we now consider upward appraisal, for example, we can see how the staff might consider the same items as the manager. For example, in respect of the three competencies listed above, the staff might take them into consideration in this form:

a) My manager takes responsibility for the effective induction of new staff.
b) My manager is able to identify the training needs of new staff and agrees a training plan.
c) My manager understands how to evaluate the effectiveness of training.

It would seem to be important that staff understand the purpose if upward appraisal is used. It is not too difficult to imagine how the difference between feedback for performance evaluation would differ from that for development. Managers might fear such appraisal for a number of reasons:

- It undermines managerial authority.

- It disturbs working relationships.
- It fosters competition between managers to get the best ratings.

Antonioni (1994) suggested that staff view upward appraisal more positively when it is anonymous, and that fear of reprisal if they provide constructive feedback was a key reason for this. There was also a tendency to give more positive feedback when staff were not anonymous, which might result in fewer development needs being identified. Upward appraisal can often be used as a stepping-stone to the more adventurous models of 360-degree/540-degree appraisal. That would allow a voluntary approach to be taken in which managers could identify the staff they wish to ask for feedback. This seems to have been the approach reported by Jones (1996), where a voluntary process eventually evolved into a mandatory 360-degree feedback system. For Jones, feedback from his staff led to 'very open and honest feedback about my behaviour and approach to managing', but he also conceded that they had been 'rather too kind' (p.48).

How managers respond to upward appraisal may depend on the current ratings of managers. Reilly *et al* (1996) found that where managers had low or moderate ratings, and feedback from staff was sustained over time, an improvement in management performance occurred. Managers who already had high ratings showed less improvement. The important feature promoted by upward appraisal was an awareness of the behaviours measured and the communication of an expectation to show improvement. However, the overall climate may militate against such a process. For example, Atwater *et al* (2000) found that feedback from staff had low impact on managers in the context of a cynical response by managers to organisational change. Managers tended to respond positively to high ratings by reinforcing their commitment to staff, but low ratings reduced commitment.

Peer appraisal

From a developmental perspective, feedback from peers can be very important to a manager – and even critical feedback is more likely to be perceived as helpful. In contrast, where feedback may lead to evaluation for non-development decisions, this may lead to rivalry, backbiting and jealousy. Bettenhausen and Fedor (1997) found that peer appraisal was viewed positively when used for development but negatively when used for evaluation. Peiperl (2001) argues that peer appraisal is difficult because it is paradoxical. For example, because managers often have to work closely and associate with other managers, their peers, they tend to give positive feedback because they do not wish to disturb the relationship or damage careers. They might be prepared to give feedback informally, as part of everyday working, but less inclined to do so formally. Similarly, peers often work as part of a team but appraisal requires individulisation. Peers may be required to make comparisons between individuals, and this may harm the working of the team. When the team is low-performing, the fear of feedback from peers may be heightened, leading to resistance and avoidance of blame.

360-degree appraisal

Clearly, the move from upward and peer appraisal to the all-round version of 360-degree appraisal requires a shift in confidence and overall trust. Because the outcome can be deeply negative and demoralising for target managers if it goes wrong, most organisations will introduce this approach carefully. Fletcher (1998) found that 360-degree appraisal could soon become unworkable if used mainly for evaluation purposes, causing some organisations to drop it within two years. The approach provides for feedback from three sources: line manager, peers, and direct staff. Some organisations also attempt to obtain information from clients or customers (540-degree appraisal), a potentially valuable concept within an organisation, but even more difficult to gain from outside the organisation.

360-degree appraisal provides more feedback – a representative sample, rather than a complete collection of peers and staff, would probably require a minimum of eight people. However, the real point is that the feedback presents not only a wider picture but potentially a more accurate one. The accuracy of the comments depends in part, of course, on the construction of the rating items, and also on guarantees to respondents of anonymity. The comparison of the views of others with a self-appraisal can produce surprising results, sometimes in a positive and sometimes in a disappointing direction. However, it is also possible that accuracy could give way to ambiguity, contradiction and confusion because each group gains a different view of a manager's performance.

Once again, it is important to establish the purpose of 360-degree appraisal. Is it to evaluate performance, to provide information to determine remuneration, or to allow managers to identify needs for learning and development? Chivers and Darling (1999), in a study of six case study organisations, found that development was the main purpose and that it was usually incorporated into new or existing MD programmes. In one organisation, 360-degree appraisal was seen as one of the features of developing a new culture. They also found that there was no attempt to link the process to remuneration and reward, although it is possible to incorporate information generated into ongoing discussions that feature as part of an organisation's performance management system. What seems to be vital is to make the objectives explicit and clear so that managers do not regard it as unfocused and confusing (Handy *et al*, 1996). Where the objectives are stated as learning and development but managers suspect that there are hidden objectives that serve a political agenda, they are likely to regard the process cynically and respond ambivalently or negatively to the results. 360-degree appraisal also requires time; most feedback is paper-based, using some form of rating scales. Increasingly, rating can be completed electronically – indeed, managers may find that feedback mediated by a computer is less daunting and less emotionally fraught, allowing a more objective analysis. Where the process is incorporated into a programme or as part of a development centre, it will also be necessary to use trained facilitators or to hire external experts.

360-degree appraisal can be a powerful MD process, but it is likely fail unless a meaningful follow-through is agreed. In development terms, managers will need to be in a position where they can identify areas of improvement which can be met by MD activities. As we indicated earlier, this requires an increase in a manager's self-awareness.

WEB LINK

Go to http://www.dti.gov.uk/mbp/360feedback/ for access to an online version of the Department for Trade and Industry's Best Practice Guidelines for 360-degree feedback. You can also download a copy of the document from this site.

REFLECT – CONCLUDE – PLAN 5

- What methods of assessing development needs are used in your organisation?
- How effective are they?
- What features from this chapter might be used in improving how needs are assessed?

Table 7 *The benefits of PDPs*

Benefits for the individual manager	Benefits for the manager of the individual
Increased ability to develop performance Reduced stress about untackled gaps in personal performance Increased chance of holding on to a desired current job Increased chance of developing potential for other jobs Clearer process for establishing personal aspirations Clear process for establishing a commitment from the higher manager and the organisation to development of the manager	Reduced performance problems Increased use of additional opportunities for effective work in the unit Reduced belief that a manager's manager does not support development More individuals capable of dealing with new or difficult tasks or complete jobs

Source: adapted from Mumford (2001)

Personal development plans

Usually, an outcome of assessment and appraisal of is the establishment of an action plan or more formally a personal development plan (PDP). This might be composed of objectives and activities for learning and development, but it could include issues for a manager's performance. What is crucial is that a PDP should involve managers in a genuine discussion with their boss about MD, including opportunities for career development and progression within the organisation (see Chapter 10). Mumford (2001) suggests that there are benefits from PDPs for both the individual manager and the manager of the individual, as shown in Table 7.

We suggest that a PDP, whatever the process used, must be constructed on a meaningful understanding of the gap between performance requirements and achievements. The performance focus and the realities of the work of managers is fundamental, as is the joint discussion and involvement between a manager and his or her line manager. A PDP, formally stated, also represents a commitment by the organisation towards its MD policy, and the key mechanism seems to be line manager's involvement and support (Thomson *et al*, 2001). The outcomes agreed in a PDP should link back to an organisation's performance management system, and it is this return to ongoing activity which will determine whether assessment and appraisal processes for managers become accepted within an organisation.

Contradictions and tensions

Throughout this chapter, we have highlighted again how the contradictions and tensions that exist between the purposes of assessment frequently lead to different interpretations with unpredictable consequences. It is very difficult to escape from the view that assessment and appraisal is a means of controlling management performance, even if senior managers espouse learning and development. One possible consequence is that assessment and appraisal processes become rituals rather than a serious means of assessing MD needs. Ritual was one of themes identified by Barlow (1989) in his study of appraisal in a petrochemical organisation. Consider the following quotations by managers from the study (Barlow, 1989; pp.505–507):

> **I think success is having the ear of higher management. To be noticed by higher management, and having opinions asked for, often.**
> **Appraisal forms are no use. It's what's left out rather than what's put in that's important.**

One of Barlow's key points is that appraisal of managers presents an appearance that an organisation makes decisions in an efficient and rational manner while simultaneously providing a 'façade' (p.512) behind which 'real' decisions can be made about managers and their development.

Other commentators have employed the work of the French philosopher Michel Foucault in a critique of appraisal in which managers become 'knowable, calculable and administrable' objects (Miller and Rose, 1990; p.5). One of the images utilised by Foucault is idea of the 'Panopticon', a model prison in which all prisoners can be seen by a guard but prisoners cannot the see the guard or other prisoners.[5] Crucially, the prisoners know they can be seen even though they cannot see how it is done, and the knowledge of this allows them to be 'dominated'. The Panopticon is designed to ensure 'surveillance' (Foucault, 1980; p.148). If we transfer this image to appraisal, it is argued that the various devices to appraise and assess managers such as BARS, BOS, standards, MSF questionnaires, etc, exert a power over managers in setting an ideal or a 'norm' to be achieved. Managers accept such measurements as a means of finding out what they need to do to improve their performance, including the identification of MD needs. Thus, even where the attention is apparently on learning and development, managers are still subject to a 'disciplinary power' set by others who are able to use the 'appraisal technology ... to gauge where the appraisee "stands"' (Newton and Findlay, 1996; p.48).

SUMMARY

- Assessing needs in MD requires judgements to made concerning a manager's performance, and there are fundamental difficulties concerning who makes the judgements, how they do it, and whether the judgements are regarded as valid by managers.
- Performance management systems (PMS) provide for the alignment of organisational objectives with a manager's performance requirements and measurements.
- An aim of feedback to managers is to increase self-awareness of strengths and weaknesses to identify issues for performance improvement and needs for MD.
- Development centres (DCs) increasingly play a role in helping managers assess MD needs – however, their similarity to assessment centres (ACs) could provide doubts that their purpose is developmental.
- Appraisal lies at the heart of a formal approach to assessing MD needs although there remain difficulties in separating the purpose of appraisal between control, development and other intended outcomes.
- Multi-source feedback (MSF) allows managers to receive feedback about their performance from different 'angles'.
- The assessment process should result in an action plan or personal development plan, but implementation requires support in the workplace and a positive learning climate.

- Critical views of assessment and appraisal point to the ritualistic nature and the hidden features of power.

DISCUSSION QUESTIONS

1. Is 'performance management' likely to follow the same road as Management by Objectives?
2. 'All feedback to managers should allow them to make their own assessment of the need to improve their performance.' Discuss.
3. Can a clear distinction be made between assessment and development centres?
4. Can managers ever identify their own MD needs accurately?
5. What are the key requirements for a successful scheme of multi-sourced feedback?
6. 'The appraisal of managers is a façade and a "ritual".' Discuss.

FURTHER READING

BALLANTYNE, I. and POVAH, N. (1995) *Assessment and Development Centres*. London, Gower.

BRUTUS, S., FLEENOR, J. W. and LONDON, M. (1998) 'Does 360-degree feedback work in different industries?', *Journal of Management Development*, Vol. 17, No. 3; pp.177–190.

FLETCHER, C. (2001) 'Performance appraisal and management: the developing research agenda', *Journal of Occupational and Organizational Psychology*, Vol. 74; pp.473–487.

McCARTHY, A. M. and GARAVAN, T. N. (2001) '360-degree feedback processes: performance improvement and employee career development', *Journal of European Industrial Training*, Vol. 25, No. 1; pp.5–32.

RYAN, A. M, BRUTUS, S., GREGURAS, G. J. and HAKEL, M. D. (2000) 'Receptivity to assessment-based feedback for management development', *Journal of Management Development*, Vol. 19, No. 4; pp.252–276.

GROUP ACTIVITY

- Form a group of four.
- Consider the following types of manager and professional staff:
  - Managers of a fast-moving fresh-food-packaging factory that must meet clear targets every day
  - The managers of various sales offices around the world in a drugs company
  - Accountants who must manage a variety of clients but must meet monthly targets for chargeable time spent with clients
  - Teachers with a large school in an inner city area where there are difficulties relating to attendance and achievement among pupils
- For each type of manager and professional, consider what might be the best approach to managing their performance.
- Consider how needs for learning and development might best be appraised and identified, including overall approach, means of assessment, methods of feedback and involvement of others.
- Evaluate the requirements in each case for the successful implementation of appraisal for development.
- Prepare a combined presentation of your findings.

REFERENCES

ABRAHAM, S. E., KARNS, L. A., SHAW, K. and MENA, M. A. (2001) 'Managerial competencies and the managerial appraisal process', *Journal of Management Development*, Vol. 20, No. 10; pp.842–852.

ANTONIONI, D. (1994) 'The effects of feedback accountability on upward appraisal ratings', *Personnel Psychology*, Vol. 47; pp.349–356.

ARMSTRONG, M. and BARON, A. (1998) *Performance Management: The new realities*. London, Institute of Personnel and Development.

ARMSTRONG, M. and BROWN, D. (1998) 'Relating competencies to pay: the UK experience', *Compensation and Benefits Review*, Vol. 30, No. 3; pp.28–39.

ATWATER, L. E., WALDMAN, D. A., ATWATER, D. and CARTIER, P. (2000) 'An upward feedback field experiment: supervisors' cynicism, reactions and commitment to subordinates', *Personnel Psychology*, Vol. 53, No. 2; pp.275–297.

BARLOW, G. (1989) 'Deficiencies and the perpetuation of power: latent functions in management appraisal', *Journal of Management Studies*, Vol. 26, No. 5; pp.499–518.

BETTENHAUSEN, K. L. and FEDOR, D. B. (1997) 'Peer and upward appraisals', *Group and Organization Management*, Vol. 22, No. 2; pp.236–263.

BOLTON, R. and GOLD, J. (1994) 'Career management: matching the needs of individuals with the needs of organisations', *Personnel Review*, Vol. 23, No. 1; pp.6–24.

BURGOYNE, J. and JACKSON, B. (1997) 'Management development as a pluralistic meeting point', in J. Burgoyne and M. Reynolds (eds) *Management Learning*. London, Sage.

CAMPBELL, D. J. and LEE, C. (1988) 'Self-appraisal in performance evaluation: development versus evaluation', *Academy of Management Review*, Vol. 13, No. 2; pp.302–314.

CARRICK, P. and WILLIAMS, R. (1999) 'Development centres – a review of assumptions', *Human Resource Management Journal*, Vol. 9, No. 2; pp.77–92.

CHIVERS, W. and DARLING, P. (1999) *360-Degree Feedback and Organisational Culture*. London, Institute of Personnel and Development.

CONWAY, J. M. (1999) 'Distinguishing contextual performance from task performance for managerial jobs', *Journal of Applied Psychology*, Vol. 84; pp.3–13.

FLETCHER, C. and WILLIAMS, R. (1996) 'Performance management, job satisfaction and organizational commitment', *British Journal of Management*, Vol. 7, No. 2; pp.169–179.

FLETCHER, C. (1998) 'Circular argument', *People Management*, 1 October; pp.46–49.

FOUCAULT, M. (1980) *Power/Knowledge: Selected interviews and other writings, 1972–1977*. Colin Gordon (ed). New York, Pantheon.

GUEST, D., MICHIE, J., SHEEHAN, M. and CONWAY, N. (2000) *Getting Inside The HRM-Performance Relationship*. Working Paper 8, ESRC Future of Work Programme. Swindon, ESRC.

HALMAN, F. and FLETCHER, C. (2000) 'The impact of development centre participation and the role of individual differences in changing self-assessments', *Journal of Occupational and Organizational Psychology*, Vol. 73; pp.423–442.

HANDY, L., DEVINE, M. and HEATH, L. (1996) *360-Degree Feedback: Unguided missile or powerful weapon?* Berkhamsted, Ashridge Management Research Group.

HOLBECHE, L. (1998) *Motivating People in Lean Organizations*. Oxford, Butterworth-Heinemann.

HOLBECHE, L. (1998) *Aligning Human Resources and Business Strategy*. Oxford, Butterworth-Heinemann.

HOLMAN, D., GOLD, J. and THORPE, R. (2002) 'Full of characters: identity and talk in practical authoring', in D. Holman and R. Thorpe (eds) *Management and Language*. London, Sage.

ILES, P. (1992) 'Centres of excellence? Assessment and development centres, managerial competence and human resource strategies', *British Journal of Management*, Vol. 3; pp.79–90.

JONES, O. (1996) 'I was upward appraised and survived!', *Career Development International*, Vol. 1, No. 2; pp.47–48.

KETTLEY, P. (1997) *Personal Feedback: Cases in point*. Report 326. Brighton, Institute of Employment Studies.

LEVINSON, H. (1970) 'Management by whose objectives?', *Harvard Business Review*, July/August; pp.125–134.

LONDON, M. and SMITHER, J. W. (1995) 'Can multi-source feedback change perceptions of goal accomplishment, self-evaluation and performance related outcomes? Theory-based applications and directions for research', *Personnel Psychology*, Vol. 48; pp.803–836.

MAIER, N. R. F. (1985) 'Three types of appraisal interview', *Personnel*, March/April; pp.27–40.

McGREGOR, D. (1957) 'An uneasy look at performance appraisal', *Harvard Business Review*, Vol. 35; pp.89–94.

MEYER, H. H., KAY, E. and FRENCH, J. R. P. (1965) 'Split roles in performance appraisal', *Harvard Business Review*, January/February; pp.123–129.

MEYER, H. H. (1980) 'Self-appraisal of job performance', *Personnel Psychology*, Vol. 33; pp.291–295.

MILLER, P. and ROSE, N. (1990) 'Governing economic life', *Economy and Society*, Vol. 19; pp.1–31.

MUMFORD, A. (2001) *How to Produce Personal Development Plans*. Maidenhead, Honey Publications.

NEWTON, T. and FINDLAY, P. (1996) 'Playing God? The performance of appraisal', *Human Resource Management Journal*, Vol. 6, No. 3; pp.42–58.

PETTIJOHN, L. S., PARKER, S., PETTIJOHN, C. E. and KENT, J. L. (2001) 'Performance appraisals: usage, criteria and observations', *Journal of Management Development*, Vol. 20, No. 9; pp.754–771.

PEIPERL, M. A. (2001) 'Getting 360-degree feedback right', *Harvard Business Review*, January; pp.142–147.

REILLY, R. R., SMITHER, J. W. and VASILOPOULOS, N. L. (1996) 'A longitudinal study of upward appraisal', *Personnel Psychology*, Vol. 46; pp.599–611.

REDMAN, T., SNAPE, E., THOMPSON, D. and KA-CHING YAN, F. 'Performance appraisal in an NHS hospital', *Human Resource Management Journal*, Vol. 10, No. 1; pp.48–62.

SANDERSON, I. (2001) 'Performance management, evaluation and learning in "modern" local government', *Public Administration*, Vol. 79, No. 2; pp.297–313.

STREBLER, M. and BEVAN, S. (2001) *Performance Review: Balancing objectives and content*. Report 370. Brighton, Institute of Employment Studies.

TAYLOR, S. (1998) *Employee Resourcing*. London, Institute of Personnel and Development.

THOMSON, A., MABEY, C., STOREY, J., GRAY, C. and ILES, P. (2001) *Changing Patterns of Management Development*. Oxford, Blackwell.

VANDEWALLE, D. and CUMMINGS, L. L. (1997) 'A test of the influence of goal orientation on the feedback seeking process', *Journal of Applied Psychology*, Vol. 82, No. 3; pp.390–400.

VANDEWALLE, D., GANESAN, S., CHALLAGALLA, G. N. and BROWN, S. P. (2000) 'An integrated model of feedback-seeking behavior: disposition, context and cognition', *Journal of Applied Psychology*, Vol. 85, No. 6; pp.96–103.

WOODRUFFE, C. (2000) *Development and Assessment Centres*, 3rd edition. London, Chartered Institute of Personnel and Development.

ENDNOTES

1. Despite the undoubted influence of this study, we should also mention that it has been criticised on the grounds of 'criteria contamination' – managers who made 'above-average criticisms' also rated the subsequent 'low goal achievement' – see Newton and Findlay (1996).
2. There are other related notions such as self-confidence, self-efficacy and self-acceptance.
3. Other purposes identified were to bring people of the same level together and to foster team spirit.
4. There were 13 competences in the framework but managers were able to focus on up to three at any one time.
5. The Panopticon is drawn from the work of Jeremy Bentham, the founder of British 'utilitarianism' in Victorian England. You can find out more about Bentham at http://cepa.newschool.edu/het/profiles/bentham.htm

Managers and learning

CHAPTER 5

Chapter outline

LEARNING OUTCOMES

After studying this chapter, you should be able to understand, explain, analyse and evaluate:

- **the meaning of effectiveness in management development**
- **the main features of how and why managers learn.**
- **the major theories affecting managerial learning**
- **the importance of reflection in learning**
- **how to assist managers in using learning opportunities effectively.**

INTRODUCTION

An understanding of how managers learn must be a major consideration in the creation of effective MD. A fundamental point here is that past generalisation about how managers learn has been found to be as badly flawed as some of the other generalisations about the work managers do. Over a 40-year period there has been a fairly consistent search for activities that can be seen not only as real but that in some sense 'involve' managers and require them to 'participate'. The ineffectiveness of such techniques as the lecture process, and the vociferous feedback of many managers bored with being its victims, has led to the development of a variety of teaching methods, and particularly of active simulations. In the course context this has meant that most course designers have tried to provide a variety of processes. This was partly because variety was seen as a good thing in itself, since managers would be more likely to remain interested if they were offered a varied process. But it also stemmed from partial recognition of a much more fundamental point.

More aware tutors frequently find themselves faced with conflicting feedback. A session marked very highly by some managers will be marked poorly by others. A process found particularly stimulating by some will be put down as wholly unreal by others. A charismatic lecturer will be marked as the highlight of a course by some managers and rejected by others as having had 'nothing concrete to say about my kind of organisation'. The result of conflicting feedback of this kind over years of experience has led at least some tutors to provide a variety of experiences, because they are aware that some participants will enjoy one form of learning whereas others will not. This provides the course designer with a basic protection: not all participants will be bored all of the time.

It ought to come as no surprise at all that managers differ in their likely response to any particular learning process. Not only is this our common experience within the formal learning environment; it is also observably true that managers differ in their ability to learn from particular kinds of opportunity on the job. We face a remarkably self-evident conclusion. People differ in their preferences for opera and pop music, for different kinds of sporting activity, in their enjoyment of different holidays. Closer to home, in MD terms we know that managers differ substantially in terms of managerial style. Some are hard-edged, directive, forceful autocrats; some are reflective and listening people who prefer to consult before making a decision. So it should be no surprise to us that people differ in their preferred approach to learning. The question for MD is how such preferences and the differences between managers can be taken into account. In this chapter, we will attempt to provide some indicators of how it might be achieved.

EFFECTIVENESS IN MD

In Chapter 1 we presented a definition of MD as 'an attempt to improve managerial effectiveness through a learning process'. We now wish to extend the idea of effectiveness to the MD itself and suggest that this is best achieved by bringing together the following three aspects:

- a contingent definition of effective managerial behaviour
- a development process which emphasises activities in which managers can be effective
- identifying learning processes which are effective for managers.

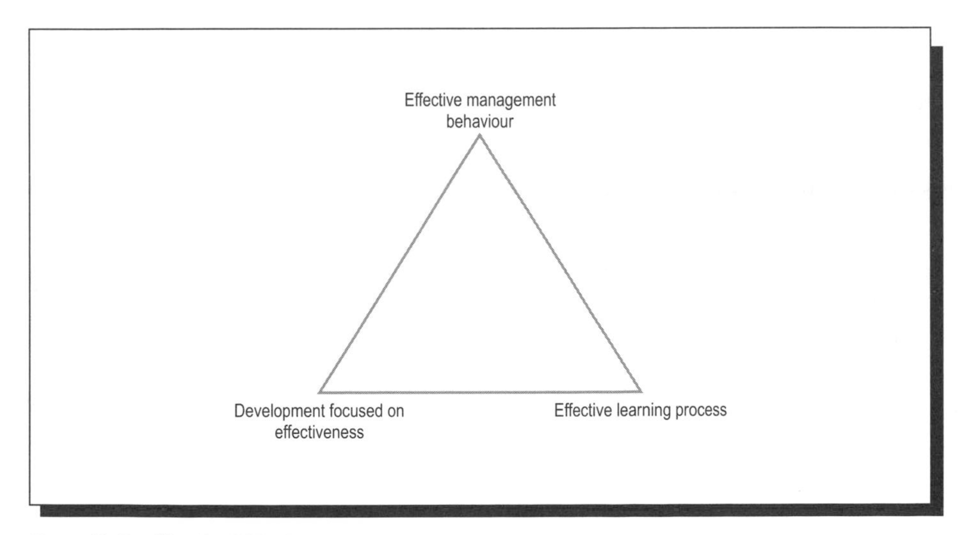

Figure 15 *The Triangle of Effectiveness*

The three points can be usefully presented visually, as in Figure 15. The point, literally, of this 'effectiveness triangle' is that the purpose of MD is not to have a particular kind of development, nor even to provide an effective learning process, but that these two both focus on and are pointed towards effective managerial behaviour.

In Chapter 1 we pointed to the contingent nature of management and the recognition that there are no single statements about management that can be applied to all managers in all organisations. What is effective behaviour for a manager in one organisation may be less effective in another. It therefore becomes crucial to help managers assess their MD needs based on definitions of effectiveness that are meaningful to them, so that any activity undertaken is based on a view of what managers need to be able to do in the specific context of their work. This leads to the second point in the triangle, where MD needs to attend to the desired results of managers and the actions to achieve results rather than detached generalisations of skills or abstract presentations of knowledge and theories. We argue that the emphasis on generalised skills and knowledge, especially in off-the-job MD, leads to a problem in the transfer of learning. Managers need to use real situations and real management problems so that results can be identified to be achieved by actions. Modern motivational theory tells us that behaviour that is not rewarded is not willingly repeated.

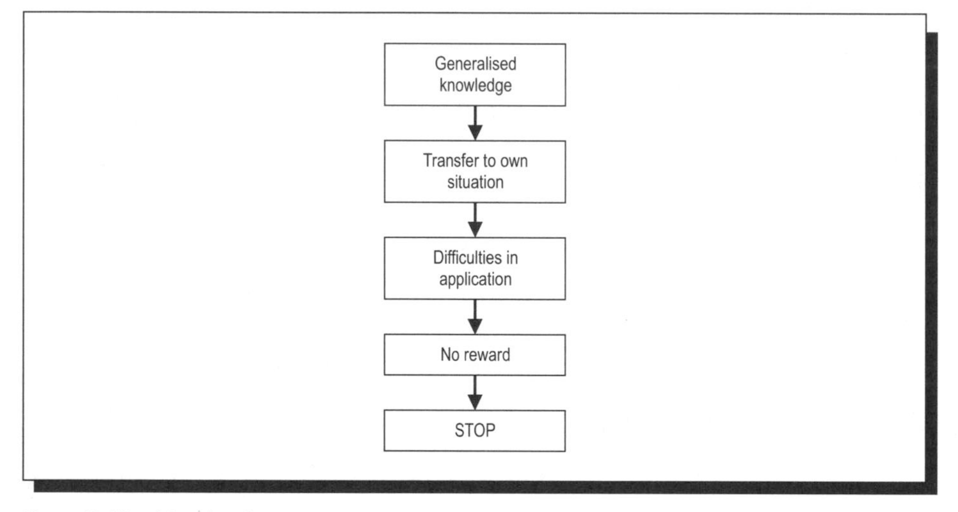

Figure 16 *The vicious learning sequence*

A vicious learning sequence

Clearly, some managers have had useful management training or educational experiences and subsequently repeat these experiences. There are at least an equivalent number who have had bad experiences which have put them off formal MD. This is the 'vicious learning sequence', shown as Figure 16.

REFLECT – CONCLUDE – PLAN 1

- How far does the vicious learning sequence accord with your own experience of training and development?
- How did you attempt to avoid the difficulties?
- How successful were you, or what could you do next time you attend any training and development?

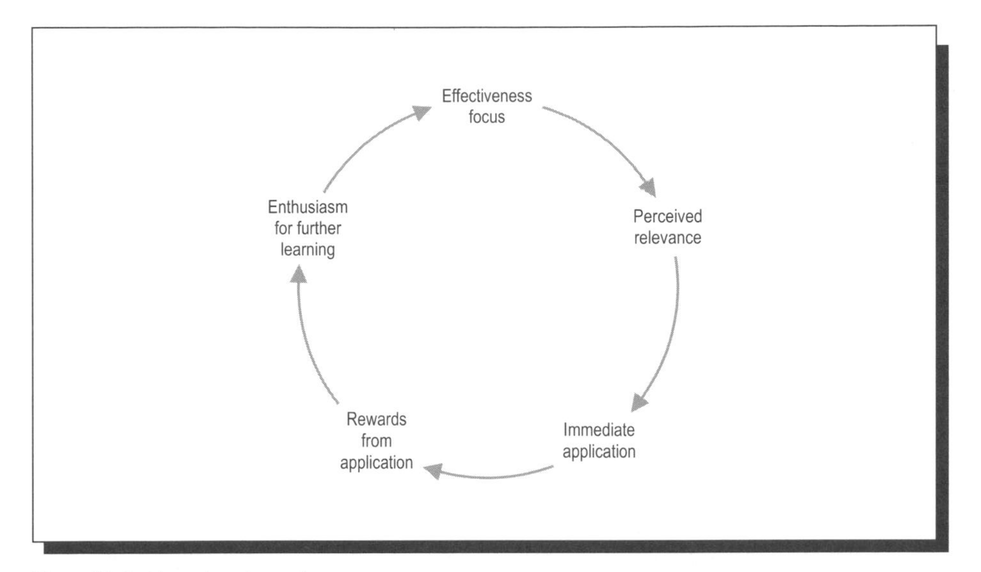

Figure 17 *A virtuous learning cycle*

A virtuous learning cycle

To avoid the worst effects of the Vicious Learning Sequence, we argue that attention needs to be given to creating the conditions for A Virtuous Learning Cycle where there is an effective focus for development, leading to perceived relevance of the activity and therefore instant application and the reward of success. This in turn leads to enthusiasm for more learning. The cycle is shown in Figure 17.

As an example of how a virtuous learning cycle works, consider the following case of an MD programme for sales managers:

> **A company which had revised its sales objectives and organisational structure had some concern that the managers involved might not have the skills necessary to achieve the changed objectives. As a result of analysis with them it became clear that although probably a number of them were lacking in some skills, the more crucial problem was that although apparently committed to the revised objectives, they had not fully set up the action necessary to implement them. The prime effectiveness concern was not therefore the skills of sales management but the identification of specific actions to implement the broad objectives agreed, and the skills involved in implementation.**

By attending to what managers understand as the requirement for effectiveness and focusing MD on such requirement, there is a stronger likelihood that managers will identify actions that could be implemented in their work. However, although these are necessary conditions for effectiveness, they are not sufficient.

People are more likely to learn if they perceive the potential benefits. Attwood (2002) provides a list of benefits to the individual, the individual's manager and the organisation. There remains the need to examine learning – in particular, how managers prefer to learn, and by implication, how they might prefer not to learn.

WHAT DO WE MEAN BY 'LEARNING'?

There are quite a few different definitions of learning. The following, provided by Kolb (1984), has been of particular importance in the history of MD:

> **Learning is the process whereby knowledge is created through the transformation of experience.**

One difficulty with this definition is that it seems to emphasise only knowledge. The definition we prefer is therefore one taken from Honey and Mumford (1996):

> **Learning has happened when people can demonstrate that they know something they did not know before (insights and realisations, as well as facts) and/or when they can do something they could not do before (skills).**

We feel this knowledge-skills-insights definition provides practical utility in the understanding of – and therefore the effective implementation of – learning. The three categories can be used to define what an individual or group of individuals need to learn, and to help them analyse subsequently exactly what it is they have learned. Both aspects of this are crucial to effective MD – a manager who has the need to learn a particular skill may, for example, be offered a form of learning that may be suitable for knowledge but not for learning a skill. The term 'insights' also has great resonance with many managers when they are asked to think about it. People who have reviewed their learning experiences quite often bring out as the conclusion from a particular experience something that is often described colloquially as the 'Aha!' Insights seems to us a much more useful third element in learning than the word 'attitudes', which used to be regarded as one of the objectives of much formal training. The attempt to cause people to learn different attitudes foundered probably because if attitudes are changed, they are changed through a variety of knowledge, skill and insight experiences.

The definition of learning has two further implications. Firstly, if managers have achieved knowledge, skills and/or insight, learning is an end result or an outcome. That is, to whatever is achieved, the noun *learning* is applicable. Secondly, to achieve an end result requires a process by which managers acquire knowledge, skills or insight. Managers to varying degrees become engaged in activities in which the verb *to learn* is deemed to be appropriate. It is worth pointing out that this distinction between 'learning' in a verbal sense and 'learning' as a noun can often lead to difficulties and misunderstandings. One particular problem relates to learning as a process that requires attention to the complexity of activity which may be difficult to observe or capture for understanding. Thus there is often a preference to focus on outcomes – *learning* as a noun – which stands as proxy for the process of learning. This point becomes more pertinent when the variety of different ways in which learning is acquired are considered. For example, training or education, formally structured with the aim of enabling managers to learn, is one way (although the aim is not always achieved). However, learning is also brought about by the experience managers have in and around work (and of course

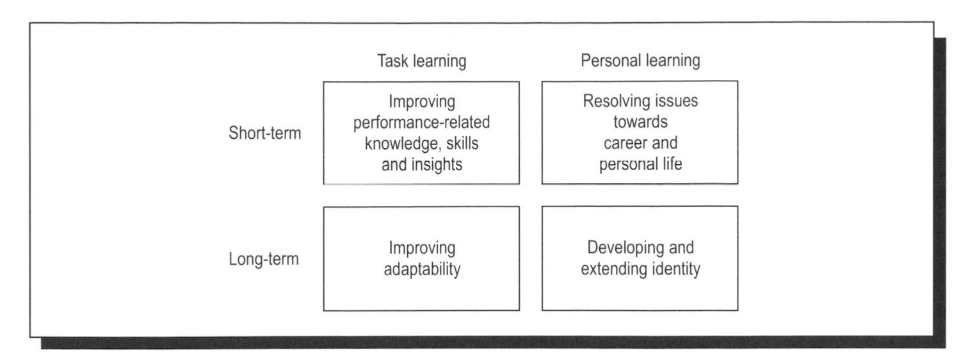

Figure 18 *Task and personal learning*
Source: adapted from Hall (1986)

also in their lives outside work), where learning occurs naturally in a non-contrived manner as part of an everyday process (Stuart, 1984). The formal experiences – education and training – are inputs designed and controlled by educators and trainers. They may be intended to add new learning, or replace inappropriate learning. The informal learning experiences we all have at and outside work, often called 'learning from experience', are especially important in managerial and professional development. Perhaps we need to see managerial learning as being much more concerned with helping managers to learn more effectively from their work experiences rather than necessarily attempting to replicate or replace them by off-the-job experiences (see Chapter 7 for similarities between a task cycle and the learning cycle).

Is 'learning' different from 'development'?

Until relatively recently the debate about the possibly different meaning of these two words contrasted current needs for learning compared with needs for the future – to which the word *development* was often attached. Distinctions have also been suggested about different kinds of content – for example, by Pedler and Boydell (1985). They saw learning as more concerned with an increase in knowledge or a higher degree of an existing skill, whereas development was, in their view, a move towards a different state of being or functioning. We do not agree that this is a viable distinction and use 'learning' and 'development' interchangeably. One useful distinction was, however, made by Chris Argyris (1991): between 'single-loop learning' and 'double loop learning' (see below).

Hall (1986) made another between task and personal learning as part of a progressive model of management growth and effectiveness, shown as Figure 18.

Managers need to learn relevant skills, knowledge and insights to improve work performance in the short term and adaptability in the long term. They also need the chance to assess themselves by exploring their views towards career and personal life. Progression can continue towards 'being truly one's own person ... to being a self-directed, self-aware organisational leader' (p.252).

REFLECT – CONCLUDE – PLAN 2

- Use Hall's typology to consider learning in your organisation.
- Is there a need for more personal learning?
- How can you extend learning beyond short-term task learning?

As a final point on definitions, it is relevant to emphasise the difference between inputs such as training or mentoring or coaching. These inputs may or may not achieve the desired output – ie learning.

THEORIES AND MODELS OF MANAGERIAL LEARNING

A statement by the American psychologist Kurt Lewin[1] provides an explanation for the selective nature of the theories we review below:

> **There is nothing so practical as a good theory.**

There are a large and growing number of ideas that purport to provide explanations of how people learn. These can be broadly grouped under the headings of 'behaviourist', 'cognitivist' and 'humanistic'. We have selected theories on the basis of the extent to which they are referred to in courses, articles and books about MD, and therefore seem to have influenced practice. We have also emphasised theories which have lasted for a number of years. So, for example, Skinner (1974) and subsequent variants of 'behaviour modification' had its period of attention, but now seems largely discarded, although their influence remains, especially in sales training. Herrmann's (1996) 'whole-brain thinking' and various left- and right-brain theorists produced interesting analyses but have not progressed into showing what to do with the results of the analysis.[2]

WEB LINK

If you want to explore the connections between various theories of learning, try the following website:
http://www.dmu.ac.uk/%7Ejamesa/learning/contents.htm

Malcolm Knowles

While his original work was outside the managerial and professional field, Knowles' (1984, 1998) identification of the differences between how adults learn ('andragogy') and how young people are taught ('pedagogy') gradually infiltrated the work of management developers and then management educators. In his view:

- The learner is self-directed but has a conditioned expectation to be dependent and to be taught.
- The learner comes with experience which means that with many kinds of learning, adults are themselves the richest resources for one another and that there is a wide range of experience in most groups of learners.
- Adults are ready to learn when they have a need to perform more effectively in some aspect of their lives.
- For the most part, adults do not learn for the sake of learning – they learn in order to be able to perform a task, solve a problem or live in a more satisfying way.
- Although adults will respond to some external motivators (eg a better job, a salary increase), the more potent motivators are internal – self-esteem, recognition, greater self-confidence, self-actualisation.

The historical importance of these statements is only partly reduced by the fact that Knowles generalised about adults without identifying the existence of individual differences.

Reg Revans

Recognised in most countries (though not always in the United States) as the originator of Action Learning, Revans (1982) in fact had three rather different contributions to learning theory.

1 The learning equation

L	=	**P**	+	**Q**
Learning		Programmed knowledge		Questioning insight

Although Revans' prime attention has been to the questioning insight element of the equation through Action Learning, and has occasionally seemed to dismiss the importance of P, the equation neatly captures the view that the acquisition of knowledge by itself is likely to be unsatisfactory, and certainly unlikely to lead to subsequent action. This equation provides a fascinating question for any method of learning – is it pure P or pure Q, or does it combine the two in some form?

2 Action Learning

Revans himself never made a single complete statement of the elements of Action Learning. He saw it (Revans, 1982; p.633) as:

> **'the development of the self by the mutual support of equals. Even if we cannot describe it as a communion of saints, it is at least a conspiracy of innocents.'**

Mumford (1991) suggested the following elements:

1. Learning for managers should mean learning to take effective action.
2. Learning to take action involves actually taking action.
3. Action for learning is work on a project which is significant for managers.
4. Learning is a social process.
5. The social process is carried out through group meetings.
6. Groups are helped to learn by exposure to problems and each other.

3 System Beta

This was Revans' concept of a learning cycle, again influenced by his scientific background, involving five distinct steps:

1. survey
2. hypothesis
3. experiment
4. audit
5. review.

In this case Revans' scientific background seems to have taken him into a model of a cyclical process which is not universally useful, especially in describing the reality of managerial learning. 'Hypothesis' is not a prime part of the learning process for most manager learners most of the time.

Chris Argyris

Like Revans, Argyris (1991) has made three major contributions, first on the difference between 'single-loop' and 'double-loop' learning. He defines single-loop learning as learning that corrects errors by changing routine behaviour. It is incremental and adaptive, rather like a thermostat that is set to turn on the heat if the room temperature drops below a comfortable level. Double-loop learning, in contrast, corrects errors by examining the underlying values and policies of the organisation. The metaphor continues – double-loop learning involves an intelligent thermostat that can evaluate whether or not the 'comfortable level' is the right temperature for optimum efficiency. Single-loop learning involves enabling people to develop knowledge and skills appropriate to and defined by present circumstances. Double-loop learning in contrast involves redefining the nature of problems faced by an individual or organisation and learning how to cope with the new – transformed – understanding. (The terms 'incremental' and 'transformational' learning are connected to but not exactly the same phenomenon.)

A second Argyris statement is literally about theories, and represents his description of the difference between espoused theories and theories in use. The former represent what we say we believe, what we say we mean to do, and what we say we actually do. In contrast, theories in use describe what we actually do and the beliefs, values and theories which have in fact determined what we do.

Finally, Argyris develops the concept of defensive routines. Double-loop learning involves challenging the here and now – understanding the difference between our espoused theory and our actual theory in use requires us to examine both the fact and the reasons for the difference. What stops either of these processes happening? Argyris says that both individuals and organisations develop defensive routines. These are the conscious, unconscious, stated and unstated ways in which an examination of underlying themes, issues, problems, beliefs is prevented. As Argyris goes on to say, the existence of defensive routines is often illustrated by the fact that people and organisations are unwilling to test whether they actually are employing them!

WEB LINK

Go to http://tip.psychology.org/argyris.html for more detail on Argyris' notion of double-loop learning.

David Kolb

Kolb's (1984) definition of learning was given earlier. His most powerful impact has been through his version of the learning cycle and his integrated theory of experiential learning.[3] Figure 19 shows the stages of Kolb's learning cycle.

The learning cycle is often quoted as an example of what should be happening within any designed learning experience – and rather less frequently as what should be happening in learning in and around the job. Kolb's unique contribution was the identification not only of the fact that individuals sometimes have strong preferences to learn in one way but not in another, but in the creation of an instrument, the Learning Styles Inventory (LSI), which could be used to identify those preferences. According to Kolb, learning occurs by grasping an experience and transforming it. Thus at CE, an experience is sensed, and then transformed through reflection (RO) leading to the emergence of ideas (AC) and extended into the world

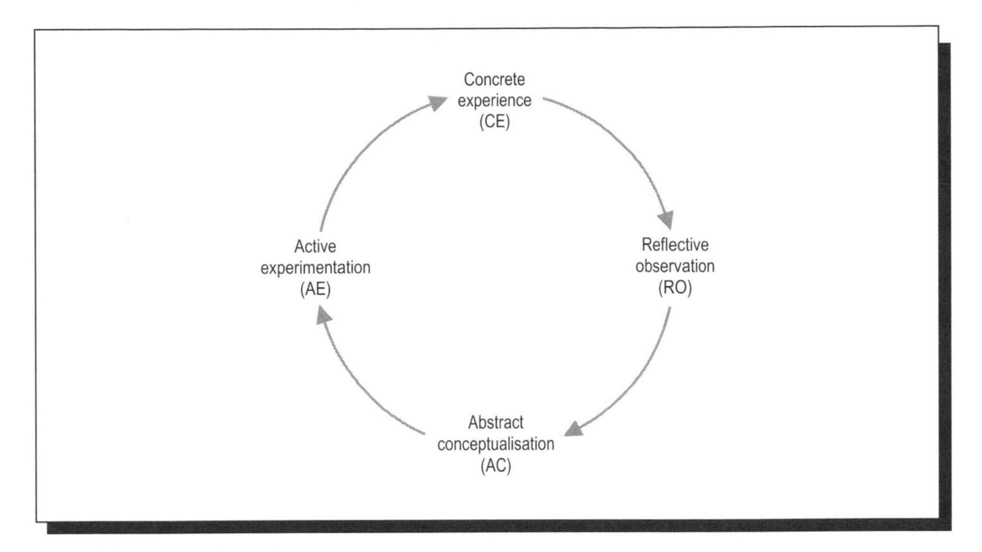

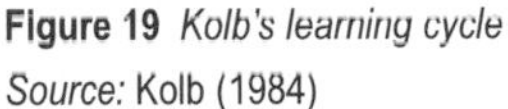

Figure 19 *Kolb's learning cycle*
Source: Kolb (1984)

by taking action (AE). Thus learning in the cycle embraces both process and outcomes. While LSI was originally criticised on technical grounds, reliability significantly improved in his later version. Further, the model of the learning has been very influential in MD and HRD more generally. It has also provided an inspiration for the work of Honey and Mumford (1996).

Honey and Mumford

These authors have created two models, rather than a grand theory. They accepted the theories of Lewin and Kolb in relation to a virtuous learning cycle; they also took on Kolb's fundamentally analytical proposition about the association of different learning styles with different stages of the cycle. However, their models developed differently from Kolb's original theories. Their learning cycle (Figure 20) has a major practical difference from Kolb's in their 'Planning the next steps' stage as compared with Kolb's 'Active experimentation'.

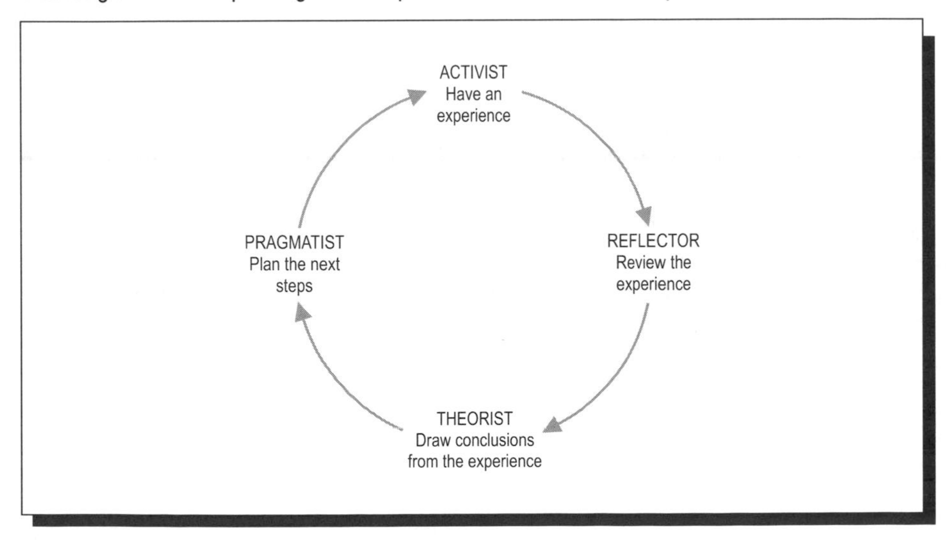

Figure 20 *Honey and Mumford's learning cycle and learning styles*
Source: Honey and Mumford (1996)

Kolb seems to imply that action takes place without being planned as a result of a thoughtful learning process. A second and major difference in theory and practice is that whereas Kolb's original theory and construct was based on the proposition that differences could be identified as polar opposites – eg between abstract conceptualisation and concrete experience – his own research seemed to show that polar opposites did not really exist in practice. A third difference is that Honey and Mumford regard their learning cycle as applying to all kinds of learning activity, whereas Kolb specified an 'experiential learning cycle'. This has been interpreted, perhaps wrongly, as meaning that his cycle applies only to learning from some kind of activity. The Honey and Mumford learning cycle proposes rather that, for example, learning can occur when a lecturer provides conclusions, where neither having an experience nor reviewing has occurred within the individual before the lecturer offers conclusions.

The learning cycle is obviously a simplified version of what occurs. It has the great virtue that managers can identify and use it. It is the description of the optimum way of learning. Individuals differ in their willingness to engage in all elements of the cycle.[4] The idea of identifying individual preferences about learning, followed through by Kolb in his LSI, was developed in a different way by Honey and Mumford in their Learning Styles Questionnaire (LSQ), now more widely used in the UK than Kolb's LSI. The box below provides abbreviated versions of preferred ways of learning for the four styles.

HONEY AND MUMFORD'S LEARNING STYLES

- *Activists* – learn best from relatively short here-and-now tasks. These may be managerial activities on the job or on courses – such things as business games and competitive teamwork exercises. They learn less well from situations involving a passive role, such as listening to lectures or reading.
- *Reflectors* – learn best from activities in which they are able to stand back, listen, and observe. They like collecting information and being given the opportunity to think about it. They learn less well when they are rushed into things without the opportunity to plan.
- *Theorists* – learn best when they can review things in terms of a system, a concept, a model or a theory. They are interested in and absorb ideas even where they may be distant from current reality. They learn less well from activities presented without this kind of explicit or implicit design.
- *Pragmatists* – learn best when there is an obvious link between the subject matter and the problem or opportunity on the job. They like being exposed to techniques or processes which can be applied in their immediate circumstances. They learn less well from learning events which seem distant from their own reality. 'Does it apply in my situation?'

These models have been shown to be very important in the design of learning experiences, and in enabling individuals to learn to learn. One important finding was that 35 per cent of individuals have a single strong preference on how to learn. This does not say that they are unable to learn outside these preferences – but does help to explain why some individuals have unsatisfactory learning experiences.

The results of the LSQ are indicative, not prescriptive, and learning styles are capable of being changed. Changes may occur because of changes in the learner's work environment or through explicit development processes (see *Learning to learn* below).

WEB LINK

For more information about learning styles, including Honey and Mumford's LSQ, try http://www.support4learning.org.uk/education/lstyles.htm#General

REFLECT – CONCLUDE – PLAN 3

- Read the descriptions of learning preferences in the *Honey and Mumford's learning styles* box.
- Which do you feel is your preferred style or styles of learning, and which do you prefer less?
- How do you think you can use your learning preference?
- What can you do to help others understand their learning preferences?

Learning styles, preferences and the concept of the learning cycle, whether based on Kolb's LSI, Honey and Mumford's LSQ, or any other typology, have proved to be a very popular approach to helping managers engage in MD activities. They appear to have significant face validity with many managers and MD providers. Nevertheless, there have been a number of criticisms. For example, the LSI has been criticised for its lack of reliability and construct validity (Allinson and Hayes, 1988). Others have criticised the measurement of learning styles as lacking in rigorous research and made difficult by 'conceptual and semantic confusion' (Moran, 1991; p.241). Reynolds (1997) provides a broad-ranging critique, but his key argument is that the learning styles approach tends to decontextualise learning and give prominence to individuals. Thus, by focusing on the measurement of a person's style or preferences, there is a distortion of the social context in which a person actually works and supposedly learns. Styles or preferences (and by implication, non-preferences) can become seen as 'psychological concepts' which not only avoids the complexity of organisation environment but can also result in stereotyping and labelling managers in particular ways. Reynolds (p.128) feels that the

> **individualistic discourse has become 'common sense' in management learning, expressed in the competencies movement and like forms of credentialism . . .**

He suggests that learning styles can be avoided by considering the following questions, developed by Caple and Martin (1994):

- What is learning?
- What learning experiences have been beneficial to you?
- Do you tend to avoid certain ways or opportunities for learning?
- How can others be of help to you in enabling you to enhance your learning and self-development?

A further critique of learning styles, particularly Kolb's model, is presented by Holman *et al* (1997). They seek to counter the idea of a manager as an individual ('isolated monad', p.140) separated from social context.[5] Their analysis gives particular emphasis to the importance of social conditions, the use of language and other tools of mediation and, especially, conversations with others for carrying the role of managing and learning. These points are linked to our final theoretical model, *situated learning*.

Lave and Wenger

Lave and Wenger (1991) argue for a social approach to learning, especially through participation in everyday activities. Learning occurs through practice in work situations which are usually informal and incidental. This is their version of 'natural' learning (p.47). There is an explicit differentiation between 'learning and intentional instruction' (p.40), the former being the focus for their work practices. Fox (1997) summarises the following key elements of situated learning:

- People who perform work practice belong to a 'community of practice', and it is within that community that learning occurs 'naturally'.
- The community of practice has an apprenticeship system which may be formal or informal, and novices learn to participate by assisting more experienced members. Novices are 'legitimate' but on the 'periphery' of a community. They can observe skilled practitioners and then copy and learn.
- Communities are dependent on other communities and are part of a network of communities.

Lave and Wenger were not explicitly concerned with MD, although situated learning has been applied by them and others to organisations with particular interest in the role of communities of practice in knowledge production and management (see Chapter 12). However, once again we are able to highlight the importance of everyday activities and natural learning for managers and others in part of what Fox calls 'the learning iceberg'. Managers and those who wish to become managers learn through their work and participation in practice. This involves watching, doing and talking, especially the sharing of stories. In this way, what they practise makes sense to their communities, and it is through practice they learn, often tacitly, what is acceptable or not. In addition, such learning is situational, contingent and improvisational, and where faced with a problem or difficulty, managers construct new possibilities for practice (Brown and Duiguid, 1991). Of course, one of the challenges to managers is for learning-in-practice to occur not just in their own communities but also across communities. By definition, such learning has to be contextual and in relationship with others.

WEB LINKS

For an overview of situated learning, try http://tip.psychology.org/lave.html
For further details on communities of practice, go to
http://www.infed.org/biblio/communities_of_practice.htm

REFLECT – CONCLUDE – PLAN 4

- Does your personal experience of learning relate to any of these theories? If you have experience of designing learning experiences, have these theories impacted on your design?
- How important do you think it to be to have a theory of learning in your work?
- How do any of these theories relate to what has occurred on learning experiences in which you have been involved?
- Do you want to acquire more knowledge of any of the theories?
- What action might you take?
- What could you do as a result of your answers to these questions?

THE VALUE OF REFLECTION

The requirement for conscious and frequent reflection about experience is a shared feature of both the Kolb and the Honey and Mumford learning cycle models, and in recent years reflection has been recognised as a crucial feature in MD. However, it is sadly absent in the working and learning practices of many managers. Theories emphasising the significance of reflection were developed by Donald Schön (1983) and later extended by Jack Mezirow (1990).

The reflective practitioner

Schön identified the possibility of reflection in the work of the best practitioners in management. He highlighted tacit knowledge as an aspect of what he referred to as 'reflection-in-action', which is the ability to respond spontaneously to surprise through improvisation and without thought. He contrasted such knowing with 'technical rationality' aimed at problem-solving, predictability and control. He referred to 'programmatic descriptions' of knowledge consisting of formulable propositions which increase in generality and abstraction. For Schön (1987; p.4) what is required is 'not a blind adherence to *one* method [emphasis in original]' but that through reflection-in-action a manager can solve new problems and 'change the situation for the better'. Indeed, by becoming 'reflective practitioners', managers can generate new insights and invent new ways of working in practice.[6] The idea of reflective practice has become very significant for managers and professionals and forms the basis of many frameworks of Continuing Professional Development. It is argued that reflective practitioners can cope with difficulty and change.

Critical reflection

Mezirow developed the idea further by emphasising the requirement that reflection should not be only a recapitulation and improved understanding of experience but should involve serious internal criticism of it. Through critical reflection, an individual becomes more open to the perspectives of others, less defensive, and able to accept new ideas. These are the features of what Mezirow referred to as 'transformative learning'. Mezirow explained that the opportunities for such learning arose when individuals face situations that do not match previous experience and understanding. Through reflection a manager can examine feelings, beliefs and actions and the assumptions that underpin them. Transformation occurs through the challenge to assumptions and the identification of new possibilities for thinking, feeling and action.

Drawing on the ideas of Mezirow and other writers in the field of adult education, the idea of the manager as a critically reflective practitioner has received a great deal of attention, especially among academics who have focused on Management Learning as an emerging field of study (Burgoyne and Reynolds, 1997). There are different versions of the meaning of the term 'critical', and indeed there is now a flourishing academic domain referred to as Critical Management Studies (Fournier and Grey, 2000).[7] One approach to critical thinking management is presented by Mingers (2000) as:

- the critique of rhetoric – whether arguments and propositions are sound in a logical sense
- the critique of tradition – a scepticism of conventional wisdom and long-standing practices
- the critique of authority – being sceptical of one dominant view and being open to a plurality of views, and
- the critique of knowledge – the recognition that knowledge is never value-free and objective.

These aspects of critical thinking were used by Gold *et al* (2002) in a programme of MD. Managers engaged in critical reflection of work experiences by examining their claims and beliefs through argument analysis, following the work of Toulmin (1958). It was found that managers were able to think critically and take a more considered approach to their work. They became more aware of their own views of the situation and the perspectives of others. Some managers were also able to uncover beliefs about their behaviour and question their feelings, especially when reflecting on difficult experiences. This led to new actions and more confidence – they also became more aware of how different views of the same situation can arise.

WEB LINKS

Read more about Donald Schön at http://www.infed.org/thinkers/et-schon.htm
Further details about Jack Mezirow can be found at
http://adulted.about.com/gi/dynamic/offsite.htm?site=http://nlu.nl.edu/ace/Resources/Mezirow.html

We will consider some of the particular techniques of reflection in Chapter 7.

APPROACHES TO LEARNING

Managers, when talking about how they have learned, tend to talk about 'learning from experience'. There is an extraordinary lack of research and analysis of the ways in which individuals learn. One study by Mumford (1995) described the results of research he and colleagues had done with senior executives, which assist the ways in which they learn from experience. His Four Approaches model identified these approaches as 'intuitive', 'incidental', 'retrospective' and 'prospective', as summarised below.

- *intuitive approach* – unconscious natural process
- *incidental approach* – events trigger post-mortem
- *retrospective approach* – regular review process
- *prospective approach* – planning to learn from experience.

The model is significant in so far as it provides a way of emphasising again the significance of reflection and planning in the development process.

Further work has been carried out by Megginson (1996), who suggested that learning strategies can be characterised by a mixture of deliberation/forethought and unpremeditated exploration. The former involves managers planning their learning, and latter allows learning to emerge. Managers engage in both processes to a greater or lesser extent.

Methods

MD has been especially subject to waves of fascination about and claims for the effectiveness of particular methods. A basic understanding of the difference between passive and active forms of learning, associated with a view that managers often preferred active methods, was an early feature in MD. Then there were innovations such as groups discussing issues in 'syndicates' and the more highly structured case study method. At one time groups were taken in a wholly unstructured direction through what were called T-Groups, which existed without any structure or content or apparent direction, but which provided people with experiences of dealing with each other and thinking about the results. Then we had outdoor training, Action Learning, mentoring, and now e-learning. Each has had advocates and for a period of time has been suggested as the most vital way of helping managers to learn. Mumford (1997) in a unique, detailed review was disturbed to find how little the proponents or their followers had actually provided as to precisely what particular methods purported to deal with. He provides four frameworks through which he analyses 16 major methods. He shows, for example, how each method can be assessed in terms of its different level of contribution to the development of knowledge, skills or insight – and how each relates to some of the major theories of management learning and to individual learning styles. His detailed analysis shows how methods are better at meeting some needs than in meeting others. His 16 'development methods' are listed in Table 8.

Table 8 *Development methods*

At work	Primarily away from work	At and away from work
■ line managers as developer ■ learning through the job ■ coaching ■ mentoring	■ Action Learning ■ case studies ■ distance learning ■ lectures ■ outdoor ■ reading ■ role plays ■ simulations and games ■ technology-based training ■ videos	■ group learning ■ learning reviews

REFLECT – CONCLUDE – PLAN 6

- Review Mumford's 16 methods of learning in Table 8.
- Which methods have you found most influential:
  - as a learner?
  - as a facilitator of learning experiences?
- What in your view has made one or other of these methods effective?
- How might you use your answers in developing yourself and other people?

LEARNING TO LEARN

There has been a general movement over the last 20 years to see people as responsible at least in major part for their own development, rather than having development thrust upon them. Indeed, learning has been promoted a part of government policy through Lifelong Learning and the Learning Society (DfEE, 1998). An underlying principle is that individuals are more likely to work more effectively at their learning needs if they have contributed substantially to identifying those needs, and if they are also encouraged to work on those needs through processes which they have themselves identified, or at least on which they have a substantial degree of choice. Principal authors here include Brookfield (1986) for self-directed learning, Cunningham (1999) for self-managed learning, and Pedler, Burgoyne and Boydell (1994) for self-development (see Chapter 7).

The idea that individuals should take more responsibility for their own development is very welcome. Part of that responsibility will be exercised more effectively if individuals understand how they learn, and exercise conscious discipline through their understanding of themselves and others in making better use of learning experiences. The Learning Declaration Group (Attwood, 2002) highlighted this issue by saying that 'learning to learn is the most fundamental learning of all'. The logic of this proposition is that, particularly in the context of increasing personal responsibility for learning, rather than accepting the learning thrust upon them, effective learning depends on people's recognising and using consciously the learning skills involved. Unfortunately, this is an area in which lip service is too often paid – brochures of, for example, business school courses may include it as a heading in their conspectus, yet they provide no explicit sessions on it.

Mumford's definition of 'learning to learn' (2001) is

> **A process through which individual or groups understand the principle of effective learning, and acquire and continuously improve the disciplines and skills necessary to achieve learning.**

He has reviewed the impact of his chosen 16 methods on learning to learn, as shown in Table 9.

Table 9 *Management development methods and impact on learning to learn*
rating scale: ●●● strong likelihood ●● moderate likelihood ● low likelihood

	Potential	Variety	Types of learning			
At work			*Cognitive*	*Affective*	*Inter-personal*	*Self-knowledge*
Manager as developer	●●●	●●●	●	●●	●●	●●●
Through the job	●●●	●●●	●	●●	●●	●●●
Coaching	●●●	●●●	●	●●	●●	●●●
Mentoring	●●●	●●●	●	●●	●●	●●●

	Potential	Variety	Types of learning			
Off the job			*Cognitive*	*Affective*	*Inter-personal*	*Self-knowledge*
Action Learning	●●●	●●	●●	●●	●●	●●
Case studies	●●	●	●●	●	●●	●
Distance learning	●	●	●●●	●●	●	●
Lectures	●	●	●●●	●	●	●
Outdoor	●●●	●	●	●●●	●●●	●●●
Reading	●	●	●●●	●	●	●●
Role plays	●●●	●	●	●●●	●●●	●●
Simulations	●●●	●	●	●●●	●●●	●●●
Technology-based training	●	●	●●●	●	●	●
Video: talking head	●	●	●●●	●	●	●
Video: case/ drama	●	●	●●	●●	●●	●

	Potential	Variety	Types of learning			
Other methods			*Cognitive*	*Affective*	*Inter-personal*	*Self-knowledge*
Group learning: process	●●●	●●●	●●	●●●	●●●	●●●
Group learning: content	●●●	●●●	●	●●●	●●●	●●●
Learning review/logs	●●●	●	●●	●	●	●●●

Each method is assessed on whether it:

- potentially helps individuals to understand the learning process
- provides a variety of learning experiences
- assists a particular type of learning.

The learning cycle and learning styles model provides an easily usable vehicle for enabling learning to learn to be highlighted and worked on. The main learning cycle contains in relation to each stage or element a potential mini-learning-cycle, which can focus on the element of the cycle. For example, the process of 'plan the next steps' is in itself 'have an experience' which can be 'reviewed', followed by 'drawing conclusions' and then planning.

This is illustrated in Figure 21. It is drawn from a plan by an individual to watch a colleague in action in order to learn from her.

This example is taken from the opportunities available from learning how to learn from work experiences. It ought to be more easily provided on structured learning experiences, for example, through a course. Unfortunately, the response here may be of incomprehension, or of different priorities. Every session on a course contains the possibility of enabling individuals

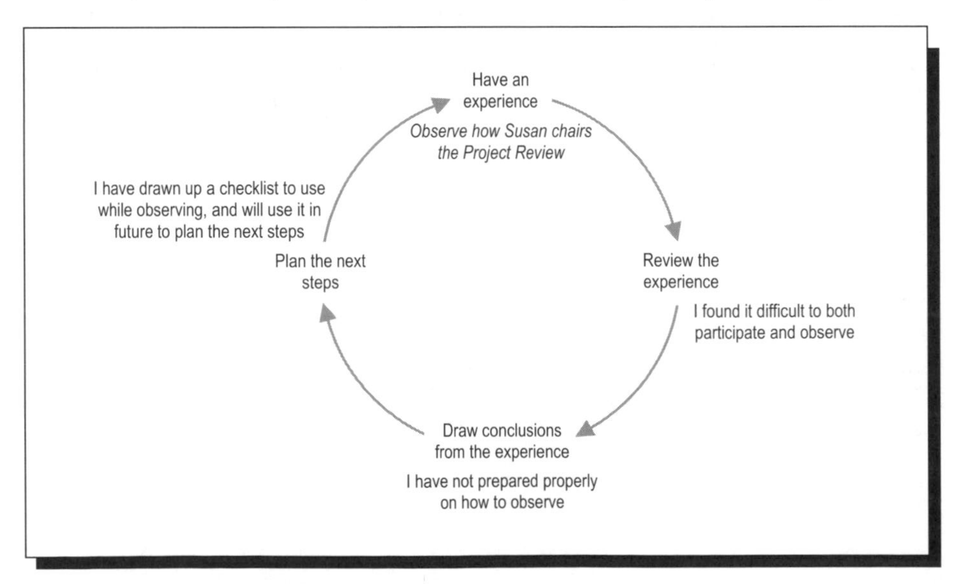

Figure 21 *Planning the next steps: stages in a mini-cycle*

to consider what they learn from it, and the particular feature of this section, how they learn from it. In practice many session leaders are exclusively concerned to meet the content requirements of the session. Burgoyne and Mumford (2001) found in discussion with a range of case study tutors, for instance, that some of them were positively opposed to the idea that their sessions should include a discussion not only of what had been learned but how individuals had learned from each other and from the case study leader in the session. The view of several of them was that their priority was to get through the content requirement – for example, on marketing or operations management – in the session, and that discussion of how individuals had learned was both a low priority and outside their remit: 'That's something for the organisational behaviour people to deal with.' While explicit sessions on learning to learn run by the OB people would indeed be desirable, it is equally desirable that the opportunities of learning how to learn available within other sessions should be taken, as some of the respondents in the research did in fact recognise when the issue was put to them. The immediate reality of the effect of particular exchanges during a case study session on how individuals' understanding of how and why they have learned is crucial for any subsequent discussion how individuals are learning to learn.

Although this section has concerned itself mainly with recommending that individuals are encouraged to pay serious attention to learning how to learn, those individuals in a managerial population will often be responsible for other people. Managers ought to understand the learning to learn processes in order to facilitate the learning of others as well as themselves. As was shown in Chapter 1, 'learning pyramid' managers learn with and from each other. The significance of group or team learning is emphasised in Chapter 7.

REFLECT – CONCLUDE – PLAN 7

- Do you agree with the statement 'Learning to learn is the most fundamental learning of all'? What is the basis for your agreement or disagreement?
- How important in your view would it be to make learning to learn an explicit element in any learning experience?
- To what features of learning to learn would you give priority?
- How important are disciplines like learning reviews and learning logs?
- How could you implement any conclusions you have reached from these questions?

Throughout this chapter, we have made an implicit assumption that learning is beneficial for managers, organisations and society as a whole. Indeed, the value of learning at these different levels was the basis of a Declaration on Learning (Attwood, 2002). However, despite the benefits, it does seem that some managers do not seek to learn or are prevented from learning. There may be a variety of reasons for this, as we have indicated in this and previous chapters, including:

- lack of recognition that a learning need exists
- lack of assessment of relevant needs
- inhibition by the organisation of learning by giving a high priority to work
- the presence of defensive routines
- a failure by a manager's manager or by the larger organisation to give stimulus, encouragement and help.

We will give further attention to barriers to learning in the following chapters.

WEB LINK

You can read the Declaration on Learning at
http://www.peterhoney.co.uk/main/declaration

SUMMARY

- Managers differ in their likely response to any particular learning process.
- Effectiveness in MD requires a contingent definition of effective managerial behaviour, development focused on results, and identifying learning processes which are effective for managers.
- Learning is both a process and an outcome concerned with knowledge, skills and insights.
- There are a growing range of theories of learning. In management learning, an understanding of learning styles in relation to a learning cycle has proved beneficial to many managers.
- Managers always learn in a context of practice.
- Reflection is recognised as crucial for a critique and improvement to practice.
- Managers differ in the way they learn from experience and approach learning activities.
- Increasingly managers and others are being asked to take responsibility for their own learning.

DISCUSSION QUESTIONS

1 Here are three statements about the significance of theory in management learning. What is your response to them?

- 'There is nothing so effective as a good theory' (Kurt Lewin).
- 'Theory without practice is empty, and practice without theory is blind' (Patricia Cross).
- 'Practice, at the end of the day, need theories to shape it. Theory on the other hand is tested and developed through practice' (John Burgoyne and Mike Reynolds).

2 Which of these statements do you think most significant in relation to the theories outlined in this chapter?

3 Can you develop a case for saying that theory is unimportant in management development, except for a small number of 'experts in learning'?

4 Is a manager's learning transferable?

5 Why should managers reflect on their practice? How critical should their reflection be?

6 How can managers learn to learn, and why should they?

7 What do you consider to be the most important principles of effective learning for managers?

FURTHER READING

MUMFORD, A. (2001) *Effective Learning*. London, CIPD.

BOUD, D., KEOGH, R. and WALKER, D. (1986) *Reflection: Turning experience into learning*. London, Kogan Page.

BOYATZIS, R., COWEN, S. and KOLB, D. (1995) *Innovation in Professional Education*. San Francisco, Jossey Bass.

HUCZYNSKI, A. (2001) *Encyclopaedia of Development Methods*. Aldershot, Gower.

FRENCH, R. and GREY, C. (1996) *Rethinking Management Education*. London, Sage.

REYNOLDS, J., CALEY, L. and MASON, R. (2002) *How Do People Learn?* London, CIPD.

GROUP ACTIVITY

- Form a group of three.
- Consider Figure 22, which shows the factors that influence learning and development.

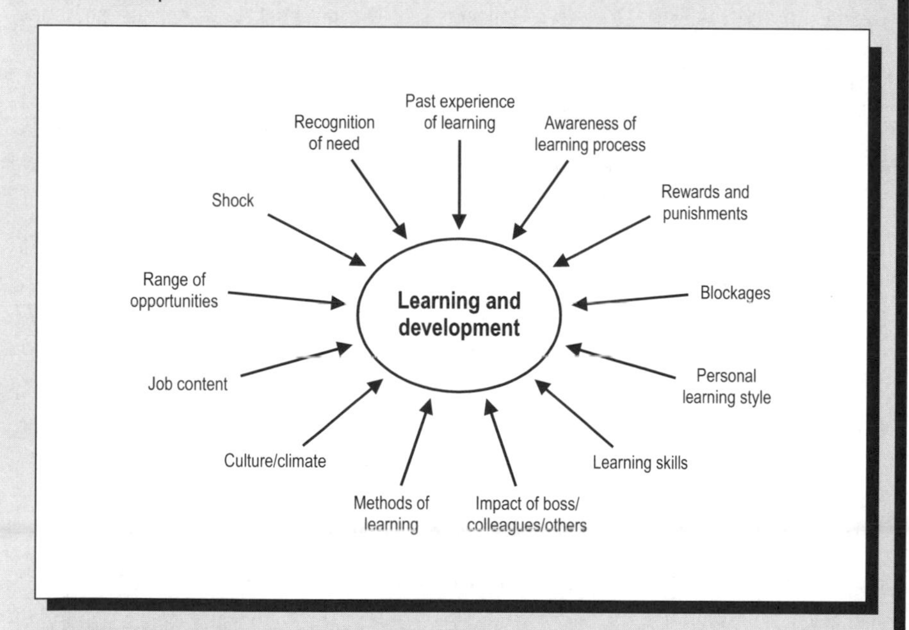

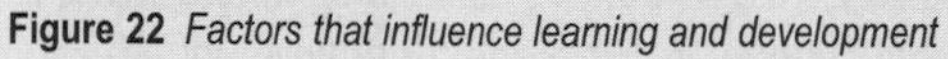

Figure 22 *Factors that influence learning and development*

- Select the three most important influences on your own learning and development, either as negative or positive influences.
- Prepare notes for discussion in a group on your selected influences.
- Be prepared to explain why the impact on you was positive or negative.

REFERENCES

ALLINSON, C. W. and HAYES, J. (1988) 'The learning styles questionnaire: an alternative to Kolb's inventory', *Journal of Management Studies*, Vol. 25, No. 3; pp.269–281.

ARGYRIS, C. (1991) 'Teaching smart people how to learn', *Harvard Business Review*, May/June; pp.99–109.

ATTWOOD, M. A. (2002) *Declaration on Learning*. Maidenhead, Honey Publications.

BROOKFIELD, S. D. (1986) *Understanding and Facilitating Adult Learning*. Milton Keynes, Open University Press.

BROWN, J. S. and DUGUID, P. (1991) 'Organizational learning and Communities-of-Practice: toward a unified view of working, learning and innovation', *Organization Science*, Vol. 2, No. 1; pp.40–47.

BURGOYNE, J. and MUMFORD, A. (2001) *Learning from the Case Method*. Lancaster, Lancaster University.

BURGOYNE, J. and REYNOLDS, M. (1997) 'Introduction', in J. Burgoyne and M. Reynolds, *Management Learning*. London, Sage.

CAPLE, J. and MARTIN, P. (1994) 'Reflections of two pragmatists: a critique of Honey and Mumford's learning styles', *Industrial and Commercial Training*, Vol. 26, No. 1; pp.16–20.

CUNNINGHAM, I. (1999) *Wisdom and Strategic Learning*, 2nd edition. Aldershot, Gower.

DfEE (1998) *Education and Training for the 21st Century*. Green Paper. Sheffield, Department for Education and Employment.

FOURNIER, V. and GREY, C. (2000) 'At the critical moment: conditions and prospects for critical management studies', *Human Relations*, Vol. 53, No. 1; pp.7–32.

FOX, S. (1997) 'From management education and development to the study of management learning', in J. Burgoyne and M. Reynolds, *Management Learning*. London, Sage.

GOLD, J., HOLMAN, D. and THORPE, R. (2002) 'The role of argument analysis and story-telling in critical thinking', *Management Learning*, Vol. 33, No. 3; pp.371–388.

HALL, D. (1986) 'Dilemmas in linking succession planning to individual executive learning', *Human Resource Management*, Vol. 25, No. 2; pp.235–265.

HERRMANN, N. (1996) *The Whole Brain Business Book*. New York, McGraw-Hill.

HOLMAN, D., PAVLICA, K. and THORPE, R. (1997) 'Rethinking Kolb's theory of experiential learning in management education', *Management Learning*, Vol. 28, No. 2; pp.135–148.

HONEY, P. and MUMFORD, A. (1996) *Manual of Learning Styles*, 3rd edtion. Maidenhead, Honey Publications.

KNOWLES, M. (1984) *Andragogy in Action*. San Francisco, Jossey Bass.

KNOWLES, M. (1988) *The Adult Learner*, 5th edition. Houston, Gulf Publishing.

KOLB, D. (1984) *Experiential Learning*. Englewood Cliffs, Prentice Hall.

LAVE, J. and WENGER, E. (1991) *Situated Learning: Legitimate peripheral participation*. Cambridge, Cambridge University Press.

MEGGINSON, D. (1996) 'Planned and emergent learning', *Management Learning*, Vol. 27, No. 4; pp.411–428.

MEZIROW. J. (1990) *Fostering Critical Reflection*. San Francisco, Jossey Bass.

MINGERS, J. (2000) 'What is it to be critical? Teaching a critical approach to management undergraduates', *Management Learning*, Vol. 31, No. 2; pp.219–237.

MORAN, A. (1991) 'What can learning styles research learn from cognitive psychology?', *Educational Psychology*, Vol. 11, Nos 3/4'; pp.239–245.

MUMFORD, A. (1991) 'Learning in action', *Personnel Management*, July.

MUMFORD, A. (1995) *Learning at the Top*. Maidenhead, McGraw-Hill.

MUMFORD, A. (1997) *How Managers Can Develop Managers*. Aldershot, Gower.

MUMFORD, A. (1997) *How to Choose the Right Development Method*. Maidenhead, Honey Publications.

MUMFORD, A. (2001) *How to Produce Personal Development Plans*. Maidenhead, Honey Publications.

PEDLER, M. and BOYDELL, T. (1983) *Managing Yourself*. London, Fontana.

PEDLER, M., BURGOYNE, J. and BOYDELL, T. A. (1994) *A Manager's Guide to Self-Development*, 3rd edition. Maidenhead, McGraw-Hill.

REVANS, R. (1982) *The Origins and Growth of Action Learning*. Bromley, Chartwell-Bratt.

REYNOLDS, M. (1997) 'Learning styles: a critique', *Management Learning*, Vol. 28, No. 2; pp.115–133.

SCHÖN, D. A. (1983) *The Reflective Practitioner: How professionals think in action*. London, Maurice Temple Smith.

SCHÖN, D. A. (1987) 'Educating the reflective practitioner', Paper presented to the American Educational Research Association, Washington.

SKINNER, B. F. (1974) *About Behaviourism*. London, Jonathan Cape.

STUART, R. 1984) 'Towards re-establishing naturalism in management training and development', *Industrial and Commercial Training*, July/August; pp.19–21.

TOULMIN, S. (1958) *The Uses of Argument*. Cambridge , Cambridge University Press.

ENDNOTES

1 Kurt Lewin is regarded as one of the most important social psychologists of the last century. You can read more about him at http://www.a2zpsychology.com/great%20psychologists/kurt_lewin.htm

2 Go to http://www.hbdi.com/ if you are interested in this approach to learning.

3 Kolb acknowledges precursors in Kurt Lewin and John Dewey – check the Dewey Center at http://www.siu.edu/~deweyctr/

4 You may have experienced this through your willingness to engage in the *Reflect – conclude – plan* exercises.

5 Holman *et al* (1997) were using ideas from Social Constructionism and Activity Theory.

6 Schön (1987) distinguishes between reflection-in-action and reflection-on-reflection-in-action where the latter, in contrast to the former, is intellectual requiring verbalisation and symbolisation.

7 You can examine the proceedings of the Critical Management Studies conferences at the site of the Electronic Journal of Radical Organisation Theory at http://www.mngt.waikato.ac.nz/ejrot/

Activities influencing the development of managers

CHAPTER 6

Chapter outline

LEARNING OUTCOMES

After studying this chapter, you should be able to understand, explain, analyse and evaluate:

- **the importance of a written management development policy**
- **whether there has been an imbalance between formal and informal modes of management development**
- **strong and weak features of formal and informal development**
- **the value of management education.**

INTRODUCTION

There has been an explosion in the amount of providers and the number of activities that purport to develop managers. The report by CEML (2002) also found a large supply of MD opportunities, but it suggested (p.4) that such supply was 'mixed on quality' and presented a 'confusing plethora of options' which was not 'sufficiently customised to meet the specific requirements of the organisation or of the individual'. This finding does not surprise us because the work of managers is contingent on contextual factors such as structure, culture, technology and the situation faced; it is therefore difficult to provide generalised statements about what managers should do. For effectiveness in MD, even if it is possible to identify MD needs that are relevant to a manager's performance and find or design activities that meet those needs, there is still the significance of whether learning will be effective for a manager. For us, one of the most important causes of a dysfunction of the MD system in the UK is the failure to address the issues that arise from the Triangle of Effectiveness (shown in Chapter 5, Figure 15).

When most people refer to MD activities, they are normally referencing and emphasising those that are planned and deliberate, such as attending a course on interviewing, doing an MBA or having a formal mentor. Such activities may be of value in themselves, but they also exclude many of the experiences that are particularly real for managers. The exclusion of those preponderant and powerful experiences is not only illogical but leads to a diminished persuasiveness in talking to managers about MD. The reality of MD is reversed, so that the minority pursuits of carefully planned and deliberate development experiences have become the only ones recognised as MD! In this chapter and the next, we hope to restore the balance somewhat by presenting a model of MD activity that gives particular significance to the learning dimension. However, before we do this we will examine the importance of an MD policy in organisations.

PROPOSING A MANAGEMENT DEVELOPMENT POLICY

In Chapter 2 it was suggested that MD gains purpose by showing a link to organisational strategy and that MD policy explicitly translates the requirements into activities – it is a central symbol and indicator of intentions. Managers may not agree with its contents, and like many policy statements in HR, it may represent an espoused view rather than actual practice. Nevertheless, as found by Thomson *et al* (2001), organisations which had formal MD policies were likely to provide more MD than those without. Policy represented a choice by organisations to give MD a priority, to devote resources and to take responsibility for it. Mabey (2003), building on these findings, showed that policy contributed to a positive HR context that took both formal and informal MD seriously. Some organisations will have set and sustained an objective that all top management appointments should be filled by people developed by the organisation itself. Others will have set some target figure for recruitment from outside, or will set different targets for different jobs.

Formal management development will normally include the following items:

- A statement of the purpose of management development, such as

  To ensure that executives are developed or recruited and trained in sufficient numbers to sufficient standards to meet the specialist and general management requirements of the group in the short and the long term.

  (See the *Management development policy* box below for a more extended version of this.)

  Some organisations have given dedicated attention and resources to formal development, without having a formal statement of policy. This may be because the organisation has such a well-established system of procedures and processes that there is no need to give it the attention and focus that production of a formal policy might achieve.

- A statement about the processes to be used in identifying and developing managers.

  Such a statement will refer usually to individual performance review or appraisal, to the identification of individual training and development needs, the possibility of individual development plans. These will be supported by statements about the disciplines, procedures and reviews involved, the timetables to be created, and the levels of decision-making involved in making a job-movement or development decision.

  Emphasis is usually given to either or both of appraisal processes, or a development needs analysis for individuals (see Chapters 3 and 4). The type of performance review/appraisal to be conducted, the philosophy behind it, and the way in which it should contribute to the identification and development needs may be set out. Variants such as 360-degree appraisal may be introduced. Where organisations separate appraisal and the identification of development needs (see Chapter 4), timetables will be set out for the achievement of these tasks. Training or guidebooks and videos about how to conduct these processes may well be provided.

Guidance on the kind of learning activities which may be provided has progressed beyond the identification of training courses in an internal catalogue, to guidance on some of the processes centred on and around the job, such as mentoring and coaching and online guidance as part of a company intranet service. For example, at Lloyds-TSB, as a feature of the infrastructure to support the organisation's corporate university, managers and others can access development material from any Internet-enabled PC in the world.

A MANAGEMENT DEVELOPMENT POLICY

Example taken from a UK organisation

Effective management is clearly vital to the success and continuing prosperity of the group, and to the security and quality of employment and morale of its staff.

We accept that it is the group's responsibility to:

- provide every manager with the opportunity to develop his/her ability and potential so that he/she does his/her existing job effectively
- ensure that there is an adequate supply of trained staff who are competent for promotion to meet the future managerial needs of the group.

We believe:

- that people derive more satisfaction from working when they themselves have helped to establish and are committed to the objective of their jobs
- that people should be encouraged to develop their own creative roles, exercise initiative and demonstrate self-discipline within the agreed limits of their jobs.

Application
The policy requires that through the divisions:

- we create an environment in which all managers contribute to the objectives of the business to their maximum ability
- we give all managers the scope for exercising initiative by allocating responsibility with authority down the line and see that decisions are taken at the lowest appropriate level; we ensure that every manager participates with his/her superior in determining the basic responsibilities of his/her job, and the results that can be reasonably expected of him/her, and accepts full responsibility for achieving those results
- we appraise every manager's performance against his/her expected results, for the purpose of helping him/her to develop his/her skills and improve his/her performance
- we assess every manager's potential on the quality of his/her performance
- we encourage and train all managers to adopt a similar policy in the management of their subordinates.

Context
We have undertaken to support this policy by:

- providing an organisational structure within which the responsibilities of each manager are clearly defined
- providing and implementing consistent personnel policies covering recruitment, salaries and promotion
- providing appropriate training and development programmes.

Expectations
We expect that increasing the influence and scope for initiative and self-motivation of managers and their subordinates will lead to increasing job satisfaction and to direct improvement in the group's commercial performance and efficiency.

REFLECT – CONCLUDE – PLAN 1

- Does your organisation have a written MD policy?
- How effectively does it operate?
- What could you do to make it work better or to convince your organisation of the need for a policy?

A MODEL OF MANAGEMENT DEVELOPMENT ACTIVITIES AND LEARNING

In Chapter 2 we examined Burgoyne's (1988) framework of levels of maturity of organisational MD (Table 2). The framework offered a very recognisable and usable statement about the formal processes of MD. One weakness, though, is that what he describes as 'natural' MD and 'usually good and destined always to be the major provider of MD', seems to disappear after Level 1: *No systematic management development*. However, managers often talk about informal and unplanned experiences as 'explicit, powerful, relevant and realistic', and as the main source of their development. Yet the same experiences can also be fragmentary, insufficient, inefficient, only partially understood and subject to the winds of circumstance. MD needs to remedy these defects.

The elimination of informal learning primarily in and around the job from what was understood to be MD was illogical and unhelpful (see Chapter 5). Those experiences continue as 'situated learning' for all managers, whatever the effectiveness of any formal processes they may have been involved in, whether on-the-job or off-the-job. To the extent that MD is placed in a separate box as a discrete activity, especially when it is carried out away from work, it carries the risk that it is seen by managers as psychologically and practically distant from the managerial world they inhabit. In that world the resolution of managerial problems is the highest – sometimes the only – priority. Formal MD became better at recognising the opportunities involved in using real managerial work in off-the-job learning activities – through the case study method, through business games. But this recognition was contained only within those formal carefully-planned and deliberate development experiences.

In Figure 23 we present a model which attempts to portray conceptually the totality of MD in an organisation by including both formal and informal learning activities and experiences.

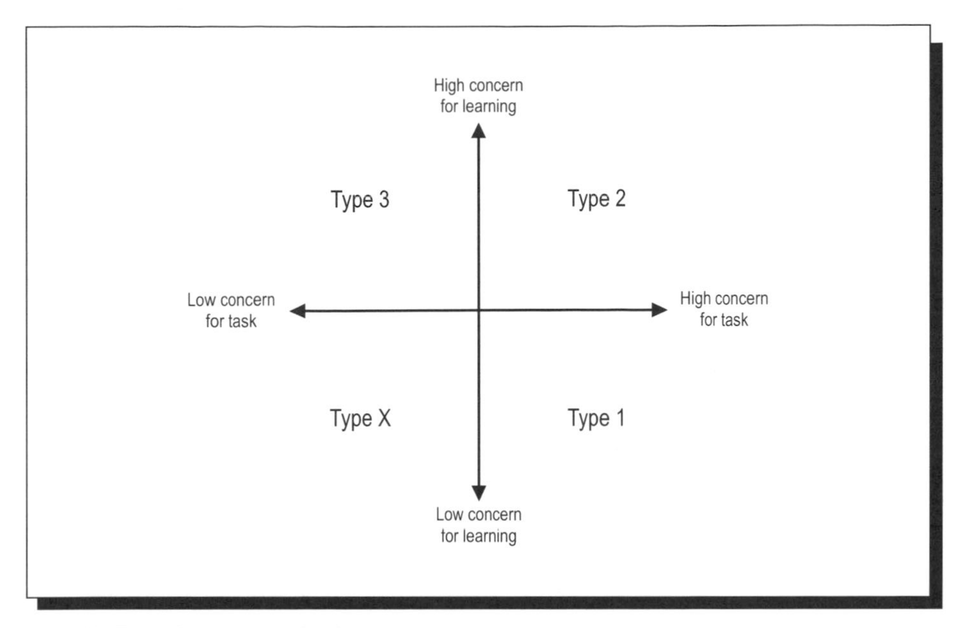

Figure 23 *Types of management development*

The model, originally developed by Mumford and his colleagues (Mumford, 1987), takes into account variations of two key features of a manager's existence. Firstly, there is a concern for working on tasks. Managers to a greater or lesser degree are responsible for the completion of tasks. However there will be times when there is less concern – eg when they are attending a conference away from work – at that moment a manager will not be completing tasks. This provides the first dimension: high concern for task versus low concern for task. The second dimension considers the concern for learning. What is suggested here is that again there is variation between two positions. There will be times and situations when concern for learning will be high – that is, a manager is both consciously and deliberately attending to learning. However, at other times, attention to learning will be low. In Figure 23 the two dimensions are combined to provide a number of types of MD. In Table 10 the characteristics of Types 1, 2 and 3 are presented. We will consider what we call Type X later in the chapter.

In the research which led to this model it was clear that some organisations were at Level 1 in the Burgoyne (1988) model, others were at the higher Levels 4 and 5. Even in those organisations in which managers had had opportunities to learn from formal structured development activities, the experiences that had been most significant were much more often from informal and unplanned experiences in and around the job. It was also clear that they had not previously thought of these experiences as learning experiences – they were tasks, jobs, problems, which had registered as important. They had learned – but often did not recognise what they had learned. Some told the researchers that they regretted that they had not 'thought more about the experience at the time'.

Type 2 learning attempts to transform the regrets expressed by managers that they had not learned more into a more productive experience by providing a conscious and disciplined process of development especially at work. The provision and encouragement of Type 2 learning is opportunistic and problematic at the same time. It is opportunistic as far as the managers themselves are concerned, because it asks them to make use of learning

Table 10 *Characteristics of Types 1, 2 and 3*

Type 1 Informal managerial – incidental and accidental processes	*Characteristics* Occurs within managerial activities Explicit intention is task performance No clear development objectives Unstructured in development terms Not planned in advance Owned by managers *Development consequences* Learning is real, direct, unconscious, insufficient
Type 2 Integrated managerial – opportunistic processes	*Characteristics* Occurs within managerial activities Explicit intention is both task performance and development Clear development objectives Structured for development by manager and direct report Planned beforehand or reviewed subsequently as learning experiences Owned by managers *Development consequences* Learning is real, direct, conscious, more substantial
Type 3 Formal management development – planned processes	*Characteristics* Often away from normal managerial activities Explicit intention is development Clear development objectives Structured for development by developers Planned beforehand and reviewed subsequently as learning experiences Owned more by developers than managers *Development consequences* Learning may be real (through a job) or detached (through a course) Is more likely to be conscious, relatively infrequent

opportunities in and around the job at the time that those opportunities occur. From a manager's point of view it brings MD into the real managerial world. From the point of view of MD professionals and academics, Type 2 is problematic because the situation in which it occurs is outside their environment and often outside their immediate influence. We will give greater attention to Type 2 MD in Chapter 7.

REFLECT – CONCLUDE – PLAN 2

- How far does your own experience confirm or challenge the model shown in Figure 23?
- Using your answers to earlier exercises, what conclusions do you draw about the relative impact of formal and informal learning on your own effectiveness?
- Using your answers to earlier exercises, what conclusions do you draw about the relative impact of formal and informal learning on the effectiveness of managers with whom you have worked?
- What actions would be necessary to move towards Type 2, if you think that desirable?

INFORMAL LEARNING (TYPE 1)

When asked how they learn to do their jobs, managers frequently reply that they 'learn from experience'. By this they mean usually experience from the work they do, rather than more experiences away from work. Type 1 learning, however, is informal learning that is not deliberately encouraged – it occurs by accident or incidentally, through everyday experience and management practice (Marsick and Watkins, 1990).[1] Such experiences must be recognised in MD – although in Chapter 7 we propose ways in which such learning can be transformed through Type 2 into more effective learning.

David Kolb (1984) argued that 'Learning is the process whereby knowledge is created through the transformation of experience.' His learning cycle, and the Honey and Mumford variant on it, is especially important in this context because it enables us to see why so often those powerful and significant work episodes which managers describe have so often been an unrecognised and underused experience. As the poet T.S. Eliot said, 'We had the experience but we missed the meaning.'[2] Managers have not been encouraged and helped to go through the process of assessing and planning what to do about the learning experience. They need to be encouraged to look at their experiences in those terms. Similarly, the 'situated learning' approach of Lave and Wenger (1991) supports the importance of natural learning within the context of practice and legitimacy received for learning through the social relations of a community of practitioners.

Managers can be helped to recognise that these powerfully experienced managerial processes are also learning experiences, but that as learning experiences they could be improved, with a significant benefit to themselves and their organisation. Informal learning is difficult to uncover; rather like the submerged part of an iceberg (Coffield, 2000). Managers can of course be helped further by looking in more specific detail at the kind of informal learning opportunities that exist, as in the *Informal learning opportunities* checklist box below.

INFORMAL LEARNING OPPORTUNITIES FOR MANAGERS

analysing mistakes
attending conferences or seminars
being coached or counselled
being mentored
budgeting
championing and/or managing changes
covering for holidays
dealings with colleagues and peers
dealings with subordinates
dealings with your boss
domestic life
familiar tasks
giving a presentation
interviewing
job change in a new function
job change within same function
job rotation
making decisions
meetings
negotiating
networking
performance appraisals
planning project work
reading
same job with additional responsibilities
secondments
solving problems
unfamiliar tasks/work
working in groups/teams
working with consultants

What else? Note additional learning opportunities below.

Adapted from Honey and Mumford (1995)

Any attention to informal learning must, however, be accompanied by a recognition of major deficiencies.

They include:

- *idealisation* – Attitudes and behaviours may predominate which say that past experience is so valued and appropriate that it is all that is necessary. Effective learning involves building successfully on properly understood past experience, not treating it as the only process of merit.
- *narrowness* – It is possible for a manager's work experience to be extremely narrow in terms of jobs, functions, kinds of organisation and sizes of organisation. While effective management development is more likely to focus on the specific than the general, this does not mean that a manager in retail needs to know nothing about, for instance, production processes.
- *obsolescence* – Painful and perhaps carefully acquired experience of how to do a managerial job may well become out of date. The appropriate attitudes and behaviour of managers in public service utilities who have had to change to meet the new demands of privatised business are a case in point. As a director said rather ruefully, 'I reached the top of this organisation by being better than most at managing a centralised bureaucratic business. Now I am here, I have to manage newly-created profit centres with managers who want a decision yesterday.' If you learn only from what you encounter in the normal and natural processes of work at a particular level, it may mean that you will not be exposed to those activities or opportunities you will actually need in future.

Of course, people develop skills from the 'natural' process of doing the job, and finding out whether the way they do it works. If it does, they understandably assume that they have a skill. However, the skill they have acquired may be either inappropriate or at an insufficiently high performance level. At worst it may even be the wrong kind of skill. One example is the process of interviewing. The skills that managers deploy in selection interviewing have often been acquired from the experience of being interviewed themselves, and then of interviewing others. Their level of skill is often, however, well below what they need to interview effectively. You might also recall the Power School of Strategy that we mentioned in Chapter 2 and the structures of everyday experience where the most important message might be 'Learn not to learn!' (Salaman and Butler, 1990). In a similar vein, Type 1 learning always occurs in a context where politics, contests and tensions may exert inhibiting influences on a manager (Garrick, 1998). These are aspects of Type X MD (see below).

FORMALLY DESIGNED DEVELOPMENT IN AND AROUND THE JOB (TYPE 3)

Formal MD attempts to overcome the major disadvantages involved in relying on accidental – informal – learning for the development of managers. Much more, and more effective, development is secured when it is actually driven through an organised plan. This may well start with the kind of appraisal and performance review discussed in Chapter 3, followed by a formal personal development plan (Chapter 4). Table 11 gives a large-scale view of opportunities in and around the job. Within each major opportunity there are a number of different learning activities involved.

In this chapter we deal with the first two major opportunities – in Chapter 9 we look at issues around coaching and mentoring.

Changes in the job

There are significant differences in the nature of the opportunities provided by different types of change, and of the difficulties involved in taking up the opportunities. Figure 24 shows some of the possibilities.

Moving into a new job with an existing or new employer poses the same development issues. What is the new manager to learn, at what pace, and through what processes? As Figure 24 indicates, the most difficult move of all – yet the one with the most potential for learning – is promotion into a new organisation. Some kind of induction programme will usually be arranged. The new manager will meet new colleagues, and will probably be given a tour of working facilities. There may be arrangements to meet a range of customers, suppliers and

Table 11 *Formally planned learning opportunities at work*

Changes in the job	Changes in job content	Within the job
■ promotion ■ same job but in different function or product job rotation ■ secondment	■ stretching boundaries of job by extra responsibility and tasks ■ special projects ■ committees or task groups ■ junior boards	■ being coached ■ being counselled ■ monitoring and feedback by direct manager ■ being mentored

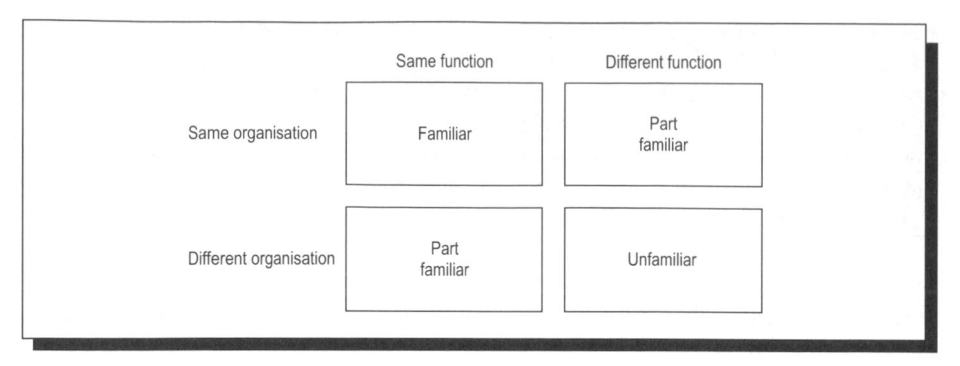

Figure 24 *Learning problems in job moves*

other useful contacts. In essence the manager has to learn about the nature and purpose of the organisation – 'getting to know the business'.

Then there is the need to find out about internal relationships: the politics of the business, the way in which people work together, or avoid working together. Finally, there is the outside world, the people and organisations serviced, as shown in the following example:

> **'A newly-appointed general manager of an overseas subsidiary of a UK multinational was brought to the UK for a week. His programme included a number of visits to different people at head office, to research division, and to several managers of similar companies. The original design of the programme filled almost the whole of the week with visits and travel, and there was no opportunity for the manager to review what he had learned and to check out that he had learned appropriately. Two review sessions with his immediate boss and the main board director concerned were therefore built in, during which he reviewed what he had learned from his visits and contacts'**

Gabarro (1985) described the stages involved when managers move into a new job:

- taking hold
- immersion
- reshaping
- consolidation
- refinement.

The example above shows that effective action can be taken to help with the stage Gabarro described as 'taking hold'. Gabarro set out the further requirements for this stage:

- Make sure that priorities are set out for the new manager.
- Provide processes by which new managers work out expectations with their new subordinates.

- Give support in areas of lack of knowledge or experience.
- Accept that taking charge takes time.

What is involved here is clearer recognition that the transition between jobs, whether promotion or movement sideways, involves a great deal more than some prior training and development activities and an initial induction period. This transition frequently provides only informal and accidental learning. In part this is because of failure by formal MD processes and organisers to recognise exactly what is involved in these transitions and to provide formal development plans during the transition. It is not simply a case of waiting for the first review of the manager's performance (probably a formal appraisal) and picking out from it the learning needs that experience on-the-job has identified. It is quite possible to see in advance what at least some of those learning needs will be, and to plan for them formally – the Type 2 approach. The review would then more usefully be of both performance and the achievement of and learning from that experience.

Secondment can be a useful MD job move (we do not include moving people across divisions, or from one company to another within a group of companies, which is a form of job rotation). A secondment may in certain instances have a dual learning objective. For example, secondment of a manager from industry to work in the civil service normally has a double objective – the individual learns from exposure to a different culture, a different environment, a different way of doing things. At a secondary level the organisation sponsoring the secondee learns about how the civil service operates, and may therefore learn how to deal with it more effectively.

Changes in the job content

Just as an agricultural crop will extract all the goodness from one location and therefore benefit by being grown in a different one, so with managers. The agricultural analogy can be developed further by considering development opportunities within existing jobs. As with job moves, too often opportunities are provided without any effective development taking place. Fertilisation is needed – the use of effective learning and development processes within the opportunities provided.

A manager may be given additional responsibilities or a greater weight of responsibility. This is stretching boundaries and acquiring new tasks. An example of this would be that of a sales director handing over to a sales manager the responsibility for a major national account previously handled by the director. Another would be delegating to a subordinate manager the task of producing a report, visiting an important customer or negotiating with a trade union. Crucial here, as highlighted by Davies and Easterby-Smith (1984), is that managers who have to face new situations and difficulties, where their existing behaviours are not adequate, will need to learn to cope. However, such learning must be recognised by senior managers in order to become 'legitimate' (p.181).

Senior line managers most frequently assign managers to special committees/working parties or task forces for purely managerial reasons. The senior manager wants a particular expert on the subject or a representative from a particular area in the business or somebody who is known to have the ear of somebody important. Such appointments may lead to Type 1 learning, but the learning can be improved – made into Type 2 or created as Type 3 if the development opportunities and ways of benefiting from them have been discussed.

Managers can stay in their existing jobs but be given experience simulating the work of their board of directors through a 'junior board', explicitly as a Type 3 objective. They may be given the same information as the board on a particular issue, and/or be required to make recommendations to the board.

Projects

Projects can be a development tool in all the processes mentioned so far. The manager in a new job can take up a major project as a development process – for example: 'Find out why repeat orders have declined by 28 per cent in the last six months.' A secondment can include a project or, indeed, be totally dedicated to one. For example, 'We are seconding you to charity X for six months. Your project is to review their management control systems, and produce a report for the chairman of their council.' Projects can also be identified within the existing job: 'We want you to do an investigation into the forecasts actually used by sales, marketing and production. Why do they have different forecasts, and what problems result?'

Any of these projects could have been set up as a purely managerial exercise, resulting at best in informal learning – Type 1. They were actually Type 3 development opportunities, because the manager selected to carry them out was chosen for development reasons as well as for managerial ones. There was also discussion with the individual about why he had been given the project as a development exercise. This was supplemented by a discussion on how the manager might take the best advantage of the development opportunity. In each case a development plan was agreed, and in both cases a short review session was held at the end of the project, separate from the managerial project presentation and review.

Projects provide major potential developmental benefits. They often involve managers in looking at a wider range of issues, in greater depth, across a wider range of functions, than might otherwise be encountered. At their best, even within a formal development context, projects of the kind described here should be real rather than invented purely for development. In some cases they carry responsibility for implementation as well as recommendation, in which case they provide for the strongest form of development (see Chapter 7 on Action Learning). Even projects in which the participant does not carry final responsibility can, if properly managed from a development point of view, provide good learning. Smith and Dodds (1993) examined the value of project-based learning with Volvo and ICI.

REFLECT – CONCLUDE – PLAN 4

- Which of the processes outlined in this chapter have been the most powerful in use in your organisation? Why were they the most powerful?
- As a result of reading this chapter so far, do you see any ways in which you could introduce some processes you do not currently use? What action could you take?
- In what ways does your organisation currently assist managers to learn from the opportunities created for them through formal management development? Could these be improved?
- Do you see any way of improving your application of any processes you do currently use?

PLANNED DEVELOPMENT OFF THE JOB (TYPE 3)

The problem with development processes centred on the job is that their greatest strength – reality – constantly poses the risk of seduction. The manager's attention is always likely to be seduced by the reality and priority of the managerial activity rather than focusing on learning. The case for taking managers away from that reality and putting them on a course is precisely that they are then able to concentrate entirely on learning rather than on managing. Nor it is only a question of focus of attention. Although we can greatly increase the productivity of learning through real-life experiences, they will still offer learning only within the limits of those experiences. You cannot learn on the job anything that is not available within or around it. You cannot develop a skill if that skill is not actually employed currently. An even more pervasive problem is that you cannot improve your level of skill if there is no one else around capable of demonstrating, coaching or facilitating your development of it.

Manager-centred learning

We regard the key elements of manager-centred learning as:

- managerial reality
- building on experience
- using familiar learning processes
- continued learning
- preferred approaches to learning.

The focus for development work ought to be reality, not only because it is real but because it engages the attention of managers. The problem with processes and content that do not engage and focus on reality is that for many managers they create learning problems rather than making learning easier and more effective. It is more sensible to build the design and content of formal MD on the experience that managers have when they arrive on a course. It takes longer and may be less exciting for the tutor – but it is more effective. Although one of the great virtues of formal training and education is precisely that it focuses on learning rather than just managing, the achieved learning of managers will be small if the process is too different and distant from what they usually do. Since managers do not customarily spend their time listening to lectures, even brilliantly delivered lecturers may not attract them. If they do not spent their time reviewing historical case studies of managerial practices in other organisations, a learning process based on this starts with some major disadvantages. Perhaps most powerfully of all, if the learning process, of whatever nature, is seen as something that is likely to be useful only on a course, not in real managerial life, learning will be limited. Causing managers to think in a different way, by giving them opportunities to listen, study reflect and generate new ideas, is attractive but insufficient.

Continued learning

A follow-on from the last point is appropriate for many courses. It is desirable that the learner should continue learning after the course. This is not simply a matter of 'further reading' or individual action plans. These are partial but low-level contributions. For any but short courses on particular techniques, participants should be given such an understanding of their own learning processes that they can seek out and use appropriate learning experiences beyond the confines of the course. A successful consequence of such attention would be a vast increase in Type 2 learning as a result of these Type 3 experiences. Trainers and educators should take on board responsibility for enhancing the capacity of managers to learn outside as well as on their courses. This means explicit sessions on learning to learn (see Chapter 5).

MD literature tells readers how to deliver particular methods of off-the-job development, usually including either an explicit or implicit claim that the particular method has special virtues. However, the literature is extremely weak on two very important issues. The first question in choosing any method is what need it is pre-eminently suited to meeting. What is the justification for using a case study, a lecture or e-learning to meet that defined need? Huczynkski's *Encyclopaedia* (2001) illustrates the variety of techniques available. What is needed is careful and objective consideration of why a particular method should be used (see Mumford's framework, Table 12, later in this chapter).

The second issue is whether that method, whatever its general suitability for a need, will actually suit the learning preferences of the people exposed to it. Course designers and tutors must enhance their capacity to deal with these individual preferences, difficult and time-consuming though this may appear to be.

Values

In-company courses can be particularly powerful in protecting and sustaining the culture and value system of the company. Indeed, this is precisely what some courses explicitly, but more often unconsciously, attempt to do. However, they may also say, explicitly or implicitly, 'Here is the way we want things done round here – do not expect to get rewarded or promoted if you behave differently.' In contrast, MD courses can also play a significant part in attempting to bring about culture change (Sadri and Lees, 2001).

The link with individual needs

What an individual recognises as development needs may differ from that person's manager's perception, or from what the organisation defines as 'what managers need' (Antonacopoloulou, 1999). One virtue of the effectiveness-centred approach is that it is more likely to secure the real participation of individuals on the course. The programme might start with a session on 'What is our business and what do we need to do to manage it well?' Or 'What are the problems and opportunities facing our organisation, and what do we need to do well to meet them?'

While this approach may mitigate, it will not overcome the different problems so frequently encountered on many management courses – failures in the nomination and preparation process. Management trainers and educators usually point to the nominator as the cause of the problem. Managers arrive on courses at short notice having been told 'It was your turn', and with no previous discussion with their bosses about why they are being sent. Some people for whom the course is, in fact, appropriate turn up but are poorly motivated. And sometimes people turn up for whom the course is not appropriate at all. It is scarcely surprising that someone whose needs have not been discussed is at best unlikely to see how a course may help or at worst be disposed to reject the course precisely because it has been imposed without discussion.

WEB LINKS

http://www.mapnp.org/library/trng_dev/gen_plan.htm provides a link to a resource which allows managers to develop their own training plans.
The Association of Management Education and Development (AMED) is a network for people interested in management and organisation development practice. The website is http://www.amed.org.uk/
You may also be interested to read some work on outdoor management development with many references and examples from the experience of managers. The link is http://www.users.zetnet.co.uk/research/index.htm

Education or training?

In the past, education has been defined as a broadly-based and broadly-directed process aimed at the whole person and total career, while training has been seen as the specific process of helping managers to learn things appropriate to particular circumstances, within specific organisations or industries. The distinction also broadly followed location: education was what happened in the further/higher education system, and training was what happened in management centres.

The distinction, if ever true, seems now to have largely lost its meaning (Holman, 2000). Although training centres probably tend to focus more on issues that are practical and specifically related to organisational needs, they also often see themselves as educating a manager for his or her total life. Similarly, education centres have increasingly taken on responsibility for developing managers who meet the specific needs of their particular organisations. The major business schools, when first set up, took a distinctly lofty and distant view about the desirability of doing in-company work (except as private ventures by senior faculty). Now many make a virtue, as well as making a great deal of money, from doing such work.

One distinctive characteristic of management education compared with management training may be that there is likely to be an academic award associated with it. Part of the case for establishing such programmes geared to a qualification is that this process ensures a rigour and discipline in both tutors and learners in that they are driven towards attempting to secure the qualification. The contrasting snag about them is that they therefore inevitably give much more attention to trying to inculcate knowledge rather than to develop skills, since the former is much easier to assess, and academic judgements about performance on knowledge are easier to justify than comments about levels of skill. This general problem extends itself to the possibility that learners become involved in a sort of karaoke form of learning, in which they deliver the words already presented to them, rather than having to invent their own words and their own tune.

Until relatively recently a different distinction could have been drawn between education and training. Education processes, particularly as exhibited on MBA programmes, were clearly knowledge-based, whereas training was much more likely to have a higher skill content and be more directly concerned with implementation. But under the impact of customer requirements there has been a considerable conceptual and practical shift towards skills of implementation and effectiveness.

A study carried out by CEML (2002a) suggested that there is little evidence that management qualifications improve organisational performance although there is likely to be a benefit to individual managers and their careers. At undergraduate levels there is a good demand for business and management degrees and graduates become eminently employable, although such a degree is not a requirement for management work.

MBA programmes receive disproportionate attention in discussion about management education and training because they are the longest and most ambitious attempt to develop managers by structured processes. The Constable Report (1987) proposed a quintupling (from 1,200) in the production of MBA graduates in the UK, although it lacked any analysis of why management training and education processes had so far been unattractive to British management. This was more than achieved; there were 11,000 in 2000 (CEML, 2002). In the UK most business schools now offer MBA qualifications, and demand for the MBA has grown, many UK-based students (80 per cent) opting for a part-time or distance learning approach (CEML, 2002a). The MBA is presented as a high-quality qualification, with an approval process developed by the Association of Business Schools (AMBA).

There are continuing concerns, however, about the application of theoretical teaching and the practice of managers and leaders (CEML, 2002a). In the United States there have been major concerns about the actual results achieved by 100,000 MBA graduates a year, and this concern has been expressed not so much by concerned industrialists as by academic researchers like Behrman and Levin (1984). Henry Mintzberg (1989), and more recently Pfeffer and Fong (2002), criticising MBA programmes as being too much oriented towards skills of analysis rather than skills of implementation. Further concerns come from those who take a more critical stance towards management education more generally (Grey, 1996) – indeed, it is claimed that management education faces a 'crisis of confidence' (p.11). The key argument is that such education purports to provide managers with 'useful knowledge'; it should instead 'expand and challenge the intellectual world' of managers (p.14), including the complex moral and political dimensions of that world.

WEB LINKS

AMBA's website is located at http://www.mbaworld.com/

If you would like to consider a free online Management Development programme with 10 modules, try

http://www.managementhelp.org/fp_progs/org_dev.htm#anchor704607

Problems in off-the-job development

Thomson *et al* (1997) found that only 4 per cent of the larger organisations and 20 per cent of the small organisations reported doing no management training. Importantly, in terms of our argument for the need to balance formal and informal methods of training, he found there was a reasonably equal amount of attention available to both. However, there are clear reasons why managers often find informal processes more effective than formal ones. These include:

- the content of development programmes, especially courses, which is experienced as unreal, irrelevant to the manager's priorities or difficult to transfer from a course to a managerial job
- processes of learning that too often reflect the interest of course designers and tutors rather than those of managers
- processes that do not take into account different individual learning preferences.

Table 12 *A framework of management development methods and their suitability for learning outcomes rating scale:* ●●● most suitable ●● moderately suitable ● least suitable

At work	Suitability for knowledge	Suitability for skills	Suitability for insights
Manager as developer	●●●	●●●	●●
Through the job	●●●	●●●	●●
Coaching	●●●	●●●	●●
Mentoring	●●●	●●	●●●

Off the job	Suitability for knowledge	Suitability for skills	Suitability for insights
Action Learning	●●	●●	●●●
Case studies	●●	●●●	●●
Distance learning	●●●	●●	●
Lectures	●●●	●	●●
Outdoor	●	●●	●●
Reading	●●●	●	●●
Role plays	●	●●●	●●●
Simulations	●	●●●	●●●
Technology-based training	●●●	●	●
Video: talking head	●●●	●	●●
Video: case/drama	●●	●●	●●

Other methods	Suitability for knowledge	Suitability for skills	Suitability for insights
Group learning: process	●●●	●●●	●●●
Group learning: content	●●	●●	●●●
Learning review/logs	●	●●●	●●●

Source: adapted from Mumford (1997)

A major cause of failures on courses has been the grotesque lack of attention paid to learning processes in institutions that provide the off-the-job learning. If individuals are not helped to develop their learning abilities in those circumstances uniquely dedicated to learning, a major opportunity has been missed (see Chapter 5). Further, the methods chosen to deliver the desired end product – learning – have not been decided through the kind of analyses recommended in courses on decision-making! Some tutors are wholly addicted to one method, demonstrating proof of the proposition that if you have a hammer you only see nails. Mumford (1997) reviewed 16 major methods, and a summary of his analysis of the contribution of each of these methods to *knowledge*, *skills* or *insight* is shown as Table 12. Huczynski (2001) provides a very large number of methods, many of which would be subsumed under one of Mumford's 16.

At the time of the research, the description 'e-learning' had not replaced 'technology-based training', but the essential content and therefore the judgements involved are the same. Mumford found that there was astonishingly little written in specific terms about individual methods which showed even what the method was intended to achieve, let alone any review of the effects of the method in relation to a proposed outcome – knowledge, skill, attitude or insight.

TYPE X

The problems inherent in formal MD, both off the job and on the job, and the uncertain learning processes that might be associated with Type 1 activities can result in a low concern for learning and a low concern for task. We refer to this as Type X MD in Figure 23. What we are suggesting here is that not all managers gain benefits from MD and that it is possible for both learning and task performance to be affected negatively. We have mentioned the deleterious effects of the power dimension in MD, and this can appear in a variety of ways. For example, it might occur where aspirations for MD are disappointed after the apparent identification of needs during appraisal. Or managers attend a programme of MD only to find that there is scant attention to what has been learned and little support for new ideas on their return to work. In both cases, managers may become unhappy or even despondent as a result of MD. They realise that there is no value in learning or even in trying to work more effectively – they have learned not to learn. Worse still, managers begin to lose confidence in the value of MD: 'There's simply no point to it.' Type X learning may be in tension with the objectives of Type 3 activities and prevent emergence in Type 2 approaches. This may go some way towards explaining the gaps between providers' and participants' perceptions which is evident in MD surveys (Mabey and Thomson, 2000).

SUMMARY

- A management development policy is a symbol of an organisation's intentions and contributes to a positive HR context to support MD.
- MD activities have to include both formal and informal learning processes.
- Informal (Type 1) learning is always present but often works inefficiently – yet can be converted into Type 2 learning.
- Formal (Type 3) management learning attempts to overcome the major disadvantages involved in relying on accidental – informal – learning but has been over-emphasised in MD.

- Formal, created, off-the-job opportunities must be converted into effective learning experiences.
- Courses have great potential as learning experiences if they focus on effectiveness and use methods appropriate to the needs specified.

DISCUSSION QUESTIONS

1. Why should an organisation develop a formally stated MD policy?
2. How convinced are you that the balance between informal and formal development ought to be changed?
3. What is the value of projects in MD?
4. Whose values are present in the design, delivery and experience of MD activities?
5. What issues are raised by Type X management learning, and how can its worst effects be ameliorated?
6. 'Orthodox' management education has failed.' Discuss.

FURTHER READING

BUTLER, J. (1994) 'Learning design for effective executive programmes', in A. Mumford (ed.) *Handbook of Management Development*, 4th edition. Aldershot, Gower.

BOYATZIS, R., COWEN, S. and KOLB, D. (1995) *Innovation in Professional Education*. San Francisco, Jossey Bass.

BARSOUX, J.-L. INSEAD (2000) *From Intuition To Institution*. Basingstoke, Macmillan Business.

GABARRO, J. (1987) *The Dynamics of Taking Charge*. Boston, Harvard Business School Press.

HERON, J. (1999) *The Complete Facilitator's Handbook*. London, Kogan Page.

WILLMOTT, H. (1997) 'Critical management learning', in J. Burgoyne and M. Reynolds (eds) *Management Learning*. London, Sage.

GROUP ACTIVITY

- Form a group of four.

You have been asked by the training director of a large chemical organisation to investigate the effectiveness of outdoor management development and then suggest how most value can be obtained from sending all managers on such a programme.

- Use the web to gather data.
- Go to http://www.aee.org/. This is home page of the Association for Experiential Education. It provides research findings on outdoor development and links to other pages.

  http://www.geocities.com/dr_adventure/activitypage.html is a page of activities for the outdoors.

  A resource for reviewing outdoor management development can be found at http://reviewing.co.uk/index.htm
- Prepare a presentation based on your findings.

REFERENCES

ANTONACOPOULOU, E. P. (1999) 'Training does not imply learning: the individual perspective', *International Journal of Training and Development*, Vol. 3, No. 1; pp.14–23.

BEHRMAN, J. N. and LEVIN, R. I. (1984) 'Are business schools doing their job?', *Harvard Business Review*, January; pp.140–147.

BURGOYNE, J. (1988) 'Management development for the individual and the organisation', *Personnel Management*, June; pp.40–44.

CEML (2002) *Managers and Leaders: Raising our game*. London, Council for Excellence in Management and Leadership.

CEML (2002a) *The Contribution of UK Business Schools to the Development of Managers and Leaders*. London, Council for Excellence in Management and Leadership.

COFFIELD, F. (ed.) (2002) *The Necessity of Informal Learning*. Bristol, The Policy Press.

CONSTABLE, J. (1987) *The Making of British Managers*. London, BIM/NEDO.

DAVIS, J. and EASTERBY-SMITH, M. (1984) 'Learning and developing from managerial work experiences', *Journal of Management Studies*, Vol. 21, No. 2; pp.168–183.

GABARRO, J. (1995) 'When a new manager takes charge', *Harvard Business Review*, May.

GARRICK, J. (1998) *Informal Learning in the Workplace*. London, Routledge.

GREY, C. (1996) 'Introduction', *Management Learning*, Vol. 27, No. 1; pp.7–20.

HOLMAN, D. (2000) 'Contemporary models of management education in the UK', *Management Learning*, Vol. 31, No. 2; pp.197–217.

HONEY, P. and MUMFORD, A. (1995) *The Opportunist Learner*, 2nd edition. Maidenhead, Honey Publications.

HUCZYNSKI, A. (2001) *Encyclopaedia of Development Methods*. Aldershot, Gower.

KOLB, D. (1984) *Experiential Learning*. Englewood Cliffs, Prentice Hall.

LAVE, J. and WENGER, E. (1991) *Situated Learning: Legitimate peripheral participation*. Cambridge, Cambridge University Press.

MABEY, C. (2003) 'Mapping management development practice', *Journal of Management Studies*, forthcoming.

MABEY, C. and THOMSON, A. (2000) 'Management development in the UK: a provider and participant perspective', *International Journal of Training and Development*, Vol. 4, No. 4; pp.272–286.

MARSICK, V. and WATKINS, K. (1990) *Informal and Incidental Learning in the Workplace*. London, Routledge.

MINTZBERG, H. (1989) *Mintzberg on Management*. New York, Free Press.

MUMFORD, A. (1987) 'Using reality in management development', *Management Education and Development*, Vol. 18, Part 3; pp.223–243.

MUMFORD, A. (1997) *How to Choose the Right Development Method*. Maidenhead, Honey Publications.

PFEFFER, J. and FONG, C. T. 'The end of business schools? Less success than meets the eye', *Academy of Management Learning and Education*, Vol. 1, No. 1; pp.78–96.

SADRI, G. and LEES, B. (2001) 'Developing corporate culture as a competitive advantage', *Journal of Management Development*, Vol. 20, No. 10; pp.853–859.

SALAMAN, G. and BUTLER, J. (1990) 'Why managers won't learn', *Management Education and Development*, Vol. 21, Part 3; pp.183–191.

SMITH, B. and DODDS, B. (1993) 'The power of projects in management development', *Industrial and Commercial Training*, Vol. 25, No. 10.

THOMSON, A., STOREY, J., MABEY, C., GRAY, C., FARMER, E. and THOMSON. R. A. (1997) *A Portrait of Management Development*. London, Institute of Management.

THOMSON, A., MABEY, C., STOREY, J., GRAY, C. and ILES, P. (2001) *Changing Patterns of Management Development*. Oxford, Blackwell.

ENDNOTES

1 Informal learning can result in tacit knowledge which is a key factor in knowledge productivity and organisational learning – see Chapter 12.

2 From Eliot's *The Dry Salvages* in *The Four Quartets*.

Combining work and learning

CHAPTER 7

Chapter outline

LEARNING OUTCOMES

After studying this chapter, you should be able to understand, explain, analyse and evaluate:

- **how managers can combine work and learning**
- **the range of learning opportunities available to managers**
- **barriers to learning and how to surmount them**
- **ways to learn more effectively from difficulties**
- **the use of learning reviews and techniques of reflection.**

INTRODUCTION

The contingent process of management practice suggests that MD could be most beneficial if it were grounded in the experience of managers and meaningful to their activities. Further, because managers face work of increasing complexity and ambiguity in the context of rapid change and turbulence, knowledge and skills acquired on a course, for example, may soon become redundant and out of date. Managers need to learn frequently and in the context of their practice. This is an experiential/practice approach to MD. It is also an approach that is receiving growing attention in the broader field of Workplace Learning.[1]

As we described in Chapter 6, Type 1 informal managerial learning processes occurring within managerial activities have:

- task performance as the explicit intention
- no clear development objective.

Our description of such processes is thus that they are both informal and accidental. Learning in such circumstances is real, direct and naturally occurs every day (Burgoyne and Hodgson, 1983), but it is usually unconscious and insufficient. In this chapter we look at the ways in which accidental processes can be converted into Type 2 MD, which we have described as 'integrated managerial opportunistic processes'. The characteristics of Type 2 learning include that it:

- occurs within managerial activities like Type 1
- has, however, the explicit intention of both task performance and development gain
- has clear development objectives
- is structured for development including the disciplines of planning beforehand and reviewing subsequently.

The consequence of Type 2 is that learning is real and direct as in Type 1 – but is now conscious and much more substantial. Some of the activities that may generate Type 2 learning are similar in task terms therefore to those identified as Type 1. Some of them will also look the same as activities we identified in the previous chapter as Type 3. The significant difference here is that Type 3 activities are constructed for development purposes, rather than using existing task-centred opportunities.

THE CASE FOR COMBINING WORK AND LEARNING

Experiential/practice approaches to learning are most suitable for learning from current situations, problems and relationships. It is most appropriate for relatively slower learning and development over time with repeated situations, and because learning is complementary to real task requirements, this approach is suitable for encouraging learning with managers who are otherwise suspicious about formal training or education. While providing opportunities to develop any or all of knowledge, skills or insight, it may have particular strengths in:

- managing problems, problem-solving and tackling dilemmas
- interpersonal relationships
- personal analysis
- absorbing behaviours and values of a particular organisational culture
- negative learning – ie learning how not to do something
- learning to follow existing policies, procedures, routines, values.

Type 2 MD

All professional and managerial work is replete with opportunities for learning. Everything we do, or that we see others doing, is potentially a learning opportunity. Learning through the job as a method is particularly attractive because it derives from imperatives around the job. This contrasts with many other forms of learning which are seen as being driven by a development agenda that may or may not have been set by the individual involved. Davies and Easterby-Smith (1984; p.180) give a less generalised view:

> **'Managers develop primarily through confrontations with novel situations and problems where their existing repertoire of behaviours is inadequate and where they have to develop new ways of dealing with these situations.'**
>
> **(See also McCall *et al*, 1988.)**

There may be personal or organisational barriers to learning effectively through the job.

- The apparent naturalness of learning through the job can lead to some impatience with efforts to make it a more disciplined process.
- While the work itself creates a huge variety of opportunities, the recognition of them or the motivational need to learn from them may be strong or weak in relation to any particular opportunity.
- It is a fundamental of management, of course, that managers learn from mistakes. Unfortunately, this learning may be inhibited by personal or organisational constraints on identifying what has gone wrong. Nor are the lessons drawn always accurately drawn because of a failure to analyse a problem, its context and the actions taken to overcome it with sufficient rigour.

Clearly, it is important for managers to recognise such difficulties and to confront them as part of a process of learning. A core principle of Type 2 MD is that managers can combine their work, including difficulties faced, with an understanding of their approach to learning so that new possibilities for action can be determined.

An important contribution by Kolb (1982) was to combine his experiential theory of learning with problem management. As he suggested (p.110), the primary skill

> **is the ability to manage the problem-solving process in such a way that important problems are identified and solutions of high quality are found and carried out with the full commitment of organisation members.**

What is particularly interesting about this view of management is that it gives attention to different aspects of a task. Managers face problems of varying degrees of difficulty[2] but depending on how the task is understood, managers need to consider:

- finding and defining problems
- analysing and understanding the causes
- deciding on appropriate solutions
- working with others to plan and implement actions
- using the results to decide the next steps.

One important aspect of this view is that managers may focus on solving problems at the expense of finding the right problems. Schön (1983) also focused on the importance of 'problem-setting' which he saw (p.40) as

> **a process in which, interactively (along with everyone who must solve it), we name the things to which we will attend and frame the context in which we will attend to them.**

Kolb claimed that the skills for problem management can be shown in relation to the phases of his learning cycle, as shown in Figure 25.

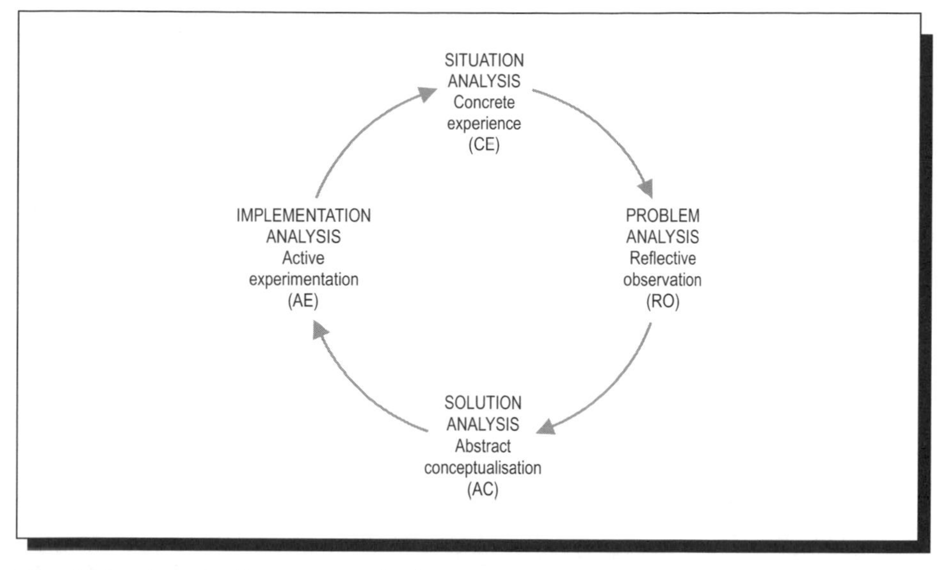

Figure 25 *Learning and problem management cycles*
Source: adapted from Kolb (1982)

Kolb explained that cycles provide managers with a normative process, and that where there was ineffectiveness in managing problems, it could be due to constraints in the organisation context or skill limitations and particular habits. For example, a low preference towards the concrete experience stage of the cycle could also mean a failure to give full attention to problem-setting. Alternatively, a stronger orientation towards abstract conceptualisation could lead to a focus on solutions rather than problem-setting and problem analysis. As some managers might say, 'Bring me your solutions, not your problems.'

In a similar vein, Mumford (1997) also sees a connection between dealing with the reality of management tasks and the learning cycle. So management is learning, and learning is a

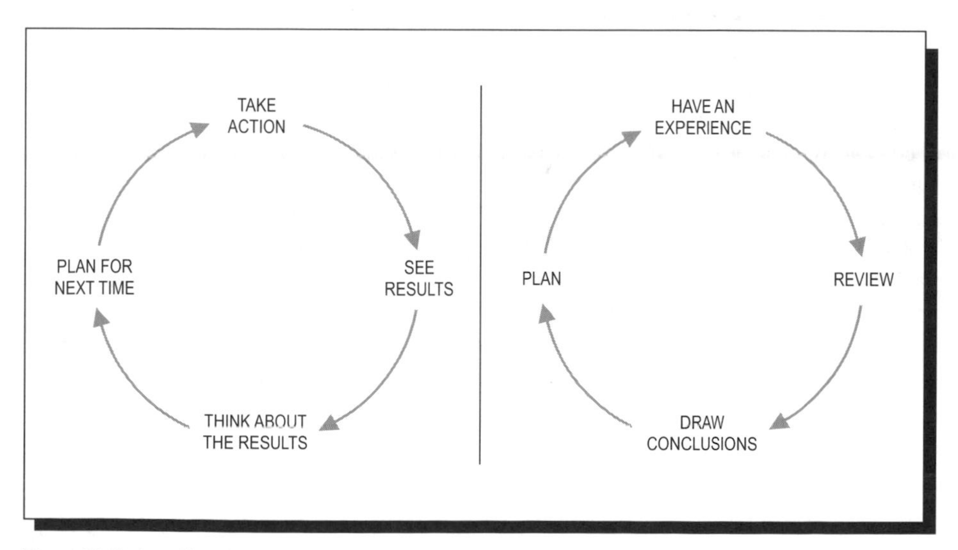

Figure 26 *Task and learning cycles*
Source: adapted from Mumford (1997)

management process, linked conceptually and practically through the learning cycle cast as a task cycle, shown in Figure 26.

The combination of the two cycles can encourage managers to see that when asked to work through a task, they can also relate it to how they learn and their preferences for learning. Managers can give consciousness to both learning and working on a task. This becomes especially meaningful when facing problems. The following is based on a manager who used the learning and task cycles to work with problems over a three-week period:

> **I went through the learning cycle many times, each time arriving back at another problem having solved one. I was very aware that as I progressed over the three weeks, one does not go around the cycle before another problem appears. More problems can arise when reflecting and conceptualising. I learnt that provided I completed the cycle with each problem, it was possible to deal with more than one problem at once. One problem or learning opportunity cannot be kept separate from others, as Mintzberg suggested when he talked about the variety of tasks completed by a managers in a day. I was constantly dealing with a variety of problems and using different skills and learning styles to deal with them.**

REFLECT – CONCLUDE – PLAN 1

- What is your reaction to the example above?
- How can you learn better from your everyday tasks?
- What help will you need to do this?

The combination of approaches to learning and tasks faced, especially current problems, can be a very powerful way to help managers begin and continue a process of MD. Many managers may not see the value of academic and theoretical views of their work, but they do appreciate help with their difficulties. Gold and Holman (2001) provide an example where learning was still prominent, although they preferred not to use a model of learning styles. Instead, they posed simple questions relating to a manager's preferences in relation to a work problem. This helped managers explore the meanings that they held about the situation and particular value-orientations held. Through talk and challenge, managers could consider new possibilities for action in work, through which they could continue this process. As we will explain below, a vital aspect of this or any other MD process that combines work and learning is the importance given to reflection as a way of both reviewing actions taken and generating new ideas.

OPPORTUNITIES FOR LEARNING

We use the term 'the opportunist learner' (Honey and Mumford, 1995) to describe the individual who recognises and uses opportunities to learn from the wide variety of managerial and professional activities in which that individual is engaged. In a way this is a subset of

LEARNING OPPORTUNITIES FOR MANAGERS

Situations within the organisation
meetings
tasks – familiar
– unfamiliar
task force
customer visit
visit to plant/office
managing change
social occasions
foreign travel
acquisitions and mergers
closing something down

Situations outside the organisation
voluntary work
domestic life
industry committee
professional meetings
sports club
processes
coaching
counselling
listening
modelling
problem-solving
observing
questioning
reading
negotiating
mentoring
public speaking
reviewing/auditing
clarifying responsibilities

Walking the floor
virtual visits
visioning
strategic planning
problem diagnosis
decision-making
selling

People
senior managers
mentor
staff
network contacts
peers
consultants
family and friends

another description – if we learn from every kind of experience including formal, structured, off-the-job processes as well, we become entitled to see ourselves as 'effective learners'. Although 'opportunistic' may initially carry a less than pleasant meaning, in the context of discussions about learning it quickly loses any such unfortunate connotation. The *Learning opportunities for managers* checklist box above shows some of the opportunities.

In Chapter 6 we looked at some of the ways of describing large changes in activities or jobs deliberately engaged with a development objective. They are designed and delivered as Type 3 experiences, and we contrasted their existence also as Type 1 learning activities, where no real attention or thought is given to them as learning experiences. People essentially are thus just dumped into the new job or task with no provision for defining the learning opportunities involved in advance, or reviewing them subsequently. They can also exist under a Type 2 heading, providing significant opportunities for a large-scale combination of work and learning. The essential reason for a change in role or major task focus is primarily driven by task requirements, but here the learning opportunities involved are recognised and used. Research by McCall *et al* (1988) in the United States established five key events as precipitating learning at work. They were:

- participation in projects or task forces
  - handling ignorance (perhaps including their own) and getting co-operation without line authority

- switching job from line to staff
  - learning the difference between hands-on action-oriented line roles and a more reflective, persuasive style necessary in staff jobs
- starting from scratch – eg a new plant or function
  - learning what is important and how to organise for it; learning how to survive and generating confidence from doing so
- turning jobs around
  - being both tough and persuasive; being instrumental in carrying things through
- taking a leap in a job to something broader or very different
  - examples of this were moves within the same function or area, but could also involve moves to a new function or area.

While the managers involved in the research presented these experiences as crucial in their own learning, their descriptions were clearly of a Type 1 experience in most cases. They were not set up as development experiences in any serious way, nor were they reviewed afterwards as learning experiences.

Mumford and his colleagues came to similar conclusions (Mumford, 1988). Senior people described the same kind of experiences but also had not identified beforehand or reviewed subsequently the experiences as learning experiences. Some of those interviewed remarked on the extent to which the questions they were asked for research purposes were in many ways those which should have been asked of them at or immediately after the time at which they had the experience. Some, indeed, made an action note about what they should now do in relation to their own future experiences, and in relation to the people for whom they were responsible. The case for converting these large-scale experiences from Type 1 learning into Type 2 is that an additional benefit is drawn from something which is occurring anyway – a bonus with no substantial cost.

Consider the following example of informal, accidental learning (Type 1):

> **‘I was a shift manager on a new production line in our plant. The line involved quite a bit of new technology and we had a number of problems with it. My immediate manager was a very ingenious guy with an engineering background. Every problem that came up he seemed to have an answer for, but the problems kept coming up. His boss, the production director, called all three shift managers and our manager to his office. He had two flipcharts. One he marked ‘Problems’; the other he divided into two columns, ‘Causes apparent’ and ‘Causes deeper?’ After 40 minutes with him we did not come out with a single answer, whereas five minutes with our manager always produced an answer. The difference was that we came out with the questions we needed to pursue in order to produce really effective answers. I learnt two things – one was about looking deeper into problems, and the other was about how to make the best use of the intelligence of five people working together.’**

Examples like this are just the tip of a very large iceberg. The iceberg analogy shows how much there is under the surface, not seen but present and yet to be discovered. These Type 1 experiences represent what is easily visible, though not always seen in a timely way in order to avoid accidents – ie failure! What is under the part of the iceberg that is visible is in a sense the Type 2 possibility – seeing the whole of what exists rather than only part of it. Converting Type 1 to Type 2 learning experiences means taking what is essentially the same activity or experience and converting it into a double-value learning experience by making the learning process itself a planned, structured and implemented part of the activity. The informal and accidental learning involved in the case mentioned above could have been enhanced by either seeing in advance what kind of learning possibilities were contained within the experience (prospective learning) or looking at the experiences afterwards (retrospective learning). Effective MD arises from using either or both of the retrospective and prospective ways of learning more frequently and more effectively. A crucial part of effective learning from projects which so often provide Type 1 experiences, for example, is to construct a structure in setting up and reviewing the projects which emphasises questions about what has been learned during and at the end of them. In addition, of course, there has to be a supportive learning environment around those attempting to learn from it.

The support for learning required

Converting Type 1 and Type 3 learning opportunities into Type 2 MD is seldom an easy process and an environment which encourages careful attention to learning is a crucial requirement. There are usually a significant number of people who can help individuals with their development (see Chapter 9). A fundamental feature of support necessary for Type 2 learning is, as we have emphasised throughout, that individuals should have been encouraged through some structured learning-to-learn process to understand *how* they learn. The concepts we advanced above relating, for example, to the close association between the problem management/task cycle and the learning cycle is particularly relevant for work-centred learning.

However, even without support individuals can often create their own learning, taking responsibility to continue learning at work. The ideas involved in self-development (see below) certainly help with this, and whatever the formal support given to them as learners by their organisations, individuals can take their own initiatives in creating Type 2 Learning. If they can do so, we can also introduce here the more sophisticated version of the Learning Cycle – the Learning Spiral (see Figure 27).

On courses, the visual image of the learning cycle as a single completed event in relation to some particular session or for a course as a whole is understandable. In the work context, Type 2 learning is more likely to involve the learning spiral, which emphasises that as you go through continuous pieces of work – for example a project – the learning you have secured at one stage is developed and employed and further reviewed at a later stage. One of the important aspects of this, which we will pick up again in Chapter 9 on helpers, is that those involved in helping other individuals to learn not only help to structure the experience but to assist learners in dealing perhaps with those aspects of learning with which those individuals are least comfortable – quite often, for example, by encouraging more reflection.

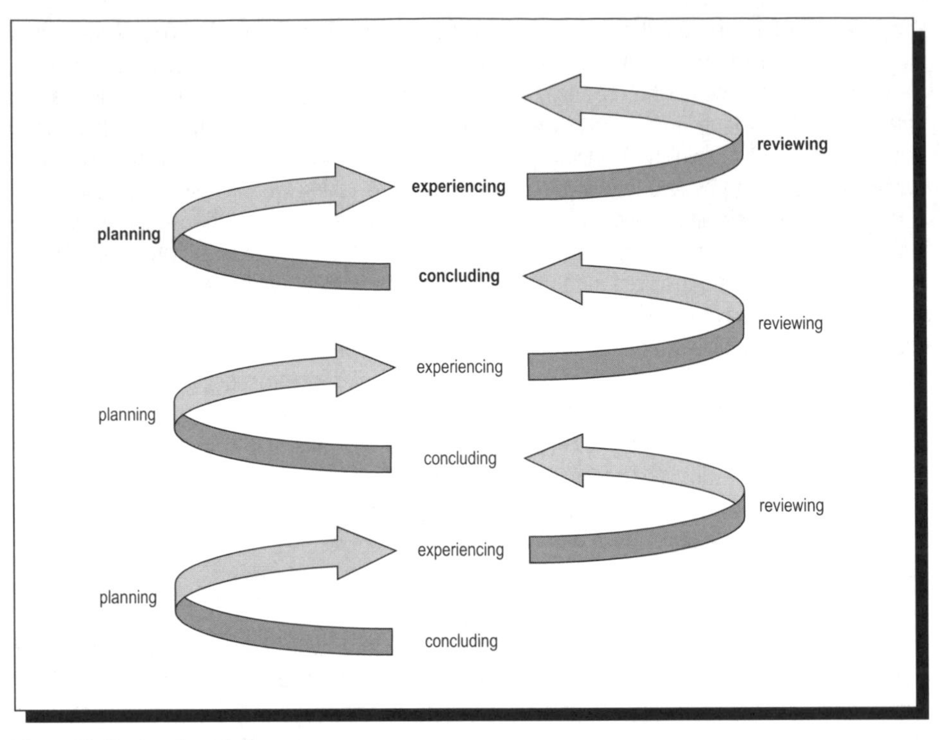

Figure 27 *The learning spiral*

REFLECT – CONCLUDE – PLAN 2

- Look back over your career and identify a learning experience you would categorise as Type 1.
- What do you think you learned from that experience at the time?
- Do you think you could have learned more?
- How might you convert the Type 1 experience into a Type 2 experience?
- What steps might you take to turn single event learning into a learning spiral?

Making learning clear

The defining feature that makes any experience Type 2 rather than Type 1 is obviously that it may be envisaged beforehand as a learning opportunity, and is certainly reviewed during and after the experience as learning. Instead of saying 'Of course people learn from experience,' we say 'People will learn more effectively from experience if that learning is consciously planned and appraised.' It has often been the case that individuals have told us that they did not realise fully at the time what they learned – and that it is only in subsequent discussion that more learning has been identified and perhaps therefore used. What managers and professionals do is an implicit statement about what they have learned (or not learned!).

Nonaka and Takeuchi (1995) tackle implicit or tacit learning in relation to knowledge. Tacit learning is 'personal knowledge embedded in personal belief, perspective, and the value system'. Explicit learning can be articulated in formal language, including grammatical statements, mathematical expressions, specifications, manuals, and so forth, and can be transmitted across individuals formally and easily. We say more about this in Chapter 12. Here, we are emphasising the importance of a learning dynamic which encourages the conversion of tacit into explicit. We do so in relation not just to knowledge, however, but to our other two elements of learning – skills and insights.

An important aspect of turning tacit into implicit is that this is not simply a solo operation but one in which the conversion is aided by and/or directed to sharing with others. It is of course much easier to talk about the desirability of sharing information with others than it is to achieve it – just as the proposition that feedback is important as a crucial aspect of individual improvement is similarly difficult for many of us in implementation. Dixon (1998) helpfully reviews many of the crucial issues around sharing, presenting both her own ideas and their association with those of others such as Argyris (1982, 1991; defensive routines) and Mezirow (1990; critical reflection). In her view, dialogue means the co-creation of meaning: 'Each individual has internalised the perspectives of others and thus is enriched by a sense of whole.' While sceptical about the extent to which such exchanges are transferred from courses to real work, she identifies for example Action Learning as one of the ways in which sharing is designed and encouraged.

BARRIERS TO LEARNING

The various models of how managers learn can represent normative or ideal views of how managers could learn rather than how they actually learn. For various reasons, managers may be prevented or blocked from learning. Several of the possible barriers come from what is often referred to as 'the learning climate'. Temporal (1978; p.95), for example, referred to the learning climate as a 'collection of variables – physical and psycho-social – subjectively perceived by managers'. The important feature of such variables is that they can prevent managers from learning. Physical barriers to learning occur in the work that a manager is required to do. Paradoxically, a major barrier to creating more Type 2 learning is precisely the strength of learning from real work activities. The task is the priority – and often overwhelms the delivery of disciplines particularly of allocating time to the consideration of the learning that could be or has been achieved. An associated element is the fact that managers and professionals see themselves in those work roles, and often do not like being described orally in associated literature as 'learners'.[3] Other barriers come from the overall structure of the organisation and the way that tasks are allocated. Managers will also feel limited where the pace of activity and time-scales for planning and delivery are intensified. Of course, the actual physical setting of work may prevent deliberate learning.

A second set of variables form psycho-social barriers to learning. These arise from a prevailing culture in which the particular relationships that managers are a part of prevent learning or only support a particular kind of learning. Managers may experience negative attitudes and the exertion of influence which prevents new ideas being tested – 'You can't do that here!' Both the environment for learning and specific individual managers may be unsupportive (Honey and Mumford, 1994).

WEB LINK

Try the Campaign For Learning's quiz at
http://www.campaign-for-learning.org.uk/law_survey/law_survey.asp

Variables that form the learning climate will influence and interact with a manager's own barriers to learning. Such internal barriers have been classified by Temporal (1978) as:

- *perceptual* – Managers cannot see problems or recognise what is happening in a situation, and have a limited view of learning possibilities.
- *cultural* – Managers cut themselves off possible MD activities by a set of norms and values which have been internalised, regarding what is right/wrong, possible/not possible, etc.
- *emotional-motivational* – Managers feel insecure and become reluctant to try new behaviours. They may avoid MD situations where they feel threatened.
- *expressive* – Managers have poor listening, speaking or presentation skills. They may avoid participating in group activities.

Unhelpful emotions may particularly inhibit learning. While emotion can be a positive factor that leads to people pursuing something worthwhile and feeling good about the pursuit, undoubtedly for some managers in some situations emotion massively inhibits learning. Although learning can be stimulated by challenges and difficulties, those same situational aspects may inhibit learning where they promote anxiety. Emotion is specific to the moment, and can therefore be a significant inhibition on learning from precisely those specific and of-the-moment work activities which in principle provide learning. Emotion can be created by an individual's general anxiety level, fear about what he or she does not know and the implications of not knowing, and past negative experiences of learning. Snell (1988) described both some emotional aspects and, still more helpfully, how to try to reduce the pain and/or discomfort involved. More recently, Vince (2002) found that even in events designed to promote learning it is possible for emotion to provide a block and become embedded within political processes that affect the learning climate. Fineman (1997) argues that working life is inevitably emotional, and that learning to be a manager requires the acquisition of an emotional literacy. Managers as learners also have emotions.

What becomes apparent when we consider both the variables of the learning climate and these internal barriers, is that any desired form of MD must contain within it the possibility of overcoming barriers to learning. Failure to do so threatens the effectiveness of MD.

Learning from difficulty

Barriers to learning may become very evident when managers have to work with difficult issues or where they are likely to make mistakes. Managers face problems of varying degrees of difficulty ranging from those which are fairly structured and easily solved to problems of equivocality (Weick, 1995) where there are different views about what is happening in a situation such that no single solution is likely to be successful. Managers face many problems of equivocality, such as how to manage employees with different goals and expectations, building teams with different cultural backgrounds, and planning for changes that might include making acquisitions, the relocation of production facilities, re-engineering work design, etc. One consequence of attempting to treat problems of equivocality or dilemmas as if they were structured problems is that managers will make mistakes.[4]

The expression commonly used by managers about 'learning the hard way' is most often a description of the fact that they believe themselves to have learned from mistakes, rather than a view that the actual process of learning is hard. Given that mistakes are an inevitable feature of the complex changing managerial world, it is certainly the case that there are plenty of mistakes which provide opportunities to learn. It is a weakness of research in management development that so little has been written about what and how individuals learn from difficulty. Morphey and Smith (1994) concluded that the opportunities for learning from mistakes had not been identified and were not supported by discussions between colleagues, and that no discipline or procedure for undertaking learning had been set up. However, we would suggest that difficulties represent superb opportunities to engage in Type 2 MD, with a special emphasis on reflection and learning to learn.

WEB LINK

Karl Weick is a prominent and influential writer on organisations. His answer for managers facing difficulties: 'Complicate yourself.' Read more at
http://www.wired.com/wired/archive/4.04/weick_pr.html

EFFECTIVE LEARNING FROM REFLECTION

From a development perspective the issue is whether and how people are encouraged to learn from difficulties and mistakes. This is partly an issue about the environment in which they work – the extent to which the attitude towards taking risks is totally negative and punitive, as compared with a cultural context in which trying new things and making mistakes, while clearly not encouraged, is seen as something from which to learn. Learning from difficulty is particularly important because most learning from difficulty occurs at times of significant job change. Managers are much more prepared to think seriously about problems, difficulties, failures than about success.

REFLECT – CONCLUDE – PLAN 3

- Do you agree that effective learning from mistakes and difficulty is an important issue in MD?
- Look at your own experiences, and those of other people. What do you think have been the constraints in learning from these events?
- How do you think this learning can be improved through action in your organisation taken by:
  - yourself?
  - others?
- What must be done to bring about that action?

If difficulties and mistakes are to provide opportunities for effective learning, a crucial contribution must be made through structured reflection on experience – and an important issue is the extent to which reviews are conducted to encourage critical reflection as described by Mezirow (1990), or by Argyris in encouraging double-loop learning and the avoidance of defensive routines (1982, 1991). As we saw above, managers have internal barriers, and such barriers – which affect learning preferences and approaches to the management of problems – are underpinned by a manager's meaning perspective combined with a range of organisational and job factors. Reflection, therefore, provides an opportunity for surfacing attitudes and meaning perspectives to reveal assumptions. The potential here is to test the validity of assumptions, gaining insight and understanding about their actions and the nature of the problems and difficulties faced. Managers can become aware of limitations and open to new and alternative perspectives.

A learning review provides for the construction or reconstruction of meaning from an experience. It achieves this through a process of recording, recall and reasoning. It is a process of reflection: 'the process of stepping back from an experience to ponder carefully and persistently its meaning to the self through the development of inferences' (Daudelin, 1996; p.38). It is a method of facilitating MD that is:

- conscious
- structured
- planned.

There a variety of ways of reflecting on experience such as sitting and thinking about experiencing, going for a jog or just talking with others.[5] However, we feel that a more deliberate approach is required and that a review should be written. We therefore recommend two methods, both quite similar, which we feel are in a real sense super-methods – ie methods to be used on top of all other MD methods. They provide a way of ensuring that any method has been squeezed for all the learning potential it contains.

Learning logs

The learning log is a written record designed to facilitate the learning review. It may focus particularly on recording experiences, but can become a total review completing the stages of the learning cycle:

- to record or 'capture' experience
- to encourage managers to think about what has been recorded
- to encourage managers to decide what the experience has meant to them
- to enable managers to consider how to move from understanding to action.

Thus, as with many diaries, the prime intention may be simply to record, but from a learning point of view this is an unhelpfully restricted purpose. Many managers will be more persuaded to keep a learning log if it is directed at least partly at identifying reasons for what has been recorded, and possibilities for further action. The learning log may exist in handwritten, PC or laptop form. It can also be dictated onto tape or disk and can then be either transcribed or not, according to the preference of the manager.

Story-telling

Gold *et al* (2002) suggest that managers can become critical reflectors by recording their experiences in the form of stories. Stories make use of all managers' abilities to think in narrative terms, which according to writers such as Polkinghorne (1997) is the most important way experience is made meaningful. By writing out stories of important events, including difficult situations or mistakes, managers can re-present the complexity of their work, including the views and actions of different characters, connected by a plot into a whole. Stories are a primary means by which managers can make sense of reality; they can also be a resource for talking over with others. An important aspect of any story, told from a personal point of view, is the beliefs and values presented. For managers to understand these for further critique, Gold *et al* used argument analysis based on the work of Toulmin (1958). After writing a story of an experience, particular claims can thus be identified and evidence sought to support the claims.

WEB LINKS

You can find out more about the growing interest in story-telling on the Internet. Try the Society for Story-telling at
http://www.sfs.org.uk
David Boje's fascinating study of story-telling in organisations can be found at his own website http://web.nmsu.edu/-dboje
The following site gives details of the Toulmin method of analysing arguments – http://writing.colostate.edu/references/reading/toulmin/index.cfm

Learning logs and story-telling can both be used further to help managers understand key patterns and themes of behaviour that occur over time so that areas for improvement can be identified along with new opportunities for MD. One such process is to chart a number of logs or stories on a single side of A3 paper, as shown in Figure 28.

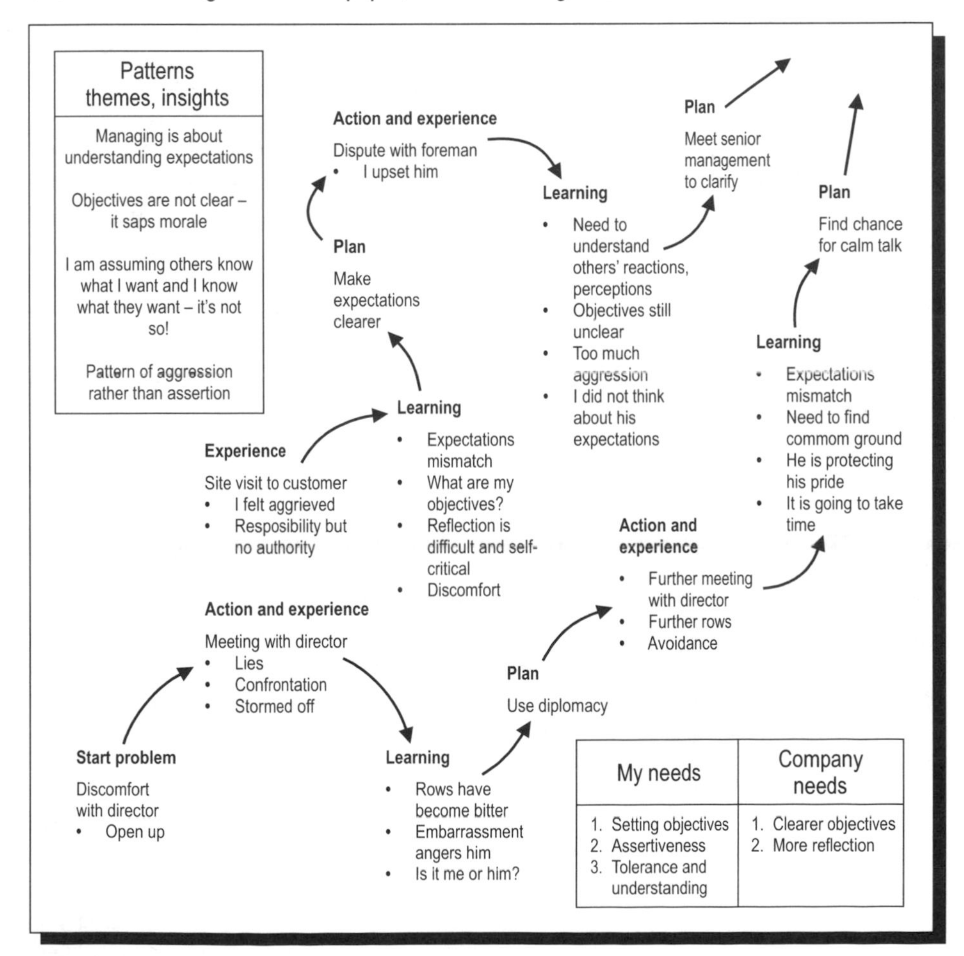

Figure 28 *A learning chart*

This particular chart is based on stages of the learning cycle, showing how events are linked together through a number of learning logs with patterns, themes and insights emerging as further reflection occurs by completing the chart. These appear in the top left corner of the chart. This can also include any assumptions made which can be checked for validity. The bottom right corner shows possible development needs. The richness of the process is based on the number of logs (or stories[6]) made which allows more themes to emerge. What is also important is that individual managers maintain control over the whole process; it can thereby add to a manager's self-development.

SELF-DEVELOPMENT

Self-development for managers emerged during the 1970s and 1980s, partly as a response to problems related to management training courses in which providers would determine what managers learned. During such times, the vicious learning sequence that we established in Chapter 5 (Figure 16) was especially in evidence. Megginson and Pedler (1992; p.3) see self-development as a process in which 'learners take the primary responsibility for choosing what, when and how to learn'. They also suggest that this implies a certain freedom in choosing what *not* to learn, although this may raise certain tensions with others in the organisation. Self-development has also been seen as part of wider view of how adults should determine their own needs for learning and taking command of the direction of that learning (Brookfield, 1995). In recent years, such ideas have become more prominent as more managers and professionals are pushed to engage in Continuous Professional Development and take more responsibility for career development (see Chapter 11).

There are many techniques and resources for self-development (Pedler *et al*, 1999), but once again there is the issue of whether managers are willing and able to take responsibility. Some of the processes that we have covered in this chapter – such as relating learning to current problems and tasks, reflecting on experiences, surfacing assumptions and revealing patterns of behaviour – can be used to help managers become aware of what they want to learn and how. Managers can also come to a similar understanding by attending a development centre and using the feedback from other assessment processes where information is used to help managers determine MD needs. Where the organisation agrees to support self-development, managers may agree a 'learning contract' (similar to a personal development plan), setting out the aims and objectives for learning, which activities will be undertaken, and what resources are needed.

Review and reflection play a crucial role in self-development not simply to analyse experiences and record learning but also to explore the learning process itself. This provides a link to many ideas relating to development, although we prefer to differentiate between qualities of learning and the ability to learn to learn. For example, there is interest in helping managers to learn to think in more complex ways (cognitive complexity – see Streufert and Swezey, 1986). This would enable managers to view problems from different perspectives so that different ideas can be considered. Managers are also able to tolerate ambiguity and less likely to make mistakes in their behaviour. To learn such skills managers must engage in activities that stretch them beyond their current capabilities (Bartunek and Louis, 1989). Stretching tasks can be set by others, or managers can find new opportunities, taking a risk and allowing experimentation with new actions. The more difficult the situation faced, the more a manager may need to explore the underlying patterns of belief which Schön and Rein (1994) refer to as a 'frame', or the way a manager perceives reality.[7] Challenging and changing such perceptions (reframing) cannot be imposed on a manager, although managers can be shocked into new views of their situations and their abilities. However, the prime method for reframing comes where a manager, through critical reflection, finds new meanings and understanding for action.

WEB LINKS

Other approaches for helping managers learn to learn include:
Personal Construct Psychology and the Repertory Grid at
http://www.brint.com/PCT.htm and http://www.repgrid.com/pcp
Neuro-linguistic programming (NLP) at
http://www.nlpinfo.com and http://www.anlp.org
Myers-Briggs indicators at
http://members.cts.com/king/saoirseTarotAndMBTI.html and
http://www.teamtechnology.co.uk/myers-briggs-type-indicator-home.html
You might also check the Centre for Self-Managed Learning at
http://www.selfmanagedlearning.org

LEARNING IN GROUPS

Self-development was never meant to be a solo process of learning. Managers always undertake MD in relation to some context, and this can made more deliberate by making groups the unit of development. Given the significance attached to them as main features of most off-the-job training, it is again significant that very little research has been done on what happens to help or hinder learning within groups at work. We deliberately use the word *groups* rather than *teams* because there are groups which are not teams. The situation may be that of direct colleagues working together closely for a specific purpose, who may actually be described as a management team. Or they may be a collection of individuals brought together to exchange information with no accountability or specific job purpose. Mumford (1997) says that group learning is achieved through 'the three-legged stool' – task, process and learning:

- knowledge, skills, insight gained by and through the task – As an example, a product launch might provide knowledge about customers, skills in carrying out analysis, and insights into how a particular sales message was delivered.
- knowledge, skills and insight gained about the process through which the task was tackled – The group carrying out a task might learn about how different members interacted with each other, how the meetings were managed, how successfully different contributions were taken in and used.
- knowledge, skill and insight about learning gained by participants understanding how they have learned from the task and the process – The group might set up regular and structured processes through which it assessed not only what had been learned from task and process, but how it was going about learning – eg through explicitly following the learning cycle.

There are different ways of looking at the kind of learning achieved. One differentiation is that learning is:

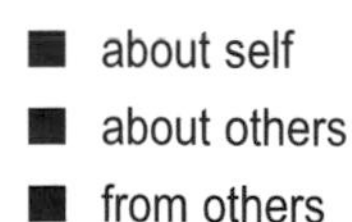

- about self
- about others
- from others

- about the processes of this particular group
- about group processes in general.

Knowledge, skills and insights may be generated in any of these categories.

Another form of analysis would be concerned with different levels of learning. In one form a group might be concerned to generate knowledge of a relatively objective type such as 'What are the different approaches to marketing used by the participants in this group?' In contrast, the group might be concerned with much more risky sharing of knowledge such as 'You never seem to be really interested in anyone else's point of view.' The question of the level at which knowledge is sought, skills are intended to be developed, or insights pursued is crucial. It may be that interpersonal issues are considered not open for discussion. As Argyris (1982) has argued on individual group and organisational levels, the fact that some issues are not discussed can itself be unmentionable.

REVIEW – CONCLUDE – PLAN 4

- In what ways have experiences in groups helped or hindered your learning?
- What lesson do you draw from those experiences?
- What action could you take to improve learning in groups in which you are involved?

WEB LINKS

If you are more interested in team roles and development, try
http://www.belbin.com
or
http://www.tms.com.au

Action Learning

Projects in general often provide examples of Type 1 learning, but can be converted into Type 2 learning through the disciplines already identified in this chapter. The most effective learning through projects is Action Learning (AL). It may be initiated through Type 3 process, but is Type 2 'task'-based rather than based on 'MD' as the stimulus. The characteristics of AL were never set out in a single statement by its progenitor, Reg Revans. Indeed, he once wrote that 'The day Action Learning becomes explicable in words alone will be the day to abandon the practice of it' (Revans, 1982; p.626). However, a useful definition is provided by Pedler (1996; p.9):

> **Action Learning is a method of problem-solving and learning in groups to bring about change for individuals, teams and organisations. It works to build the relationships which help any organisation improve existing operations and learn and innovate for the future.**

Table 13 *Action Learning contrasted with traditional management education*

	Traditional management education	**Action learning**
World view	There is some notion of correct management practice established through research that defines the curriculum.	The curriculum is defined by the manager or organisation.
	Managers should learn theories and models derived from research.	Managers should join a 'set' tutored by a facilitator, in which each member is in a similar position, where they learn to solve problems, learn management competencies and develop self.
	Self-development is unimportant.	Self-development is very important.
	The world is something to learn about.	The world is somewhere to act and to change.
Practical objective	Management development is 'to' the manager.	Management development is 'by' the manager.
	Experts are seen as the highest form of knowledge.	Experts are viewed with caution.
	Experts decide what should be learned, when, and how much.	The manager takes responsibility for his/her own development in deciding what to learn, including how and when to stop, and to value what has been learned.
	Management education requires distillation of approved research and ideas, which people then relate to how they might use them to either do things differently or do different things.	Delivers management education via self-development in tackling problems with set support to manage change and build management competencies.
	Models, concepts, ideas are provided to offer tools for thinking and action.	Models, concepts, ideas are developed in response to problems.
	Learning is individualist.	Learning is social – 'comrades in adversity'.
Manifestation	Theoretically-oriented research.	Practically-oriented research.
	It is held that a properly tested theory is able to offer reliable knowledge, which allows situations to be predicted, and ideally brought about. Requires prior knowledge of past models both to test and use as foundations for new theories.	Based on the assumption that research into organisational systems and, paradoxically, that one of the best ways of understanding issues relating to organisations, people and self as manager is an attempt to change them.

Source: McLaughlin and Thorpe (1993)

McLaughlin and Thorpe (1993) argue that AL can be viewed as a philosophy and set of beliefs representing a different 'world view' (p.20) by which managers must take responsibility for their own development (as in self-development). They contrast AL with traditional management education as shown in Table 13.

A key assumption is that managers can overcome problems that are important to them by working in a group or 'set' as 'comrades in adversity' (Revans, 1982; p.636) who can help each other by asking questions, discussion, exposure to critical comment and allowing time for reflection and planning action. Managers work on real projects which ensures that action and learning occur in a work context, and through participation in a set and reflection they gain an understanding of power and politics in organisation. The process is not without risk, and for Revans it was vital that managers understood change in themselves, expressed as the 'principle of insufficient mandate' (p.545):

> **Managers unable to command change in themselves cannot constructively change the conditions in which they command others.**

Although the explicit function of Action Learning is to pursue the twin goals of real work and learning from real work, many Action Learning authors give surprisingly little attention to *how* learning is achieved (as distinct from the 'what' which is secured through task completion). Mumford (1997) has attempted to fill this gap. He has also argued strongly that the task which requires to be undertaken is best one in which a participant or group of participants is actually involved in implementation, rather than acting as a group of consultants to others. This view is not accepted by all other authors. Of course, projects of a consultancy nature – for example, those often set up as part of a traditional business school programme – may lead to good development. But they are not the full version of Action Learning.

WEB LINKS

Go to http://www.ifal.org.uk/ifalhomesi5.html
for the home page of the International Foundation for Action Learning.
Information about the Revans Collection at Salford University can be found at
http://www.isd.salford.ac.uk/specollect/revans.php
For papers on Action Learning and Action Research, try
http://www.scu.edu.au/schools/gcm/ar/arp/actlearn.html

SUMMARY

- It is the work, the job, the task and its problems that are the prime features for MD, in contrast to most other approaches where the central feature of the method is the learning content.
- While the work itself creates such a variety of opportunities, the motivation or need to learn may be strong or weak in relation to any particular opportunity.
- Although an opportunity to learn is available, there may be personal or organisational barriers to learning effectively through the job.
- Learning from difficulties or mistakes provides strong opportunities for development through reflection and learning to learn.

- The apparent naturalness of learning through the job can lead to some impatience with efforts to make it a more disciplined process.
- Structured planning makes it possible to identify learning opportunities – prospective learning must be supported by retrospective learning via learning reviews and reflective techniques such as learning logs and stories.
- Self-development allows managers freedom to choose what and how they learn.
- Action Learning projects allow managers to work in sets on issues of importance to them.

DISCUSSION QUESTIONS

1. What are the key organisational and personal factors that can ensure the effective combination of work and learning for managers?
2. What kind of support in learning and developing at work do managers need?
3. How can organisational barriers to learning be overcome?
4. 'Both self-development and Action Learning are too focused on individual managers.' Discuss.
5. Do managers need to engage in double-loop learning? What are the requirements?
6. Do managers need to be 'shocked' into learning to learn? What are the dangers and the prospects?

FURTHER READING

BOUD, D. and GARRICK, J. (eds) (1999) *Understanding Learning at Work*. London, Routledge.

DECHANT, K. (1994) 'Making the most of job assignments', *Journal of Management Education*, Vol. 18, No. 2; pp.188–211.

MEGGINSON, D. (1996) 'Planned and emergent learning', *Management Learning*, Vol. 27, No. 4; pp.411–428.

LEE, M. (2003) *HRD in a Complex World*. London, Routledge.

MUMFORD, A. (1997) *Action Learning at Work*. Aldershot, Gower.

GABRIEL, Y. (2000) *Storytelling in Organizations*. Oxford, Oxford University Press.

GROUP ACTIVITY

A manager's place of work and real issues are increasingly been seen as a source of learning – what we have referred to in this chapter as Type 2 MD. Apart from Action Learning, other approaches include:

work-based learning (WBL)
problem-based learning (PBL)
Action Research (AR)

- Form a group of three.
- Use the Internet and other sources to find more information on each of these approaches to management learning. Pay particular attention to:
  - the main features of each approach and how they are incorporated into programmes of learning
  - examples of practice
  - evidence of the effectiveness or otherwise on management learning.
- Meet to integrate your findings and prepare to report back.

REFERENCES

ARGYRIS, C. (1982) *Reasoning, Learning and Action.* San Francisco, Jossey-Bass.

ARGYRIS, C. (1991) 'Teaching smart people how to learn', *Harvard Business Review*, May/June; pp.99–109.

BARTUNEK, J. M. and LOUIS, M. R. (1989) 'The design of work environments to stretch managers' capacities for complex thinking', *Human Resource Planning*, Vol. 11, No. 1; pp.13–22.

BROOKFIELD, S. (1995) 'Adult learning: an overview', in A. Tuijnman (ed.) *International Encyclopedia of Education and Training.* Oxford, Pergamon Press.

BURGOYNE, J. and HODGSON, V. (1983) 'Natural learning and managerial action: a phenomenological study in the field setting', *Journal of Management Studies*, Vol. 20, No. 3; pp.387–399.

DAUDELIN, M. (1996) 'Learning from experience through reflections', *Organizational Dynamics*, Winter; pp.36–48.

DAVIS, J. and EASTERBY-SMITH, M. (1984) 'Learning and developing from managerial work experiences', *Journal of Management Studies*, Vol. 21, No. 2; pp.168–183.

DIXON, N. (1998) *Dialogue at Work.* London, Lemos & Crane.

FINEMAN, S. (1997) 'Emotion and management learning', *Management Learning*, Vol. 28, No. 1; pp.13–25.

GOLD, J. and HOLMAN, D. (2001) 'Let me tell you a story: an evaluation of the use of story-telling and argument analysis in management education', *Career Development International*, Vol. 6, No. 7; pp.384–395.

GOLD, J., HOLMAN, D. and THORPE, R. (2002) 'The role of argument analysis and story-telling in critical thinking', *Management Learning*, Vol. 33, No. 3; pp.371–388.

HONEY, P. and MUMFORD, A. (1996) *How to Create a Learning Environment*. Maidenhead, Honey Learning.

KOLB, D. (1982) 'Problem management: learning from experience', in S. Srivastva (ed.) *The Executive Mind*. San Francisco, Jossey-Bass.

McCALL, M., LOMBARDO, M. M. and MORRISON, A. M. (1988) *The Lessons of Experience*. Lexington, KY, Lexington Books.

McLAUGHLIN, H. and THORPE, R. 'Action learning – a paradigm in emergence: the problems facing a challenge to traditional management education and development', *British Journal of Management*, Vol. 4, No. 1; pp.19–27.

MARSICK, V., VOLPE, M., and WATKINS, K. (1999) 'Reconceptualizing informal learning', in V. Marsick and M. Volpe, *Informal learning in the workplace*. Advances in Human Resource Development Series. San Francisco, Berrett-Koehler.

MEGGINSON, D. and PEDLER, M. (1992) *Self Development*. Maidenhead, McGraw-Hill.

MEZIROW, J. (1990) *Fostering Critical Reflection in Adulthood*. San Francisco, Jossey-Bass.

MORPHEY, G. and SMITH, B. (1994) 'Tough challenges: how big a learning gap?', *Journal of Management Development*, Vol. 13, No. 9; pp.5–13.

MUMFORD, A. (1988) *Developing Top Managers*. Aldershot, Gower.

MUMFORD, A. (1997) *How to Choose the Right Development Method*. Maidenhead, Honey.

MUMFORD, A. (2001) *How to Produce Personal Development Plans*. Maidenhead, Honey.

NONAKA, I. and TAKEUCHI, H. (1995) *The Knowledge-Creating Company*. Oxford University Press.

PEDLER, M. (1996) *Action Learning for Managers*. London, Lemos & Crane.

PEDLER, M., BURGOYNE, J. and BOYDELL, T. (1999) *A Manager's Guide to Self-Development*, 3rd edition. Maidenhead, McGraw-Hill.

POLKINGHORNE, D. E. (1997) *Narrative Knowing and the Human Sciences*. New York, University of New York Press.

REVANS, R. (1982) *The Origins and Growth of Action Learning*. Bromley and Lund, Chartwell-Bratt.

SALAMAN, G. and BUTLER, J. 'Why managers won't learn', *Management Education and Development*, Vol. 21, Part 3; pp.183–191.

SCHÖN, D. A. (1983) *The Reflective Practitioner: How professionals think in action*. London, Maurice Temple Smith.

SCHÖN, D. A. and REIN, M. (1994) *Frame Reflection*. New York, Basic Books.

SNELL, R. (1988) 'The emotional cost of learning at work', *Management Education and Development*, Vol. 19, No. 4.

STREUFERT, S. and SWEZEY, R. (1986) *Complexity, Managers and Organizations*. Orlando, Academic Press.

TEMPORAL, P. (1978) 'The nature of non-contrived learning and its implications for management development', *Management Education and Development*, Vol. 9; pp.93–99.

WEICK, K. (1995) *Sensemaking in Organizations*. San Diego, Sage.

VINCE, R. (2002) 'The impact of emotion on organisational learning', *Human Resource Development International*, Vol. 5, No. 1; pp.73–85.

ENDNOTES

1 In the UK, the Learning and Skills Research Centre's project is the question: what is the nature of non-formal learning, and how does it contribute to the pursuit of further learning and employment opportunities? Details at http://www.lsda.org.uk/pubs/dbaseout/download.asp?code=LSRC447NR1. Also, see the work of Marsick *et al* (1999).

2 Kolb (1982) distinguishes between tasks to be accomplished, structured problems, unstructured problems and 'opportunities'.

3 Of course, some managers may take the opposite view, seeing themselves as champions of learning.

4 Problems of equivocality and difficulties from dilemmas have variously been described as 'messes' or 'wicked'.

5 A manager once told us that one of the most fruitful approaches to reflection occurred while he was cooking!

6 Stories can be charted in the same way.

7 The psychologist Paul Watzlawick distinguishes between two realities – a first-order reality referring to the world 'out there', and a second-order reality referring to our opinions and thinking which provide the images of that world. See http://www.doyletics.com/art/changart.htm

Evaluating Management Development

CHAPTER 8

Chapter outline

LEARNING OUTCOMES

After studying this chapter, you should be able to understand, explain, analyse and evaluate:

- **the purpose of and various approaches to the evaluation of management development**
- **different models of evaluation and ways of collecting evaluation data**
- **the key factors that influence the transfer of learning**
- **the role of an organisation's learning climate.**

INTRODUCTION

In Chapter 2 we referred to the key concern of whether MD, in whatever shape or form it is delivered, could be shown to result in an improvement of management performance. We also suggested that the reasoning behind this view was based on what Garavan *et al* (1999; p.193) referred to as a 'functional performance rationale' by which a linear connection between MD, good managers and successful performance of managers, success in organisations and, even, national economic success can be proposed and sought. It therefore follows that evaluation must be concerned with proving the validity of claims relating to such a connection. However, it has long been recognised that proving impact as a kind of cause-and-effect relationship is far from easy in MD (Smith, 1993), not least because of the difficulty of isolating the variables that are required to make any claim of a successful link, once managers return to the complexity of their everyday lives.

This has not prevented a continuing effort to find the evidence, but more often than not, it can lead organisations to try to evaluate MD with limited methods based on a general lack of knowledge and understanding about evaluation. The result is that most evaluation is cursory and it is left to chance whether MD activities can be shown to contribute to management effectiveness and organisation results. In this chapter we will attempt to explain why this occurs and show how, by taking the time to consider key questions relating to the purpose of evaluation and overall approach, it is possible to develop a strategy for evaluating MD.

MEANINGS, PURPOSE AND APPROACH

A single meaning for the term 'evaluation' is not easy to find. Weiss (1972; p.1) saw evaluation as 'an elastic word that stretches to cover judgements of many kinds'. One starting point is the old French word *évaluer* meaning 'to value'. We might therefore suggest that one meaning of 'evaluating' in MD is concerned with judgements relating to the *value* of particular MD products and processes. Taken in this way, we can see that evaluating is closely connected with people's view of MD and the criteria used to make judgements. Since MD is inevitably the concern of a variety of people with different interests, we can also see that the judgements they make about MD and the criteria used to form such judgements will strongly influence the value they will seek. This will inevitably affect the purpose of evaluation and the overall approach, including the methods used.

Placing a value on MD can occur at different points in time. Valuing may begin before, during and/or after delivery. We can also distinguish between the evaluation of programmes of MD activities and the evaluation of the activities themselves. This distinction gives rise to a number of other terms relating to evaluation. For example, if we consider the managers who participate in MD activities, we would expect them to arrive at an event with a set of expectations, sometimes formulated as explicit objectives in terms of what each manager wants to know or do better on completion of the activity. For such managers, what may be important is that those expectations are met, and these set the criteria for judgements of value. Evaluation might therefore be concerned specifically with the extent to which an MD activity meets expectations and objectives specified – this is referred to as 'internal validation'. We would also expect providers of MD activities or the trainers to be interested in this kind of evaluation, although an immediate issue arises on the extent to which managers do set objectives for their participation and whether these match the objectives set by providers. One particular interest for providers, especially when they are testing a new product or process, is in being able to show that managers achieve particular objectives set. Of course, they would wish to show that such achievement occurs with different managers in a variety of settings thus demonstrating the reliability and validity of the activity in a systematic or scientific manner.

A managing director might be interested in internal validation but probably more interested in whether internally valid MD activities contribute to organisation performance and the various criteria of effectiveness. This requires an answer to the question whether the objectives of MD activities relate sufficiently to organisation objectives – an aspect of evaluation that is referred to as 'external validation' and that could also be a feature of a management development audit (see Chapter 3).

A finance director might take this further. The crucial questions would concern whether MD activities provided financial benefits for an organisation that were greater than the cost of providing the activities. Evaluation therefore means undertaking a cost-benefit analysis so that value-added can be proven, usually in financial terms. This has always been difficult to carry out in most areas of MD and, more widely, in HRD. It would require some measurement of performance, preferably quantitative and financial, before attending an event or participating in a programme and at various times afterwards too. Where a number of managers participated in the same activities, measurements could be used to show statistically that benefits achieved were due to participating in MD activities rather than by chance.

There may be a desire to consider all such meanings in a single framework, showing evaluation at different stages. A well-known approach has in this respect been provided by Kirkpatrick (1983), as shown in Figure 29.

Level I: Reaction
– of the learners following an activity

Level II: Learning
– skills, knowledge gained as a result of the activity

Level III: Behaviour
– the effect on the performance of the learner within the workplace

Level IV: Results
– the effect of changes in performance on measurable results at work
e.g. production/service figures, costs, etc.

Figure 29 *Evaluation of MD at different stages*
Source: adapted from Kirkpatrick (1983)

This view of evaluation has become the conventional wisdom with regard to evaluation where evaluation at different levels can be linked in a chain of consequences (Hamblin, 1974). Thus, if evaluation of MD occurs at the *reactions* level, this can be used to evaluate at the next level of learning. If it can be evaluated that a manager has learned new skills, it might then be possible to evaluate at the next level of behaviour and eventually at Level 4: Results. Beyond this level, Phillips (1996) added a Level 5 to enable a cost-benefit analysis to measure net programme benefits (NPB) by calculating programme benefits divided by programme cost. The beauty of this view is that it could provide a direct link between MD and an organisation's results, so long as each level of evaluation is completed in sequence.

WEB LINK

Evaluation is a vibrant field of activity and you may be interested learn more about its theory and broader practice. Try the UK Evaluation Society's page at
http://www.evaluation.org.uk/
and the American Evaluation Association's which can be found at
http://www.eval.org/
A particularly useful starting point with access to resources and many other sites is the Virtual Library on Evaluation at http://www.policy-evaluation.org/

Formative and summative evaluation

The various meanings of evaluation have tended to focus on the outcomes of MD activities. However, we should also consider that such activities involve managers in a learning process, and this will affect their expectations and the value they derive from it. It suggests also that such value can change throughout participation and that objectives at the start of the process are not the same during the process and on completion of it. Here we could make use of a distinction that is frequently made in education (Tessmer, 1993) between 'summative evaluation', which occurs on completion of an activity, and 'formative evaluation', which occurs while the activity is happening either to improve it and/or to enhance the experience of the participants and the value they gain. Similarly, Rackham (1973) made a useful distinction between 'long-cycle' and 'short-cycle' evaluation, in which long-cycle evaluation is concerned with a whole programme whereas short-cycle evaluation is concerned with quick feedback for participants within a programme.

These variations in the meaning of the term 'evaluation' and the presence of different interests make evaluation a complex process since it has to take account of and respond to the different interests and their judgements, which are always value-laden and frequently permeated by organisational politics (Easterby-Smith, 1994).

REFLECT – CONCLUDE – PLAN 1

- What are the meanings of 'evaluation' in your organisation?
- How do such meanings affect the way evaluation is carried out?
- What can you do to make the meaning of evaluation relevant to managers?

Purpose

A broad distinction can be made between evaluation as a form of research and evaluation as a provider of practical knowledge which can help decision-making. The former is the concern of those who seek to explore and explain social activities to provide generalisable hypotheses, models and theories of the working of particular features of the world. The latter is more concerned with providing information about programmes and activities in response to various interests so that decisions can be made and actions taken. While these two perspectives towards research and the practical lead to differences in methods and approach, there is considerable overlap between them (Clarke, 1999). In general, evaluation in MD is oriented towards the practical perspective, but there are also examples of research-oriented evaluation.

Easterby-Smith (1994) suggests that there are four consistent purposes that can be identified for evaluating MD. These are:

- proving
- improving
- learning
- controlling.

The first purpose – proving – is probably the most obvious and logical. Evaluation is concerned with showing that a particular outcome has been achieved as a result of MD activities. The proving purpose also matches conventional wisdom on how evaluation should proceed, informed by models of evaluation that suggest that data can be collected systematically and rigorously as though the impact of MD activities occurred in a linear fashion. Thus the purpose of proving could be applied at all levels of evaluation and, in theory, provide satisfaction for all stakeholders. However, there may be difficulties in making the necessary links in MD, especially once the influence of contextual factors of the workplace are taken into account.

The second purpose – improving – arises partly from some of the difficulties of proving the impact of MD. In the absence of a definitive link between MD and, for example, organisational outcomes, it might be argued that the least that should be done is to make sure that evaluation contributes to the improvement of activities.

The purposes of proving and improving provide data that allow decisions to be made about MD. For example, if a programme is proved to meet objectives, it could be repeated, and if proved not to, information from evaluation might help providers decide how to improve it. The third purpose – learning – however, focuses on how data can be used by managers and others as part of the learning process within MD events. For example, it is often difficult to specify how climbing a mountain or crossing a river can relate to the work of a manager. But through a process of review, such as completing a learning log or conducting a discussion, managers are able to evaluate the experience and identify key learning points. It is important to stress the focus of learning – that is, that whatever data is generated in reviews, it is part of the process. Possible confusions may arise if such data is also used for other purposes.

The control purpose of evaluation is a reminder that MD events seldom take place without some aspect of surveillance, whether in the form of financial control via a budget or the need to show that MD provision operates within particular boundaries with respect to content and delivery.

There is also another related purpose – influence. Evaluation provides data which can be manipulated to ensure a persuasive portrayal of MD for particular reasons. For example, a pilot programme might be evaluated in such a way to ensure the continuation of the programme. It is a reminder that information collected as part of evaluation can be presented as a revelation of real facts or the 'truth' (Clarke, 1999).

While the choice of evaluation purpose in MD is significant, there is a frequently a requirement to respond to a variety of different needs, and this may result in a mix of purposes. Easterby-Smith (1994) suggests that purpose can be decided on the grounds of expediency, where an activity is under threat, or by prioritising the interests of stakeholders.

Approach

Allied to the purpose of evaluation are issues relating to

- the approach taken concerning what data is collected
- who it is collected from, when and how
- the analysis and presentation of results
- the evaluation methodology and the strategy adopted to meet the purposes.

Methodology will partly depend on the beliefs held about what happens in MD and how what is happening can come to be known. There are significant debates relating to evaluation methodology, and at the heart of the debate are questions about what is meant by 'knowledge' and what is a reliable claim to 'know' something.

Two broad approaches to the issue of methodology can be identified:

- positivist methodologies
- phenomenological methodologies.[1]

The two categorisations are underpinned by very different sets of assumptions made about the world and the explanations that can be developed.

To explain the relevance and possibilities for evaluation of MD, we will consider methodology in relation to an organisational example. The company in question, a software project management company, was seeking to enhance a 'coaching culture' among managers and team leaders. An MD programme for 30 managers and team leaders was set up with the overall aim of enhancing managers' coaching skills and the ability of team leaders to improve team performance. The programme ran over 10 weeks with an initial training event, followed by work application and reviews. The evaluation design needed to be rigorous in seeking to prove the effectiveness of the programme but had also to be useful to trainers and participants.

Considering the overall methodology, the key ideas of *positivism* are:

- the world exists externally and objectively
- knowledge of this world can only be based on observation and measurement of its properties.

The first idea is a statement about the reality of MD, and especially the view of it. As a positivist, you would believe that the MD activities you wish to understand do exist, and that you can separate them sufficiently from other factors. Thus, the coaching programme would actually take place with real managers and team leaders.

The second idea is based on the view that if MD activities exist, the only valid way to claim knowledge about their value is to observe and measure. If you cannot do that, how could you claim to know it? For example, to explain the behaviour of coaches and team leaders at work following training, there must be a way of measuring and observing what happens in terms of skills, the application of knowledge and the values of participants. You can believe that managers and team leaders really have values which affect their performance, but how do you know this? Can you observe and measure values?

Positivist evaluation is also closely aligned with what is referred to as 'the scientific method' in research, from which a number of implications for evaluation can be derived:

- The evaluator is independent of what is observed and measured, and his or her values and subjective opinion are held in check.
- Observations and measurements provide knowledge which can be used to produce generalisations about what is happening.
- Generalisations can be used to make claims about cause and effect, anticipate what will happen, and, if necessary, control events.

The important values of rationality and objectivity make a positivist view so attractive in evaluating MD, particularly the emphasis on seeking data that systematically provides a logical flow of cause and effect – ie to suggest that MD events lead to particular outcomes. Thus in the coaching programme, an external evaluator sought to find out what was happening both during and after the initial training, with an attempt to measure impact on the performance of participants.

REFLECT – CONCLUDE – PLAN 2

- Think of a recent MD programme in your organisation. Write out a description of the programme striving to maintain independence as an evaluator.
- What do you conclude about maintaining independence in your observations of what happened?
- What can you do to enhance accuracy?

Phenomenological methodologies in evaluating MD are concerned with understanding how a manager's behaviour is formed from meanings held by a manager (and others) in the various situations that he or she faces as part of an MD event and beyond. In the coaching programme, the starting point of phenomenological evaluation is that managers and team leaders define and interpret what goes on around them and make their own sense of coaching. They use their own interpretations to evaluate the usefulness of coaching in terms of what they consider to be important. Throughout their participation, new interpretations are made, new meanings may be constructed,[2] and the value given to coaching may change. Further, there are like to be a variety of interpretations, meanings and values for different managers from the same coaching activities. For example, both managers and team leaders will share informal evaluation through anecdotes which show the benefits or otherwise of the experience. The passing on of anecdotes or stories is probably the most common form of evaluation and could significantly affect the success and value given to MD.

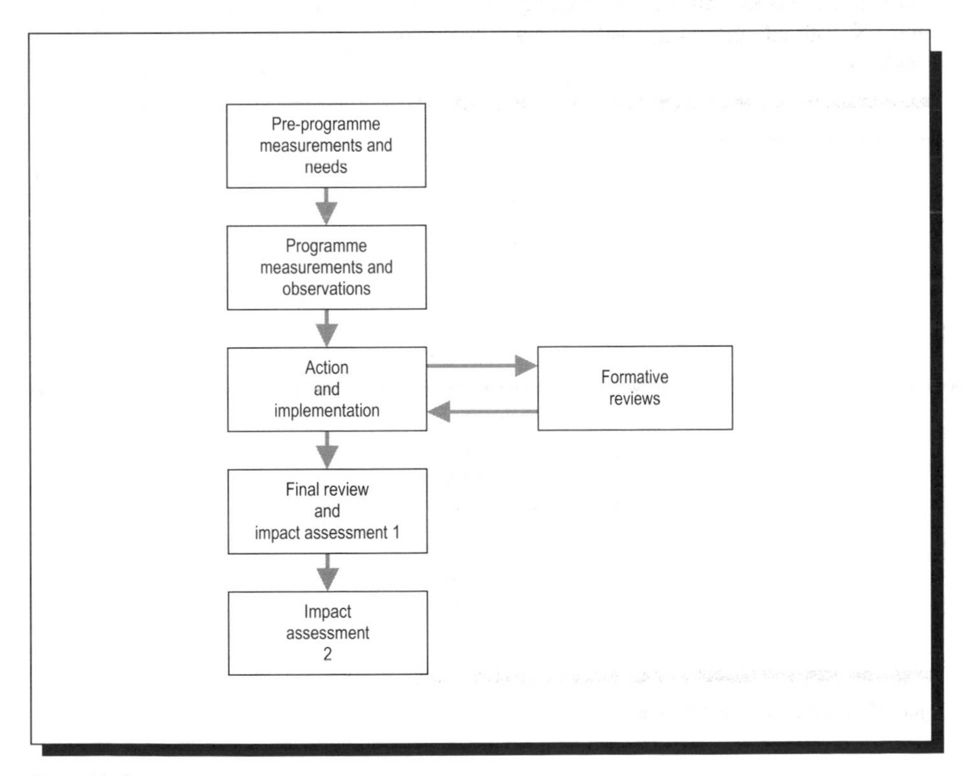

Figure 30 *Evaluation design for a coaching programme*

For the evaluator, a consequence of accepting the phenomenological approach is that it is difficult to make generalisations of cause and effect in relation to the coaching programme. Rather, a multiplicity of values exists – there are many voices, including the evaluator's, and what is seen as social reality is a social construction. The way this construction is built up and sustained by managers and team leaders is a legitimate issue for evaluation. Indeed, it is within the ongoing events before, during and after the programme that meanings are made, and actions are carried out and valued. The evaluator can seek to access such meanings to gain a richer understanding of the programme and provide feedback for use by the participants.

The contrasting approaches give rise to a wide variety of evaluation methodologies, models and methods. The sponsors of the coaching programme were happy for an evaluation design which encompassed aspects of both approaches, as shown in Figure 30.

In the programme positivist methods are used at various stages for measurement, observation and assessment of impact during and beyond the duration of the programme. Phenomenological methods are used to gain access to the meanings of participants at all stages of the programme, including the formative reviews[3] and the final review which allow learning to be used to enhance action and implementation and to collect qualitative data relating to participants' valuation of the experience.

WEB LINK

http://www.sosig.ac.uk/social_science_general/social_science_methodology/ provides access to the Social Science Methodology of the Social Science Information Gateway in the UK, with information and links to many resources on evaluation methodology and methods.

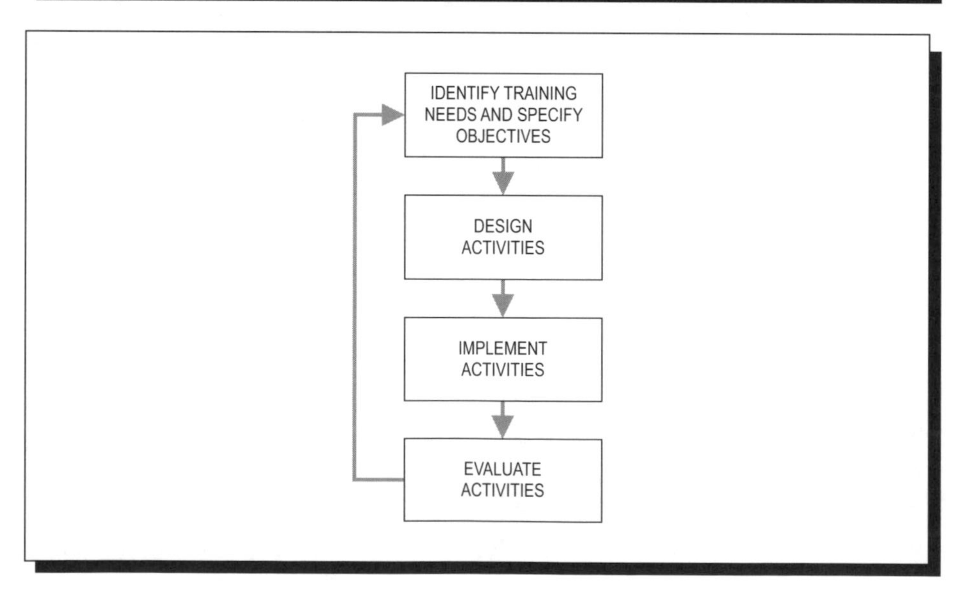

Figure 31 *A systematic model of training*

SYSTEMATIC AND SYSTEMS MODELS

The differing perspectives offered by positivism and phenomenology provide evaluators of MD with different schools of thought to inform the choice of evaluation models and methods. In the UK, for many years, a systematic model of training and evaluation has been regarded as the orthodoxy. A typical presentation of this model is shown as Figure 31.

The four-stage model emphasises the need to evaluate at the conclusion of activities. Data collected can then be analysed and decisions made on the value of the activities and the extent to which the objectives set were valid. This model has become deeply ingrained into the thinking of organisations as a way of proving the effectiveness of activities. Further, the model can incorporate a feedback loop from evaluation back to identifying needs and specifying objectives. Thus, as well as being systematic and logical, the model is also systemic in that feedback provides information about activities so that necessary improvements can be made.

There are some obvious consequences of this model for the evaluation of MD. Firstly, evaluation appears as the final stage of a process. This tends to mean that the evaluation of MD activities becomes something of a ritual and perhaps an afterthought. Usually it is completed after the close of the 'official' activities with a certain amount of pressure to do it quickly before departing.[4] The favoured technique in such situations is to issue a questionnaire to gain overall reactions to the activities (a 'reactionnaire') and collect data on enjoyment ('happiness' or just 'happy' sheets). The consequence is that data gathered may be subject to bias and distortion, dependent on the feelings of the group at the time of completion (Smith, 1990). Secondly, MD providers may be able to influence matters so that adverse reactions are screened out or regarded as anomalous. Thus, starting from the premise that 'good activities' are provided, good activities must lead to good experiences for participants and positive evaluation, as shown in the 'happiness' sheets. Negative evaluation can be disregarded.

The restriction of this view of evaluation has long been recognised and has prompted various attempts to adjust the model so that evaluation occurs not just at the end of a course. Kirkpatrick's (1983) model (Figure 29 above) showed that evaluation can take place at different stages or levels. Further elaboration has been provided by Warr *et al* (1970), who presented an integrated model of evaluation covering all stages of MD activity. The CIRO model covers:

- **C**ontext – the organisational situation that requires change through training
- **I**nputs – the methods used to meet training objectives
- **R**eactions – of managers to their training
- **O**utputs – immediate, intermediate (behaviour in the work context) and ultimate (the impact on organisation results).

This version provides a basis to evaluate stages other than those that follow the end of MD activity. Because there are so many factors that could affect the performance of managers once they return to work, it was suggested by Warr *et al* (1970) that trainers might have difficulty in linking training to outputs beyond the activities themselves. Trainers might do better, therefore, to evaluate the context that produces the need for training and the effect of their activities, the inputs, as the training happens. In this way, trainers can ensure that training meets the requirements of managers and make improvements as required. Of

Table 14 Techniques of evaluation

Context (before MD)	Interviews and questionnaires, briefings, written tests, 360-degree assessment
Inputs (during MD)	Session reviews, questionnaires, written and practical tests, observation of behaviour, interviews, repertory grids[5]
Reactions (to MD)	Questionnaires, interviews
Outputs (following MD)	Interviews, questionnaires, debriefing meetings, 360-degree feedback, appraisal, performance measures, results measurements

particular importance is the idea that evaluation can provide feedback for learning so that opportunities for work application can be identified (Burgoyne and Singh, 1977) and stimulate Type 2 MD.

Evaluation at different stages throughout MD allows the use of a wide variety of data collection techniques ranging from the quick (and dirty?) to the more complex and sophisticated. Table 14 shows some suggestions for evaluation techniques at each stage.

WEB LINKS

If you are seeking further tools and techniques for evaluation, a good starting point is the National Evaluation Project, Resources for Evaluators at
http://www.lancs.ac.uk/fss/projects/edres/itsn-eval
For a more training-oriented web-site try
http://reviewing.co.uk/

The systematic model of evaluation and the various elaborations would appear to have a strong appeal – however, in MD a number of difficulties can be highlighted:

- The systematic model is mainly applied to training – that is, Type 3 MD – but this is just one feature of MD. As we have indicated throughout this book, MD incorporates many activities including formal education programme and Type 2 learning at work.
- Managers can undertake a mix of MD activities such as training and education programmes, and these often overlap or occur in relation to each other. Identifying the effect of one activity may be contaminated by the effect of other activities.
- Managers learn in different ways. We have indicated that learning preferences can affect how managers respond to activities. There are also time-lags for some managers in responding to MD activities.
- Management work always occurs in a context. Even when managers have been able to improve their knowledge and skills, unless they are able to implement what they have learned, it may be impossible to link the effects of MD to changes in a manager's behaviour. Ideally, an evaluator would seek to minimise the impact of random or unknown factors – however, this is impossible in management work where a wide range of variables are likely to affect behaviour and performance.[6]

The incorporation of feedback allows evaluation to occur more frequently and for more data to be collected and used. It also allows evaluators to respond to activities and participants during activities (Bramley, 1999) – a feature of responsive evaluation which we will consider below. However, even a systems model of evaluation has its limitations.

Even if adjustments are made in response to feedback, the adjustments may be limited by the language of the feedback and prevent more critical or radical responses. This is a feature of what Easterby-Smith (1994; p.35) calls the 'systems fallacy'. Negative feedback may explain that participants dislike a technique and may provide a way of improving the technique – but a provider may continue to use the technique. What is not provided is an alternative technique or a true decision on whether such techniques should be used at all. Easterby-Smith also suggests that the systems model tends to focus on outcomes, which assumes a mechanistic view of how managers learn. Further, the model assumes that MD starts with objectives with little reference to the status of such objectives, to who set them, or to how they might change or be disregarded during the unfolding of MD activities.

More generally, there are doubts about the applicability of the systemic idea or metaphor to the complexity, uncertainty and difficulties of reality – especially the reality of organisations. Specifically, can the systems model of evaluation capture the multiple values that are present in MD in all its forms? Could it, for instance, cope with conflicting values, dilemmas and paradoxes and power relations? Evaluation models must therefore accord with the complexity these factors bring.[7]

REFLECT – CONCLUDE – PLAN 3

- Does your organisation evaluate MD systemically?
- What difficulties are there? Do they match those presented in this section?
- What can you do to counter the difficulties?

RESPONSIVE MODELS

The difficulties inherent in systematic and systemic models have resulted in a move to understand different perceptions, respond to requirements, and make improvements rather than directly prove the success of MD (Simpson and Lyddon, 1995). There is an acceptance that within any situation there is likely to be a variety of different meanings and understandings. Thus in evaluating MD, different groups or stakeholders will have different interests, and this will affect their requirements for evaluation. It would not be surprising to find conflicts of interest between stakeholders, and this can create difficulties in meeting requirements. Evaluation that attempts to take account of various perspectives and respond to their requirements has been called 'responsive evaluation' (Stake, 1975). Of particular importance is the attention that is given to cultural and contextual factors within evaluation and a revision of the purpose of evaluation away from proving towards feedback and learning.

Utilisation

Patton (1997) presents a model of utilisation-focused evaluation, the key characteristic of which (p.21) is:

> **'Involving specific people who can and will use information that enables them to establish direction for, commitment to, and ownership of evaluation every step along the way.'**

By involving stakeholders, the evaluator is active, reactive and adaptive to decision-makers and those who will make use of evaluation information. As stated by Patton (p.21), 'The evaluator facilitates judgement and decision-making by intended users rather than acting as a distant, independent judge.' Users are able to act on the evaluation findings because it meets their requirements and they have a personal interest in the findings. Evaluation is mainly formative and begins by analysing the context. This is particularly important in MD, and it allows evaluation to occur throughout an MD process. Tasks of utilisation-focused evaluation include:

- the development of relationships with intended users so that it is understood what kind of evaluation is required
- the facilitation of meetings between stakeholders to examine findings, assess progress against expectations and reconsider the next steps
- the organisation of dialogues about the evaluation data where there are different interpretations.

One key task is to identify the key stakeholders, their desires and interests, the roles they will play and the various situational factors that will affect how evaluation will occur and be used.

Action Evaluation

A concern with finding ways to make action possible in MD, especially in the face of the difficulties and complexities facing managers, could find some connection with what has become referred to as Action Evaluation (Rothman, 1997). Action Evaluation (AE) has its roots in Organisation Development (OD) and Action Research and was developed during the 1990s with a particular orientation towards the resolution of conflict. However, it also emerged as an evaluation methodology for complex situations in organisations composed of multiple stakeholders each with their own interests. AE is 'designed to develop rich, nuanced and context-specific definitions of success' (Rothman, 1998; p.2), which allow stakeholders to share understandings and which therefore make the achievement of success more likely. The stages of AE can be represented by a simple cycle, as shown in Figure 32.

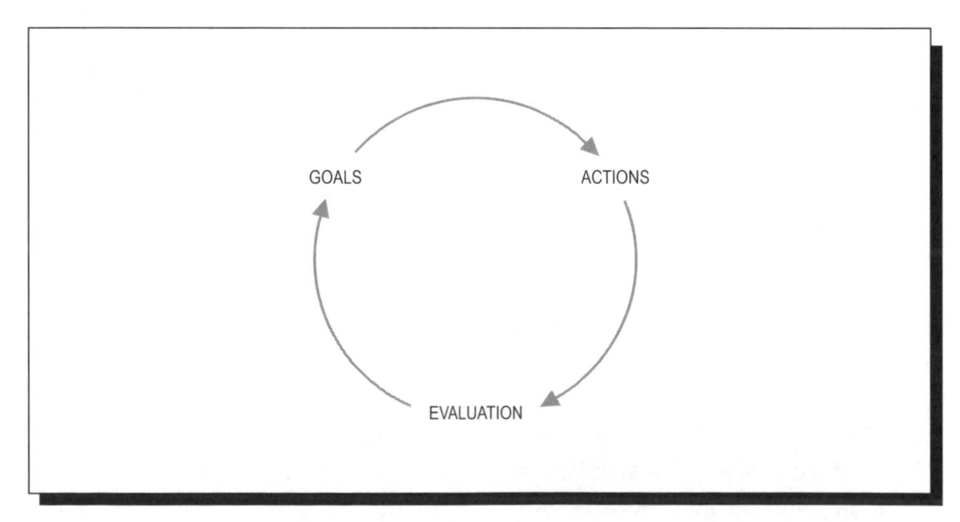

Figure 32 *An Action Evaluation cycle*

At first glance, AE would seem to have some similarity to the systems model of evaluation that we explored earlier in this chapter. However, the approach has some important differentiators. A key feature is the stage of setting goals where AE is concerned, asking the various stakeholders to identify their goals and express values and motivations attached to the goals. By participating in such a process, the various parties are able to move to what Rothman (1998; p.3) refers to as 'intersubjective agreement' about goals. In this way, goals of the different stakeholders become explicit. Actions emerge from goals set and can then be evaluated. That is, the goals set become the source of feedback to participants and the source of reflection. Reiteration and a continuous focus on defining/redefining goals and what is required for success make AE responsive to context and an integral part of the learning process, especially Type 2 MD. Similarly, in Action Learning evaluation is integrated into the learning process. An example is provided by Pedler (1996) from a programme with head teachers. Evaluation consisted of:

- using a stakeholder map to identify critical success factors for projects
- visits to each other's schools to check on how far stakeholder criteria had been met and what benefits had been achieved – eg attendance at open evenings, communication between staff members, use and practice of techniques, interviews with stakeholders
- regular reviews and developmental evaluation within learning sets
- a final summarising evaluation on the worth of the programme.

WEB LINKS

You can find out more about Action Evaluation at the Action Evaluation Research Institute at
http://www.aepro.org/
Information about a related idea of Empowerment Evaluation can be found at
http://www.stanford.edu/~davidf/institute.html

Stories

A phenomenological stance on evaluation is an invitation to enter the murky waters of how managers and others value MD and how such values change throughout the experience of MD and beyond. It is not always easy to gain access to values but one opportunity is provided by story-telling and what is referred to as narrative evaluation[8] (Abma, 2000).

Stories can be significant in evaluation because stories of personal experience provide an opportunity to give an interpretation and meaning to events. In addition, stories told capture uniqueness and richness of experience. So a manager who has undertaken some of MD will be able to present feelings and emotions relating to the experience by story-telling. Narrative evaluation provides a more formal attempt to make use of the anecdotes that surround MD but are rarely captured.

Narrative evaluation is a complex approach – but it is its complexity that makes it attractive for the capture of the value of the dynamic and often ambiguous learning activities that form MD. Further, evaluation through story-telling can be highly participative since stories told orally or written are a means of reflecting on MD to make sense of participation, revealing key arguments and values which can provide managers with new ways of understanding and ideas for actions (Gold *et al*, 2002).

WEB LINK

Narrative evaluation is strongly connected to 'narrative analysis' and the work of William Labov. Go to his home page at http://www.lingupenn.edu/~wlabov/home.html

TRANSFER OF LEARNING

Because Type 3 MD is a planned process, occurring away from normal managerial activities but with the potential to help managers bring new skills back to the organisation, managers face problems in how to ensure that learning is transferred back into their performance as managers at work, so that it becomes Type 2 MD. These problems are concerned with what is referred to as the transfer of learning.[9] If we take a simple approach to the evaluation of MD, we might ask the following crucial questions:

- Can managers show they have learned something?
- Can managers apply what they have learned?
- Can someone show that that the organisation has benefited?

Answering such questions raises the following key points to consider in the transfer of learning:

- managers do learn new skills, ideas and attitudes
- managers are able to apply learning to work in various ways
- the application is sustained over time leading to some impact.

Baldwin and Ford (1988) provided a framework for this process, and an adapted version is shown as Figure 33.

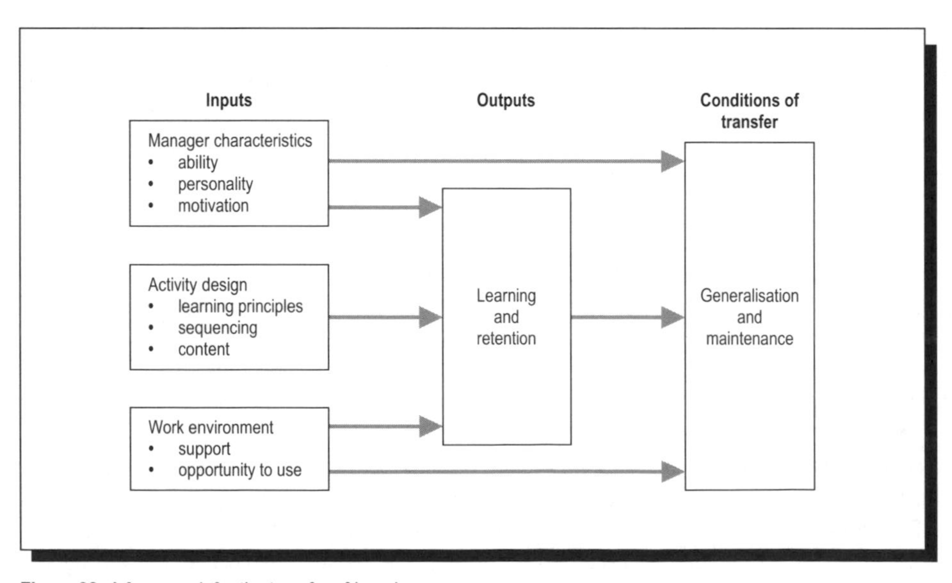

Figure 33 *A framework for the transfer of learning*
Source: adapted from Baldwin and Ford (1988)

The value of the framework is the prominence it gives to some of the key factors that affect transfer of learning. Transfer occurs when skills, knowledge and attitudes are not only learned and retained but also generalised sufficiently for application in various work activities and maintained by further application over time. The framework suggests that learning, retention, generalisation and maintenance are all influenced by manager characteristics and the work environment. Thus, even where MD activities are well designed for positive learning and retention – with good reaction-level evaluation – it is still possible that transfer will be inhibited by a lack of motivation on the part of a manager. There may also be a lack of opportunity to use the learning and/or no support from others such as peers and line managers; these are crucial features of what is referred to as an organisation's learning climate (see below).

REFLECT – CONCLUDE – PLAN 4

- Think back to some form of MD or other training and development activity you have undertaken.
- What were the factors that contributed to the successful or unsuccessful transfer of learning?
- How can you help others to improve transfer?

Manager characteristics

Motivational factors, personality and existing abilities will influence learning and retention and overall transfer. Huczynski (1977) suggested that it was the individual working with self-interest that made the key decisions about transfer, although this was on the basis of an 'inner debate' (p.98) that took into account the organisational context. There are a number of ways to consider manager characteristics. One approach is to examine how managers prefer to learn, or better still, to help managers understand their learning orientation, including how managers may prefer not to learn. If a manager, for example, prefers to avoid trying new actions, or planning new actions which involve others, and so on, this preference will influence how that manager might participate in MD, learn from participation, and attempt to transfer ideas and skills back into practice.

In addition to learning preferences, there are other ways to consider characteristics. For example, a study by Cheng (2000) considered the following key elements from an MBA programme to examine transfer of learning:

- a measure of personality type to indicate a degree of ambition to succeed and achievement striving
- the 'locus of control', which measures the inner belief that rewards and outcomes in life are controlled by a person's own actions or by outside forces
- self-efficacy, which corresponds to a person's confidence that he or she can carry out certain behaviours and deal with threatening situations.

Self-efficacy has been particularly interesting, especially in the context of how managers cope with difficulties in trying to apply ideas or use skills. This refers to the conviction that a manager has about his/her ability to execute the behaviour needed to produce particular outcomes (Bandura, 1977). Robertson and Sadri (1993) suggested that high self-efficacy is associated with high performance and low self-efficacy is associated with poor performance. For example, if a manager does not believe he or she is able to chair a meeting, it indicates low self-efficacy for chairing meetings. So even if this skill is 'learned' on a training course, the manager may try to avoid using it because of fear and inhibition, and if the manager is forced to chair a meeting, the low self-efficacy may result in poor performance and reinforce the negative expectations about chairing meetings held by the manager. Indeed, the manager may even be more pessimistic about carrying out such a task in the future. Accordingly, it may be important to prepare managers for the possibility of dealing with difficult applications of new skills and ideas so that they can cope and prevent the negative impact on self-efficacy. Marx (1982) referred to this process of preparing managers as 'relapse prevention'. By becoming aware of high-risk situations in advance and developing coping skills, self-efficacy can be enhanced so that when a difficult situation arises, a manager will believe that success can be achieved, and through accomplishment, will use the skill again, leading to generalisation and maintenance.

WEB LINK

For more information about self-efficacy, try
http://www.emory.edu/EDUCATION/mfp/effpage.html
A general measurement of self-efficacy can be found at
http://userpage.fu-berlin.de/~health/selfscal.htm

The learning climate

Manager characteristics will influence and be influenced by external factors that form part of an organisation's context. In particular, we are interested in that part of context which will impact on how a manager learns: the learning climate. In Chapter 7 it was suggested that the learning climate is composed of perceived variables that affect a manager and others in whether they realise learning potential (Temporal, 1978). With reference to the transfer of learning, it is a reminder that MD does not begin with attendance at a Type 3 event. Managers work, assess needs for MD and identify how needs will be met all in a context, and they return to that context after attending events that should have been designed to meet their needs.

Features of a positive learning climate for managers include:

- the structuring of a manager's work to match and stretch capabilities
- ongoing discussions to set objectives and review performance focused sufficiently on development
- Type 3 MD events and activities identified to match requirements
- opportunities to use new skills and learning on return to work, together with support from line managers to investigate how work can be extended or deepened to allow application
- ongoing coaching and informal support.

One of the key factors identified in research (Ford *et al*, 1992) is that opportunities to use new skills can be created, and this is connected with the degree of autonomy within work. Essentially, this would require support from superior managers. An implication here is that managers who receive support should also support others, thereby reinforcing a positive learning climate (Axtell *et al*, 1997). We would also expect to find the positive HRM context involving the use of planned career structures, succession planning and fast-tracking which were found by Mabey (2002) to contribute significantly to MD in organisations, along with an importance given to informal learning and development or Type 2 MD.

In identifying the key features of a positive learning climate, we should not forget that many managers face less favourable circumstances. Instead of support, managers find themselves blocked by factors such as lack of autonomy in their work, insufficient stretch to allow the application of learning, and the psycho-social factors such as the negative reactions of others and lack of help from superiors. At best, managers returning from Type 3 MD might be greeted by ambivalence or mild disinterest; at worst, power and politics may prevent any attempts to try something different, leading to disillusion about MD in general and overall cynicism.

REFLECT – CONCLUDE – PLAN 5

- What are the features of a less positive learning climate in your organisation?
- What is the impact on transfer of learning?
- What steps can you take to improve the learning climate?

Evaluation and transfer

This consideration of transfer of learning suggests that there are a number of ways evaluation can be utilised:

- The organisational context will influence who undertakes MD, and how and what MD is undertaken. Through management development audits and other organisational review processes (see Chapter 3), contextual factors can be influenced to support effectiveness.
- MD needs can be identified through discussions with superiors and feedback from others in the organisational context. MD should be driven by a manager's problems and by business issues. Preparation for attending Type 3 MD may include a plan on how to apply learning on return to work.
- The goals set by managers for MD provide information for providers.
- Consideration for transfer begins during a programme by identifying possible new ideas, setting goals and/or identifying what is needed to manage transfer and how to cope with difficulties in transfer.[10]
- Reviews with managers soon after their return to work should identify the need for support for transfer.
- Further reviews will allow new ideas for transfer to emerge after a programme.

Evaluation for learning becomes the main purpose by providing feedback for managers and others that facilitates the transfer of learning and continues it as an ongoing process. One important consequence of this is that evaluation becomes purposeful in enhancing an organisation's learning climate. It has been a feature of many organisational approaches to change, organisational learning, the 'learning company' and knowledge production and management (see Chapter 12). By taking a whole-organisation approach, evaluating MD can become an integrated and continuous activity rather than an add-on at the end of courses.

Clearly, evaluation is a complex activity. The temptation not to make a serious effort is understandable. If there is no serious attempt, MD will live – or die – by anecdotes and stories: a most uncertain basis. At the least, we advocate a form of evaluation which assesses whether people have learned something from an activity.

SUMMARY

- Proving the value of an investment in MD is a key purpose of evaluation, but is difficult to achieve.
- In MD, evaluation is concerned with criteria-based judgements relating to its value. Placing a value on MD can occur at different points in time.
- The main purposes of evaluation in MD are *proving*, *improving*, *learning*, *controlling* and *influencing*.
- There are significant debates concerning evaluation methodology affecting what data is collected, who it is collected from, when and how it is collected, and the analysis and presentation of results.
- Evaluation can occur at different stages to form a chain of consequences, providing a direct link between MD and organisational results.
- Responsive models of evaluation are concerned with understanding and meeting the needs of different stakeholders in MD.
- Many managers face difficulties in transferring learning from MD into their work as managers – this is the transfer of learning problem.
- There are a number of ways evaluation can be used to support the transfer of learning.

DISCUSSION QUESTIONS

1. Should evaluating MD be more than an 'act of faith'? If so, why?
2. Can evaluation be designed to prove the *added value* of MD?
3. How can competing interests in MD be reconciled through evaluation?
4. 'Evaluation of MD serves no purpose unless results lead to action.' Discuss.
5. Is transfer of learning an issue only for off-the-job MD?
6. How do organisational power and politics affect MD?

FURTHER READING

HALE, R. (2003) 'How training can add real value to the business: Part 1', *Industrial and Commercial Training*, Vol. 35, No. 1; pp.29–32.

HASKELL, R. E. (1998) *Reengineering Corporate Training: Intellectual capital and transfer of learning*. Westport, Conn., Quorum.

KESNER, I. F. (2003) 'Leadership development: perk or priority', *Harvard Business Review*, May; pp.29–36.

TAMKIN, P., YARNELL, J. and KERRIN, M. (2002) *Kirpatrick and Beyond: A review of models of training evaluation*. Brighton, Institute for Employment Studies.

OLSEN, J. H. (1998) 'The evaluation and enhancement of training transfer', *International Journal of Training and Development*, Vol. 2, No. 1; pp.61–75.

GROUP ACTIVITY

- Form a group of four or five members, preferably from different organisations.
- Select one management development activity from each organisation and carry out a stakeholder analysis by completing the chart represented by Table 15. What roles should be carried out by each stakeholder?

Table 15 *Stakeholder analysis chart*

Stakeholder	Evaluation Interest	Stakeholder Roles
Names/Department/Position	Desires, requirements, expectations	Actions by the stakeholder Response to evaluation findings

- Report back with your findings to the group.
- Consider the variety of interests in each organisation – what are the similarities, differences, sources of tension?
- How are competing interests reconciled?

REFERENCES

ABMA, T. (ed.) (2000) Telling Tales: On evaluation and narrative. Volume 6 of *Advances in Program Evaluation*. Boston, JAI Press.

AXTELL, C. M., MAITLIS, S. and YEARTA, S. (1997) 'Predicting immediate and longer-term transfer of training', *Personnel Review*, Vol. 26, No. 3; pp.201–213.

BALDWIN, T. T. and FORD, J. K. (1988) 'Transfer of training: a review, and directions for future research', *Personnel Psychology*, Vol. 41; pp.63–105.

BANDURA, A. (1977) *Social Learning Theory*. New Jersey, Prentice-Hall.

BRAMLEY, P. (1999) 'Evaluating effective management learning', *Journal of European Industrial Training*, Vol. 23, No. 3; pp.145–153.

BURGOYNE, J. and SINGH, R. (1977) 'Evaluation of training and education: macro and micro perspectives', *Journal of European Industrial Training*, Vol. 1, No. 1; pp.17–21.

CHENG, E. W. L. (2000) 'Test of the MBA knowledge and skills transfer', *International Journal of Human Resource Management*, Vol. 11, No. 4; pp.837–852.

CLARKE, A. (1999) *Evaluation Research*. London, Sage.

EASTERBY-SMITH, M. (1994) *Evaluating Management Development, Training and Education*, 2nd edition. Aldershot, Gower.

FORD, J. K., QUINONES, M., SEGO, D. and SORRA, J. (1992) 'Factors affecting the opportunity to perform trained tasks on the job', *Personnel Psychology*, Vol. 45; pp.511–527.

GABRIEL, Y. (2000) *Storytelling in Organizations*. Oxford, Oxford University Press.

GARAVAN, T., BARNICLE, B. and O'SUILLEABHAIN, F. (1999) 'Management development: contemporary trends, issues and strategies', *Journal of European Industrial Training*, Vol. 23, Nos 4/5; pp.191–207.

GIST, M. E., BAVETTA, A. G. and STEVENS, C. K. (1990) 'Transfer training method: its influence on skill generalisation, skill repetition and performance level', *Personnel Psychology*, Vol. 43; pp.501–523.

GOLD, J. (2001) 'Storying systems: managing everyday flux using Mode 2 soft systems methodology', *Systemic Practice and Action Research*, Vol. 14, No. 5; pp.557–574.

GOLD, J., HOLMAN, D. and THORPE, R. (2002) 'The role of argument analysis and story-telling in facilitating critical reflection', *Management Learning*, Vol. 33, No. 3; pp.371–388.

HAMBLIN, A. C. (1974) *Evaluation and the Control of Training*. London, McGraw-Hill.

HUCZYNSKI, A. (1977) 'Organisational climates and the transfer of learning', *BACIE Journal*, Vol. 31, No. 6; pp.98–99.

KIRKPATRICK, D. L. (1983) 'Four steps to measuring training effectiveness', *Personnel Administrator*, November; pp.19–25.

MABEY, C. (2002) 'Mapping management development practice', *Journal of Management Studies*, Vol. 39, No. 8; pp.1139–1160.

MARX, R. D. (1982) 'Relapse prevention for managerial training: a model for maintenance of behavior change', *Academy of Management Review*, Vol. 7, No. 3; pp.433–441.

PATTON, M. (1997) *Utilization-focused Evaluation*, 3rd edition. Newbury Park, CA., Sage.

PEDLER, M. (1996) *Action Learning for Managers*. London, Lemos & Crane.

PHILLIPS, J. (1996) 'Measuring ROI: the fifth level of evaluation', *Technical and Skills Training*, April; pp.10–13.

RACKHAM, N. (1973) 'Recent thoughts on evaluation', *Industrial and Commercial Training*, Vol. 5, No. 10; pp.454–461.

ROBERTSON, I. T. and SHADRI, G. (1993) 'Managerial self-efficacy and managerial performance', *British Journal of Management*, Vol. 4; pp.37–45.

ROTHMAN, J. (1997) *Resolving Identity-Based Conflict in Nations, Organizations and Communities*. San Francisco, Jossey-Bass.

ROTHMAN, J. (1998) 'Integrating evaluation into the intervention process'. Available from http://www.aepro.org/inprint/conference/rothman.html

SIMPSON, P. and LYDDON, T. (1995) 'Different roles, different views: exploring the range of stakeholder perceptions on an in-company management development programme', *Industrial and Commercial Training*, Vol. 27, No. 4; pp.26–32.

SMITH, A. (1990) 'Evaluation of management training – subjectivity and the individual', *Journal of European Industrial Training*, Vol. 14, No. 1; pp.12–15.

SMITH, A. (1993) 'Management development evaluation and effectiveness', *Journal of Management Development*, Vol. 12, No. 1; pp.20–33.

STAKE, R. (ed.) (1975) *Evaluating the Arts in Education: A responsive approach*. Columbus, OH, Merrill.

TEMPORAL, P. (1978) 'The nature of non-contrived learning and the implications for management development', *Management Education and Development*, Vol. 9; pp.93–99.

TESSMER, M. (1993) *Planning and Conducting Formative Evaluations*. London, Kogan Page.

WARR, P., BIRD, M. and RACKHAM, N. (1970) *Evaluation of Management Training*. Epping, Gower Press.

WEISS, C. H. (1972) *Evaluation Research*. Englewood Cliffs, NJ, Prentice-Hall.

ENDNOTES

1 The different approaches are sometimes referred as quantitative and qualitative evaluation. However we avoid such a distinction here. Quantitative methods may be use in phenomenological approaches and qualitative methods may be used in positivist approaches.

2 The phenomenological approach may also be referred to as a 'Constructivist' approach (see Easterby-Smith, 1994; p.23).

3 Formative reviews were learning reviews held every two weeks, using learning logs and stories which were posted on a secure web location so that the evaluator could access such data.

4 Anecdotal evidence suggests that participants while recognising the need to evaluate would rather go home, especially where activities have been completed off-site and participants become 'demob-happy'.

5 The repertory grid is a multi-purpose technique based on Personal Construct psychology. The technique can be used to gather data about a manager's personal meanings in relation to a particular issue and aspects of that issue. In MD, a grid could be used to evaluate attitudes towards activities, situations and people and how these might change during MD.

6 The Kirkpatrick model has been subjected to considerable criticism – see Tamkin *et al* (2002).

7 Some systems approaches do claim to be able to cope with the complexity of human activity. See Gold (2001) for an examination of 'soft systems methodology' in management learning and the Systems Dynamics Society at http://www.albany.edu/cpr/sds/

8 'Narrative' is a broader term covering a wide variety of forms such as myths, fables, tragedy, painting, pantomimes . . . as well as stories. See Gabriel (2000).

9 Sometimes called the transfer of training, since it is off-the-job programmes which suffer most from lack of transfer.

10 Research by Gist *et al* (1990) suggested that 'self management' skills were more effective in transfer for complex work than 'goal-setting'.

Helpers in management development

CHAPTER 9

Chapter outline

LEARNING OUTCOMES

After studying this chapter, you should be able to understand, explain, analyse and evaluate:

- **the full range of potential help for managers**
- **differences in what may be offered by different kinds of helper**
- **how help might be offered effectively**
- **how relationships can be systematised but always remain highly personal**
- **actions necessary for self and others.**

INTRODUCTION

Until the early 1990s it was often assumed that the prime responsibility for ensuring that managers developed lay with the managers themselves. However, partly as a result of interest in the importance of informal learning and the ideas relating to situated learning, there has been growing attention paid to the social context of learning and the role of others in encouraging, delivering and monitoring MD both formally and informally. Others can be particularly significant in helping the conversion of Type 1 experiences into Type 2 and Type 3 experiences. Like all opportunities in MD, though, the offer of help, requests for help and the ways in which these are received are substantially affected by personal feelings, present and past relationships, managerial styles and learning orientations. Further, organisational culture, especially in its attitude to mistakes, affects both where the help is offered and the perceptions of it on the part of helpers and learners. As we have indicated earlier, the effect of power may indicate to managers exactly how much or how little help they can expect in MD and the limits on learning. National culture, ethnicity or gender can also affect both the 'what' and the 'how' of helping relationships. Then there is the issue of how helpful the help is – help is defined as such by the person receiving the help, not by the person offering it. In general, the success of most relationships is improved when the participants in the relationship recognise that learning is reciprocal and the effectiveness of help is improved by the adoption of learning structures and disciplines, especially in an understanding of the learning process and specific objectives within the helping relationship

Table 16 *The range of potential helpers in MD*

On the job	Off the job
■ direct manager	■ tutors/trainers/facilitators
■ manager's manager	■ consultants
■ colleagues/peers	■ friends
■ direct reports	■ partner
■ mentors	■ participants on events
■ clients	■ participants in professional activities
■ internal advisers	■ participants in voluntary activities
■ external advisers	
■ management development committee	

Source: adapted from Mumford (1997)

THE RANGE OF POTENTIAL HELPERS

There is an extensive range of people who can provide help to the learning manager. Often such help is provided within formal processes or Type 3 MD, such as assessing needs, creating and reviewing personal development plans and attending MD events. But help may be less formal in processes such as mentoring, which can often become a Type 2 activity in supporting the integration of work-based learning. In particular, helpers can be very influential in providing support for the transfer of learning and overcoming both internal and external barriers to learning (see Chapter 6). The range of potential helpers is set out in Table 16.

As we have indicated throughout this book, management work is characterised by frequent and ongoing interactions with others. It was Kotter (1982) who noted that managers get their work done by building networks involving others and spending time within relationships. The value of relationships with others has been increasingly recognised as a form of 'social capital', defined by Nahapiet and Ghoshal (1998; p.243) as the

> **sum of actual and potential resources embedded within, available through and derived from the network of relationships possessed by an individual or social unit.**

This view of relationship development highlights the importance of investing time in building trust and respect with others whose help can then be called upon when needed. It also focuses attention on relationships and interactions as learning opportunities for Type 2 MD, as a form of social capital development (Tymon and Stumpf, 2003).

WEB LINKS

Find out more about social capital at
http://www.worldbank.org/poverty/scapital/whatsc.htm
A key writer is Robert Putnam at Harvard University and you can read a paper by him at
http://www.apsanet.org/PS/dec95/putnam.cfm

REFLECT – CONCLUDE – PLAN 1

- Who have been the helpers in your learning and development?
- What do you need to do develop your social capital?
- How can you help others develop theirs?

THE DIRECT MANAGER

For a long time formal MD schemes or policies identified line managers as being 'responsible for developing their subordinates'. This was primarily to be achieved by appraising the performance of their subordinates, thereby identifying what were often referred to as 'training needs', although as we suggested in Chapter 4, there was a danger that this process would become little more than a ritual, and that the real decisions about MD would take place elsewhere. London (1986) identified the 'boss' as the controller of important situational factors that affect career development for managers and opportunities to advance. He found that there were variations in whether managers were treated as a person to meet current needs or as a resource for the future.

Responsibilities

The recognition that individuals could and should be given significant responsibility for their own development led to a reassessment of the role of the manager towards facilitating the development of others rather than always proposing or providing development in an authoritarian way. Moreover, the responsibility of the line manager was now seen not to be a rather distant process of diagnosing needs and then asking someone else to meet them, but one in which line managers took personal action to facilitate the development of subordinates. This led, first, to the identification of coaching as a desirable on-the-job process, followed by an increasing recognition of the general availability of learning opportunities on the job. Then ideas about the 'learning organisation' identified more learning-related activities.

Organisations are at different levels of recognition and action in terms of what they expect of line managers in developing others. Some still give exclusive attention through formal processes of development, through structured MD systems and procedures, organised through human resource or management development specialists. Others try to influence the use of learning opportunities on the job, integrating formal and informal development. The line manager has the potential to convert the cliché about learning from experience into a more effective development process. But the central characteristic of the role of line managers as a method of MD will increasingly be based on the recognition that development is drawn from tasks, highlighting the importance of coaching (see below). The line manager is also influential in the learning of new managers once they are in post. Watson and Harris (1999) found that 'being thrown in at the deep end' was the main learning experience, combined with watching others as role models. The process was 'slow, often painful' (p.107), typical of Type 1 MD.

An effective MD process not only encourages direct managers to take up their formal managerial responsibility in the Type 3 mode, but would also encourage them to improve the contribution they make in their day-to-day informal relationships. Processes necessary for converting the direct manager's contribution from Type 1 to Type 2 are shown in Table 17.

Table 17 *The direct manager's contribution to MD*

Within a formal system of development (Type 3)	Within the direct managerial context (Type 2)
■ appraising performance ■ appraising potential ■ analysing development needs and goals ■ recognising opportunities ■ facilitating those opportunities ■ giving learning a priority	■ using management activities as learning ■ establishing learning goals ■ accepting risks in subordinate performance ■ monitoring learning achievement ■ providing feedback on performance ■ acting as a model of managerial behaviour ■ acting as a model of learning behaviour ■ using learning preferences ■ offering help ■ coaching directly

Reasons a line manager may have for choosing to engage in direct development processes with someone else may correspond, more or less strongly, to the following situations and ideas:

- Improving performance is necessary to overcome problems, to meet the needs of the organisation.
- Improving the performance of an individual would reflect favourably on the manager's own managerial ability.
- Satisfaction would be derived directly from helping someone to grow.
- The manager's own skills, knowledge and insights would be developed as a result of discussions with the individual.
- The manager would be meeting the requirements of the organisation which are to the effect that direct involvement in development activities with subordinates is a 'good thing' and is a measure of perceived managerial effectiveness within the organisation.
- Developing the skills of a subordinate can help to take problems off the manager's desk.
- This in turn affords more space for the manager to do other things.

The least satisfactory reason for line managers to offer help on learning is that a policy, system, form or workbook requires them to undertake the task. If the only reason line managers have for undertaking development is to satisfy the system, it is likely to be the system that will be satisfied, not the potential learners.

An example of the direct manager's large-scale provision of learning opportunities can be seen in the history of one of the biggest and most successful companies in the United States, GE. Jack Welch describes (2001) both the way in which he was developed in order to become chief executive officer, and the process he used for developing subordinates through a specific programme to succeed him. Although there were differences in what happened for him and what he provided for others, essentially the point worth emphasising here is the personal involvement of the two chief executive officers, and their focus on providing different kinds of learning opportunity to stretch and test out their potential successors.

The collective of managers, and particularly the board of directors, has the responsibility for actually determining the nature of MD in their organisation. Their responsibility for the total system – again usually seen purely in terms of the formal processes set up for the organisation as a whole – is also important, although different in kind from that discussed so far. The general rather than personal involvement of the direct manager in the total system will include:

- helping to determine the formal MD system, and perhaps contributing to a written policy
- giving evidence of the priority attached to MD by allocating resources, participating in decision-making meetings and courses
- giving personal evidence of interest by calling for reports on what has been done and evaluating results, by discussing development issues with managers at various levels on both a formal and an informal basis, by making achieved development of direct reports one of the criteria for selection for promotion.

Honey and Mumford (1995) have identified four roles for direct managers. They focus on the specific actions which direct managers must undertake:

- *role model* – explicitly demonstrating through behaviour and actions an enthusiasm for learning and development
- *provider* – consciously and generously providing learning and/or development opportunities for others, and active support/encouragement whenever the opportunities are taken up
- *systems provider* – building learning into the system so that it is integrated with normal work processes and is firmly on the conscious agenda
- *champion* – promoting the importance of learning for other parts of the organisation and the organisation as a whole.

REFLECT – CONCLUDE – PLAN 2

- How clear do you think managers in your organisation are about how they can help others to learn?
- Does your understanding need to be improved?
- How might this be done?

Coaching

Coaching is now recognised as a crucial means to achieve results in the context of rapid change (Parsloe, 1999). Impetus was provided when coaching was transferred from the sporting field with the aim of improving performance (Evered and Selmen, 1989). During the 1970s and 1980s coaching also focused on employee development as part of a general movement to increase management responsibility for learning and development at work.[1]

Megginson and Boydell (1979; p.5) defined coaching as

> **A process in which a manager, through direct discussion and guided activity, helps a colleague to solve a problem, or to do a task better than would otherwise have been the case.**

This definition remains useful because:

- it refers to guided activity
- it is aimed at solving a problem
- it talks about colleagues, with the useful indication that the manager can be working with peers as well as with direct reports
- it helps to distinguish coaching from counselling.

The weakness of the definition is that it refers only to managers – but coaching can be carried out by a wide variety of people. It also does not give sufficient attention to the development part of the equation. If the meaning of coaching is confined to performance, there is the tricky problem of a manager's accountability for the work of staff, which may pose a dilemma for a manager as a coach (Phillips, 1995). There is significant potential for managers to retreat to task focus, with the possibility of tension if coaching becomes confused with performance assessment for performance management. When it is done well, coaching is a powerful and very effective method of developing managers. Unfortunately, it is not always done well (see Berglas, 2002).

While formal training in coaching can help, one problem that arises is that courses and books tend to emphasise the creation of special coaching sessions in which a problem is clearly identified, time is set aside, manager and colleagues sit down and discuss objectives, plan their session and conduct themselves in an effective interactive way. Coaching experiences are likely to be nothing like this. Problems arise and are tackled there and then. A direct report brings a problem to the manager: help and decision is required *now* – not through a planned session two or three weeks ahead. People such as mentors, consultants, advisers provide effective structured help on coaching, and it may be that in these different roles effective coaching is more likely to take place. Particularly, they are more likely to fit into the conventional wisdom of human resource specialists about what 'good' coaching would be like. Essentially, they tend to emphasise the virtues of non-directive coaching.

Directive forms of coaching tend to emphasise explicit guidance – instruction on how to do something. Although managers certainly have often adopted too readily the directive approach, it is not always entirely inappropriate. The situation may require, or the absolute level of past experience and knowledge may indicate, that the directive approach is in fact the right one. From the point of view of coaching as a learning method rather than an immediate manager requirement, the non-directive approach will often provide a fuller learning experience for both coach and participant. The idea of the manager as facilitator and guide rather than instructor will usually suit the values of management developers – but those values are not necessarily those of the managers.

To a considerable extent the focus of coaching can differ between:

- problem management
- performance improvement
- personal growth
- career development.

In the first two cases coaching arises naturally in a Type 1 mode of learning. In fact, probably neither coach nor the recipient would actually describe them as coaching – they just see them as work-centred problem-solving, although this can be adapted to Type 2 MD. Type 2 or Type 3 coaching might have different purposes for the coach and for the learner – especially where this is created through a personal development plan.

Coaching skills and characteristics

Books and articles on coaching present lists of skills and behaviours required which have a great deal in common. Useful though these are, at least at the level of improving an understanding of what is involved, there is little research evidence on how successful courses on coaching skills are (although that comment could be applied to a lot of skills courses). The lists do not typically include skills related to designing the coaching experience as a learning event, and the processes of learning from it. Emphasis on listening skills is appropriate – not least because it may introduce some coaches to the idea of non-directive coaching. The skills involved in active listening and the provision and receipt of feedback are desirable priority items. Mumford (1993) emphasises the non-directive skills of effective coaching and lists them:

- active listening
- reflective listening
- open listening
- drawing out
- recognising and revealing feelings
- giving feedback
- agreeing goals
- deciding which coaching style to use – questioning for reflection, questioning for challenge, instruction
- adapting to preferred learning styles.

In recent years, the pressures of change have lent urgency to replacing a command-and-control approach to management with coaching. This has been the vision at Vodafone, where coaching is seen as a way to change values and a channel of communication (Eaton and Brown, 2002). The coaching programme included skills training, follow-up coaching and review seminars with action plans to ensure transfer of learning. A further stimulus for managers to become coaches is part of the drive towards making managers responsible for the development of their staff, again in contrast with models that emphasise control and task performance. Ellinger and Bostrom (1999) found that the transition from manager to coach is not easy and requires time and encouragement to practise new behaviours.

Counselling

In many MD systems the processes of coaching and counselling are confused – probably because they are, in fact, difficult to separate. Counselling may clearly be taking place when a manager discusses issues of domestic significance and difficulty with a subordinate. It may still be counselling when the discussion centres on problems with personal relationships at work. But is it counselling or coaching if the discussion focuses on how the subordinate's aggressive instincts towards the head of another department can be reduced to a level acceptable to both sides? A discussion about an individual's career may also be counselling. The extremes of coaching and counselling are distinguishable, yet both of them require rather similar skills in areas of common interest. Some managers will be able to make direct statements under either coaching or counselling umbrellas, while being unable to carry out a gentler non-evaluative process under either heading.

Indeed, the whole problem of these distinct MD processes of coaching and counselling is that managers do not readily key in to them. They are seen as formal MD processes which have no direct association with what happens in real life. Many managers do not see themselves as coaches or counsellors, feeding the general pessimism towards the adoption of high-performance HR practices (Taylor, 2003). They deal with business issues, with management problems and management activities. They provide guidance and help on these. If MD advisers choose to call the process by which the help is offered 'coaching', well – with a politely resigned shrug – so be it. When one of the authors worked with a manager on the 'coaching' aspects of his normal behaviour, the light dawned – 'You mean, if I am helping somebody with a problem, without telling him what the answer is, that's coaching. If you want to call it that, OK. I call it helping him with his problem.' Again formal MD processes are seen by the managers they are intended to help as separate from the world in which they live.

WEB LINKS

The website of the International Coaching Federation can be found at http://www.coachfederation.org/
The Coaching and Mentoring Network in the UK has a resource centre at http://www.coachingnetwork.org.uk/ResourceCentre.htm

OTHER MANAGERS AND STAFF

Other managers can help to set the priority given to MD. For example, a manager's manager is normally required to review appraisal forms and probably also any development plans associated with that review. This ought to involve proper discussion with the direct manager and the addition of ideas not only about an individual's performance but about the appropriate development actions to take. This 'one-level-up' manager might be involved personally with providing opportunities – for example, attending meetings and discussing what has happened at them.

Mentoring

The historical origins of mentoring can be found in the Greek myth of the entrustment of Telemachus, the son of Homer's Odysseus, to the wise Mentor.[2] Since then mentoring has been a development process in many walks of life and continues to be so. However, mentoring as an MD intervention came to prominence in the late 1970s. For example, Roche (1979) found 66 per cent of respondents in a study of US managers had had a mentor or someone who took an interest in their career and provided guidance and sponsorship. Such studies revealed and named a helping process as mentoring, a process that is most likely to have existed in organisations and elsewhere for many years – an archetypal Type 1 MD but with elements of Type 2. However, since the late 1970s there has been growing interest in mentoring, again as part of the drive towards making managers responsible for the development of their staff. The result is a growing plethora of ideas, models and prescriptions relating to mentoring in organisations.[3]

There are some issues of definition, and of what is involved, which are very important in establishing mutual expectations. Here are two definitions:

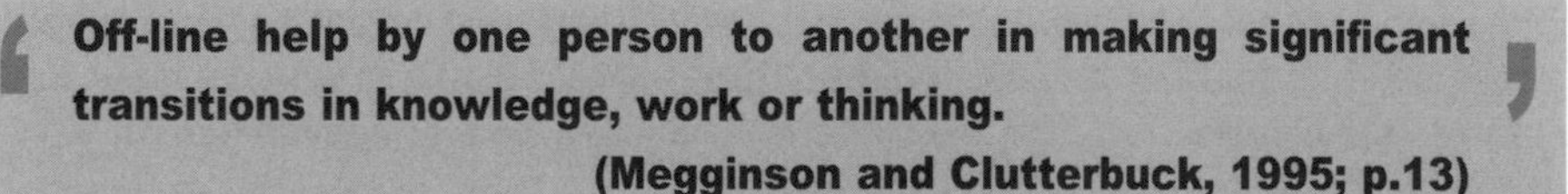

'Off-line help by one person to another in making significant transitions in knowledge, work or thinking.'
(Megginson and Clutterbuck, 1995; p.13)

> **A protected relationship in which experimentation, exchange and learning can occur and skills, knowledge and insight can be developed.**
>
> **(Mumford, 1993; p.103)**

There are important variations of understanding contained within these definitions (and of course there are many others in the considerable library of books on mentoring). From an MD point of view, Mumford's definition has the virtue of identifying that the relationship is about learning, and about particular kinds of learning.

The second major issue is the need for clarity on the difference between being a mentor and being a direct manager. Much of the American literature has introduced confusion, no doubt repeating what occurs in practice, by including the activities of direct managers operating in a particular style which they then describe as mentoring. There is a crucial difference between the kind of relationship which occurs with an 'off-line' mentor and that which exists with an individual to whom you are directly responsible for managerial performance. That is why Mumford describes it as a 'protected relationship' – the mentor's responsibility is for development, the direct manager's responsibility is for managerial performance, although this may also include coaching. By contrast with coaching, a mentor:

- is able to take a long-term view
- can be more concerned with issues such as career and personal growth
- is more interested in significant and broad issues of performance rather than detail
- takes an interest in the general direction of a person's life
- is able to offer both distance, independence and perhaps greater clarity of thought about issues.

Megginson and Clutterbuck (1995) in their research found four roles for the mentor:

- performance improver
- career developer
- counsellor
- sharer of knowledge.

This seems to confuse purpose (the first two) and process but supports Kram's (1983) distinction between career and psycho-social development within a mentor relationship. The career function includes sponsorship, coaching, protection, exposure-and-visibility and challenging work. Psycho-social functions include role modelling, counselling and friendship. One obvious group for mentoring are graduates and employees identified to have talent. This was the purpose of a mentoring programme at Halifax plc (HBOS) in the UK (Garvey and Galloway, 2002). The programme was designed to help participants make the transition to manager. Volunteer mentors were sought and asked to complete a questionnaire providing information on functional experience and perceptions of mentoring style. The information was used to match mentors and mentees.[4] Workshops were held for both groups before the process began. What was particularly interesting was that evaluation showed that the process often started off oriented towards content and purpose but became more process- and development-oriented over time.

The organisation, the mentor, the mentee and the mentee's manager may all have different requirements or understandings about what the purpose of a mentoring relationship should be (Mumford, 1997). However, mentoring is most suitable:

- for escaping from sole dependence on the boss as developer
- for providing alternative views about managerial problems, structure, objectives and strategy
- for feedback on the mentee's reported or observed behaviour
- for providing a role model of effective managerial and learning behaviour
- especially for development purposes grounded in managerial reality.

While mentoring in organisations was under-researched and the overall benefits little appreciated, as a Type 1 activity it occurred informally and without direction or planning. Mentors in a Type 1 role have often been door-openers – they try to ensure that their mentees are considered for important jobs, assignments, projects. They ensure that those who make decisions about people know what their mentee has achieved and why that level of achievement is noteworthy. The door-opening role is more that of a sponsor than of someone who provides direct help in learning. Such a process could easily lend itself to advancing the power-base of both the mentor and mentee. A critical view of mentoring emphasises the way a mentee is required to adopt the values and norms of a dominant group within an organisation (Townley, 1984). Mentoring could also have a discriminatory impact on potential mentees who might not be able to find a compatible mentor – eg females, members of ethnic minorities, etc (Hunt and Michael, 1983). Once interest grew and research findings appeared, there was an effort to make mentoring a Type 3 development process, making the relationship explicit and turning it from an informal into a formal MD process. With formality came a degree of specification of roles and skills. Thus in the early 1990s Gibb (1994) was able to show how formal schemes might be defined by either:

- a competence approach – expressed as skills and activities in checklists, usually prescriptive

or

- a typology approach – types of mentoring such as 'instrumental', 'developmental', 'professional', involving roles left for negotiation.

One of the interesting findings was that these differences affected the degree of structure and perceptions of value. Gibb presented a continuum between systematic mentoring and process mentoring. The former is highly structured with pre-set requirements. Such schemes were seen as valuable but not important developmentally. By contrast, process mentoring is more concerned with the development of the relationship and the learning within the relationship, which may become the main purpose. This presents organisations with something of a dilemma – how far should mentoring be formally structured, or should the participants themselves be responsible for the process? It is a tension which is unlikely to be fully reconciled. As Gibb (2003; p.48) more recently suggests, 'The theory and practice of mentoring . . . evolves with blooms and with thorns', with different views on how far it is possible to specify and institutionalise its practice.

Change seems to be the main driving force, often connected to restructuring to provide greater autonomy and teamworking. Garvey (1999)[5] found that there was increased attention to mentors as agents of change.

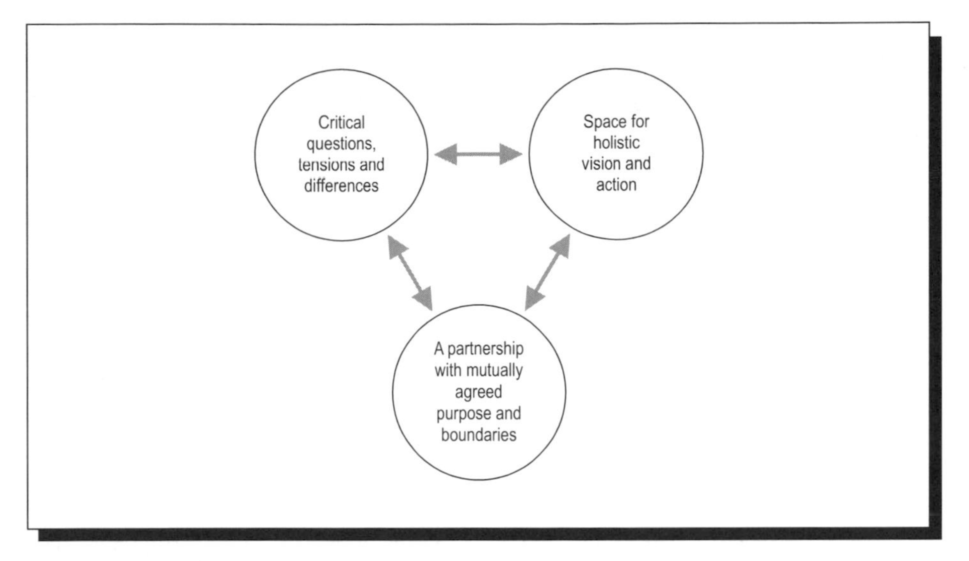

Figure 34 *A model of the mentoring process*
Source: Borredon (2000)

Mentoring is a highly personal relationship, and problematic as it might be, it forms the focus of considerable research. There are many case study examples, sometimes produced in collaboration with participants (Clutterbuck and Megginson, 1999), and large-scale surveys that attempt to measure effectiveness and satisfaction (Ragins *et al*, 2000). Data from research allows a degree of model-building seeking to explain the key variables of a mentoring relationship. For example, Borredon (2000) produced a simple model of the mentoring process, as shown in Figure 34.

The model highlights the importance of 'space', where mentors use critical questions to stimulate reflection by the mentee. The result is learning which is shared and becomes mutual for the mentor as well as the mentee. However, this does require mentors who are reflective and have an understanding of the different learning processes and the differing learning preferences of individuals to make the interaction a Type 2 MD event.

Hale's (2000) research was concerned with the match between mentors and mentees. He found that where the aim was to speed the development of the relationship, the emphasis had to be on matching similarities of interests, professional background and function. However, if the aim was to optimise learning, there had to be differences in behaviour and learning styles, strengths and development needs, but there had also to be similarities in terms of values, beliefs and life-goals.

REFLECT – CONCLUDE – PLAN 3

- What is the approach to mentoring in your organisation?
- How far is the process pre-specified? Are mentors and mentees prepared for a learning approach to their interactions?
- What can you do to learn more from mentoring?

WEB LINKS

The European Mentoring and Coaching Council's website is located at
http://www.emccouncil.org/
A mentoring for change site can be found at
http://www.mentoringforchange.co.uk/

Colleagues

Kram and Isabella (1983) found that relationships between colleagues or peers offered an alternative to traditional mentoring. Such relationships were more likely to be mutual, both parties giving and receiving emotional and information support which help in career progress. In most cases the help offered by colleagues is not formal MD but arises from normal managerial activities – shared problem-solving, discussion of a difficult forthcoming meeting, a chat about a difficult colleague, a review of organisational necessities and political requirements. It is only afterwards that they recognise that they have learned something from a colleague. Peters (1996) shows how National Semiconductors in the USA incorporated peer coaching to reinforce feedback received from 360-degree assessment.

Another form of learning from colleagues is that of modelling or observation. This can be either positive or negative: a manager may base future behaviour on what he or she admires in a successful colleague, or on the opposite of an unsuccessful process. Managers can pick up useful behaviour even from people they do not like and/or admire.

Perhaps the most powerful aspect of a learning relationship with colleagues revolves around the kind of feedback one offers another. Managers often have quite incorrect ideas about how they achieve what they do. Accurate feedback, particularly if presented in a helpful rather than a negative way, is the first stage of learning and a necessary precursor to learning to do things better. Colleagues may agree to become learning partners, forming a relationship explicitly to support each other in Type 2 MD. Figure 35 shows a process used with peers in an MD programme with managers in a professional organisation.

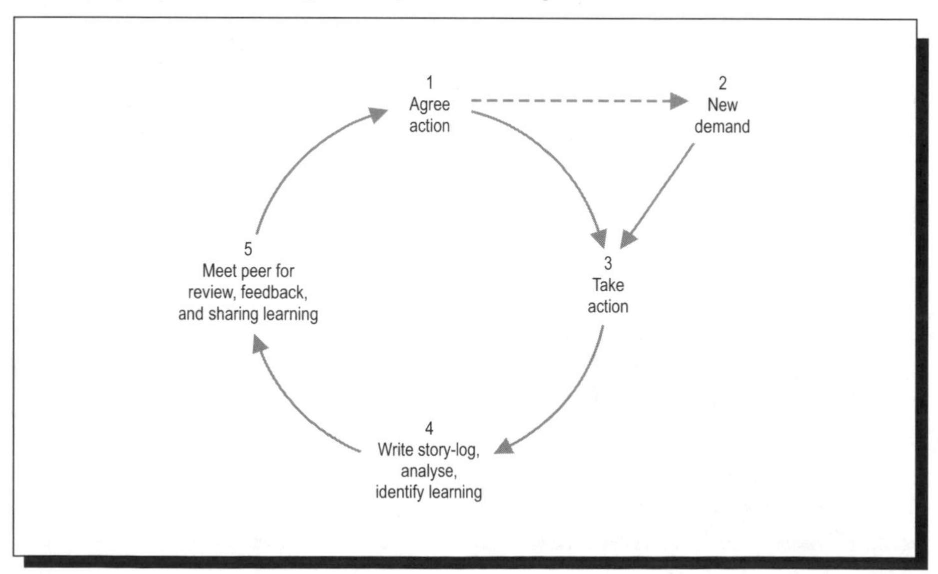

Figure 35 *A learning partner process*

Managers met every two weeks to review and share learning and receive feedback. Actions were agreed but it was accepted that action plans could be changed as new demands were made. The focus of the partnership was to hold a learning conversation with a trusted colleague, having already reflected on key actions by the use of a story-based learning log.

Most managers will also be member of a group or team. We referred to these as constituting a potential learning opportunity in Chapter 7.

WEB LINK

http://www.peer.ca/coachingnews.html
– this is a US site but provides interesting links to resources relating to peer coaching, mentoring and networking.

Direct reports

The growing use of 360-degree assessment including upward appraisal (see Chapter 4) brings about the possibility of using the feedback of direct reports and others for help. Based on the principle that others can see aspects of a manager, especially performance, which the manager cannot see, staff can provide important information.

Internal professional advisers

Personnel specialists, MD advisers, management trainers and human resource specialists of a variety of titles are covered in this section. In larger organisations, the HR director ought to direct the development processes and ensure that any separate specialisms are co-ordinated. This responsibility is not always met, especially where training and development are compartmentalised. The different roles depend on the size of the organisation and more particularly on the amount of resources it is prepared to put into this whole field.

In some cases internal professionals will act as counsellors or advisers to managers on problems concerned with effective performance. So an MD adviser might help set up a two-day event 'Problems and opportunities to 2005', or 'Clarifying relationships between our divisions'. The adviser might give individual advice on development in terms of a total career plan or in terms of advice on a particular need or a developmental process.

In some organisations, an MD Committee is concerned with the organisation of formal opportunities through succession planning, job rotation and nominations for courses. Such a committee can:

- generate interest amongst senior management about MD
- give symbolic significance to MD
- act as the focus for decision-making
- provide an opportunity to generate a consensus decision or corporate view.

While such committees fill a very necessary place in the formal structure, they are much less likely to discuss the kind of help that might be available for individual managers, and most are stuck at the stage of defining opportunities. They are unlikely to enable managers to take advantage of those opportunities to achieve learning.

THE WIDER NETWORK

Beyond a manager's immediate context, help for MD can be available by establishing relationships with others. This is networking, defined by Orpen (1996; p.245) as the process of

> **building up and maintaining a set of informal, co-operative relationships with persons other than the manager's immediate superior and subordinates in the expectation that such relationships will help or assist the manager to perform his or her job better**

– and, we would add, to support the learning process. Every activity undertaken by a manager and every interaction (virtually or otherwise) carries the potential for learning and a widening of the network. Managers who make use of their network are referred to as 'high-dependency managers' (p.246), and it is suggested that such managers, by engaging in networking behaviour, are more likely to advance their careers – so long as such behaviour leads to support and co-operation from the network to perform more effectively. There is also increasing interest in networking behaviour in the construction of new knowledge and ideas. Knowledge-based organisations require the continuous production of knowledge to prosper. Managers are often at the hub of different processes and cross-functional/organisational teams, both inside and beyond organisation boundaries. By networking, shared understandings can be co-ordinated into new knowledge (Swan *et al*, 1999).

Clients and customers

The increasing growth of e-business and customer choice highlights the importance of customer relationship management and the use of feedback for learning. It is not always understood that any interaction in providing a product or a service can also be a learning situation. It can be primarily about knowledge – but it might be about the skills observed in those with whom the interaction is taking place. This is of course usually an implicit learning process, not one in which the client or customer is actually asked to structure and provide a learning experience within a work situation – but it could and should be.

External professional advisers and consultants

One of the reasons for going outside the organisation for help was indicated earlier. The greater the level of intimacy of the development counselling and advice, the greater the likely worry of managers about the terms under which it is offered. While the internal adviser potentially has the great advantage of knowing much more about the reality of the organisation, the problem of confidentiality inevitably arises. Can a manager really get highly personal advice from an internal adviser and trust that details of her or his thoughts and problems are not going to be passed on or used internally? Or the organisation might wish to test its internal knowledge against the wider view.

One trend in recent years is for managers – usually those working at more senior levels in organisations – to seek help from an external consultant, acting as an 'executive coach' (Hall *et al*, 1999). Executive coaching (EC)[6] represents the latest variation in the coaching movement, and the key idea is that even though he or she has reached the top, a senior manager's performance, like that of a sporting champion, can be sharpened up and improved. In the UK, Carter (2001) suggests that EC has arisen through the failure of more traditional sources of MD to provide feedback for senior managers who often have to operate in lonely and isolated contexts. There has been a phenomenal growth in EC – although, like many other notions metaphorically transferred from other fields, EC has been subjected to a great deal of confusion and, some would say, mystery (Carter, 2001). Perhaps this is part of the reason for a daily charge of £3,300. Research suggests that EC can lead to more specific goals and better ratings from staff (Smither *et al*, 2003).

WEB LINK

Learn more about executive coaching at
http://www.theexecutivecoachingforum.com/
and
http://www.execcoach.net/

Tutors/trainers/facilitators

Individuals in these roles have a clear formal responsibility for aiding development, as compared for example with a manager for whom this is an additional and potentially very secondary purpose in his or her life. The extent to which tutors/trainers/facilitators actually do help development depends on:

- the needs, interests and preferred learning style of the manager being developed
- the extent to which the tutor's style and abilities relate to those needs
- the extent to which the content and the process being delivered by the tutor are appropriate to the individual's needs
- the values held by the tutor, and how those values relate to those of the manager under development
- the appropriateness of the method being used.

Participants in training, professional meetings, voluntary activities

There is a significant difference between the first of these – participants on a training or education course – and the latter two. In the former case, particularly if the institution providing the course uses learning theory and especially the concept of learning to learn advanced earlier in this book, learning from and with each other becomes a conscious and structured part of the programme. It is a specific element in Action Learning, for example. While individuals often talk about what they have learned from others on courses, it is sadly the case that in few instances the course has been designed explicitly to achieve this. It is something which for both the runners of the course and for the participants is 'expected to happen', rather than being the focus of particular information, discussion or even specific sessions. Courses often get credit for their success in providing opportunities to exchange information and ideas – but they ought to be much more effective than most of them are at ensuring that it happens.

The second and third categories of participation, on professional activities such as attending meetings of the CIPD or the Chartered Management Institute, or voluntary activities such as chairing a committee for a sports club, or leading a charitable appeal, do not provide 'helpers' in the same way. They are more people who provide opportunities for others to learn by providing their knowledge or exemplifying skills. Increasingly, however, professional associations are incorporating the idea of the 'reflective practitioner' into their accreditation frameworks.[7]

Domestic partners

There has been a considerable change in the way partners discuss careers and career moves. The advent of dual-career families is one obvious cause, but in general the trend has been towards a less clear-cut, less autocratic process of decision-making on the managerial career of one partner.

Jack Welch (2001) gives an unusual illustration – he improved his own golf by teaching his wife how to play.

Most partners carry out a range of roles as listener, prompter, or commentator. Whereas some managers want to leave their work at the office and not discuss it at home, others find it at least therapeutic and sometimes positively helpful to do so. For managers in small business, domestic partners and the family as a whole are often a key influence on learning, although usually as part of a problem-solving process (Gibb, 1997).[8]

Friends

Friends outside work sometimes carry out the role of the mentor. Like the partners in a marriage they can provide helpful guidance on questions about career or about particular problems. Just as managers often look for someone at work who can act as a sounding-board, so they may look for someone outside who carries out a similar function. Because of increasing loneliness as you move up the managerial hierarchy, the availability of such a person can be very important. More advice ought to be provided on how to identify and use potentially helpful friends. They can give advice unsullied by direct managerial responsibility or competitiveness – offering a friendly ear. Many managers do use friends in this way, but informally and accidentally, perhaps as a result of a meeting on a course. Useful though those accidental processes are, they could be improved through Type 2 and Type 3 learning – someone outside the organisation might help with identifying or meeting development needs.

REFLECT – CONCLUDE – PLAN 4

- Which part of your wider network has provided the most help for you on learning? Which has provided the least help for you on learning?
- Why was the help useful, or not useful? What conclusions do you draw?
- In what ways could you change for the better your own use of 'helpers'? In what ways might you help others provide more effective help?

The relationship between the person willing to receive help and the person offering it is so important that it is worth repeating an earlier point:

- Help is defined by the person receiving help, not by the person offering it.

One of the oldest clichés is particularly appropriate here: 'You can take a horse to water, but you cannot make it drink.' Ideally, the person offering help tailors both the content of the help and the way in which it is offered to the needs of the individual recipient, and into the style of help which will facilitate the individual's acceptance of that help. Unfortunately, this means, however, that some individuals are asked in principle to behave towards a learner in a way that is quite outside their normal behaviour. Understandably, they do not always manage this. More manage with a reasonable degree of effectiveness if they are given specific behaviour-focused training.

GROUP ACTIVITY

- Form a group of four.
- Each person should take a plain sheet of A3 paper and, placing themselves one at a time in the centre, identify who are the key influences on how they perform their work. Consider influences both inside and outside the organisation.
- Now identify to what extent such influence have been helpful or a hindrance to learning and development.
- Provide an explanation for your classification.
- Share your findings and prepare a presentation on help and hindrance in learning at work.

The Campaign for Learning's website may be of interest at http://www.campaign-for-learning.org.uk/

REFERENCES

BERGLAS, S. (2002) 'Dangers of executive coaching', *Harvard Business Review*, June; pp.87–92.

BORREDON, L. (2000) 'Capturing essential meaning', *Career Development International*, Vol. 5, Nos 4/5; pp.194–201.

CARTER, A. (2001) *Executive Coaching: Inspiring performance at work*. Report 379. Sussex, Institute of Employment Studies.

EATON, J. and BROWN, D. (2002) 'Coaching for a change with Vodafone', *Career Development International*, Vol. 7, No. 5; pp.284–287.

ELLINGER, A. and BOSTROM, R. P. (1999) 'Managerial coaching behaviors in learning organizations', *Journal of Management Development*, Vol. 18, No. 9; pp.752–771.

EVERED, R. D. and SELMAN, J. C. (1989) 'Coaching and the art of management', *Organizational Dynamics*, Autumn; pp.16–32.

CLUTTERBUCK, D. and MEGGINSON, D. (1999) *Mentoring Executives and Directors*. Oxford, Butterworth-Heinemann.

GARVEY, B. (1999) 'Mentoring and the changing paradigm', *Mentoring and Tutoring*, Vol. 7, No. 1; pp.41–53.

GARVEY, B. and GALLOWAY, K. (2002) 'Mentoring at the Halifax plc (HBOS) – a small beginning in a large organisation', *Career Development International*, Vol. 7, No. 5; pp.271–278.

GIBB, A. (1997) 'Small firms' training and competitiveness: building upon the small business as a learning organisation', *International Small Business Journal*, Vol. 15, No. 3; pp.13–29.

GIBB, S. (1994) 'Inside corporate mentoring schemes: the development of a conceptual framework', *Personnel Review*, Vol. 23, No. 3; pp.47–60.

GIBB, S. (2003) 'What do we talk about when we talk about mentoring? Blooms and thorns', *British Journal of Counselling and Guidance*, Vol. 31, No. 1; pp.39–49.

SUMMARY

- There is a significant role for others in providing help for MD but there are variations in how managers respond to help.
- The value of relationships with others has been increasingly recognised as a form of 'social capital', and managers are encouraged to engage in social capital development.
- Direct managers have a growing responsibility for MD, especially through coaching.
- Coaching is increasingly associated with attempts to change values and management priorities towards learning and development.
- Mentoring enables young managers to benefit from the experience and guidance of more senior managers.
- There are variations in both coaching and mentoring by which relationships are formed with peers for mutual benefit.
- Use of a wider network enables managers to draw on support for learning and to perform more effectively.

DISCUSSION QUESTIONS

1 How helpful are organisations in providing support for MD?

3 'Direct managers' accountability for the performance of managers is bound to conflict with their role as supporter of the managers' learning.' Discuss.

3 Is mentoring simply a way of socialising managers into the 'old boys' network'?

4 What do you see as the advantages and/or disadvantages of formal/informal mentoring?

5 What is the importance of feedback from customers in management development? How can such learning be optimised?

6 What are the key skills of the helper in management development? What are the key skills of the helped manager?

FURTHER READING

ALRED, G., GARVEY, B. and SMITH, R. (1998) 'Pas de deux – learning in conversation', *Career Development International*, Vol. 3, No. 7; pp.308–313.

HAYES, J. (1996) *Developing the Manager as a Helper*. London, Routledge.

HONEY, P. (1994) *One Hundred and One Ways to Develop Your People*. Maidenhead, Honey.

MACLENNAN, N. (1996) *Counselling for Managers*. Aldershot, Gower.

SCANDURA, T. A. (1998) 'Dysfunctional mentoring relationships and outcomes', *Journal of Management*, Vol. 24; pp.449–467.

WHITMORE, J. (1992) *Coaching for Performance*. London, Nicholas Brealey.

HALL, D. T., OTAZO, K. L. and HOLLENBECK, G. P. (1999) 'What really happens in executive coaching', *Organizational Dynamics*, Winter; pp.39–53.

HALE, R. (2000) 'To match or mis-match? The dynamics of mentoring as a route to personal and organisational learning', *Career Development International*, Vol. 5, Nos 4/5; pp.223–234.

HUNT, D. M. and MICHAEL, C. (1983) 'Mentorship: a career training and development tool', *Academy of Management Review*, Vol. 8, No. 3; pp.475–485.

HONEY, P. and MUMFORD, A. (1995) *Managing Your Learning Environment*. Maidenhead, Honey Publications.

KRAM, K. E. (1986) 'Phases of the mentor relationship', *Academy of Management Journal*, Vol. 26, No. 4; pp.608–625.

KRAM, K. E. and ISABELLA, L. A. (1985) 'Mentoring alternative: the role of peer relationships in career development', *Academy of Management Journal*, Vol. 28, No. 1; pp.110–132.

KOTTER, J. P. (1982) *The General Managers*. New York, Free Press.

LONDON, M. (1986) 'The boss's role in management development', *Journal of Management Development*, Vol. 5, No. 3; pp.25–34.

MEGGINSON, D. and BOYDELL, T. A. (1979) *Manager's Guide to Coaching*. London, Bacie.

MEGGINSON, D. and CLUTTERBUCK, D. (1995) *Mentoring In Action*. London, Kogan Page.

MUMFORD, A. (1993) *How Managers Can Develop Managers*. Aldershot, Gower.

MUMFORD, A. (1997) *How to Choose the Right Development Method*. Maidenhead, Honey Publications.

NAHAPIET, J. and GHOSHAL, S. (1998) 'Social capital, intellectual capital and the organizational advantage', *Academy of Management Review*, Vol. 23, No. 2; pp.242–266.

ORPEN, C. (1996) 'Dependency as a moderator of the effects of networking behavior on managerial success', *Journal of Psychology*, Vol. 130, No. 3; pp.245–248.

PARSLOE, E. (1999) *The Manager as Coach and Mentor*. London, CIPD.

PETERS, H. (1996) 'Peer coaching for executives', *Training and Development*, March; pp.39–42.

PHILLIPS, R. (1995) 'Coaching for higher performance', *Executive Development*, Vol. 8, No. 7; pp.5–7.

RAGINS, B. R., COTTON, J. L. and MILLER, J. S. (2000) 'Marginal mentoring: the effects of type of mentor, quality of relationship and program design on work and career attitudes', *Academy of Management Journal*, Vol. 43, No. 6; pp.1177–1194.

ROCHE, G. R. (1979) 'Much ado about mentors', *Harvard Business Review*, January/February; pp.14–28.

SMITHER, J., LONDON, M., FLAUTT, R., VARGAS, Y. and KUCINE, I. (2003) 'Can working with an executive coach improve multi-source feedback ratings over time? A quasi-experimental field study', *Personnel Psychology*, Vol. 56, No. 1; pp.23– 44.

TAYLOR, R. (2003) *Managing Workplace Change*. Swindon, ESRC.

TOWNLEY, B. (1994) *Reframing Human Resource Management: Power, ethics and the subject at work*. London, Sage.

TYMON, W. G. and STUMPF, S. A. (2003) 'Social capital in the success of knowledge workers', *Career Development International*, Vol. 8, No. 1; pp.12–20.

SWAN, J., NEWELL, S., SCARBROUGH, H. and HISLOP, D. (1999) 'Knowledge management and innovation: networks and networking', *Journal of Knowledge Management*, Vol. 3, No. 4; pp.262–275.

WATSON, T. and HARRIS, P. (1999) *The Emergent Manager*. London, Sage.

WELCH, J. (2001) *Jack: What I've Learned in Leading a Great Company and Great People*. London, Headline.

ENDNOTES

1 The more recent idea of 'executive coaching' is examined later in the chapter.

2 To add further confusion to the myth, the original Mentor was the female goddess Athene in disguise.

3 Mentoring as process of learning and development can be found in many areas of human activity other than organisations – eg teaching, and social and community work.

4 On the question of what the individual receiving help from a mentor should be called, 'mentee' seems to have won out over 'protégé'.

5 Others terms found by Garvey (1999) included 'godfather/mother' scheme and 'sponsorship'.

6 Executive coaching overlaps with other expensive forms of external help for senior managers such as personal coaching and personal mentoring. There is also a connection to career counselling (see Chapter 10).

7 The CIPD refers to the idea of the 'thinking performer'.

8 See also Chapter 11.

The future supply of managers

CHAPTER 10

Chapter outline

Introduction
Selecting managers
Careers for managers
Self-management of careers
Succession management
Summary

LEARNING OUTCOMES

After studying this chapter, you should be able to understand, explain, analyse and evaluate:

- **approaches to selecting managers**
- **how management careers are developed**
- **the importance of the self-management of careers**
- **the importance of succession planning.**

INTRODUCTION

In Chapter 2 we highlighted concerns at a macro level relating to the supply and quality of managers in the UK. It has been noted over a long period of time that managers in the UK tend to be under-qualified and receive low levels of qualifications (Johnson and Winterton, 1999). However, as acknowledged by Williams (2002), although most organisations are able to find recruits for management positions, that is crucially no guarantee of their quality. At the micro level, it is up to organisations to ensure that they have the right number of managers with the potential for high performance through MD. Evidence suggests that a positive psychological contract forms the basis for commitment and motivation (Guest *et al*, 1998) and that it is during times of selection that managers will form and reform their expectations and assess the organisation's offer. At different points in their lives, managers face selection processes. Thus, each time a manager moves to a new area of responsibility, the changed situation has to be seen as a new beginning to the relationship between the manager and his or her employer. Although employers have the power to select managers and set the conditions of employment, managers will also be assessing their employers and part of this assessment will relate to factors such as the potential for further promotion, the opportunities for training and development, and how they will continue to be supported in the management of their careers.

SELECTING MANAGERS

The availability of a management position provides a range of opportunities for both the organisation and potential recruits. A strategic view would suggest two key questions:

- Should the position be filled internally by developing current staff?
- Should the position be filled by seeking someone externally with the required profile of skills and attributes?

Filling a management vacancy by internal promotion of staff provides the need for, and justification of, MD and prevents managers from leaving through lack of opportunities (Holbeche, 1999). The importance of this 'grow-your-own' approach is highlighted by the survey of over 500 managers by Thomson *et al* (2001), according to which many managers spent most of their career in the same organisation. Findings from the same survey, however, indicated that nearly half the managers expected to stay less than five years, which suggests that organisations must find ways of retaining managers throughout their careers. There may be certain problems with internal recruitment, though, such as accusations of favouritism or the 'blue-eyed boy' syndrome. Further, while it may in the short term be more cost-effective to recruit internally, it may also lead to recruitment below the standard required.

The alternative of external recruitment allows an organisation to seek managers with particular skills and attributes that have not been developed internally, such as the formation and implementation of strategy and/or acting as a 'champion of change'. In addition, graduates are a key source of external recruits for the stock of future management.

Competences

An organisation's management competences (MC) framework, according to Whiddett and Hollyforde (1999), can be used to provide information in the assessment of applicants against the requirements of work, perhaps through assessment centres (ACs; see Chapter 3). The BBC provides a good example of how MC are being used strategically in recruitment. In 2003, after extensive consultation with staff as part of the 'One BBC' change programme, six core values (including 'Lead more, manage better') and 53 behaviours for managers and leaders were developed. These formed the basis of an MD programme for 7,000 managers over five years, but they will also form the basis of recruitment.[1] For external applicants, evidence suggests that ACs enhance the attraction of an organisation. It is also important for successful applicants to use the information gained from ACs as an input into discussions for further MD.

WEB LINKS

Some useful information on ACs can be obtained at http://www.jobsitc.co.uk/career/advice/assessment.html

Go to http://www.topjobs.co.uk/ase/asetjn8.htm for more information about psychometrics in assessment.

Selection for learning

Increasingly, managers may be required to undertake new responsibilities and learn new skills caused by changes in work requirements. During the 1980s and 1990s, for example, many organisations chose to reduce costs by adopting flexible working practices, often within projects such as business process re-engineering or Total Quality Management. One result, associated with delayering, was the emergence of flatter organisation structures with the consequence of fewer grades for managers to move into and a widening of responsibilities within grades. Managers in so-called 'lean' organisations were required to adopt styles of management which were suited to multi-skilled teams empowered to make key decisions (Holbeche, 1998). This had implications for career development (see below). In addition, it has meant that many managers are required to lead change in their areas of responsibility. As Doyle (2002) suggests managers have become change agents, although many may not have had previous experience of change management processes. Projects of change are excellent opportunities for MD but managers will need help to realise the learning potential of such projects. Doyle's research found that 'change competence' was recognised but seldom measured or used in selecting managers. Instead, there was an *ad hoc* approach which was subjective and posed a risk to both the individuals involved and the direction of the change project. Such findings would support taking a more strategic view by combining projects of change with MD – as, for example, can be found in some approaches to Action Learning (see Chapter 7).

CAREERS FOR MANAGERS

It was not so long ago that managers could apply a number of fairly reliable 'rules' in relation to their careers. Firstly, careers would follow a progressive path through a number of stages. Through selection, assessment and appropriate MD, a manager could move 'up the ladder', taking on roles of increasing responsibility and rank. Although not all managers could be sure of reaching the top, most managers and potential managers could expect some degree of certainty about how their careers would develop. It was within careers which provided a 'well-made road' (Sennett, 1998) that managers could reach their desires for status and fulfilment. Career and managerial identity were thus tightly linked and organisations were expected to support this link by providing a structure for career progression composed of plans for developing managers. Organisations could play a key role in how careers were managed. In recent years, however, there has been growing scepticism whether the rules to do with careers and the meanings of 'career management' continue to apply (CIPD, 2002).

The meanings of 'career'

Adamson *et al* (1998) have explored the roots of the term 'career' and its implications. They suggest that:

- 'Career' implies a route to be followed which has direction and purpose.
- There is movement over time which has order, logic and meaning between successive positions.
- In organisations, employers and employees can plan the logical progression through work-related events and experiences.
- Over the course of one's life, a career can pass through a number of phases or stages.

Models of career and development have matched such views. For example, Super (1957) suggested that careers were determined by a range of socio-economic factors, mental and

Table 18 *Super's stages of career choice*

Stage	Characteristics
Growth	Forming the self-concept, developing attitudes, needs, interests and abilities relating to work
Exploration	Trying things out through classes, work experience, hobbies. Beginning to consider work choice
Establishment	Building necessary skills. Stabilising through work experience, adjusting as required
Maintenance	Adjusting to improve position
Decline	Moving towards retirement

Source: adapted from Super (1957)

physical abilities, personal characteristics and the opportunities from which a person can choose. A key idea in Super's model was that career maturity was achieved by matching tasks with stages of development over a life-span. Career satisfaction could be obtained if, at the appropriate stage of development, people could choose a work role that allowed them to develop their self-concept.[2] Table 18 shows Super's stages model.

Super's model has been a significant influence in thinking about careers. For example, Schein (1990) has focused on the importance of self-concept and the way key themes and values established earlier in life remain resonant in his idea of 'career anchors' (see below). Since 1957, the model has been adapted and adjusted several times. One such adjustment related to the flexibility of career stages and the fact that each stage can be repeated or recycled (Super and Kidd, 1979). Other writers have also pointed to a more flexible and evolutionary perspective of careers. Kanter (1989) pointed out that the 'bureaucratic career' based on a logic of advancement was only one form of career, and Arthur *et al* (1995; p.8) referred to the 'evolving sequence of a person's work experiences over time', highlighting the importance of the relationship between people and those who provide positions in organisations. That relationships are always subject to change raised the prospect that a career route may have to deviate from an intended path, perhaps coming to a standstill or even closing down altogether.

Adamson *et al* (1998) suggest that during the 1990s, in response to economic and competitive pressure, the notion of a career for life began to disappear. There have been three consequential changes in organisational career philosophy:

- an end to the long-term view of employer-employee relationship
- an end to hierarchical movement as career progression
- an end to logical, ordered and sequential careers.

As the certainty of the career path disappears, those who seek management careers and managers already working cannot rely on organisations for advancement. Instead, they must take more responsibility for their own career management. Arnold (1997; p.16) shifts the emphasis towards individuals by considering a career to be 'the sequence of employment-related positions, roles, activities and experiences encountered by a person'. Arnold includes leisure activities, education and domestic work within the notion of career if they link with employment. It is very much up to individuals to define their careers, and this includes moving around from one post to another and not necessarily seeking promotion. It also shifts the responsibility for managing careers towards the individual – although a variety of stakeholders may influence how a career develops. During the 1990s the notion of the 'portfolio career' gained prominence (Cawsey *et al*, 1995), and it became the responsibility of individuals to develop a range of skills which enhanced their marketability and employability. The more they did this, the less they needed to restrict themselves to employment within one particular organisation; managers could consider their careers 'boundaryless' (Arthur and Rousseau, 1996).

REFLECT – CONCLUDE – PLAN 1

- Do you agree with the view that a 'career for life' has disappeared?
- What have been the consequences for career management in your organisation?
- What can you do to increase your employability and marketability?

Career management

Managers perform their work in organisations so it should be self-evident that organisation context and systems are immensely important to the way a manager's career is managed and developed. Edgar Schein (1978) took a particular interest in career systems, arguing for their strategic importance. He presented a Human Resource Planning and Development system which was composed of minimum-level activities to match individual and organisation needs. The activities included:

- at organisational level: organisation planning, human resource planning
- at individual level: individual work history, individual self assessment
- matching processes: performance appraisal (in respect of present and future performance), human resource inventory.

The outcomes of the system covered individual career plans and a 'specific human resource plan'. Schein argued that because organisations were likely to face increasing turbulence from the environment, it was important to maintain a balance between activities which serve the needs of individuals and those that serve the needs of the organisation. In particular, Schein highlighted the importance of dialogue to achieve such balance in the form of jointly negotiated plans for work and development.

WEB LINK

For more about the work of Edgar Schein, go to his web page at
http://web.mit.edu/scheine/www/home.html
which includes links to more work on career dynamics.

Further work for matching activities in career management was carried out by Hirsh (1984). In her framework, organisational environmental features such as history, the future, culture and power all impacted on career policies and the career development philosophy, and on how these in turn influenced career management systems and practices. Career management systems concerned:

> **Job design, recruitment and selection, appointments and promotion, separation, pay, appraisal, training and development, counselling and succession planning.**

Mayo (1991) saw career management activities as a spectrum ranging from those that benefit the organisation, such as succession planning, to those that benefit individuals, such as counselling, and to those that bring the two together, such as appraisal. The key is to ensure that mutual objectives are agreed.

The line manager's role in career management seems particularly important in light of findings relating to perceptions of equity with career management processes. For example, an organisation's concern with the management of careers, especially where it is seen to be fair, has been found to be a significant contributor to satisfaction with career management (Herriot *et al*, 1994). There is a clear link between fairness of promotion procedures and honouring agreements and satisfaction with career management, even if managers do not make career progress. Career management can therefore be seen as a feature of the psychological contract between managers and their organisations in respect of attitudes and perceptions towards what each expects from the other. During the 1990s the psychological contract relating to management careers was thrown into flux and, for some, broke down. The need for competiveness, customer service and a response to global change, combined with technological advances, all served to impact on organisational structures and decision-making that had been a source of relatively stable management careers. Managers' expectations on promotion and job security were changing (Goffee and Scase, 1992).

One consequence was a movement in what Hirsh and Jackson (1997; p.9) referred to as the 'pendulum of ownership of career development'. Some organisations swung the responsibility for career development towards individuals' taking the initiative for managing their own careers. A new psychological contract for managers was on offer; organisations could provide a job and opportunities, but it was the managers' responsibility to make use of these and develop their own careers – a move which could match a self-development MD policy. However, Hirsh and Jackson also found that there could be an over-emphasis on individual responsibility, and more shared responsibility where information from career development processes could provide useful data for both the organisation and individuals. For example, 360-degree feedback could be used by individual managers and the organisation. They suggested that career development could be managed in a variety of ways, as shown by Figure 36. It is quite possible that variations in responsibility and career development offer exist in the same organisation.

A survey by the CIPD (Hirsh and Rolph, 2003) of career management practices in the UK found a confusing and conflicting pattern, most organisations advocating the view that staff should take responsibility for their careers while also emphasising the need to grow future managers and retain key staff. One example of excellent practice was from KPMG, which gave strong input to supporting career development. Everyone had regular discussions with their managers about performance and career aspirations. The organisation also provided internal career coaches, group workshops on career management, one-to-one advice as required and web-based guidance.

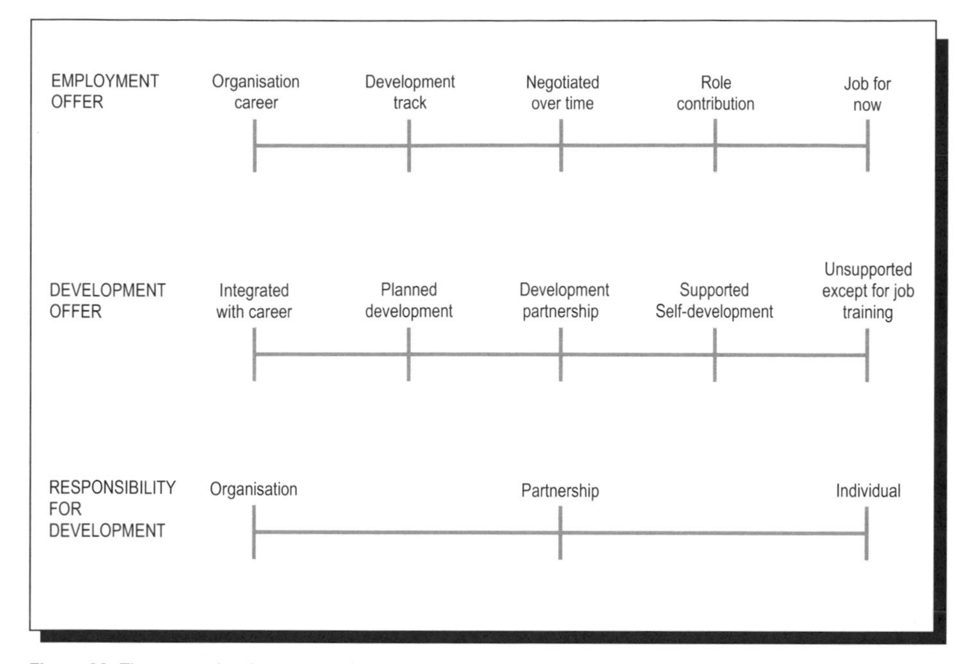

Figure 36 *The career development continuum*
Source: Hirsh and Jackson (1996; p.26)

WEB LINK

Check KPMG's approach to careers at
http://www.kpmgcampus.com/

REFLECT – CONCLUDE – PLAN 2

- What is your organisation's position on responsibility for career development?
- How can more support be provided for career development?
- What action can you take to help others develop their careers?

Middle managers

Flatter organisations and downsizing was meant to have serious implications for the career progress of middle managers. Some managers found their careers in their preferred organisations curtailed but even those that remained at work after a period of downsizing might experience lower commitment and insecurity as well as guilt as they felt sympathy for those made redundant – a feeling referred to as 'survivor syndrome' (Thornhill *et al*, 1997). Another finding has been that middle managers had to take on increased work responsibilities with greater pressure to achieve results (Doherty *et a*l, 1995). Thomas and Dunkerley (1999) found in their case study research of 50 organisations that middle managers had experienced intensification of work with the loss of a career structure particularly significant in the public sector. For example, in the civil service the loss of a career structure was seen as 'betrayal' by middle managers, little alternative being offered in the form of career development and personal career plans. In some cases, however, restructuring meant an early promotion for middle managers as more senior colleagues took the option of retirement. Applebaum and Santiago (1997; p.13) suggest that in the context of what they refer to as 'career plateauing', managers must take control of their career development by becoming 'career strategists'. This includes:

- viewing career paths as fragmented and subject to change
- equating career success with personal satisfaction and charting progress by the degree to which career decisions satisfy personal needs
- developing a multi-dimensional plan clustered around several objectives that fulfil career needs at a particular point in life.

For organisations, the experience of middle managers and others in the 1990s has important implications in the 2000s, especially in the context of continuing changes to expectations about careers. As Hirsh (2002) has argued, the idea of career is still very important to people. Organisations need to combine the achievement of high job performance with active career development, aiming for 'win-win' outcomes (p.49).

Dual-career couples

There has been an increasing tendency for women to become managers and to seek career development. Where both partners in a domestic relationship work in management roles, they become a Dual-Career Couple. This may allow both to fulfil ambitions with respect to their careers as managers but such ambitions need to be reconciled and balanced with the demands of family and the jointly established home (Smith 1997). Even where couples work in different organisations, there are some key implications for managing the careers of either partner. A study by Pierce and Delahaye (1996) suggested that organisations need to consider:

- the necessity for relocations for either partner in a dual-career couple
- a wider view of costs with respect to decisions on issues like relocation where there could be knock-on effects within the couple's relationship
- the assumption that the male partner's career always take precedence – female partners are unlikely to subordinate their careers to male partners
- the culture and values relating to career couples including issues such as work scheduling and the home/work link and family arrangement.

Dual-career couples represent a particular problem for organisations that operate globally where managers may resist appointments overseas on the basis of family ties. In development terms, partners in dual-career contexts have no option but to consider their careers with reference to each other and organisations need to acknowledge and understand such issues.

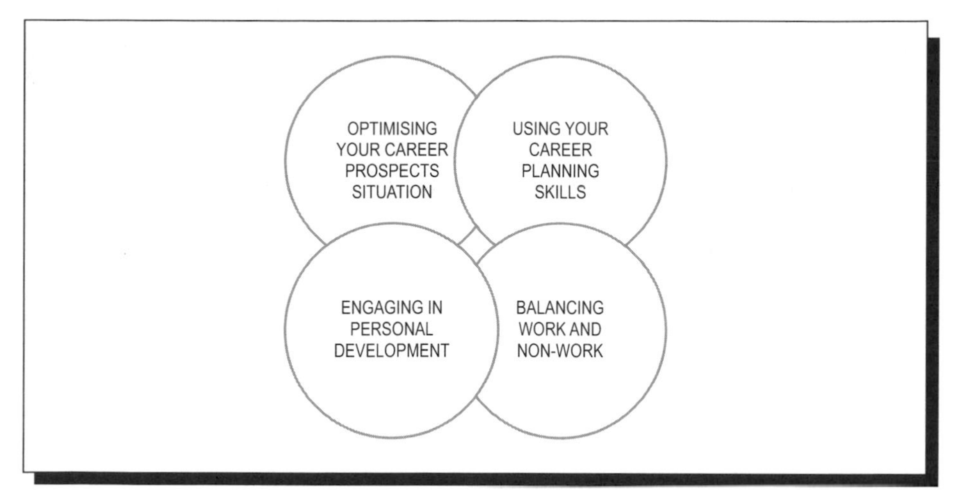

Figure 37 *A model of career competences*
Source: Ball (1997; p.76)

SELF-MANAGEMENT OF CAREERS

In the 2000s managers have to be more strategic about their own careers and learn skills centring on self-management of careers, while at the same time organisations must facilitate career learning through a climate of supporting relationships and structures.

Career competences

If managers are faced with a diverse choice in their careers, they require skills of self-management. One such model has been provided by Ball (1997), who used data from case studies that took an individual perspective on career changes to develop four overlapping career competences. These are shown in Figure 37.

Ball explains the competences as follows:

- *optimising career prospects* – taking a goal-directed approach to career planning, anticipating the future and promoting one's own career interests. In addition, managers can make use of mentors and engage in activities that get the manager noticed
- *career planning* – playing to strengths by frequent reviews of career and personal development. In effect this involves completing the stages of the learning cycle but applying each stage to career considerations. It corresponds to Mumford's (1990) view that the learning process should be prominent in career planning. Managers take advantage of learning opportunities within work roles and put less reliance in formally constructed plans; we referred to this as Type 2 MD
- *engaging in personal development* – as well as learning within roles, identifying other learning opportunities both to increase fulfilment and satisfaction and also to enhance marketability. Managers identify needs, learn from the opportunities and find others to support them – such as becoming part of an Action Learning set
- *balancing work and non-work* – using opportunities for learning that might include non-work openings such as voluntary work, although this seems more likely in the USA than in the UK (Whymark and Ellis, 1999). It could also be important to counter stress that occurs from working long hours.

REFLECT – CONCLUDE – PLAN 3

- How far have you developed career competences?
- Which career competence do you think requires attention?
- What will you do to develop this competence, and what action should your organisation take?

WEB LINK

Achieving work-life balance is now being promoted by the UK Government – the website is located at
http://www.dti.gov.uk/work-lifebalance/

Self-management of careers by managers also implies that careers can be made by managers. As Adamson *et al* (1998) suggest, the concern is with careers as a subjective property of managers rather than through objective determination by the organisation. Stewart and Knowles (1999) point to the crucial importance of self-awareness as a process of reflection to match what knowledge and skills a manager has to offer with the work that will provide satisfaction. Self-knowledge is also identified by Butcher and Harvey (1998; p.76) as a meta-ability for managers 'as a first step toward developing flexibility in dealing with diverse and complex managerial situations'.[3]

One source of self-awareness could be a manager's talents, values and motives which form the self-concept and are acquired through experience and learning. As managers advance through their careers, the self-concept may form into a pattern and provide the basis for decisions about career choices. Schein (1990) refers to the idea of 'career anchors' as features of a person's self-concept which have a significant impact on career choice and behaviour. The crucial impact of a career anchor, according to Schein, is that it is an element of self-concept that 'he or she will not give up' (p.18). This means that where work does not match a career anchor, a manager will have a sense that what he or she is doing is 'not really me, not really what I would like to be doing or am capable of doing' (p.19). Eventually, this will cause dissatisfaction and attempts to move to work that matches the career value more closely. Schein (1990) outlines eight career anchors, as listed below.

- *technical/functional competence* – skills in a technical or functional area which provides a sense of identity
- *general managerial competence* – desire to seek responsibility and accountability for total results
- *autonomy/independence* – the opportunity to define one's own work and remain in work that allows flexibility
- *security/stability* – a concern for security, including financial, and seeking achievement to allow relaxation
- *entrepreneurial creativity* – the desire to create organisation by taking risks and using one's own abilities
- *service/dedication to a cause* – pursuing work that achieves something of value, such as making the world a better place and doing something for others

- *pure challenge* – working on difficult problems and overcoming obstacles
- *lifestyle* – balancing personal, family and career needs into an integrated whole.

Complexity and careers

Career anchors offer a degree of persistence and continuity to managers in the face of uncertainty with respect to their careers. In recent years there has been an interest in the application of chaos and complexity theories to provide some explanation of how careers might be developed. Career systems are complex and dynamic, but according to chaos theory such systems follow basic and simple rules even though the effects may seem random and unpredictable. Gibb (1998), for example, argues that the beliefs of people in the system offer an indication of 'attractor states' – that is, of the point at which complex systems settle into an apparent equilibrium. Gibb suggests that the messiness produced by career chaos can be better explored by an examination of beliefs and assumptions of various interests. For individual mangers, beliefs and values lie at the heart of a self-organising process that creates the order of their lives. However, this image of the individual manager must be augmented by the degree of interdependence between managers and others that form a network of relationships. Parker and Arthur (2001) work with the concept of an 'intelligent career', in which interaction feeds three features of 'ways of knowing' for careers – *knowing-whom* in terms of relationships, *knowing-how* in terms of skills, and *knowing-why* in terms of career motivation. Interactions are non-linear where small actions can have large effects and are subject to feedback which can prevent any degree of settlement or equilibrium.[4] It is suggested that the principles of 'new science' can offer an alternative range of tools and ideas for career learning in the future.

Further support to the importance of interaction is provided by attention to relationships as a form of social capital (see Chapter 9).

WEB LINKS

If you want to explore further the way chaos and complexity theories can be used in thinking about careers, you might like to visit M@n@agement, an online journal at http://www.dmsp.dauphine.fr/management/
where Vol. 5, No. 1, 2002 – a special issue on 'Careers and new science' can be downloaded.
Go to http://www.humaxnetworks.com/socialcap.html for more information on social capital and how it is measured.

SUCCESSION MANAGEMENT

While managers may be concerned about making their own careers and organisations may well seek to support such efforts, there will also be the need to consider the identification of managers to fill key management positions both in the present and the future. This is the concern of a succession management system (SMS) incorporating the process to review the potential of managers, the plan of implementation (the succession plan) and the overall policy to cover contingent issues such as the approach to high flyers and promotion. In the light of what we have suggested above about careers for managers, we would also expect an SMS to include some consideration on how to ensure that the adverse effects of reduced opportunities for promotion, the likelihood of 'plateauing' and the threat or actuality of redundancy due to downsizing are ameliorated.

The evolution of succession management systems

The simple view of succession rests on two basic propositions:

- There are fewer management positions as the shape of an organisation's hierarchy narrows.
- There is a pool of staff within an organisation's internal labour market who may have the potential to fill management positions within the hierarchy.

Succession management activities are therefore concerned to reconcile the tensions between identifying the requirements for managers now and in the future in terms of numbers and key skills in relation to business strategy and the desires of managers who aspire to such positions. At the heart of an SMS lies the succession plan, which is formed by consideration of the direction of the business and future requirements for management and information about the capabilities and potential of the management pool. The process by which the plan is produced and discussed varies between organisations, but some fairly common elements are:

- collecting information from appraisals and making an assessment of the individuals concerned (where they exist) including attendance at assessment or development centres[5]
- summarising that information, often by the HR function
- alternatively, presenting the line manager with a chart empty of everything except the name of the job and job-holder, and then asking for the insertion of comments on the blank, or asking the manager to talk through his or her comments with an HR adviser
- collecting the information and putting it together in a file or binder to be presented to a decision-making group or to the chief executive alone
- the group or chief executive reviewing the comments made and making a final decision about the comments recorded on the succession plan
- a process by which the succession plan is eventually reviewed and adopted, including a special meeting either of the board or management committee, or of a special MD committee created for the purpose
- development plans for individual managers.

Of course, there was a time when the shape of an organisation's hierarchy was relatively predictable and sufficiently tall to accommodate enough levels and grades to meet aspirations to 'climb the ladder', with 'fast tracks' available for those identified with the potential to reach the top. In such circumstances, managers could expect frequent promotions into clearly specified jobs until they reached the point where their abilities were matched to the requirement of the role. One approach to measuring the match between people's ability and the task to perform over time is 'career path appreciation' (Stamp, 1989). The key idea of this approach is the matching of individual capabilities[6] with challenges the person is to tackle, as measured by the requirements for decision-making. If the challenge is greater than a person's capability, there are negative consequences for individuals and organisations such as stress and rising costs. If the capabilities of the manager are greater than the challenge of the work, resources are wasted and boredom and frustration creep in. Since challenges occur within tasks that are set in an organisation's structure, for balance, flow and effectiveness, managers must be performing work at the right level or stratum for their stage of development with projections to continue the process of development over time. The basic notion of path appreciation is shown in Figure 38.

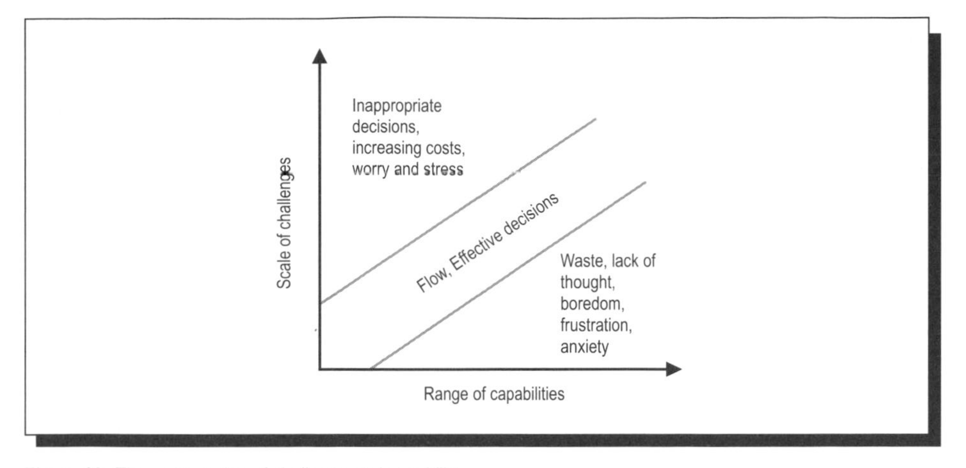

Figure 38 *The appreciation of challenge and capability*
Source: adapted from Stamp (1989)

WEB LINK

You can find out more about career path appreciation at http://www.bcoss.com

By the end of the 1980s and into the 1990s, organisations were facing an increasingly volatile context which was affecting structures and the nature of work. As a result, succession planning became increasingly problematic. This suggested that continuous learning and development were needed, a theme also highlighted by Hirsh (1990), who pointed to a 'developing potential' (p.18) model of succession as a response to high business uncertainty. Organisations develop all staff as part of a culture of self-development, and succession plans are used only for emergencies; the main onus is on individuals to manage their own careers.

Through the 1990s and into the 2000s, varied patterns of SMS have continued to unfold, often within single organisations. There is emerging a segmented pattern of succession. For example, some managers and high-potential staff may have their careers managed and supported by their organisation with succession planning to fill senior positions. Such managers may face frequent assessments of their capability, especially where management competencies provide a link to strategy and a potential means of identifying high-performers.[7] Others, including managers, face more limited development opportunities and uncertainty over career paths, with an expectation that they should look after themselves. Taylor (2002) found, in an in-depth survey of the attitudes of nearly 2,500 employed people towards their jobs and life at work, trends of a decline in organisational commitment and in a sense of obligation to the firms that employed them. He suggests, 'The disgruntled manager has joined the disgruntled manual worker' in complaints about 'the long hours culture' (p.10).

Career success

If most managers are unable to gain rapid promotion or achieve hierarchical advance, how do they judge whether they have been successful in developing their careers? This was an issue explored by Sturges (1999) in a UK telecommunications company. Interviewing 36 managers of different ages and both genders, meanings of 'career success' were examined. Managers identified both external and internal criteria for success. External criteria included pay and position but also intangible criteria such as influence and personal recognition. Internal criteria related to accomplishment in terms of feeling good about work carried out, a sense of personal achievement from work, enjoying and finding work interesting, feeling that work was worthwhile and combing work with successful home life. Four orientations for career success were suggested:

- *climbers* – who described success in terms of external criteria, such as moving up the organisation hierarchy to gain status
- *experts* – who saw success as achieving competence in their jobs and being recognised personally for being good
- *influencers* – for whom success was defined as being able to do things that had a clear and positive effect, whatever their hierarchical position
- *self-realisers* – for whom success was based on achievement on their own terms for personal fulfilment, with a balance between work and home life vital.

There is evidence here that managers use criteria other than position in the organisational hierarchy to judge success in their careers. This may be a response to the reality that managers now face – ie reconciling the limitations on external indicators of success by focusing on what is achievable, such as influence or high competency in work. It also suggests that SMS need to focus less on formal plans and more on the values and beliefs of managers, helping them to understand how they can continue to develop their careers in line with their own criteria for success. One way of doing this is for organisations to provide career development workshops to deliver a range of processes for the self-management of careers. Jackson (1990) identified career workshops as one of the most effective interventions to promote career planning. For example, as part of a workshop provided for young managers in Leeds, the following processes were used:

- an introduction to career competences, based on Ball (1997)
- a consideration of key influences on the career, surfacing values and beliefs
- a personal SWOT analysis
- the completion and analysis of Schein's Career Anchors Inventory and Honey and Mumford's Learning Styles Questionnaire
- the compilation of a personal action plan, followed two months later by a one-day review.

Increasingly, an organisation may support career development by providing access to materials for self-help and continuous learning, often available online.

WEB LINK

An online career development e-manual can be found at http://www.cdm.uwaterloo.ca/steps.asp

High flyers

High flyers are one group that customarily expected few problems with promotion, succession and their careers. Organisations have traditionally spent a great deal of time and money identifying managers of the future who have high potential and are destined to climb the career ladder at a rapid pace; they are on the fast-track to success, starting with graduate entry. Those identified have, until recently, symbolised an ideal of how careers are meant to develop, especially in the Anglo-American context. A good deal of organisational language is action- and achievement-oriented, so high flyers embody most closely the expectations that such language brings (Altman, 1997). However, even in the 1980s the upward path was being superseded by the horizontal path which implied sideways moves with the opportunity to acquire different skills before advancing upwards (Baruch and Peiperl, 1997). By the 1990s many organisations began to close off their fast track because there could not be any certainty about such a track's existing in the future. As Holbeche (1999, p.270) suggests, 'In a "flat" structure, where was a "high flyer" to "fast track" to?' However, some organisations have continued to maintain an offer for managers of high potential, so as to remain competitive in the market for talent. For example, at Rabobank in Holland, young high-potential managers attend an MD programme, including attendance at an assessment centre, coaching and mentoring. The programme acts as a signal of management commitment to young managers. Loyalty is expected in return, and personal development is strongly linked to organisation development.[8]

Learning from redundancy

For some managers, the illusion of a career for life in an organisation is shattered by the loss of their position, and this is often accompanied by financial, social and psychological losses. As reported by Hallier and Lyon (1996), both the threat and the actuality of redundancy affect a manager's feelings of security, commitment to the company and the working of the psychological contract. Long-serving managers in particular tend to assume that they will be protected from redundancy, even in the face of objective information. Managers that remain may suffer from 'survivor syndrome', as we mentioned above. One way to soften the impact for managers is to include within SMS a proactive and creative approach to managing redundancy – one that helps managers move to a new stage in their career and that is based on learning and development. For example, an organisation can offer managers help through outplacement.[9] This involves providing a programme of support to develop a CV and review skills, to consider how to access the job market and to receive counselling from qualified occupational psychologists. Managers may receive outplacement support as part of a termination package providing off-site access to specialist consultants.[10] During the 1990s outplacement became a central feature of HRM strategy in managing redundancy (Doherty, 1998). While outplacement may lead to a new job, another transitional opportunity is to become an 'interim manager'. This involves managers taking on short-term projects and attempting to transfer their knowledge and experience to a new situation. Sometimes referred to as 'troubleshooters' (Voudson, 2002), interim managers may be required to manage projects and carry out mergers using their experience and wisdom. Most are senior managers in their fifties, and although they may be 'comfortably over-qualified' (p.122), the opportunity offers a manager a chance for MD.

WEB LINKS

http://www.ioim.org.uk/ provides a link to the recently formed Institute of Interim Management.
http://www.interimmanagement.uk.com/ is the trade body, the Interim Management Association,
and http://www.entegria.co.uk takes you to one of the leading providers of interim management.

SUMMARY

- Management positions are either filled internally, offering an opportunity focusing MD on future supply, or externally, affording the chance to seek managers with particular skills which may take too long to develop internally.
- An organisation's management competence framework can be used to provide information in the assessment of applicants against the requirements of work.
- Fuller information about candidates can be obtained from assessment centres and via the use of valid and reliable methods such as psychometrics.
- Managers may be required to undertake new responsibilities and learn new skills caused by changes in work requirements.
- Models of career and development have tended towards the view that careers have a logical route to follow which can be planned – but more recently, predictable career paths have become difficult to achieve.
- Career management in organisations has to maintain a balance between activities which serve the needs of individuals and those that serve the needs of the organisation.
- Managers can learn skills of career self-management including self-awareness and self-knowledge, especially relating to their talents, values and motives which form the self-concept.
- Succession management systems can range from simple reaction to departures and retirements to a more sophisticated consideration of future supply, succession and development.
- Proactive redundancy management though the provision of outplacement and interim management opportunities can help managers move to a new stage in their career, based on learning and development.

DISCUSSION QUESTIONS

1. Consider the costs and benefits of internal selection of managers versus external selection.
2. How can assessment centres be made attractive to managers in selection?
3. How can the needs of organisations and the needs of individuals be reconciled in career management?
4. 'I am fed up with people asking me about careers in the organisation. There are none.' Discuss, with reference to career development for managers.
5. What is meant by the 'survivor syndrome', and how can it be avoided?
6. Do succession plans work? What are the requirements for successful succession management?

FURTHER READING

CIPD (2002) *The Future of Careers*. London, Chartered Institute of Personnel and Development.

GUEST, D. and CONWAY, N. (2001) *Organisational Change and the Psychological Contract*. London, Chartered Institute of Personnel and Development.

HIRSH, W. (2000) *Succession Planning Demystified*. Report 372. Brighton, Institute of Employment Studies.

HUANG, T.-C. (2001) 'Succession management systems and human resource outcomes', *International Journal of Manpower*, Vol. 22, No. 8; pp.736–747.

IBARRA, H. (2003) *Working Identity: Unconventional Strategies for Reinventing Your Career*. Boston, MA., Harvard Business School Press.

VINEY, C., ADAMSON, S. and DOHERTY, N. (1997) 'Paradoxes of fast-track career management', *Personnel Review*, Vol. 26, No. 3; pp.174–186.

GROUP ACTIVITY

- Form a group of four.
- Each person should complete a career time-line as follows:
  - Starting from your first 'job', draw a line that shows the path of your career (see Figure 39).

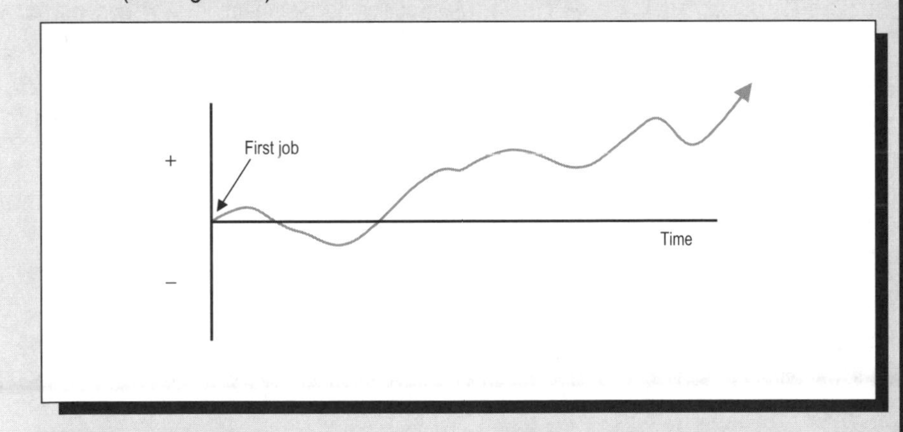

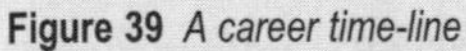

Figure 39 *A career time-line*

The line can move below or above the horizontal time-line according to how you felt your career was moving: above the line represents positive movement; below the line, negative.

  - Explain the various turning points – what did you value about each move?
- Meet together to share your findings. Identify what beliefs each person has about career success, the values that underpin career choices and the development needed to move to the next stage.

REFERENCES

ADAMSON, S. J., DOHERTY, N. and VINEY, C. (1998) 'The meanings of career revisited: implications for theory and practice', *British Journal of Management*, Vol. 9, No. 4; pp.251–259.

ALTMAN, Y. (1997) 'The high-potential fast-flying achiever: themes from the English-language literature, 1976–1995', *Career Development International*, Vol. 2, No. 7; pp.324–330.

APPELBAUM, S. and SANTIAGO, V. (1997) 'Career development in the plateaued organization', *Career Development International*, Vol. 2, No. 1; pp.11–20.

ARNOLD, J. (1997) *Managing Careers into the 21st Century*. London, Paul Chapman Publishing.

ARTHUR, M. B., HALL, D. T. and LAWRENCE, B. S. (eds) (1994) *Handbook of Career Theory*. Cambridge, Cambridge University Press.

ARTHUR, M. B. and ROUSSEAU, D. M. (eds) (1996) *The Boundaryless Career: A new employment principle for a new organizational era*. New York, Oxford University Press.

BALL, B. (1997) 'Career management competences – the individual perspective', *Career Development International*, Vol. 2, No. 2; pp.74–79.

BARUCH, Y. and PEIPERL, M. (1997) 'High-flyers: glorious past, gloomy present, any future?', *Career Development International*, Vol. 2, No. 7; pp.354–358.

BUTCHER, D. and HARVEY, P. (1998) 'Meta-ability development: a new concept for career management', *Career Development International*, Vol. 3, No. 2; pp.75–78.

CAWSEY, T., DESZCA, G. and MAZEROLLE, M. (1995) 'The portfolio career as response to a changing job market', *Journal of Career Planning and Employment*, Fall; pp.41–47.

CIPD (2002) *The Future of Careers*. London, Chartered Institute of Personnel and Development.

DOHERTY, N. (1998) 'The role of outplacement in managing redundancy', *Personnel Review*, Vol. 27, No. 4; pp.343–353.

DOHERTY, N., BANK, J. and VINNICOMBE, S. (1995) *Managing Survivors: The experience of survivors in BT and the British financial sector*. Bedford, Cranfield University.

DOYLE, M. (2002) 'Selecting managers for transformational change', *Human Resource Management Journal*, Vol. 12, No. 1; pp.3–16.

GIBB, S. (1998) 'Exploring career chaos: patterns of belief', *Career Development International*, Vol. 3, No. 4; pp.149–153.

GOFFEE R. and SCASE, R. 'Organisational change and the corporate career: the restructuring of managers' job aspirations', *Human Relations*, Vol. 45, No. 4; pp.363–385.

GUEST, D., DAVEY, K. and PATCH, A. (1998) *The Impact of New Forms of Employment Contract on Motivation and Innovation*. London, ESRC.

HALLIER, J. and LYON, P. (1996) 'Job insecurity and employee commitment: managers' reactions to the threat and outcomes of redundancy selection', *British Journal of Management*, Vol. 7, No. 2; pp.107–123.

HERRIOT, P., GIBBONS, P., PEMBERTON, C. and JACKSON, P. R. (1994) 'An empirical model of managerial careers in organizations', *British Journal of Management*, Vol. 5; pp.113–121.

HIRSH, W. (1984) *Career Management in the Organisation: A guide for developing policy and practice*. Report 96. Brighton, Institute of Manpower Studies.

HIRSH, W. (1990) *Succession Planning: Current practice and future issues*. Report 184. Brighton, Institute of Manpower Studies.

HIRSH, W. (2002) 'Careers in organisations – time to get positive', in CIPD, *The Future of Careers*. London, Chartered Institute of Personnel and Development; pp.45–52.

HIRSH, W. and JACKSON, C. (1997) *Strategies for Career Development: Promise, practice and pretence*. Report 305. Brighton, Institute of Manpower Studies.

HIRSH, W. and ROLPH, J. (2003) 'Snakes and ladders', *People Management*, Vol. 9, No. 9; pp.36–37.

HOLBECHE, L. (1998) *Motivating People in Lean Organizations*. Oxford, Butterworth-Heinemann.

HOLBECHE, L. (1999) *Aligning Human Resources and Business Strategy*. Oxford, Butterworth-Heinemann.

JACKSON, C. (1990) *Career Counselling in Organisations*. Report 198. Brighton, Institute of Manpower Studies.

JOHNSON, S. and WINTERTON, J. (1999) *Management Skills*. Research Paper 3. London, Skills Task Force.

LIEVENS, F. (2002) 'An examination of the accuracy of the slogans related to assessment centres', *Personnel Review*, Vol. 31, No. 1; pp.86–102.

MABEY, C. (2003) 'Mapping management development practice', *Journal of Management Studies*; forthcoming.

MAYO, A. (1997) *Managing Careers*. London, Institute of Personnel Management.

MUMFORD, A. (1990) 'Making a career through learning', *International Journal of Career Management*, Vol. 2, No. 1; pp.8–16.

KANTER, R. M. (1989) *When Giants Learn to Dance*. New York, Simon & Schuster.

PARKER, P. and ARTHUR, M. B. 'Bringing "New Science" into careers research', M@n@gement. Vol. 5, No. 1; pp.105–125. Available from http://www.dmsp.dauphine.fr/management/PapersMgmt/51Parker.html

PIERCE, J. and DELAHAYE, B. L. (1997) 'Human resource management implications of dual-career couples', *International Journal of Human Resource Management*, Vol. 7, No. 4; pp.905–923.

SCHEIN, E. (1978) *Career Dynamics: Matching individual and organisation needs*. Reading, MA., Addison-Wesley.

SCHEIN, E. (1990) *Career Anchors*. San Diego, CA., Pfeiffer & Company.

SENNETT, R. (1998) *The Corrosion of Character*. New York, Norton.

SMITH, C. R. (1997) 'Career transitions of dual-career couples: an empirical study', *Career Development International*, Vol. 2, No. 5; pp.229–237.

SONSINO, S. (2003) 'Reach for the stars', *People Management*, Vol. 9, No. 7; pp.31–34.

STAMP, G. (1989) 'The individual, the organisation and the path to mutual appreciation', *Personnel Management*, July; pp.28–31.

STEWART, J. and KNOWLES, V. (1999) 'The changing nature of graduate careers', *Career Development International*, Vol. 4, No. 7; pp.370–383.

STURGES, J. (1999) 'What it means to succeed: personal conceptions of career success held by male and female managers at different ages', *British Journal of Management*, Vol. 10, No. 3; pp.239–252.

SUPER, D. E. (1957) *The Psychology of Careers*. New York, Harper & Row.

SUPER, D. E. and KIDD, J. M. (1979) 'Vocational maturity in adulthood: toward turning model into a measure', *Journal of Vocational Behavior*, Vol. 14; pp.255–270.

TAYLOR, R. (2002) *Britain's World of Work – Myths and Realities*. Swindon, Economic and Social Research Council.

THOMAS, R. and DUNKERLEY, D. (1999) 'Middle managers' experiences in the downsized organization', *British Journal of Management*, Vol. 10, No. 2; pp.157–169.

THOMSON, A., MABEY, C., STOREY, J., GRAY, C. and ILES, P. (2001) *Changing Patterns of Management Development*. Oxford, Blackwell.

THORNHILL, A., SAUNDERS, M. N. K. and STEAD, J. (1997) 'Downsizing, delayering – but where's the commitment?', *Personnel Review*, Vol. 26, No. 1; pp.81–98.

VOUDSON, P. (2002) 'Interim management: now a permanent feature of the workplace', *Industrial and Commercial Training*, Vol. 34, No. 3; pp.120–122.

WATKINS, J. (2003) 'Get with the programme', *People Management*, Vol. 9, No. 12; pp.14–15.

WHIDDETT, S. and HOLLYFORDE, S. (1999) *The Competencies Handbook*. London, Institute of Personnel and Development.

WHYMARK, K. and ELLIS, S. (1999) 'Whose career is it anyway? Options for career management in flatter organisation structures', *Career Development International*, Vol. 4, No. 2; pp.117–120.

WILLIAMS, S. (2002) *Characteristics of the Management Population in the UK: Overview Report*. London, Council for Excellence in Management and Leadership.

ENDNOTES

1. More details on the 'One BBC' programme can be found in Watkins (2003).
2. In Chapter 4 we highlighted the importance of the self-concept in how managers responded to feedback.
3. In addition to self-knowledge, Butcher and Harvey (1998) identified cognitive skills, emotional resilience and personal drive as four meta-abilities for MD and taking personal career decisions.
4. This seems to contradict the notion of 'attractor states' and equilibrium mentioned above, although the key point is that the dynamics of a complex system may give the appearance of stability while remaining in flux.
5. Some organisations may require attendance at an assessment or development centre as a qualification for consideration in succession plans. A concomitant factor may be that failure to attend could indicate a lack of desire for promotion.
6. Career path appreciation has its origins in the work of the famous organisational psychologist Elliot Jacques.
7. Some behaviour approaches to management competence specify characteristics which are linked to high performance or excellence in management work.
8. See Sonsino (2003) for more details of this case.
9. Outplacement is often referred to by providers as 'career transition'.
10. Some managers and other staff may receive their support within the organisation – sometimes referred to as 'inplacement'.

Management development for particular groups

CHAPTER 11

Chapter outline
Introduction
Diversity and management
Women managers
Ethnic managers
National cultures
Professions and MD
Small and medium-sized enterprises
Summary

LEARNING OUTCOMES

After studying this chapter, you should be able to understand, explain, analyse and evaluate:

- **the relationship of MD to diversity management**
- **the difficulties faced by female and ethnic minority managers**
- **the importance of national cultures in management learning**
- **approaches to management within the professions**
- **how small business managers learn and develop.**

INTRODUCTION

There are particular issues in relation to some groups of managers. Women managers and people from minority ethnic groups face discrimination or stereotyping which may require separate MD programmes. Managers of professional firms or operating in an essentially knowledge-based environment, and managers in small organisations, have different needs. We have excluded discussion on the different needs of directors.[1] It also seems likely that some managers will retire later than age 60 or 65. Capacity to learn among older managers is not necessarily less, but willingness to learn may suffer.

DIVERSITY AND MANAGEMENT

Diversity moves beyond the idea of equality of opportunities in organisations, towards the recognition of the value of difference. Such differences, when applied to organisations, may be visible and obvious – such as gender and ethnicity – but they may also be less visible and even suppressed, such as religion and sexuality. What is important is that such differences play a vital part in people's self-concept but also in how others relate to them. Stereotyping and discrimination may be ameliorated by adjustments to structural factors such as job descriptions but may persist in actions and attitudes. Diversity is concerned with making the best use of differences and removing barriers to such use. Singh (2002) suggests that diversity matters for several significant reasons:

- the business case – Including all staff in the development pool is a source of competitive advantage.
- the fairness case – Barriers to those who are different are removed.
- the merit case – Stereotyping of the management role as white and male excludes those of talent who are not.

Singh argues that legislation has not sufficiently changed attitudes and awareness. Diversity must therefore become a strategic issue, and managers must have a vital role in leading progress and changing practices.

REFLECT – CONCLUDE – PLAN 1

- To what extent is diversity management a key issue in your organisation?
- How can you advance the business case for diversity management?
- What steps can you take to make diversity a strategic issue at work?

WEB LINK

A 'diversity excellence model' can be inspected at
http://www.cmps.gov.uk/diversity/chart.asp
It provides a means of assessing an organisation's ability to manage diversity.

WOMEN MANAGERS

At least 40 per cent of the UK workforce are women – but only somewhere between 25 and 30 per cent of managers are women (EOC, 2003). There is also a strong degree of segregation by gender in particular sectors: women make up 73 per cent of managers in health and social services; in production the figure is 6 per cent; and more generally in the private sector the figure is 28 per cent. At the level of director and senior management, the differences are even more striking: women comprise less than 1 per cent of chairpersons and occupy around 4 per cent of executive director posts. It is a pattern repeated throughout public life in the judiciary, civil service and local government. There are also significant differences in earnings, female managers suffering a 30 per cent shortfall at an average of £13.99 an hour compared to men at £20.05 an hour (ONS, 2003).[2] Historically, the view of most managers (of course predominantly male) was that this disproportion was in some sense 'natural'. It was seen to reflect women's actual competence or their own inevitable career choices as actual or potential mothers. This view was gradually challenged as ethically inappropriate and as an ineffective use of a total potential resource for the managerial population. Singh (2002) reports that one in four women remains childless, and more women are returning to work after maternity expecting to resume their careers, so there is concern that the apparent 'glass ceiling' and 'sticky floor' for managers remains.

Obstacles facing women managers

There remain a number of stereotypes about women and their position in organisations which are perceived to work against their development. One view, held by some successful women, is that the 'queen rises to the top'. Such people tend to argue that although there are special problems for women managers, it is the successful overcoming of those problems that demonstrates that you are special. One of the authors was told by his own direct manager, when he proposed some special attention for women managers, 'I got here without that kind of help; other women should do the same.' Some women – and some men – deprecate any special measures to redress what others see as problems, on the grounds that such actions lead to tokenism or even to the view that those who do progress up the managerial ladder have done so through 'politically correct processes' rather than their own abilities. Nevertheless, there are common stereotypical presentations that prevent progress for many women. Probably the most prevalent is that management and leadership is a male role in contrast to which women should play supportive followers.

Such perceptions are reinforced by the low numbers of females in high positions who can act as role models for others, which restrains their attempts to make progress (Cooper Jackson, 2001). Women face stereotypes along the whole route of their careers, and it becomes harder – and perhaps more political – the higher women attempt to rise. Davidson and Cooper (1992) pointed out that men may feel threatened by women managers and may take action to inhibit their progress.[3] The distaste for internal politics may further reinforce perceptions held by women. Vinnicombe and Singh (2002) found that although there could be much talk about the value of women and acknowledgement of the importance of equal opportunities, stereotypes and prejudices could still pervade how guidelines are implemented by line managers. A key issue therefore is what factors are consciously and less consciously considered by those who make decisions in organisations about selecting managers for higher positions. One obvious and traditional explanation is based on the idea that managers are selected for higher positions on the basis of an attraction-similarity paradigm (Byrne, 1971). Thus white male managers promote people like themselves, perpetuating a culture of male dominance which devalues women. However, there is emerging evidence from the USA that the 'glass ceiling' is less a result of male prejudice and more related to perceptions held by women that prevent them for applying for top management positions (Powell and Butterfield, 2002).

There are undoubtedly career choice issues for some women. Some leave employment in order to have children at a crucial time in terms of their development as managers. Organisational attitudes and policies in the past were certainly dominated by that. Changes towards policies which make it easier for women (and indeed men) to be both managers and responsible for their children are slowly emerging. Liu and Wilson (2001) found that women tend to regard their careers in phases, and that those who choose to have families may find themselves restricted when seeking career advancement. Family women may be prevented from participating in social networks which put them in the 'know' for advancement (p.171). During pregnancy, women may find themselves facing changed views of their abilities and accusations of less commitment to their careers and the organisation. It is therefore argued (Wajcman, 1998) that career structures favour males, supporting the male lifecycle, with the family man as norm at senior management levels rather than mothers. Some organisations – for example, the major banks and the National Health Service to some extent encouraged by the Equal Opportunities Commission – have gradually become less accepting of traditional views about women's careers, promoting themselves as 'family-friendly'.

Formal MD action to change both the actuality and the expectations of career opportunities for women includes:

- developing a clear policy statement directed at increasing the number of women managers, and accompanying it with procedures, the identification of opportunities, and monitoring

- reviewing selection processes and selection criteria in order to reduce, if not eliminate, bias against women
- developing special arrangements such as extended maternity leave, career breaks with accompanying fast-track training programmes and processes to enable women to return to work more quickly or more effectively.

There has been a shift in the expectations of at least a minority of men about the women with whom they share their lives. Women will no longer necessarily surrender their careers to the demands of child-bearing or to their husbands' careers. The issue of dual-career families (see Chapter 10) is the sharpest instance of this. Cavalier assumptions that men will go where they are sent, and that wives will go with them, have ceased to be tenable for male managers – and the parallel opposite is equally true for women managers.

Critics such as Wajcman (1998) would argue, however, that the various policies tend to reinforce the view of women as a problem, preserving the norm of the male manager. Others point to the need to change ideas about careers, understanding the differences between male and female expectations. Women are clearly as well qualified as men, especially at the start of their careers, and there is a business case for helping women reach higher levels of management (Mavin, 2001). Increased understanding would utilise research that has shown that women tend to define success in their careers differently (Sturges, 1999), giving prominence to the content of work, achievement and personal recognition for their contribution. Women also tended to take a broader view of their careers, defining success as a balance of work and other parts of their lives.

WEB LINK

The Women Returner's Network supports women who take a career break and wish to return to work. Their homepage is
http://www.women-returners.co.uk/wrn/individ/individ.asp
The Women's Management Development Network also provides help at
www.womenandmanagement.org.uk

Differences in management behaviour

General views about the reason for the lower number of women managers, to some extent depending on managerial folklore, are accompanied by more specific issues about women as managers. How women perform as managers, and how their performance is perceived by their male colleagues, is complicated by further questions. Should women managers behave like male managers? Do they bring special kinds of behaviour which actually produce more effective results? Perhaps male managers should try to employ some of the behaviours evidenced by some successful women managers.

Both men and women tend to agree that women managers behave differently from their male colleagues. While women who accept the 'difference' argument will tend to say 'different, but as good as', men will more characteristically say 'different, and less effective than'. However this commonly held view is challenged, for example, by Fraker (1984) who showed no difference in the way women managed as compared with men in a match study of 2,000 managers. Marshall (1991), however, argued that similarities in male and female managerial behaviour have been over-emphasised in order to support women managers. In her view these similarities have been overstated at the expense of legitimate and useful differences:

- Women tend to emphasise people management over task structuring, whereas men have opposite priorities.
- Women are often inhibited in exercising position power because other people reject or undermine their use of authority, or stereotype them in devalued female roles.

Like other authors she commented on the male emphasis on individualism, competition and control (in contrast to interdependence, collaboration and acceptance) as defining the values to which women managers are supposed to adhere if they wish to join the managerial club. There has been a tendency to push women into 'caring' functions. To some extent this process is a reflection of social stereotypes of desired female behaviour, of the failure to provide effective choice at school (eg for girls to do science), and of subsequent early career options. Further research by Burke and Collins (2001), based on self-ratings of styles in the use of management skills, found that there were differences between males and females, and that females were more likely to be effective in communicating and coaching and developing staff. They were strong in using contingent reward behaviour, to make expectations clear, and in using a transformational leadership style, to motivate staff. Females were more likely to:

- be positive role models for staff
- inspire staff to believe in and work for a common purpose
- encourage others to be creative and question assumptions
- spend time developing and coaching.

In the same study, male managers were more likely to engage in monitoring staff and focusing on errors or deviations.

Women managers – different development needs?

Women managers actually face a different situation from male managers. The predominant managerial style is most likely to be male in orientation. Female managers are therefore faced with the issue of whether, and how, to adopt managerial forms of behaviour that may contradict or conflict with their existing style of behaviour. Some women have obviously long since adopted male forms of behaviour and have no problems of such adaptation. For others the need to adapt may include:

- coping with competition
- adopting at least some of the behaviour of male clubs (post-work socialising, discussion of predominantly male sports)
- the use of personal and role power
- developing individual self-awareness
- acquiring a positive self-image as a woman manager
- self-confidence and assertiveness skills
- dealing with stress.

The traditional divide between rational male managers and emotional and caring female managers, with the dominance of the former over the latter, has been challenged by calls for a model of management that values both male and female talents – what Marshall (1995) referred to as the 'androgynous' manager. Singh (2002) suggests that masculinity and femininity can be regarded as two dimensions, and that both male and female managers should consider their styles in relation to both. Senior managers and those responsible for MD can work to use both dimensions in setting values and designing activities.

Different development processes

Male attitudes and behaviour on courses tend to follow the stereotypes about women found in the real world outside. Behaviour that is seen by men in men as normal, such as managerial assertiveness, is seen by men in women as aggressive and strident. Alternatively, women who do not behave like most men are pushed towards the supposedly 'feminine' behaviour corner. Women are expected to be concerned about the comfort of the group, to pour out the tea, and to express emotion rather than to conceal it. They are treated with a form of superficial gallantry that emphasises the fact that they are being treated as women, not as managers. Or their capacities may be belittled by reference to their sexuality: 'I bet it's difficult having a serious discussion with a beauty like Jane in the group.'

Because of the difficulties women have in largely male managerial training and education situations, and because of the view that they have special needs anyway, women-only training groups were developed. There are two conflicting arguments over this. One says that since women have to survive in a predominantly male environment, it is unreal to provide them with women-only management training. Whatever else this may achieve, the absence of men will reinforce the exclusion and isolation of women and create a future problem of transferring any learning achieved (Lewis and Fagenson, 1995). The alternative view is that the absence of men removes some unnecessary obstacles to learning, and opens opportunities for more women to be more experimental with behaviour. This may be helpful to them subsequently in the male environment, but it may also reinforce the view that women must change rather than the organisation. Some women feel they have benefited from women-only courses in the ways indicated above. It is also the case that since some women nowadays are less prepared to accept inappropriate male behaviour towards them on courses, mixed courses can sometimes become a battleground for male/female issues rather than a learning experience related to the original objectives (Reynolds and Trehan, 2003).

If women are in a minority in a learning group they may be dealt with differently from their male colleagues by a tutor, by a facilitator or by participants in the learning group. Hite and McDonald (1995) claim that women are often constrained in the classroom by having to conform to male modes, by materials constantly using 'he', and by the kind of management style favoured by tutors and colleagues. Their research showed further that there was a significant difference in the amount of interaction with the tutor and the kind of response made to their contribution. Moreover, males were more often called on to make a contribution. Tanton (1995) also concludes that male tutors behave differently towards male and female students. She also says that women prefer small group discussions where these problems are either less visible or capable of being managed by women themselves. They are said to like role plays and the keeping of journals. No reasons are given for these preferences (and they are not supported by the Hite and McDonald research). It may be that journal-keeping is particularly favoured because it is a solitary process of learning which is not immediately affected by the intervention of tutors or colleagues.

Case and Thompson (1995) reviewing behaviours on an MBA programme found that women engaged in more frequent self-reflection than men, and that reflecting on their own actions provides a more accurate depiction of their role in events that occur. These two aspects would suggest that women might learn better than men from the same event. One criticism of MBAs and formal management education in general is the lack of women lecturers to present a female view of management. Miller *et al* (2002) suggest that where MBAs 'replicate patriarchal orthodoxy in the classroom' (p.27), this can engender a sense of alienation among women which is not conducive to learning.

A further proposition is that women are more likely to learn through relationships and empathy, and through collaborative discussion rather than argumentative debate. Tannen (1991) described this as report talk. These points would seem to relate particularly to, for example, a large group case study discussion. Research about women's way of knowing by Belenky (1987) showed that women valued, for example, co-operation rather than competition and discussion over debate. This is interesting in its own right, but there is no comparative analysis of men on the same issues.

In multinationals additional complications arise from the unacceptability of women managers in some countries. Van Velsor and Hughes (1990) and Ohlott *et al* (1994) argue that in relation to large-scale developmental assignments women have to overcome more obstacles. The research was focused on preferred learning experiences rather than on how women actually learned from experiences. Research on whether women learn more or less readily from bosses, colleagues or mentors does not seem to exist. Case and Thompson (1995) do not support the view expressed in Van Velsor (1990) that women were more likely than men to learn from others.

There is little information on whether women are more or less likely to learn from solo methods such as reading, video, technology-based training, where they are unaffected by male company. Hammond (1992) suggested that they have a stronger inclination than men to learning alone. On the Honey and Mumford Learning Styles Questionnaire (LSQ), the norms for 174 women differed scarcely at all from men on the Reflector and Theorist dimensions, and by only one point on the Activist (higher for women) and Pragmatist (lower for women) scores. These differences are not at a level of significance to suggest that women characteristically learn differently from men. On Kolb's Learning Styles Inventory women have a much higher preference for what he calls 'abstract conceptualisation', as compared with 'concrete experience'. The male scores are almost exactly opposite to the female on these dimensions. The difference in results from the LSQ may be related to the fact that the LSI brings in 'feelings' in a more overt way.

REFLECT – CONCLUDE – PLAN 2

- Do you think 'women only' development activities are appropriate?
- To what extent might your experiences and your views about them be affected by your own gender?
- What conclusions can you draw about gender and MD?
- What action can be taken to enhance MD for women?

Mentoring and networking

Mentoring has been a particularly useful method of learning for women. Powerful male mentors may have helped, but some women prefer a female mentor – although it may be difficult to find one within the organisation (see Chapter 10). Recent interest in diversity management in organisations has highlighted the importance of mentoring by senior and line managers as a significant contributor to cultural change and the advancement of women

(Mattis, 2001). Sponsoring women for key positions is identified as a key role for senior managers and a vital requirement in driving an initiative through the organisation. Veale and Gold (1998) found that mentoring by senior managers often gave women managers the confidence to aim higher.

Networking has also been identified in previous chapters as an important MD activity. The key issue here is that women often find themselves excluded from the so-called 'old boy networks' that seem so important to male managers. Ibarra (1992) found that men were more likely to benefit from networks while women could find themselves caught between a social network of women and a task network of men and women; the consequence was potentially conflicting advice and tension. One problem for women is that they may have less time for networking compared to men. Nevertheless, networking is suggested as a method of improving women's career development (Veale and Gold, 1998), breaking down isolation and allowing the sharing of experiences to break down barriers (Linehan, 2001).

WEB LINKS

Catalyst is a North American organisation working to advance women in business. Its home page is http://www.catalystwomen.org/
Formal network for women include Women in Business and Finance at
http://www.wibf.org.uk/
and the Women's IT Network at
http://www.witnet.org.uk/aims.html
The European Women's Management Development Network is located at
http://www.ewmd.org/

ETHNIC MANAGERS

Many of the difficulties faced by women managers are also faced by managers from ethnic minorities. Ethnic minority managers accounted for 6 per cent of all managers in 2001, approximately equal to the proportion of ethnic workers in the workforce (EOC, 2002), although there is a wide variation by sector (13 per cent in hospitality/leisure, 3 per cent in production) and seniority. A benchmarking report on race and diversity covering 99 private and public organisations (RfO, 2002) showed that only 44 ethnic managers held posts at senior levels, and there were no black or other ethnic minority chief executives in the private sector organisations nor black or Asian Permanent Secretaries in any of the central government departments. However, it was also noted that there had been an improvement since the previous survey in 2001.

WEB LINK

Find out more about Race for Opportunity at
http://www2.bitc.org.uk/programmes/programme_directory/race_for_opportunity/index.html

The disproportionate presence of ethnic managers in certain sectors results in what Singh (2002; p.20) refers to as 'ghettoising'. Ethnic managers may also face stereotyping and exclusion from certain activities that help in career advancement – eg after-work drinks. In the USA Powell and Butterfield (1997) found that it was probably access to internal networks that gave white managers an advantage over other managers. Of course, many organisations are now able to prevent overt racist practices, but it is more difficult to deal with deep-seated stereotypes and negative images.

Women managers from ethnic groups face something of a double jeopardy. Davidson (2002) found that ethnicity was a greater hurdle than gender. Women managers often felt they were tokens, subject to stereotyping and had to deliver higher performance. There were also fewer role models. However, it was also found that many women could maintain a positive self-image and that their visibility allowed them to make their good performance more well known. Mattis (2001), using US findings for 'women of color', highlighted the importance of opportunities for visibility as well as help with career goals and explanation of organisation politics from senior managers.

NATIONAL CULTURES

Increasingly, managers will need to learn to work in and with different cultural contexts. There is evidence that lack of understanding of differing cultural assumptions can hamper learning and joint working among managers from different countries (Liu and Vince, 1999). Multinational organisations, and advisers working in countries different from their own, have to recognise that:

- There are differences in national culture with consequent differences in the required styles and behaviours of managers.
- Mixed management teams, particularly, require the effective integration of different cultures and styles.
- Different MD systems require a recognition that a system that works in one country may not work at all or in certain respects in another.

Dimensions of culture

Hofstede (1980) provided the major original work on cultural issues still widely used in MD. Hofstede described culture as 'a collective programming of the mind'. Because his research was conducted in one major organisation with a strong managerial culture, the differences in national style that he drew out were identifiably national rather than influenced by other variables such as organisation structure, techniques or processes. He developed four dimensions from his empirical research across 50 countries:

- *power distance* – concerned with the extent to which those with less power within a country expect and accept that power is distributed unequally
- *collectivity/individualism* – determining the levels of sharing and achievement, competition and collaboration. Individualist societies lead to expectations that people will look after themselves and their own interests; collective societies give preference to the interest of the group as a source of identity
- *masculinity/femininity* – being concerned with the degree to which gender roles are distinct (masculinity – eg men are tough, women are tender) or overlap (femininity – both men and women are models, tender and concerned with quality of life)
- *uncertainty avoidance* – being concerned with feelings of threat when there is uncertainty or unknown situations.

Organisations can use frameworks such as this to consider how to provide MD for managers who will work across cultural boundaries. For example, when Volkswagen were seeking to transfer know-how to new operations with Skoda in the Czech Republic, they identified the importance of 'intercultural sensitivity and open-mindedness' as a key competence for managers (Syrett and Lammimam, 1999; p.137).

WEB LINKS

Geert Hofstede's homepage can be found at
http://geerthofstede.com
The results of his research for different countries against each of his dimensions can be found at
http://www.pittstate.edu/mgmict/culture.html

Hofstede's definitions provide a good starting point, although he emphasised that individuals differ within a country 'norm'. (An alternative analysis by Trompenaars, 1996, challenges Hofstede.[4]) Working abroad – or working in your own country with managers from other countries – creates culture shock because your idea of the right way of doing things differs from those of other nationals. The difficulties are, of course, exacerbated by language. The old joke about the United States and England being countries separated by a common language has the major merit of reminding us that it is all too easy to believe that another person has understood you. When the other person's prime language is not English, difficulties are even more likely to arise.

Managing across cultures

The research studies are important not least because they sometimes contradict stereotypes, or perhaps provide clarification of the existence of a stereotype. As throughout this book, however, it is necessary to warn against generalisation. Of course the casual informality of many American managers demonstrates the truth of a stereotype – but informality in personal relationships does not necessarily go with informality in communication within the managerial hierarchy. One of the authors while working with German and English managers found one group complaining that the other was far too bound by rules of precedent and hierarchy. The British managers were astonished to find that it was the Germans who were making this complaint about *them*!

The comments about different cultures and management styles is significant for the design of systems. An appraisal scheme built on free and open exchange, including self-appraisal, may be well accepted in the United States, partly accepted in the UK, and not accepted at all in some other countries. Furthermore, there has been a major change in the patterns of job movement. The opportunities that used to exist in multinationals to send people abroad for a desirable period of experience in other countries are now much reduced. Understandably, many countries prefer, and need, to develop their own managers instead of creating vacancies for managers from the parent organisation. Desirable as it is that other countries should look after their own needs, this has substantially reduced certain kinds of management development opportunity for people from the parent company. An unfortunate consequence of this is that parent company senior managers may increasingly have had only visiting experience of the countries for which they may have senior responsibility at corporate headquarters. As Laurent (1986) showed, perceptions about careers and what it takes to develop careers may differ. American managers relate career to 'ambition and drive', whereas French managers see it as 'being labelled as having high potential'.

From a systematic MD point of view it may well be that the opportunities for posting abroad are diminishing at exactly the time when there is greater understanding of what needs to be done in order to make for a successful management appointment abroad! The advantage of distance and greater autonomy, which in many respects provide a good test of management competence, have to be balanced against the more solitary and isolated nature of the manager's work. There may well be greater risks, both political and commercial, involved in working abroad. Domestic problems can contribute to failure at least as often as they contribute to success. There is also the re-entry difficulty – finding the right slot at the right time for the returning manager, or even promising to do so before his departure abroad, can cause major headaches.

The main problem is the ethnocentric view of the world held in the corporate headquarters of many multinationals. It is not only that other countries and other cultures may respond negatively to the 'house' style: they may well have a substantially different view of appropriate MD practices. Handy's report (1987) described practices in France, West Germany and the United States, and was clearly an important source for any adviser in a multinational. His description of the Japanese processes were very close to the Type 2 processes described in this book. Storey *et al* (1997), while not wholly contradicting Handy, explodes some of the established myths about Japanese MD, as they were expressed at a time when Japan was seen as an exemplar of especially good management.

Work on learning style differences suggests that national differences ought not to be expressed too broadly in relation to structure or open-ended learning. However, data on the Honey and Mumford Learning Styles Questionnaire shows for example that there are no significant differences between the USA, the UK and Australia. Allinson and Hayes (1988) showed significant differences between Indian, East African and British managers. Pun (1990) compared Chinese and Western managers on features such as participation and preferred learning design, and also points out that the delivery through the English language to non-native English-speaking people often means that people do not understand the nuances.

Within the general context of an absence of research on the impact of different methods of learning, it is not surprising that as with women there is little available on whether a particular method is more, or less, suitable within a particular culture. One exception is Conway (1998) on mentoring. He provides a very detailed picture of different responses to mentoring in different countries. Marquardt (1999) also provides a detailed analysis of the impact of different cultural factors on the acceptability of Action Learning. In his case he is particularly helpful in relating the processes within Action Learning to their acceptability to different cultures.

REFLECT – CONCLUDE – PLAN 3

- What has been your experience of differences in national culture in relation to the provision of MD?
- How far does your experience confirm or deny the propositions advanced above?
- What actions might you take personally, or attempt to introduce within your own organisation?

PROFESSIONS AND MANAGEMENT DEVELOPMENT

Professional status is granted to those who have technical and theoretical expertise which is recognised by others to help them tackle what Dietrich and Roberts (1997; p.16) refer to as 'decision-making complexity'. Recognition of expertise grants professionals an authority as a group who, through their professional body, are able to set standards and ethics for practice. They might also attempt to license those who wish to practise, but most provide an education scheme for new entrants to show the acquisition of professional expertise.[5]

Managers and professionals

A crucial feature of professionals at work is that, on the basis of their expertise, they are able to act with independence, autonomy and discretion (Middlehurst and Kinnie, 1997). These particular features pose certain difficulties and dilemmas for those who wish to manage the work of professionals, as highlighted by Raelin (1986). Many professionals work in managed contexts, where they are employed on the basis of their expertise but are subject to the alternative authority of a line manager, who may not always be professionally qualified. For example, in public services such as health, local government, public administration and education, there are many professional staff who in recent years have experienced what is referred to as New Managerialism. Managers are made responsible for service delivery and improvement, frequently by setting and monitoring measurable targets (Exworth and Halford, 1999), the achievement of which may be formulated into league tables. Such managers are pressed to take a more proactive stance towards 'modernisation', especially where vested interests are perceived to provide restrictions on reform – eg professionals and trade unions. However, what is apparent is that traditional management styles of command and control are usually not appropriate, especially where staff are themselves highly qualified. As argued by Vermak and Weggeman (1999), traditional styles are a recipe for conflict with professionals, although this may be a manager's reflex to dealing with problems. Yet 'it is easy to get into a vicious circle: the manager tries to control things – the professionals sabotage this' (p.33).

The concept of management has spread into other areas of professional life with a shift towards diverse professions such as the law, the Church and armed services (Dawson, 1994). The authors, for example, have experience of working with senior people in trade unions and in the legal profession. The starting point for MD for them was not the concept of MD but helping them to recognise that they were indeed managers. Managerialism is becoming a feature in other sectors such as professional organisations. For example, Cooper *et al* (1996) argued that in the 'managed professional business', professional firms are increasingly organised as a business to be managed with more emphasis on strategy and planning, and managers accountable for the performance of teams and the delivery of results. There is an increased focus on client surveys and feedback and the introduction of organisation and business professionals such as marketing and HRM. Staff, while still working within the framework of their professional standards, may also be accountable to a line manager or 'partner-in-charge' (Hinings *et al*, 1999).

Learning about management

The principles of MD within the professions do not differ from those applied in those areas which are more traditionally understood to include management, but the different values and beliefs on standards of performance may cause difficulties in MD. In the UK, the Council for Excellence in Management and Leadership recommended that professional associations introduced 'elements of management and leadership into their pre-qualification and Continuing Professional Development programmes' (CEML, 2002; p.23). In addition, the

Profession's Working Group set out what they referred to as an 'irreducible core' of management and leadership abilities as a foundation for every professional.

Interestingly, the professions have made a contribution to MD because of their attention to their professional needs for development. So, for example, the engineering profession and the Chartered Institute of Personnel and Development have contributed the idea of Continuing Professional Development (CPD), in part so that their members can cope with change (Gold *et al*, 2001). For some, CPD is a compulsory feature of professional membership, and a growing number of associations provide formal systems to monitor and support CPD activities. Although management is not necessarily a feature of all professional association views of CPD, there are increasing pressures to bring this about. Further, managers can seek a professional standing in the UK through the Chartered Management Institute for which CPD is a core feature. The Institute's 'smart CPD' programme is based on:

- assessment – against core management skills using a self-assessment tool
- benchmarking – by the individual and colleagues, of knowledge, understanding and ability in individual management skills and techniques
- feedback – personalised information on the results of assessments
- signposting – to learning and development opportunities
- the development of learning skills – feedback on potential and capacity for learning.[6]

The ideas and processes involved in CPD have made a significant input to the idea that managers are involved also in continued development – in lifelong learning. The fact that CPD has increasingly emphasised the value of reviewing and explicitly learning from experience fits into the strategy advocated in this book. Early reliance on ticking off the number of conferences and courses attended has been replaced by this wider definition. Lifelong learning does not necessarily involve contributing profit to training and education institutions.

WEB LINKS

As part of its approach to CPD, the Institution of Electrical Engineers has created a number of online 'profession networks', including one on management which you can examine at
http://www.iee.org/OnComms/pn/management/aboutus.cfm
The CPD Forum provides an online resource at
http://www.cpdforum.org/cpdforum/control/Home
The Professional Associations Research Network provides up to date information on CPD at
http://www.parn.org.uk

REFLECT – CONCLUDE – PLAN 4

- Does your professional status conflict with management?
- What do you conclude about learning to manage professionals?
- What can you do to help managers learn about managing professionals in your organisation?

SMALL AND MEDIUM-SIZED ENTERPRISES

As with the other groups identified in this chapter, we see no difference in terms of purpose or processes in the development of managers in small and medium-sized enterprises (SMEs).[7] What differs are the likely difficulties in actually carrying out the processes. Most SMEs are owned and managed by one or two persons, and are family-based. This tends to mean that owner-managers run the business day-to-day in addition to having overall management responsibility (Johnson, 1999). The result is often that time is not available to send people away on courses, in contrast to larger organisations where loss of individuals for a period of time may be more easily borne. Yet the need for a stimulus of knowledge and experience gained from others is often even more crucial in small organisations. They may be too dependent on a narrow form of past experience, particularly where firms have been passed down through generations of one family. Alternatively, they may be first-generation businesses perhaps set up by entrepreneurs or innovators who know very little about management and organisations.

Managing and learning

It is not surprising that research suggests that few SMEs have a formal policy on MD and few managers hold qualifications in management (Johnson, 1999). However, this does not mean managers do not want MD. As Thomson *et al* (1997) found, SMEs would undertake MD if they saw value in it and it was in line with their interests; size alone is not the main barrier to MD. Although most SME managers would regard their activities as unique to their own situation, making it even more difficult to generalise in terms of skills, there have been some attempts to specify management in SMEs. For example, in the UK, the Small Firms Lead Body has provided a set of 'Standards for competitiveness' that fit within the NVQ framework. Evaluation by Atherton and Philpot (1997) showed the need to link the standards to the business development needs of SMEs in order for managers to see their value. Perren and Grant (2001) found that SME managers and entrepreneurs could identify important skills such as selling, accounting, strategic/analytical abilities and people abilities as important. However, there was a lot of emphasis on informal mechanisms for learning, such as opportunities to share experiences, networking and mentoring and coaching.

This highlights a very significant point about MD in SMEs – that it is closely related to moving the business in the direction that meets the desires of the managers. Indeed, because of the pressures of everyday work, most managers learn accidentally and reactively by solving problems (Type 1 MD). In such a process, managers by necessity draw on a network of others such as family, employees and many others who can advise SME managers – eg banks, accountants and other professionals (Gibb, 1997). However, those outside the network, such as policy-makers, can find it very difficult to intervene to stimulate managers to do more MD, especially Type 3 courses. The result has been a fragmented and often confusing pattern of activities aimed at SMEs, often funded by government and European agencies, but these seldom penetrate the micro-world of the SME. There is a greater need to develop Type 2 activities which use the real issues of managing in SMEs as a stimulus for learning. For example, Devins and Gold (2000) report on an MD programme for owner-managers where an external business coach worked on business issues over three years. The crucial feature was the importance of finding the interests of managers and working with them over a period of time. Such interests included succession planning, innovation, managing reorganisation and, most importantly at the time, surviving recession. However, it took up to six months before the coach became sufficiently trusted to pursue more adventurous activities.

WEB LINKS

Read more about the Small Firms Lead Body at
http://www.lifelonglearning.co.uk/iln4000/iln4113.htm
The Small Business Service at http://www.sbs.gov.uk/ is part of the Business Link service at http://www.businesslink.gov.uk, providing research and support for managers in SMEs.
The Small Business Research Portal at http://www.smallbusinessportal.co.uk/index.php contains a mass of information and links relating to small business learning.

SUMMARY

- Managers are required to learn about the importance of valuing difference in an organisation as part of the growing interest in the benefits of diversity management.
- Career opportunities are more limited for women managers than for men where women face problems of stereotyping and prejudice.
- There are contrasting views of whether women have different management styles and development needs, and whether there should be separate male/female MD activities.
- Managers from ethnic minorities may face stereotyping and exclusion, forcing them into 'career ghettos'.
- There are features of national cultures which cause differences in the acceptability of some MD processes, disciplines and systems.
- There is a recognition that MD for professionals must take into account the independence, autonomy and discretion of professional work.
- Managers in SMEs mostly learn by reacting to and solving everyday problems. Business issues must form the basis of MD activities.

DISCUSSION QUESTIONS

1. How can diversity management contribute to an organisation's ability to achieve strategic advantage? What are the implications for developing managers?
2. Do you think that most management courses are based on a 'masculine' view of management? Should women have separate courses?
3. What MD activities can be provided to support ethnic minority managers?
4. What are the key skills required for managers from the UK who are required to work abroad?
5. Can managerialism and professionalism ever be reconciled?
6. 'A radical rethink is needed of the whole management and leadership provision for SMEs.' Discuss.

FURTHER READING

BRYANS, P. and MAVIN, S. (2003) 'Women learning to become managers: learning to fit in or to play a different game?', *Management Learning*, Vol. 34, No. 1; pp.111–134.

DAVIDSON, M. and FRIEDMAN, R. A. (1998) 'When excuses don't work: the persistent injustice effect among black managers', *Administrative Science Quarterly*, Vol. 43, No. 1; pp.154–184.

MURREL, A. J., CROSBY, F. J. and ELY, R. J. (eds) (1999) *Mentoring Dilemmas: Development relationships within multicultural organisations.* Hillsdale, New Jersey, Erlbaum.

PERREN, L. (2001) *Management and Leadership in the Professions.* London, Council for Excellence in Management and Leadership.

SINCLAIR, M. (1997) 'The MBA through women's eyes: learning and pedagogy in management education', *Management Learning*, Vol. 28, No. 3; pp.313–330.

YORKS, L. (ed.) (2003) 'Cross-cultural dimensions of team learning', in 'Advances in Development', *Human Resources*, Vol. 5, No. 1, February.

GROUP ACTIVITY

- Form a group of three
- Carry out research on crucial issues in your organisation in relation to ethnicity, diversity and women managers.
- How do these affect MD, and what actions should be taken on MD policies and courses?
- Prepare a presentation based on your findings.

REFERENCES

ALLINSON, C. W. and HAYES, J. (1988) 'Cultural differences in the learning styles of managers', *Management International Review*, Vol. 28, March.

ATHERTON, A. and PHILPOT, T. (1997) *MCI and Small Firms Lead Body Standards and SME Development in Practice*. Report to MCI/DfEE. Durham University Business School.

BELENKY, M. F. (1987) 'Women's ways of knowing', in P. S. Laver and C. Hendrick (eds) *Sex and Gender.* London, Sage.

BURKE, S. and COLLINS, K. M. (2001) 'Gender differences in leadership styles and management skills', *Women in Management Review*, Vol. 16, No. 5; pp.244–256.

BYRNE, D. (1971) *The Attraction Paradigm.* New York, Academic Press.

CASE, S. and THOMPSON, L. (1995) 'Gender differences', in R. Boyatzis, S. Cowen and D. Kolb (eds) *Innovation in Professional Education.* San Francisco, Jossey Bass.

CEML (2001) *Meeting the Need.* London, Council for Excellence in Management and Leadership.

CEML (2002) *Managers and Leaders: Raising our game*. London, Council for Excellence in Management and Leadership.

COOPER, D., GREENWOOD, R., HININGS, C. R. and BROWN, J. (1996) 'Sedimentation and transformation in organizational change: the case of Canadian law firms', *Organization Studies*, Vol. 17, No. 4; pp.623–647.

COOPER JACKSON, J. (2001) 'Women middle managers' perception of the glass ceiling', *Women in Management Review*, Vol. 16, No. 1; pp.30–41.

CONWAY, C. (1998) *Strategies for Mentoring*. Chichester, Wiley.

DAWSON, S. (1994) 'Changes in distance: professionals re-appraise the meaning of management', *Journal of General Management*, Vol. 20, No. 1; pp.1–21.

DAVIDSON, M. J. (2002) 'The black and ethnic minority women manager', in R. J. Burke and D. L. Nelson, *Advancing Women's Careers: Research and practice*. Oxford, Blackwell.

DAVIDSON, M. J. and COOPER, C. L. (1992) *Shattering the Glass Ceiling*. London, Paul Chapman Publishing.

DEVINS, D. and GOLD, J. (2000) '"Cracking the tough nuts": mentoring and coaching the managers of small firms', *Career Development International*, Vol. 5, Nos 4/5; pp.250–255.

DIETRICH, M. and ROBERTS, J. (1997) 'Beyond the economics of professionalism', in J. Broadbent, M. Dietrich, and J. Roberts (eds) *The End of the Professions?* London, Routledge.

EOC (2003) *Women and Men in Britain: Management*. Manchester, Equal Opportunities Commission.

EOC (2003) *Facts About Women and Men in Great Britain*. London, Equal Opportunities Commission.

EXWORTHY, M. and HALFORD, S. (eds) (1999) *Professionals and the New Managerialism in the Public Sector*. Buckingham, Open University Press.

FRAKER, S. (1984) 'Why women aren't getting to the top', *Fortune*, April.

GIBB, A. (1997) 'Small firms' training and competitiveness: building upon the small business as a learning organisation', *International Small Business Journal*, Vol. 15, No. 3; pp.13–29.

GOLD, J., RODGERS, H. and SMITH, V. (2001) *The Future of the Professions*. London, Council for Excellence in Management and Leadership.

HAMMOND, V. and HOLTON, V. (1992) *Information Technology Environments*. Berkhamstead, Ashridge Management Research.

HANDY, C. (1987) *Making Managers*. London, NEDO.

HININGS, C. R., GREENWOOD, R. and COOPER, D. (1999) 'The dynamics of change in large accounting firms', in D. M. Brock, M. J. Powell and C. R. Hinings (eds) *Restructuring the Professional Organization*. London, Routledge.

HITE, M. and McDONALD, K. S. (1995) 'Gender issues in management development', *Journal of Management Development*, Vol. 14, No. 4; pp.5–15.

HOFSTEDE, G. (1980) *Cultures Consequences*. London, Sage.

IBARRA, H. (1992) 'Homophily and differential returns: sex differences in network structure and access in an advertising firm', *Administrative Sciences Quarterly*, Vol. 37; pp.422–447.

JOHNSON, S. (1999) *Skills Issues for Small and Medium-sized Enterprises*. Research Paper 13. London, Skills Task Force.

LAURENT, A. (1986) 'The cross-cultural puzzle of international human resource management', *Human Resource Management*, Vol. 25, No. 1; pp.91–102.

LEWIS, A. E. and FAGENSON, E. A. (1995) 'Strategies for developing women managers: how well do they fulfil their objectives?', *Journal of Management Development*, Vol. 14, No. 2; pp.39–53.

LINEHAN, M. (2001) 'Networking for female managers' career development: empirical evidence', *Journal of Management Development*, Vol. 20, No. 10; pp.823–829.

LIU, S. and VINCE, R. (1999) 'The cultural context of learning in international joint ventures', *Journal of Management Development*, Vol. 18, No. 8; pp.666–675.

LIU, J. and WILSON, D. (2001) 'The unchanging perceptions of women as managers', *Women in Management Review*, Vol. 16, No. 4; pp.163–173.

MARQUARDT, M. (1999) *Action Learning in Action*. Palo Alto, Davies Black.

MARSHALL, J. (1991) 'Women managers', in A. Mumford, *The Handbook Of Management Development*. Aldershot, Gower.

MARSHALL, J. (1995) 'Researching women and leadership: some comments on challenges and opportunities', *International Review of Women and Leadership*, Vol. 1, No. 1; pp.1–10.

MATTIS, M. C. (2001) 'Advancing women in business', *Journal of Management Development*, Vol. 20, No. 4; pp.371–388.

MAVIN, S. (2001) 'Women's career in theory and practice: time for change?', *Women in Management Review*, Vol. 16, No. 4; pp.183–192.

MIDDLEHURST, R. and KENNIE, T. (1997) 'Leading professionals: towards new concepts of professionalism', in J. Broadbent, M. Dietrich and J. Roberts (eds) *The End of the Professions?* London, Routledge.

MILLER, S., ROUELLA, H. and JOHNSON, M. (2002) 'Divergent identities? Professions, management and gender', *Public Money and Management*, January-March; pp.25–30.

MUMFORD, A. (1988) *Developing Top Managers*. Aldershot, Gower.

OHLOTT, P. J., RUDERMAN, M. N. and MCCAULEY, C. D. (1994) 'Gender differences in managers' developmental job experiences', *Academy of Management Journal*, Vol. 37, No. 1; pp.46–67.

ONS (2003) *New Earnings Survey 2002*. London, Office of National Statistics.

PERREN, L. and GRANT, P. (2001) *Management and Leadership in UK SMEs*. London, Council for Excellence in Management and Leadership.

POWELL, G. N. and BUTTERFIELD, D. A. (1997) 'The effect of race on promotions to top management in a federal department', *Academy of Management Journal*, Vol. 40, No. 1; pp.112–129.

POWELL, G. N. and BUTTERFIELD, D. A. (2002) 'Exploring the influence of decision makers' race and gender on actual promotions to top management', *Personnel Psychology*, Vol. 55; pp.397–428.

PUN, A. (1990) 'Managing the cultural differences in learning', *Journal of Management Development*, Vol. 9, No. 5.

RAELIN, J. A. (1986) *Clash of Cultures*. Cambridge, Mass, Harvard Business Corp Press.

REYNOLDS, M. and TREHAN, K. (2003) 'Learning from difference', *Management Learning*, Vol. 34, No. 2; pp.162–180.

RfO (2002) *Race: Creating business value*. London, Race for Opportunity.

SINGH, V. (2002) *Managing Diversity for Strategic Advantage*. London, Council for Excellence in Management and Leadership.

STOREY, J., EDWARDS, P. and SISSON, K. (1997) *Managers in the Making*. London, Sage.

STURGES, J. (1999) 'What it means to succeed: personal conceptions of career success held by male and female managers at different ages', *British Journal of Management*, Vol. 10, No. 3; pp.239–252.

SYRETT, M. and LAMMIMAN, J. (1999) *Management Development*. London, The Economist Books.

TANNEN, D. (1991) *You Just Don't Understand: Women and men in conversation*. London, Virago.

TANTON, M. (ed.) (1995) *Women in Management*. London, Routledge.

THOMSON, A., STOREY, J., MABEY, C., GRAY, C., FARMER, E. and THOMSON. R. A. (1997) *Portrait of Management Development*. London, Institute of Management.

TROMPENAARS, F. (1996) *Riding the Waves*. London, Nicholas Brealey.

VEALE, C. and GOLD, J. (1998) 'Smashing into the glass ceiling for women managers', *Journal of Management Development*, Vol. 17, No. 1; pp.17–26.

VERMAK, H. and WEGGEMAN, M. (1999) 'Conspiring fruitfully with professionals: new management roles for professional organisations', *Management Decision*, Vol. 37, No. 1; pp.29–44.

WAJCMAN, J. (1998) *Managing Like A Man*. Oxford, Blackwell.

ENDNOTES

1 Useful material for director development is available in Mumford 1988 and from the Institute of Directors at http://www.iod.co.uk/

2 Up to date information about gender differences can be found at the Equal Opportunities Commission:

http://www.eoc.org.uk/EOCeng/dynpages/research_stats.asp

and National Statistics Online at

http://www.statistics.gov.uk/about/genderstatistics/default.asp

Wider concerns about equality and opportunity for women can be found at the Women and Equality Unit at http://www.womenandequalityunit.gov.uk/

3 Various studies have revealed the difficulties faced by women from apparently threatened male managers – eg playing down achievements, undermining authority, aggression and bullying, sexist behaviour – see Liu and Wilson (2001).

4 In Hampden-Turner and Trompenaars (1993), seven valuing processes are presented as dilemmas that require reconciliation. The seven dilemmas are: universalism *v.* particularism, analysing *v.* integration, individualism *v.* communitarianism, inner-directed *v.* outer-directed orientation, time as sequence *v.* time as synchronisation, achieved status *v.* ascribed status, and equality *v.* hierarchy.

5 In the UK there are around 400 professional bodies all providing a qualification education scheme.

6 Check the CMI's website at www.inst-mgt.org.uk/ for more details.

7 SMEs are usually those organisations employing between 10 and 250 employees. Together with micro-businesses (less than 10), they account for more than 50 per cent of all people employed.

The future of management development

CHAPTER 12

Chapter outline

LEARNING OUTCOMES

After studying this chapter, you should be able to understand, explain, analyse and evaluate:

- **different approaches to dealing with the future**
- **key trends affecting the future of management development**
- **how managers must learn to deal with complexity and unpredictability**
- **the link between management development, strategic and organisation learning, and innovation.**

INTRODUCTION

Predicting the future of MD is a 'central problem' (Hirsh and Carter, 2002; p.45). Nevertheless, there are clearly significant and identifiable trends and drivers for change which will affect what managers must learn and how learning will be delivered. For example, Winterton *et al* (2000) noted that managers in the future will need greater cultural awareness and skills of learning, innovation, managing change and flexibility. It is also commonly suggested that the rate of change is accelerating and that managers and others must learn at an equal rate. We would also propose that it not just the rate of change which requires a response – there is an important difference between change that is incremental or simply an adjustment to restore equilibrium and change that is more radical, transformational and discontinuous. For the latter, learning involves a challenge to existing assumptions and frames of thinking – what Argyris (1999) referred to as 'double-loop' learning. Managers have a key role in leading and learning from change, providing the link between individual learning and such concepts as the learning organisation.

APPROACHING THE FUTURE

There are a variety of social, technological, demographic and political developments which are having and will have a significant impact on how we live and how organisations are structured and are managed. They will also constrain some of the choices. Although some of the trends may be clear, there is not always predictability about their impact. How managers respond will depend on how they learn to develop new ways of thinking and acting with

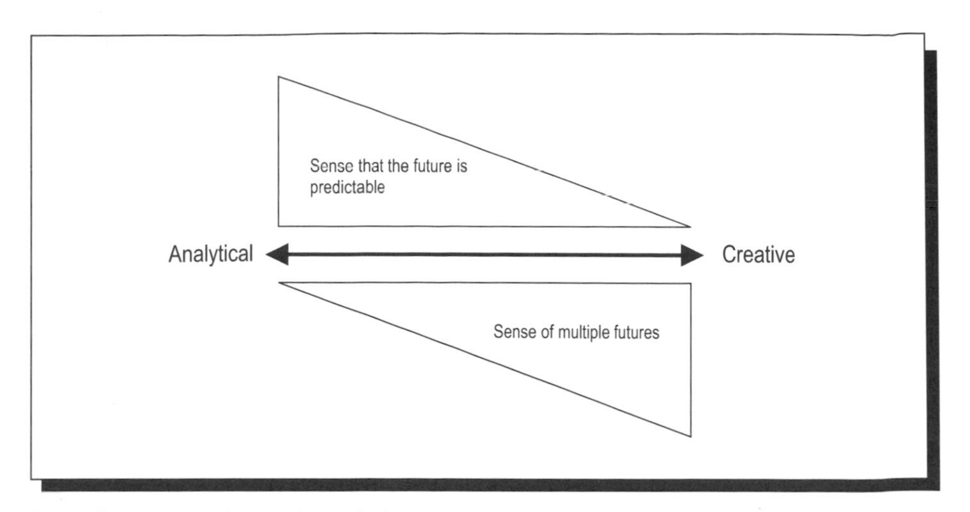

Figure 40 *A spectrum of approaches to the future*
Source: PIU (2001; p.15)

others. In the UK, the Performance and Innovation Unit (PIU, 2001)[1] highlighted a divergence between analytical thinking for predictability and creative thinking where there is unpredictability, complexity and multiple future possibilities. Figure 40 shows this spectrum of approaches to the future.

Analytical approaches work with trends and predictive models which allow managers to attempt to plan and control events. By contrast, creative approaches are required where the presence and interaction of large numbers of factors make prediction, planning and pre-specification more difficult. In such situations managers need to learn to think differently, perhaps drawing on ideas from complexity and chaos theories (Stacey, 2002). There is a difference between a future which is uncertain and one which is complex. In the former, there is a search to remove the uncertainty mainly by gathering information and subjecting it to analysis. This can occur even when there are large numbers of factors – the crucial point is that uncertainty can be made understandable. With complexity, there are too many factors interacting in a dynamic and non-linear way for analysis to reduce the uncertainty and increase predictability. Patterns of interaction between the factors produce results that cannot be set out in rules of cause and effect. Instead, more creative approaches are required.

Given the difficulty of making predictions about the future with certainty, managers will need to learn new skills, drawing from the field of *futurism.* According to Slaughter (1999), a futurist studies the future and understands how to use the knowledge gained to enable others to identify choices and options. Dator (1993), a leading futurist,[2] has suggested that various essential attributes and skills are required:

- creativity, imagination, the willingness to think new thoughts, to make unmade connections, to be ridiculed, laughed at, and to laugh at yourself
- the ability to synthesise, combine, invent, create
- a willingness to be politically active, to test out new ideas on yourself first and while trying actually to create a better world, or some portion of it

- the ability to try to anticipate the consequences of actions before you act, but also a willingness to risk failure and to learn from mistakes and criticism – indeed, to seek out and provoke criticism – but to keep trying to do better, and constantly to relearn what 'better' might be
- insatiable curiosity, unbounded compassion, incurable optimism, and an unquenchable sense of humour and delight in the absurd.

REFLECT – CONCLUDE – PLAN 1

- Does your organisation favour analytical or creative approaches to thinking about the future?
- What do you think can be done to enhance both analytical and creative approaches?
- What will you do to bring this about?

TRENDS FOR MANAGEMENT DEVELOPMENT

Spotting trends is an analytical approach to dealing with the future. If the right trend can be identified, managers can take appropriate action. A variety of trends are affecting what managers need to learn and how such learning occurs.

Globalisation

Organisations have to stretch thinking beyond local and national boundaries. Facilitated by developments in information and communications technology (ICT) and the Internet (see below), increasingly goods and services, capital and knowledge have become more mobile. Organisations will seek to exploit new markets. In the public and quasi-market sectors, there are increasing possibilities for sharing knowledge and understanding across the globe. Managers must learn to work in and across different national cultures (see Chapter 10), and interest in the skills of global, cross-cultural and transnational management is resulting in a significant adjustment to company MD.

Globalisation has also increased awareness of the effect of business activities on the environment. There may be ongoing tensions between national governments on setting limits on emissions, etc, but many organisations are attempting to adopt green management and sustainability policies and practices involving the development of environmentally-friendly products and processes. There are international standards for environmental management such as the ISO 14000 series[3] which can result in cost savings through waste management and recycling. Graham (2002), however, suggests that more radical thinking and critical reflection is required for eco-effectiveness.

WEB LINKS

Samsung's approach to green management can be found at
http://www.samsung.com/AboutSAMSUNG/SocialCommitment/EHSreport/index.htm
http://www.naturalstep.org provides a link to the Natural Step, an organisation which provides a framework to help organisations move towards sustainability.

REFLECT – CONCLUDE – PLAN 2

- How eco-friendly is your organisation? Is there a green policy?
- What ideas do you have to train managers to meet green standards or to think radically about green issues at work?
- What can you do to make this happen?

Technology and science

Developments in technology and science have always been at the heart of change in industrial societies with implications for organisational structures, skills requirements, work patterns, location and times. There has been added impetus given by the way information and communication technologies are being used to store, retrieve, analyse and communicate information. Castells (1996) referred to the 'information technology revolution' involving the convergence of micro-technologies, computing, telecommunications, broadcasting and opto-electronics.

As more attention is focused on the flows of information and processes of production, the flattening of management hierarchies moves decision-making closer to the point of production, with a greater emphasis on the development of flexible and multi-skilled teams. Managers must move away from command-and-control practices towards more progressive HRM involving opportunities to innovate within roles and the promoting of a positive psychological contract with a positive outcome in terms of organisation commitment (Guest *et al* (1998). Similarly, the International Labour Office's model of 'high-performance working' (ILO, 2000; p.1) implies that managers and leaders are to provide a vision and a 'sense of momentum and direction' so that learning becomes the only strategy to cope with change. However, according to Michie and Sheehan-Quinn (2001; p.302), organisations and managers may still be tempted by the 'wrong sort of flexibility' which preserves the traditional frame of management command and control.

WEB LINKS

The ESRC's Future of Work site can be found at
http://www.leeds.ac.uk/esrcfutureofwork/
The International Labour Office's skills and knowledge site is
http://www.ilo.org/public/english/employment/skills/index.htm

During the 1990s many organisations were able to begin the process of dispersing activities away from a single location, leading to many staff tele-working from home or in more local tele-centres. In the 2000s there are trends toward the formation of virtual organisations by which ICT allows a separation of physical and information components in production. According to Pearson (1999), information resources can be accessed from anywhere in the world, and this includes the expertise of people. Through virtual meeting spaces and conferencing, such resources can be brought together for particular projects regardless of geographical distance. In such circumstances, managers increasingly do not work with physical resources or the presence of people.

Distance provides no hurdle for MD too. It has long been possible for managers to learn at a distance, but recently there has been a significant shift towards e-learning including computer-based training (CBT), Web-based training (WBT) and online learning. According to research by Pollard and Hillage (2001), the benefits of e-learning include the ability to learn 'just in time' at the learner's pace and convenience, and the provision of updatable materials with reductions in delivery costs. Sloman (2001) suggests that in the future there will be a shift away from classroom learning and organisations will develop their intranets as vehicles for delivery, perhaps formalising resources into a corporate university (Clarke and Hermens, 2001). For example, at the University for Lloyds TSB there are computer-based facilities and access to learning materials via 2,000 computers throughout branches and offices. A significant feature of e-learning for managers is how power in learning shifts towards consumers. That is, some of the hurdles that managers may face in accessing MD can be bypassed. For example, managers can access many free materials and articles via the Internet; they can also join virtual learning communities or engage in collaborative activities with other managers (but see Chapter 5 for reservations about badly designed e-learning).

New knowledge

The generative power of ICT has contributed to an explosion in the availability of new information and knowledge,[4] with rapid dissemination. The last decade has seen the development of knowledge-intensive services in education, communication and design, expert advice and consultancy employing 'knowledge workers' in the 'knowledge-based economy'. Knowledge workers are more highly qualified, and as they apply their skills, the knowledge generated becomes part of an organisation's intellectual capital. There is a greater emphasis on people's ability to construct, manipulate and apply new knowledge, adding value to what is produced, and human capital accumulation has become one of the new reasons for an investment in continuous learning and HRD (Garavan *et al*, 2001). Knowledge is now regarded as part of an organisation's intangible assets, challenging traditional accounting practices which may fail to capture the potential of knowledge in organisations. These trends are of course also feeding the interest in knowledge management and productivity and the management of knowledge workers (see below).

For managers and MD, a key part of the knowledge society is the development of new ideas about organisations and management (and increasingly, leadership) presented in the work of academics, consultants, gurus and others. Such knowledge appears in various guises ranging from popular magazines in paper or electronic format to 'Heathrow hero' books to research findings appearing in peer-reviewed academic journals. Much of this knowledge, to a greater or lesser extent, is used to train managers.

REFLECT – CONCLUDE – PLAN 3

- What has been the impact of business process re-engineering (BPR), Total Quality Management (TQM), human resources management (HRM), neuro-linguistic programming (NLP), customer relations management (CRM) and Culture Management and Transformation in your organisation?
- How have these and other ideas affected how managers are developed?
- What conclusions do you draw from this review?
- What might you do to improve the effective use of these ideas?

Business schools and universities are key sources of many new ideas and research relating to management. There is an incredible diversity in management research which is informed by a large array of different frameworks of understanding or paradigms. Indeed, some of this research seems so obscure that there has been talk of a 'relevance gap' between the generation of knowledge and its use by managers in their work (Starkey and Madan, 2001; p.3).

WEB LINKS

Management researchers in the UK are represented by the British Academy of Management at http://www.bam.ac.uk/
If you would like to look at an online academic journal of management, try http://www.dmsp.dauphine.fr/management/
For a critical perspective, try http://www.ephemeraweb.org

In response to the outputs of management research from whatever source, academic or otherwise, managers are coming under increasing pressure to update and develop their knowledge and skills through Continuous Professional Development (CPD). Along with other initiatives relating to lifelong learning, CPD is providing an important impetus in MD (see Chapter 11). Further, it is often framed in individual terms so that managers can determine what they want to learn. However, there is the danger that it could become like other Type 3 approaches and not sufficiently owned by managers, especially if it is made compulsory. We need also to remember that managers do not work in a cultural and political vacuum. What managers learn and how they learn is strongly influenced by an organisation's learning climate which impacts on a manager's performance and by whether new skills can be applied. As identified by Kellie (2002), there is a danger that CPD processes become demonstrations of acquiring and documenting functionally relevant skills at the expense of important learning issues such as reflection on experience and the consideration of theoretical and conceptual underpinning to practice, which includes aspects of organisational life that prevent managers from learning.

Deregulation/regulation

Since the 1980s there has been an emphasis on the deregulation of markets. The overall aim has been to stimulate competition and promote entrepreneurialism across the economy. In many sectors, the drivers of technology and globalisation have already led to the restructuring of many industries. In the provision of public services, key elements have included privatisation, applying market principles to services, performance management, and giving individuals an expression of choice. To support managers in acquiring management skills and techniques, qualifications are increasingly being developed within specialist colleges. However, because many managers in the public sector are professionally qualified – eg head teachers are qualified teachers too – there is a blurring of management and professional work, and with the trend toward qualification, a dual professionalisation is in process.

Socio-economic factors

There are a variety of trends under this heading, ranging from the composition of the population and then the workforce to changing values in the information age. One clear trend is the pattern of increasing skill levels. The 2001 Skills Survey (Felstead *et al*, 2001) found that employers increased their qualifications requirements so that more jobs required more training time. The number of graduates is likely to rise as higher education both expands and provides easier access, creating expectations that work of sufficient complexity and challenge will be available. Perhaps in response, there has been an increase in the importance of coaching skills among managers (Felstead *et al*, 2001). A clear implication for MD is the growing importance attached to equality and diversity in the workplace and in society in general (see Chapter 11).

More broadly, managers will need to understand the values and ethics of their role. In the past and even in the present, managers have often presented their roles and activities using a scientific and technical way of talking which emphasised rationality and objectivity as idealised processes. There is apparently little room for emotions and values; management is value-neutral. However, even a cursory analysis would reveal that managers are continually faced with dilemmas and choices between competing alternatives – their decisions are inevitably based on judgements about what is right or wrong. We all conduct our lives according to a set of moral values which are made manifest in what we say and do. Most of the time at work, such values remain undiscussed and buried in the assumptions that make an organisation's culture, but during times of change such values are more likely to be revealed. In particular, fundamental change will require a questioning of current assumptions and the presence of different views about change, including negative views, all of which will provide managers with difficult choices. The choices managers make are ethical and reveal their values.

REFLECT – CONCLUDE – PLAN 4

- How do managers learn about values and ethical behaviour?
- What are the implications for MD?
- What could you do personally and for your organisation on ethics and values in an MD context?

WEB LINKS

You can find a *Complete Guide to Ethics Management: An ethics toolkit for managers* at http://www.mapnp.org/library/ethics/ethxgde.htm#anchor26548
The Institute for Business Ethics provides information about developing a code of conduct and other resources at
http://www.ibe.org.uk/

A key dilemma facing managers is whether their activities should focus exclusively on the interests of their organisations or whether they should also consider wider concerns relating to the interests of society. Organisations in the private sector, in the main, aim for maximum profits – the 'bottom line' – to ensure an adequate return on shareholder investment. However, there are a number of adverse consequences that result from the pursuit of purely financial returns – eg short-term targets, failure to consider the impact of activities on the environment, corruption over pay, etc. In extreme situations there may be dramatic consequences, such as the collapse of Enron in the USA. Many managers may come under pressure to conform to unethical practices, and some, unwilling to suffer the torment, may actually be prepared to reveal publicly what is happening –whistle-blowing.[5] Over the last 15 years there has been increasing concern about ethical standards in both private and public sector organisations. In the former, concern over the behaviour of senior managers has led to an interest in corporate governance. Increasingly, organisations are likely to face pressures to prove that they have adopted corporate social responsibility (CSR) as a policy to reconcile the competing demands of financial performance and business ethics. CSR is not an easy term to define and 'can mean anything to anybody' (Frankental, 2001; p.20). However, a number of practices have been identified as a feature of CSR, such as:

- corporate citizenship as a way of presenting an image of responsibility for social impact and being a member of the local community
- stakeholder management to identify individuals and groups who have an interest in organisational performance and may be impacted upon by its activities.

There are doubts about whether managers will be able to resist the requirements to meet short-term targets related to financial performance, especially where CSR is not rewarded by financial markets (Frankental, 2001).

WEB LINKS

The International Corporate Governance Network's homepage can be found at http://www.icgn.org/
Shell's report on how it contributes to sustainable development can be found at http://www.shell.com/home/Framework?siteId=shellreport2002-en
An online CSR magazine can be found at http://www.business-ethics.com/

One trend that will undoubtedly support ethical behaviour in management is the process of professionalisation. Despite doubts that management can ever be a profession (see Chapter 1), in the UK there are variety of professional associations whose members perform as managers. This includes more traditional associations, such as those in accountancy, marketing and HRM, but also those which cover management as a generic profession, such as the Chartered Management Institute. As managers seek professional standing, they become bound by a code of conduct including a requirement to behave ethically. However, although managers may improve their professional status in the future, there are also critical voices that question the institutionalisation of management. Certainly, by use of the Internet, such voices can combine to provide an alternative view of the globalised power of large organisations. Grey (1999) argues that while it is suggested that the distinction between managers and the managed will be eroded as staff become 'empowered', he challenges the idea that this has to mean that more people in organisations become managers too. He argues that managers are characterised by 'an inescapable manipulativeness' and the treatment of people 'instrumentally – as means rather than ends' (p.579). If more people become managers, they also become part of the manipulation. This critical view conflicts with past views such as those of Douglas McGregor (Theory X and Theory Y), which influenced MD in the past. Parker (2002) also takes a critical view. He argues that managerialism does not represent the only way for human beings to be organised, and that it could be possible for production and employment to take place in smaller and more local units which encourage 'more face-to-face senses of responsibility' (p.203). He cites the example of Scott Bader, an organisation in Northampton producing polymers, which claims that it is 'governed by its employees'.[6] Another example might be Semco in Brazil (Semler, 2003).

LEARNING IN COMPLEXITY

Whereas trends may be relatively easy to identify, their impact is less predictable. Even so, it might still be possible for managers to learn to cope – managers can reflect critically on their assumptions, challenge their mental models and find new ways of proceeding. The answer would seem to be to endure a period of discomfort as long-held beliefs are overturned so that eventually managers can return to some form of equilibrium, albeit with new assumptions. The difficulty here is that managers might remain with a way of thinking and behaving which continues with the assumption that events can be controlled and engineered by uncovering rules of cause and effect. The influence of this approach to management persists with the specification of skills and competences that is claimed to link to analysing the work of managers and predicting performance.

In contrast, there is increasing attention being given to discontinuity in the world, the unpredictability of events and ongoing and continuous flux in which disequilibrium becomes the norm. To help managers cope, a more creative approach to learning is suggested using the idea of complexity and complex systems. According to Cilliers (1998), while not subject to a simple definition, complexity occurs when:

- there are a large number of interacting elements behaving in a non-linear fashion
- interactions can have the effect of feedback that can be positive or negative
- systems are usually open to interaction with the environment
- systems operate far from equilibrium, subject to continuous movement and flux.

One of the main principles of complexity is that interaction between elements produces a sense of order through self-organisation. Such order emerges, but due to the non-linear dynamics cannot be predicted with certainty or planned. Instead, there are a variety of possible effects. For managers in organisations, this might mean that plans for change do not occur as expected, the acquisition of particular skills or competence do not produce a desired performance (and may even produce the opposite result), and groups of staff may be beyond control – at least by a top-down command approach to management.

WEB LINKS

The Complexity Research Programme at the LSE is focusing on complex social systems to study organisations. The home page is http://is.lse.ac.uk/complexity/
Go to http://www.santafe.edu/, the home of the Santa Fe Institute and a key source of ideas on complexity.

We can see the influence of complexity in a number of recent approaches to management and learning. For example, Watson and Harris (1999) argue that managers need to take a more process-oriented view of organisations and their own positions as managers. Instead of focusing on the idea of fixed things, like teams, the department, the business, or even the self as manager, there is a need to see everything as in a process of continuous movement. Thus a person performing a management role, managing, is never a fixed entity with permanent features such as static and unchangeable skills and competences. He or she is always 'becoming' (p.19). Similarly, organisations become more difficult to understand as ordered entities, designed for a particular purpose such as profits or serving the public. Organisations are always composed of people who through ongoing interaction carry out meaningful activities which may or may not correspond with the purposes of senior management. One way of understanding such interaction and the meanings made between people is through what Czarniawska-Joerges (1993) referred to as 'nets of collective actions',[7] and any workplace will be composed of a variety of nets. The difficulty for managers is that 'what is publicly acknowledged and recognised is just the tip of the iceberg' (p.61). Managers need to understand the meanings made within nets of collective action to understand what happens in organisations. Capra (2002) also stresses the 'livingness' of organisations, pointing out that as living beings, people have the ability to regenerate, change and evolve, and that these are the characteristics required for survival in a complex, fast-changing and knowledge-intensive environment.

Stories and systems

How can managers learn to cope with complexity, in the present and the future? Bruner (1986) referred to a narrative mode of thinking, as a contrast to a logico-scientific mode. Narratives give prominence to the way we make sense of what is happening and how events are explained. Some narratives are deeply embedded in the past – for example, in the form of myths and folktales. However, they are often employed to make sense of the present. Recent years have seen some interest in narrative and stories in organisations (Gabriel, 2000) and we would suggest that in the face of complexity in their work, they allow managers to make sense of ideas, actions and events through reflection; they also provide a resource for sense-making with others. But it is not only managers that use narratives. Managers have to recognise that far from the common assumption of a unified and single understanding of an organisation, they are more likely to have to respond to and understand a story-telling system that reflects a plurality of viewpoints. One suggestion is that managers learn to match the complexity by thinking systemically. Capra (2002), for example, argues that a systemic understanding of the organisation highlights the importance of the workplace as a living system and represents a contrast to more mechanical beliefs based on the command and control of parts. There are number of approaches to systemic thinking for managers, and probably the best-known are Soft Systems Methodology (SSM), usually associated with the work of Checkland (1999), and System Dynamics, based on the work of Senge (1994) and others. Although there are important differences between these two approaches, they both use systemic ideas to examine complex, confusing and difficult situations. Managers use data from 'real' situations and develop systemic models so that alternative thoughts can be stimulated and new actions generated.

WEB LINKS

Find out more about storytelling at http://cbae.nmsu.edu/~dboje/
This is the homepage of David Boje who has been a key writer about storytelling in organisations.
http://www.albany.edu/cpr/sds/index.html is the homepage of the System Dynamics Society, and if you would like to learn about System Dynamics, try the System Dynamics Education Project at http://sysdyn.clexchange.org/

Managers and learning at work

Systems Thinking was one of the disciplines suggested by Senge for the 'learning organisation',[8] which was a key image during the 1990s and proved to be very attractive to many organisations. In the UK, Pedler *et al* (1991; p.1) defined the learning organisation[9] as an organisation which 'facilitates the learning of all its members *and* continuously transforms itself' (italics as in the original). There followed an ongoing search for models and prescriptions for the learning organisation popularised through books, journals and conferences. The idea also became a feature of government policy in the UK. Some of the key characteristics of the development were:

- It offered a very wide view about the nature of the learning organisation, which often seemed to embrace every conceivable aspect of good managerial practice.

- The learning organisation was seen as one that constantly probed at its own values and mission.
- The thrust of thinking was towards 'transformational learning' rather than 'incremental learning'.
- The link between effective individual learning and organisational learning was recognised but not fully worked through.

There were always a variety of concerns about the learning organisation – such as that it was perceived as idealistic or elusive (Garavan, 1997), and that managers found they simply did not have the access within their organisations to enable them to initiate, promote or sustain approaches that required 'expansive patterns of thinking' or an organisation that 'continually transformed itself'. One consequence is that it was frequently regarded, in practice, as another training and development initiative concerned with improvement rather than radical change. Keep and Rainbird (2000) point out that although the idea of the learning organisation has value, there are too many factors in UK organisations which prevent its realisation. Such factors include cost-based competition, little space for creativity and a continued reliance on command-and-control approaches to people management. One particular consideration for managers is how far jobs are designed and work is organised to under-utilise skills and talent.

We would suggest that rather than being an elusive ideal, the learning organisation could better be seen as a peak of achievement in a pyramid of learning (see Figure 3 in Chapter 1). Rather than being focused on the broad set of values or behaviours that many people seem to understand by the learning organisation, the model provides an opportunity to consider the learning system of an organisation, and the processes, activities and values that have to work within and between the levels. For example, to move from the first level to the second level requires managers to become learners and to overcome anxiety towards learning and change (Schein, 2002). They can also become champions for learning and persuaders for change (Honey and Mumford, 1996). Gold and Smith (2003), for example, found that managers have to find a variety of ways to enrol others in undertaking learning activities. They have to build alliances with other managers and dissuade sceptical voices. Further, persuading staff more generally was not always easy and managers have to use every opportunity to extol the virtues of learning and development as well as undertaking key activities such as coaching and mentoring.

As we suggested above, the link from individual through groups and teams to organisation level has not been fully worked through. In particular, the explanation of learning at the level of the organisation raises certain difficulties. Here we are drawing on ideas that have been associated with 'organisation learning', a field of understanding which is related to but different from the learning organisation (Easterby-Smith *et al*, 1999).[10] The main difficulty is using learning – which is clearly what people do – as an attribute of organisations. How do organisations learn? One view, presented by Dixon (1994), is that organisations, because they can be understood as living systems, learn like humans. Thus the learning cycle can become an organisational learning cycle. Another view is to understand organisations as cultures (Yanow, 2000). This allows organisations to be seen as a collection of groups that base what they learn and practise on values, beliefs and norms that they share by telling stories and in everyday conversations. Such a cultural view is allied with research that suggests that learning in groups is mostly informal and situated in a particular and localised context (Lave and Wenger, 1991) within 'communities of practice' (CoPs). Recent years have seen a significant interest in CoPs, and managers are advised to support them as a source of creativity (Wenger and Snyder, 2000). How can managers cope with CoPs? Gherardi and Nicolini (2002) suggest that brokering activity is need for learning between CoPs to create a 'constellation of interconnected practices'. Managers may find it difficult to join or intervene in the various CoPs, but by operating at the boundaries between them, managers can facilitate processes of exchange of information and sharing of knowledge. It becomes important for interdependent CoPs to have sufficient understanding of each other – a process referred to as 'perspective-taking' (Boland and Tenkasi, 1995).

REFLECT – CONCLUDE – PLAN 5

- Would your organisation, or part of it, meet the requirements of a 'learning organisation'?
- How can you facilitate perspective-taking?
- What can you do to make it happen?

Knowledge management

Much of the learning that occurs in CoPs is informal, but increasingly in the future such learning will provide the knowledge for organisations to compete in the knowledge-based society. Managers will be required to put greater value on the skills of employees as the owners of intellectual capital. In addition, the information, knowledge and experience generated by activity must be captured and stored so that it can be used in the future – a process referred to as 'knowledge management'. Here, it is useful to distinguish between knowledge about facts which is explicit, codified and communicable (knowing-that) and knowledge which is more personal and concerned with dealing with particular or unexpected situations (knowing-how). The former forms the focus for the introduction of knowledge management systems – that is, knowledge that is codified and communicable can be more easily captured, stored and retrieved in a system based on advanced information and communication technology. However, preoccupation with technology in knowledge management can easily result in less attention being given to learning in organisations involving 'complex and intangible aspects of human behaviour' (Scarborough and Swan, 2001; p.8). This highlights the significance of knowing-how and knowledge which enables people to respond to difficult situations, often spontaneously – referred to as 'tacit knowledge'. Such knowledge is perceived as crucial to the creation of new ideas and practices in organisations. For example, Crossan (1999) provides a framework for organisation learning which begins with a process of 'intuiting', providing for the expression and surfacing of tacit knowledge. This is followed by other processes of interpreting, integrating and institutionalising, although Crossan acknowledges the presence of inhibiting factors such as structures, group dynamics and relationships. Managers who take a proactive approach to working with informal and tacit knowledge can create a learning climate that is conducive to knowledge productivity (see below).

WEB LINKS

For access to the Online Book on Knowledge Management and other resources, go to http://www.kmbook.com/

'Futures work' for managers

It is clear that managers will need to reject or reassess commonly held views about the controllability of the future and give more prominence to creativity and imagination. To help managers, a variety of processes and activities have been developed. In the UK, work by the Performance and Innovation Unit has sought to benchmark best practice for what they refer to as Strategic Futures Work (PIU, 2001), a process that enables complex analysis to explore multiple possibilities. Managers need to 'open up' the thinking process, although as futurists Rogers and Tough (1996; p. 495) stated, 'Facing the future is definitely not for wimps.'

One obvious implication of futures is that managers cannot work alone. As Slaughter (1999; p.845) warns, 'Futures work cannot be based on ego; it is an expression of shared transpersonal aspirations to help create a better world.' This also applies to thinking about strategy, and there has been growing interest in how strategy emerges and in 'strategy innovation' (Hamel, 1998), the process whereby new value for customers and new wealth for all stakeholders is created. A major implication is the need to shift attention for strategy as a plan or product to strategy as a process. Managers must adopt a learning approach to strategy, like any other management activity. However, for new ideas to emerge from activities throughout an organisation requires a climate and processes where learning is designed into activities and given priority (Mumford, 2000). Inevitably, this means that managers must delve more deeply into the process of how knowledge is produced within local contexts. For example, our earlier comments about CoPs suggest the key activities of brokering and perspective-taking. According to Garvey and Williamson (2002), organisations that learn new ways of doing things become knowledge productive. Importantly, this requires learning that goes beyond formal and codified knowledge (and narrow conceptions of knowledge management) to reach informal and tacit knowledge. There has to be a climate of trust and openness which encourages the sharing of knowledge. This cannot be achieved where politics, ego and fear feed routines that prevent discussions of significance (Argyris, 1999).

WEB LINK

There is growing interest in the process of making strategy, sometimes referred to as strategising. More information is available from www.strategy-as-practice.org

We are encouraged to find that there is significant recognition of the importance of learning from work activities for managers – what we referred to as Type 2 MD – and the extension of this to everyone else in an organisation. What also emerges is that the achievement of notions such as the learning organisation, knowledge production/management or strategy innovation, requires managers to reassess how they behave in relation to others at work. While many trends affecting the future of MD can be identified, how they are dealt with is subject to local interpretation. How do managers achieve such interpretations – especially when faced with the complexity of life at work – and proactively define the future and set a path that makes it happen? One image, presented in Holman and Thorpe (2003), is that of the manager as a 'practical author',[11] where managers learn to work in the present and make the future through talk and conversation with others. The beauty of this image for MD is that every day there are opportunities for managers to engage in conversations with others during which they are able to argue and persuade others of the need to act and respond to what they hear. By reviewing and reflecting on events that occur, through the same processes of talk and conversation, managers can learn with others how the future can be made.

SUMMARY

- There are predictable trends that are affecting the content and delivery of MD, but managers also face unpredictability.
- In facing the future, managers must learn analytical thinking for predictability and creative thinking for where there is unpredictability, complexity and multiple future possibilities.
- Trends of globalisation require MD for managers who work across cultural boundaries. There is increased awareness of the effect of business activities on the environment.
- Developments in ICT require MD for multi-disciplined teams and the delivery of MD by e-learning.
- There has been a significant growth in ideas for MD, but there are concerns about making research more relevant to the practice of management.
- Managerialism has become a significant force in the delivery of public and professional services.
- More attention is being paid to the importance of diversity at work and of an understanding for managers of the values and ethics of their role.
- MD can use ideas from complexity theory to help managers cope with discontinuity in the world, the unpredictability of events and flux where disequilibrium becomes the norm.
- Narrative and systemic thinking have been presented as approaches to learning for complexity in MD.
- Ideas about the 'learning organisation', knowledge management and productivity and 'strategy innovation' suggest the need for continuous learning from everyday activities.

DISCUSSION QUESTIONS

1. Is there a relevance gap between management research and the practice of managers?
2. 'Management is a moral and social craft.' Discuss.
3. Can management development be delivered via e-learning?
4. How can managers learn skills of complex thinking?
5. Has the idea of the learning organisation fulfilled its promise? What is the role of managers in a learning organisation?
6. 'Any useful statement about the future should seem ridiculous.' Discuss the implications of such a statement for MD.

FURTHER READING

BURGOYNE, J. (1999) 'Design of the times', *People Management*, Vol. 5, No. 11; pp.38–44.

HUFF, A. S. and JENKINS, M. (2002) *Mapping Strategic Knowledge*. London, Sage.

KIRTON, G. and GREENE, A.-M. (2000) *The Dynamics of Managing Diversity: A critical approach*. London, Butterworth-Heinemann.

STACEY, R. (2003) *Strategic Management and Organisational Dynamics: The challenge of complexity*. Harlow, Prentice Hall.

STEWART, J. and TANSLEY, C. (2002) *Training in the Knowledge Economy*. London, Chartered Institute of Personnel and Development.

VAN DER HEIJDEN, K., BRADFIELD, R., BURT, G., CAIRNS, G. and WRIGHT, G. (2002) *The Sixth Sense: Accelerating organisational learning with scenarios*. Chichester, John Wiley.

GROUP ACTIVITY

- Form a group of four.
- You have been asked to consider various approaches to learning about the future which can be incorporated into a learning programme for managers and others.

  The four approaches to consider are:

  scenarios

  open space technology

  future search

  search conferences.
- Allocate one approach to each person and find out:
  - how the approach operates, the main requirements, and the underlying theories
  - examples of how the approach has been used, and evidence of outcomes
  - advantages, and possible problems.
- Meet to combine your findings and prepare a presentation with recommendations.

REFERENCES

ARGYRIS, C. (1999) *On Organizational Learning*. Malden, MA., Blackwell.

BOLAND, R. J. and TENKASI, R. V. (1995) 'Perspective making and perspective taking in communities of knowing', *Organisation Science*, Vol. 6, No. 4; pp.350–372.

BRUNER, J. (1986) *Actual Minds, Possible Worlds*. Cambridge, Harvard University Press.

CASTELLS, M. (1996) *The Rise of the Network Society*. Oxford, Blackwell.

CAPRA, F. (2002) *The Hidden Connections*. London, HarperCollins.

CHECKLAND, P. (1999) *Systems Thinking, Systems Practice*. Chichester, Wiley.

CLARKE, T. and HERMENS, A. (2001) 'Corporate developments and strategic alliances in e-learning', *Education and Training*, Vol. 43, No, 4; pp.256–267.

CILLIERS, P. (1998) *Complexity and Postmodernism*. London, Routledge.

CROSSAN, M. M. (1999) 'An organizational learning framework: from intuition to institution', *Academy of Management Review*, Vol. 24, No. 3; pp.522–538.

CZARNIAWSKA-JOERGES, B. (1993) *The Three-Dimensional Organization*. Lund, Studentlitteratur.

DATOR, J. (2003) 'Futures studies and sustainable community development'. Available at http://www.soc.hawaii.edu/future/dator.html

DIXON, N. (1994) *The Organizational Learning Cycle: How we can learn collectively*. Maidenhead, McGraw-Hill.

EASTERBY-SMITH, M., BURGOYNE, J. and ARAUJO, L. (eds) (1999) *Organizational Learning and the Learning Organization*. London, Sage.

FELSTEAD, A., GALLIE, D. and GREEN, F. (2001) *Work Skills in Britain 1986–2001*. London, Department for Education and Skills.

FRANKENTAL, P. (2001) 'Corporate social responsibility – a PR invention?', *Corporate Communications: An international journal*, Vol. 6, No. 1; pp.18–23.

GABRIEL, Y. (2000) *Storytelling in Organizations*. Oxford, Oxford University Press.

GARAVAN, T. (1997) 'The Learning Organization: A Review and Evaluation', *The Learning Organization*, Vol. 4, No. 1; pp.18–29.

GARAVAN, T. N., MORLEY, M., GUNNIGLE, P. and COLLINS, E. (2001) 'Human capital accumulation: the role of human resource development', *Journal of European Industrial Training*, Vol. 25, Nos 2/3/4; pp.48–68.

GARVEY, B. and WILLIAMSON, B. (2002) *Beyond Knowledge Management*. Harlow, Pearson Education.

GHERARDI, S. and NICOLINI, D. (2002) 'Learning in a constellation of interconnected practices', *Journal of Management Studies*, Vol. 39, No. 4; pp.419–436.

GOLD, J. and SMITH, V. (2003) 'Advances toward the learning movement: translations at work', *Human Resource Development International*, Vol. 6, No. 2; pp.139–152.

GRAHAM, S. (2002) 'Tidy town or radical rethink? Connecting management education to the webiosphere'. Paper presented at the Connecting Learning and Critique Conference, Cambridge University, July.

GREY, C. '"We are all managers now"; "We always were": On the development and demise of management', *Journal of Management Studies*, Vol. 36, No. 5; pp.561–585.

GUEST, D., DAVEY, K. and PATCH, A. (1998) *The Impact of New Forms of Employment Contract on Motivation and Innovation*. London, ESRC.

HAMEL, G. (1998) 'Strategy innovation and the quest for value', *Sloan Management Review*, Vol. 39, No. 2; pp.7–14.

HIRSH, W. and CARTER, A. (2002) *New Directions in Management Development*. Brighton, Institute for Employment Studies.

HOLMAN, D. and THORPE, R. (2003) *Management and Language*. London, Sage.

HONEY, P. and MUMFORD, A. (1996) *How to Manage Your Learning Environment*. Maidenhead, Honey Publications.

ILO (2000) *High-Performance Working: Research project overview*. Geneva, International Labour Organisation. Available at http://www.ilo.org/public/english/employment/skills/training/casest/overvew.htm.

KEEP, E. and RAINBIRD, H. (2000) 'Towards the learning organization?', in S. Bach and K. Sisson, *Personnel Management*. Oxford, Blackwell.

KELLIE, J. (2002) 'Continuing professional development – is it about learning?' Paper presented at the Connecting Learning and Critique Conference, Cambridge University, July.

LAVE, J. and WENGER, E. (1991) *Situated Learning*. Cambridge, Cambridge University Press.

MICHIE, J. and SHEEHAN-QUINN, M. (2001) 'Labour market flexibility: Human resource management and corporate performance', *British Journal of Management*, Vol. 12, No. 4; pp.287–305.

MUMFORD, A. (2000) 'A learning approach to strategy', *Journal of Workplace Learning*, Vol. 12, No. 2; pp.265–271.

PARKER, M. (2002) *Against Management*. Cambridge, Polity Press.

PEARSON, I. (1999) 'The power of information', *Foresight*, Vol. 1, No. 5; pp.413–426.

PEDLER, M., BURGOYNE, J. and BOYDELL, T. (1991) *The Learning Company: A strategy for sustainable development*. Maidenhead, McGraw-Hill.

PIU (2001) *Benchmarking UK Strategic Futures Work*. London, Performance and Innovation Unit.

PIU (2001a) *Understanding Best Practice in Strategic Futures Work*. London, Performance and Innovation Unit.

PIU (2001b) *A Futurist's Toolbox*. London, Performance and Innovation Unit.

POLLARD, E. and HILLAGE, J. (2001) *Exploring e-Learning*. Report 376. Brighton, Institute for Employment Studies.

ROGERS, M. and TOUGH, A. (1996) 'Facing the future is not for wimps', *Futures*, Vol. 28, No. 5; pp.491–496.

SCARBOROUGH, H. and SWAN, J. (2001) 'Explaining the diffusion of knowledge management: the role of fashion', *British Journal of Management*, Vol. 12, No. 1; pp.3–12.

SCHEIN, E. (2002) 'The anxiety of learning', *Harvard Business Review*, March; pp.100–106.

SEMLER, R. (2003) *The Seven-Day Week-End*. London, Century.

SENGE, P. (1994) *The Fifth Discipline*. New York, Doubleday.

SHOTTER, J. (1993) *Conversational Realities: Constructing life through language*. London, Sage.

SLAUGHTER, R. (1999) 'Professional standards in futures work', *Futures*, Vol. 31; pp.835–851.

SLOMAN, M. (2001) 'Sharing the power of learning', in *The Future of Learning for Work*. London, Chartered Institute of Personnel and Development.

STACEY, R. (2002) 'The impossibility of managing knowledge'. Paper presented to the Royal Society of Arts, London, 27 February.

STARKEY, K. and MADAN, P. (2001) 'Bridging the relevance gap: aligning stakeholders in the future of management research', *British Journal of Management*, Vol. 12, Special Issue; pp.3–26.

WATSON, T. and HARRIS, P. (1999) *The Emergent Manager*. London, Sage Publications.

WENGER, E. C. and SNYDER, W. M. (2000) 'Communities of practice: the organizational frontier', *Harvard Business Review*, January-February; pp.139–145.

WINTERTON, J., PARKER, M., DODD, M., McCRACKEN, M. and HENDERSON, I. (2000) *Future Skill Needs of Managers*. London, Department for Education and Employment.

YANOW, D. (2000) 'Seeing organizational learning: a 'cultural' view', *Organization*, Vol. 7, No. 2; pp.247–268.

ENDNOTES

1 This report emerged from the Strategic Futures project at http://www.pm.gov.uk/output/page696.asp Other government projects to consider include the UK Foresight programme at http://www.foresight.gov.uk/

2 Jim Dator is based at the Hawaii Research Center for Futures Studies at http://www.futures.hawaii.edu/

3 More details at http://www.quality.co.uk/iso14000.htm#intro

4 'Information' and 'knowledge' are not synonymous. Information exists in the form of data which is codified and available for communication. Information becomes a form of knowledge when it is accessed by others for some purpose. However, there are other forms of knowledge which managers work with, including their experience and tacit understandings and collective knowledge shared with others.

5 In the UK the Public Disclosure Act 1998 is designed to protect 'whistleblowers' – employees who identify a serious wrongdoing at work and speak about it publicly.

6 Go to the Scott Bader homepage at http://www.scottbader.com/pub.nsf and read about their principles for organisation.

7 The idea of 'nets of collective action' is similar to the idea of 'communities of practice'.

8 Senge's (1994) five disciplines were
personal mastery
shared vision
team learning
mental models
systems thinking.

9 Pedler *et al* (1991) always preferred the term 'learning company'.

10 Organisation learning might be understood as the field of study concerned with learning at the level of the organisation; the learning organisation is a set of practices and activities to bring about individual and group learning within an organisation.

11 This image is drawn from the work of John Shotter (1993).

Index